Comments from Readers

...a splendid book—one that should be a text in every MBA program. Everything in life is about people. We can finish our MBA studies, Poly Sci or J-School studies, or whatever, but we're never done with our study of people. And Park has written a great one. Thanks also for the author's thought I intend to drill into my children "God gave us a soul. Our duty is to give it meaning, and He wants it back! —**P.J. O'Rourke**, Author, Peterborough, NH

...fascinating to read...a business primer that should be read in the business schools and corporate offices. Park radiates the aura of a worthwhile human being who makes the world a better place... —**Peter D. Novelli**, P.E., Ithaca, NY

...compelling...teared up when read the grandson's letter to his father...a powerful intimate work.... reads like a movie. I feel that I have lived these people's lives. —**Jennifer Magar**, Editor, Austin, TX

...a frank, lively account of a remarkable family history... —**David J. Skorton**, M.D., Secretary, The Smithsonian Institution, Washington, D.C.

...honest, reflective, deeply philosophical and personal...many lessons worth sharing with anyone experiencing this journey called life. Particularly enjoyed the father's and grandson's letters. One feels a palpable sense of love, respect, reconciliation and closure. —**Charles W. Dent**, Congressman, Bethlehem, PA

Park should be so proud, and his dad has to be shouting from the heavens. I had tears in my eyes on many pages as it brought back so many truly fond memories of bygone times and experiences. Thanks to Park for chronicling his father's amazing careers and creativity and the deep friendship that existed between our fathers. I can only imagine the time that the research and writing took, but it sure was well worth it for generations to come. —**Cathleen P. Black**, former President, HEARST Magazines, New York, NY

…a compelling read…I highly recommend it… —**Morton C. Blackwell,** President, The Leadership Institute, Arlington, VA

I am a Cornellian and work for my father…I could not put the book down. It had so many different and fascinating story lines, some of which parallel experiences I have had or know of within our family businesses…I felt a kinship to Park, Jr and his excellent job illustrating "examples of warnings" and "examples of examples" encountered in his fambiz life. Having done this makes the author an even better example for entrepreneurs and their families. —**Louis S. Gimbel, 4th**, Greenwich, CT

… kept rolling it over in my mind… old memories …filled in the blanks… my own father's idea for the Duncan Hines name. The biggest impact… was reading the deep and profound influence the senior Park had on my dad and our family for all those years he worked for Park... The final meeting between Roy and John Babcock, who was probably my dad's best friend, characterized the man perfectly. I have to admire the son's tenacity to endure what he did for those several decades. Not many would have. I am pleased that he somehow found it in his heart to forgive, and that in itself makes him a much greater man than his dad... —**Robert F. Flannery,** Traverse City, MI

…the tale of a son's resilience and perseverance….told objectively and honestly…a lesson on how to face life without bitterness in order to end up with compassion. Red Smith, the journalist turned writer, once was asked if it were difficult to write. His answer, 'It's simple. I just sit down at the typewriter and open up a vein.' It is the way to great writing, and Park has done it. —**Roger O'Neil**, London, England

…Praise is well earned…loved the story of the encounter with Donald Trump and Marla Maples! —**James O' Shea Wade**, Former Executive Editor, VP, Crown Publishers, Inc./Random House, Inc., Yorktown Heights, NY

…well written in a journalistic style that becomes to a non-business person an educational adventure into the business world and adds to knowledge of life in general. —**J.S. Aldridge**, M.D., Juniper, FL

A great job of capturing an important part of a family's history. —**Elizabeth L. Quick,** Esq., Womble Carlyle, Sandridge and Rice, Winston-Salem, NC

…lays out the history of the post-war American communications industry through the careers of the two Parks. Equally interesting is the author's "Mad Men" years in the ad agency world of New York…there's a Shakespearean quality to the disparate stories as they run parallel paths. One longs for some closure in the relationship between father and son, but Park steers clear of the maudlin aspects of this. —**John Roberts**, Newtown, PA

…an amazing read… reveals the joy and tensions of working in a family business.…wonderful writing style and wit…Surviving the family business as an SOB - Son of the Boss, tells it all!… learned much about business, the changing world of media from mid- to late-20th century, the relationship of fathers and sons, and enjoyed every minute of it. —**Susan R. King**, Dean, School of Media and Journalism, The University of North Carolina at Chapel Hill, NC

In spite of the epic nature of the story, the book is an easy read in a conversational tone full of anecdotes and humor. —**Kathryn Torgeson**, editor, Ithaca, NY

An extremely heartfelt, compelling, and inspirational read…vividly detailed…the lessons and advice springing from the interaction of a son with his father I found most moving and inspirational. —**Patrick Carollo**, Esq., Mechanicsville, VA

This account of a son working for a demanding entrepreneurial father offers a unique insight into the hidden dynamics of such family relationships. —**Hoyle S. Broome, Jr.**, Birmingham, AL

…a great book…must contain something that we can take to heart; to recognize enough of ourselves to allow us to see the world more clearly… *Sons in the Shadow* is such a book…an honest portrayal of an intimate subject…the book spoke to me because of its universality…I believe history will remark it as unique. —**John Siegfried,** retired attorney, Cleveland, OH

Park's relationship with his dad was far different than mine…(which) allows me to express my sincere respect for him in accomplishing many things that took an enormous amount of courage and determination. The book is more than a just another personal momento, it is a piece that will influence other S.O.B.s, and I hope they have a chance to read it. —**Jeffrey Lewis**, M.D., D.M.D., Ithaca, NY

Park is blunt and honest... he also tells the truth about the troubles facing any family that hopes to keep its business intact when Washington politicians are doing their worst... another wake-up call: successful business people can't be too careful when setting up a foundation. So many foundations soon end up funding the opposite of what their original donors wanted. Read this book! —**Terrence M. Scanlon**, President, Capital Research Center, Washington, D.C.

...like the way the book laments the fact that the Park Foundation is likely to go the way of other foundations, which have become very liberal because of the actions of board members.... —**William J. Troy, III,** Esq., Troy & Troy, P.C., Ithaca, NY

... tremendously impressive work, very honest and well-written...Certainly a 'must read' for anyone...interested in understanding the difficulty in family relationships that can in fact be exacerbated by business success. —**Ted Quirk**, Esq., Las Vegas, NV

What a great story!...stayed up until 2:00 am to finish it and...recommended it to a childhood friend who also graduated from Lawrenceville. Congratulations to the author on his spectacular career at JWT, success with Park Outdoor...and his work with the Triad Foundation maximizing his father's legacy. Thanks for sharing this journey. —**Frank Sparks,** New Canaan, CT

...A truly inspiring, honest and insightful account of a highly successful family business from the perspective of a loving son ...A wonderful and highly recommended book on the blessings of liberty and the American dream! —**David J. Theroux**, President and Founder, The Independent Institute, Oakland, CA

One of the best business books I have read, even though it's not a business book....overlaps with the refinement of marketing and the rise of consumerism following World War II...fascinating but the book is ultimately a human-interest story...(leading to) a foundation that is true to the father's legacy. —**Peter Flaherty,** President, National Legal Foundation, Falls Church, VA

... I hearby designate Park...a Poet Laureate for the poems he wrote in the book. —Professor Emeritus **William B. Ward**, Department of Communication, Cornell University, Ithaca, NY

What a monumental work! …exhaustive in its detail and exhausting for someone who knew how demanding the father was in the workplace. The book is an empathetic read for sons (or daughters) of high achievers and a cautionary tale for anyone aspiring to make it to the top in any field."
—**Sheldon L. Smith**, Austin, TX

This book was very well written and is fascinating because of the interaction between a self made billionaire father and his more sensitive son. Human interaction is often complex and this book illustrates this fact. That alone makes it a great read. —**Jonathan E. Emerson**, Farmington, CT

Especially intriguing is the "SOB' title. I like too, that early on Park made clear that he loved and admired his father. His handling of the unfortunate and difficult break-up of the original foundation was done with such finesse and skill that it was most appropriate. —**Senator Harry F. Byrd, Jr.**, Winchester, VA

…if you have ever in your life imagined what it must be like to grow up as the son of someone at the top of the Forbes 400 list…I suspect you will find comfort in knowing you are not alone in the tribulations about which the author writes with startling candor. Park lets us in on the human side of commercial success and lends first person insight on the familial implications of wealth. —**Steven W. Magacs**, Ithaca, NY

This true story depicts the challenges and strengths of business and family…(and) keeps the reader anxious for what comes next.
—**Keefe Gorman**, Merrill Lynch, Ithaca, NY

A best seller in my eyes…although Babcock isn't here now to share this, I'm sure he's looking down with a smile. —**Kerry Leipold**, Elmira, NY

Having a highly successful father myself, I understand the pressure to succeed on ones owns terms and the allure of working in a family business...—this story does not disappoint. —**Donald F. Douglas**, Woodland, CA

… really could not put the book down. I have been in a lot of companies over my 15 years as a CPA, and many were private families with multi generations involved. Park's experience is as tough as I've ever seen and I congratulate him on his successes outside of his father's shadow.
—**Lewis Cosby**, Naples, FL

Sons in the Shadow brought me and my father together. After reading the book, my father visited Mr. Park who told him that having read the book, he was more than half way to making things work out if his son joined the family business. As I approached the six month milestone at our software company, and having also read *Sons in the Shadow*, I was amazed at the parallels between the author's early career and mine. The book gave me the benefit of the author's foresight to deal with the early struggles of working as an SOB following what my father said after he met with Roy Park.
—**Matthew Larson**, Our-Hometown, Inc., Clifton Springs, NY

A fascinating presentation of harsh facts and emotional tributes…I'm addicted to the book. —**Virginia Laux**, Ithaca, NY

With *Sons in the Shadow*, Roy Park has achieved the seemingly impossible task of writing two excellent books in one: the compelling biography of a larger-than-life father and an insightful, self-reflective autobiography of his own amazing and successful journey. Both books would have been very interesting on their own, but the creativity shown in weaving them together and incorporating the perspective of a third and objective player in Johnnie Babcock make the book truly distinctive. Bringing it all together into one seamless whole is an incredible accomplishment….The two key words that arose over and over again at the recent memorial service for my friend Dr. Jack Templeton, son-of-the-boss of Sir John Templeton, were "gratitude" and "generosity." The story of Park and his father is a reminder of the importance of these values, along with "persistence" and "determination." As William F. Buckley, Jr. would say, "it was a good read." —**Christopher Long,** President, Intercollegiate Studies Institute, Wilmington, DE

From the guy who first put Roy H. Park in the billboard business, I enjoyed reading *Sons in the Shadow*. —**Stewart Underwood**, Ithaca, NY

This is the story of a quintessential American entrepreneur. Author Roy H. Park Jr., self-described "SOB," or Son of the Boss, offers the ultimate insider insights in this well-told, multi-generational family business saga. … the father-son relationship described here, in often poignant detail, was at times a rocky one. Park's reflections on his experiences in the business are what elevate this book several cuts above the standard self-made billionaire bio-cum-management manual. —**Edward J. McMahon,** President, Empire Center for Public Policy, Inc., Albany, NY

Hard…to put down, once I began…because the story is so well told, balanced, and compelling… fascinating to me how the author kept his own voice, professionally and personally, while being part of such a powerful family and business structure. —**Amy Russ**, Public Affairs, Cornell University, Ithaca, NY

Having worked in the outdoor business for 30 years for three privately held companies, the story really hits home. I thank Park for setting high standards as a valuable privately held outdoor advertising business. —**Mark E. Moyer**, President, Fairway Outdoor Advertising, Augusta, GA

…was interested in the foundation discussion but soon found myself reading much deeper… fascinating and reaffirms my sense of the author's character…well done, not a 'tell-all' or 'gotcha' story like many such books are…most enjoyable. —**Mark Tryniski**, President & CEO, Community Bank, N.A., Dewitt, NY

…written with a very daring sense of honesty. It embodies a genuine study of the family life of a dedicated businessman…father-son relationship… also delighted to read about other relationships with businessmen such as Donald Trump…a fascinating, entertaining and compelling story of challenges, success and frustrations of a perceptive and compassionate man who can touch the reader's heart when counseling his son that "God gave us a soul, and our duty is to give it meaning. He wants it back"…a moving and enjoyable read! —**Roger Fernandez**, Glendale, CA

I especially liked what was written with respect to the human soul. I felt that it was a beautifully articulated way to describe something everyone can relate to regardless of religious affiliation…people seem to get so caught up in the particulars these days. —**Gustavo Reis**, Floranopolis Santa Catarina, Brazil

There are countless thousands of S.O.B.s and grandsons of the Boss, the original entrepreneur who started a family business. All those sons or daughters working for dad or grandfather should read this book, no matter how big or small the business is. In addition, the book should be the basis of a case study at all business schools. There are dozens of lessons here written by the Son Of the Boss about his relationship with his ambitious dad; both men did it all. The big lessons are perseverance, loyalty and love. —**Grey Perry**, Chairman Emeritus, Sigma Phi Society, Vonore, TN

If character is forged on the anvil of adversity, Park's story of compassion and accomplishment is especially compelling. Written with great honesty and grace, his biography/autobiography is fascinating on its own...will provoke thoughtful reflection in many readers. It is a wonderful gift. Instead of shadow, Park Jr.'s legacy illuminates. Inspirational! —**Roger Sibley**, retired Executive Director, Franziska Racker Centers, Ithaca, NY

I was so touched by what the author had to say and so moved, I went from laughter to tears, and back again. That Park would so honestly and openly expose his life is in itself a wonder, but he did it so well. ...we are fortunate that what he shared expresses what all of us have felt...this book is a treasure! —**Prin Williams**, Chapel Hill, NC

...a fine history and compelling personal story... provides a wealth of detail and insight about an extraordinary man and his son's work in a warm tribute to him, as well as a reflective narrative of his own journey. —**Mark Gearan**, President, Hobart and William Smith Colleges, Geneva, NY

Unvarnished, entertaining, intimate. —**David Stern**, President, Boyce Thompson Institute, Ithaca, NY

I, too, grew up in the shadow of a powerful person and am very grateful my father and I reconciled during our lifetimes... people...respond favorably to compassion and kindness. The author comes across in his book as putting this knowledge into action. I thank him for taking on such a huge project and seeing it through to completion. I also enjoyed his poetry and reflections on the popular music that often says things for us so well.
—**John E. Butler**, Ithaca, NY

Nearly fifteen years after graduating as a Roy H. Park Leadership Fellow, I still relish an opportunity to glean words of wisdom (and caution) from those who have gone before me. Roy Park provided many. Especially insightful was his success dealing with potential unionization in the outdoor advertising business. The book also provided me a detailed understanding of the Parks' values and how the Triad Foundation is successfully propagating them. I share their foundational belief in the capitalist system...
—**Marshall L. Stocker**, Capitalist, Hanover, MA

Reading the fascinating *"Sons"* book, and getting a chance to have three radio interviews with the author, will always be among my Ithaca 'highlights'. —**Fred Antil**, former Vice President, American Management Association, Ithaca, NY

I have read *Sons in the Shadow* and am struck by how hard the author tried to be fair and balanced in discussing his father. The elder Park treated employees harshly, often with contempt, and they came to expect that. But I could not believe a father would treat his son as he was treated— ridiculed, often scorned in front of others. Park's compassion after all this is remarkable. —**Conrad C. Fink**, Grady College of Journalism and Mass Communications, The University of Georgia, Athens, GA

Having worked as first as a sales and then a general manager for 27 years at one of the Park Communications television stations, I literally could not put the book down! The more I read, particularly as the story entered the mid-eighties, memory after memory flooded back …and the memory of the spotlight…When an employee got called down during a meeting by Mr. Park, no one wanted to look at the person…It was a sacrificial ceremony that could have easily been one of us. I can't remember being as enthralled with a story, actually a saga, as the one shared in the book. —**Jack D. Dempsey**, Vice President & General Manager, Bonten Media Group, Inc., Bristol, VA

I thank the son for writing and sharing the Park story…will help open the eyes of young family business successors and allow them to carefully consider what they may face…to imagine and plan the legacies they will leave. …of most significance is the opportunity Park offers us to consider something that Samuel C. Johnson, another Cornellian, said near the end of his life, "As I thought about …what my father had done, and then thinking also about the future, I came to the conclusion that as a son I shouldn't worry too much about whether I have lived up to the expectations of my father…but whether we as fathers live up to the expectations of our children." Park invites…us…to join him in considering that as the true measure of family business success. —**Dr. Carol B. Wittmeyer,** New York Family Business Center Consultant and Associate Professor of Management and Family Business Club Advisor, St. Bonaventure University, Olean, NY

Glowing reader reviews are fully deserved…a great story about capitalism and free enterprise, complete with epic characters…a warm and wise tale about family and growing up…a stirring reminder of what has made our country great and what we need to defend and promote today. —**Barry Strauss**, Program on Freedom and Free Societies, Cornell University, Ithaca, NY

This is a meaningful book by the son of a media mogul who had become a billionaire. It's about their business and personal relationship, the good and the bad. Author Roy Park Jr. did an excellent job in writing it, and I know that some of the material was mighty hard to put down on paper. It's a wonderful, informative read. —**Richard Cole**, Kerr Distinguished Professor Emeritus and Dean Emeritus, School of Media and Journalism, University of North Carolina at Chapel Hill, NC

I enjoyed reading the passages about Skipper Bowles. Erskine and I would love it if our two dads were here to see all this. —**Holden Thorpe**, Provost, Washington University, St. Louis, MO

I'm impressed by the writing and the story. —**L. Joseph Thomas**, Interim Dean SC Johnson College of Business, Cornell University, Ithaca, NY

The careers of Roy Park, Sr. and Roy Park, Jr. are both fascinating, but the best part is the interaction between the two… —**David S. Foster**, Esq., Partner, Nixon Peabody, San Francisco, CA

Sons in the Shadow…is an important contribution to the historical record of media and business in 20th century America. Roy H. Park was an accomplished entrepreneur who added values to the lives of his customers, employees, and the communities where he operated. His was a life well-lived. It would serve the rising generation well to read this story of someone who had common sense and a business acumen. I congratulate Roy Park Jr. for writing this account of his father's life "in order to remember." His epilogue makes it clear that by making a positive difference in this world and serving others through enterprise and public service, one's impact will reverberate for generations to come. —**Roger Ream**, President, Fund for American Studies, Washington, D.C

Excellent read. Very well written and fascinating look inside the family dynamics of one of the original media empires. A must-read for anyone in business. I have always admired people who work very hard and have a natural ability to sell any and everything, and Mr. Park was perhaps the godfather of those ideals. Getting the perspective from someone who grew up learning from a self-made tycoon is absolutely riveting. The book is also loaded with wise tidbits, original and referenced, that will benefit any reader. Be prepared to sit for a while, because it is very difficult to put down! —**Max Drachman**, Vice President, Kalil & Co., Inc, Tuscon, AZ

5 Stars to Roy H. Park, Jr. for sharing his story and the incredible story of his dad. *Sons in the Shadow* is a true testament of God's plans to pass faith, freedom, vision, and hard work through family. —**Star Parker**, Founder & President, CURE, Center for Urban Renewal and Education, Syndicated Columnist with the Creator's News Syndicate, Washington, D.C.

While reading *Sons in the Shadow* I noted the author's aversion to flattery except where it might apply to his book and hope this mindset allows him to accept my compliments whole-heartedly. The book was truly exceptional, many of his anecdotes were so detailed and well-recollected I felt like I personally experienced the events, myself. The nature of the book was inspirational and the strength of the author was evident when life knocked him down he stood back up ready for even more. —**Stuart Ganzon**, Student, Bentley University, Boston, MA

Sons in the Shadow is a good read and of special interest to a Cornell alumnus and a retired ad executive who worked at TIME and Smithsonian Magazines for many years. —**Sandy Gilbert**, Chairman, START "Solutions to Avoid Red Tide," Tallevast, FL.

The manuscript filled in some of the gaps that have eluded me for years, The book is very interesting and well-written. —**Louis Hatchett**, Author, Duncan Hines: The Man Behind the Cake Mix, Henderson, KY

This is the story of a man who started from nothing and made a billion dollars in media and advertising written by the son who followed in his footsteps. It is candidly written and should appeal to anyone who has ever worked in a family business. Highly recommended. —**Jack of Alltrades "Just another soul,"** Yellow Mountain, United States

Sons in the Shadow is a story that contains a geographical and occupational link with my background. Growing up with dairy farming uncles who always needed help with milking, haying, stone-picking, manure spreading, etc, the author's opening paragraph on page 133 about "an old farmer's advice" means a lot more to me today than it did back in those Alleghany County days. And as a "small business" man myself, running the Right to Work operation, I try to read as many books about successful operations as I can. This book appears to be right over-the-plate. Helping to defend individual freedom to control the fruits of your labor is a passion and a privilege the Park family understands. —**Mark Mix**, National Right to Work Legal Defense and Education Foundation, Inc., Springfield, VA.

Having also grown up as a Son of the Boss with a loving, caring mother that balanced me, Roy's grit in writing this book reaches out and touches my soul. It is an adventure in life to which I can relate, especially as I recall the moments in my life when my Pop was "all there" with me and our time was cherished as a lifetime memory...good or bad... —**Frank Towner**, CEO, YMCA of Ithaca and Tompkins County

Sons in the Shadow is a great contribution to the American spirit.A forceful yet conversational reflection on the life of an extraordinary man, told through the lens of the tenacious relationship between father and son. This book serves as a reminder not only of the possibility of the American Dream, but of the humanity that is both gained and lost along the road to its fruition. It is apparent that the Parks sought a future not only for themselves but for the millions of American citizens who have of late been cast aside in the public square. The inter-generational devotion to hard work, determination, and a belief in the meritocracy of young Americans rings true in every page of the narrative. Mr. Park tells a unique story, yet it is one that strikes a chord with every aspirational child who has ever looked with reverence upon the accomplishments of a parent. Highly entertaining and unusually honest, this is a story that you don't want to miss.
—**Daniel Stein**, President, The Federation for American Immigration Reform, Washington, D.C.

Roy Park, Jr. shares with the reader, "an old farmer's advice is to live a good honorable life so when you get older you can think back and enjoy it a second time." Mr. Park has written a poignant tale of living that good and honorable life in the full shadow and certain shelter of a remarkably successful father. His reward is, indeed, enjoying it a second time and sharing it with us. —**Cindy Rushing**, Development Director, Clare Boothe Luce Policy Institute, Herndon, VA

Roy Park Jr.'s book shines a much-needed light on the unique challenges of family businesses. Families are the bedrock of the American civilization. Family businesses are the bedrock of the American economy...of entrepreneurialism...of the American Dream. Let me point out: the 2,300,000 family owned business, farms and ranches represent 29% of all firms with employees in the U.S. They provide a total 49,000,000 jobs. But as Roy Park Jr. points out, dysfunction between generations is a predictable challenge to family business' survival to the next generation. Survival is made even more difficult by the Death Tax. I write these words from an autobiographical perspective. Roy, you have my respect...from one S.O.B to another! —**Dick Patten**, President, American Business Defense Foundation, Washington, D.C.

SONS IN THE SHADOW
SURVIVING THE FAMILY BUSINESS AS AN SOB*
*SON OF THE BOSS

by Roy H. Park, Jr.

2018 Edition

With Commentary by John B. Babcock
Former CEO and Executive VP of Park Communications, Inc.

ELDERBERRY PRESS, INC.

OAKLAND

Cover art by Roy H. Park III

ELDERBERRY PRESS, INC.
1393 Old Homestead Drive, Second Floor
Oakland, Oregon 97462-9506
EMAIL: editor@elderberrypress.com
TEL/FAX: 541.459.6043
www.elderberrypress.com

Books are available from Elderberry Press and Amazon in both print and e-book.

Publisher's Catalog – in – Publication Data
Sons in the Shadow: Surviving the Family Business As An SOB
Roy H. Park, Jr.
ISBN: 978-1-934956-67-0 [Hard cover]
Library of Congress Control Number: 2012939446

1. Business.
2. Family Business.
3. Advertising.
4. Media.
5. Outdoor Advertising.
6. Entrepreneurship.
7. Franchising.
8. Philanthropy.
9. Family Foundations.
10. Memoir.
I. Title.

First Hard Cover Edition: August 2007
First Soft Cover Edition: June 2008
Revised Hard and Soft Cover Editions: June 2011, May 2012,
January 2015, February 2016, May 2016, August 2018

This book was written, printed and bound in the United States of America.

*For My Wife, Children and Grandchildren
and my Mother and the Father who inspired this work.*

*And to my dear friend and co-author, John B. Babcock,
who died on April 12, 2008, just before the first publication
of this book came out. Johnnie dedicated this work to his late
wife, Nancy, and daughters, Susan, Nancy and Jeanne.*

Roy H. Park, Jr.

A sign at an intersection in Massena, New York where Park Outdoor's Northern Division owned billboards along the Canadian border until 1995.

FOUR GENERATIONS – The Park family in the summer of 1963 before I received an MBA from the Cornell University Johnson Graduate School of Management and left to join the J. Walter Thompson Co. in New York City.

From left to right: my maternal grandmother Mildred Goodwin Dent; daughter Elizabeth; me; my mother Dorothy Dent Park; maternal grandfather Walter Reed Dent; my father Roy H. Park; and my wife Tetlow Parham Park.

CONTENTS

ACKNOWLEDGMENTS

Our deepest thanks to:

James O'Shea Wade, independent editor and former senior executive with seven major publishing companies, for his professionalism and perseverance; life-long friends of the Park family Dr. Richard R. Cole, former dean of The University of North Carolina School of Media and Journalism and the late Professor Emeritus William B Ward of the Cornell University Department of Communications Arts, for their painstaking time and personal input; and Bonnie Angelo, another native of North Carolina and former TIME London Bureau Chief, Woman's National Press Club president and author of *First Mothers and First Families*, for her support and critique.

Also to the late Sam Johnson of S.C. Johnson, one of the most successful family businesses in the county, who worked with two Park generations on behalf of Cornell University's Johnson School of Graduate Management, and was the first to suggest this book be written; to D. Bryan Mangum, professor of American Literature at Virginia Commonwealth University for his knowledge and insight; and to our attorneys with Womble Carlyle Sandridge & Rice, LLP and Clifton & Singer, LLP in North Carolina; Barney, Grossman, Dubow & Troy, LLP, True, Walsh & Sokoni, LLP and Williamson, Clune & Stevens in Ithaca, New York and Bryan Cave, LLP in New York City.

As well as to former and current employees of Park Outdoor Advertising, and to the small but dedicated staff of the Triad Foundation with special thanks to Joanne Florino, the first Executive Director of the Park Foundation who followed us to Triad in that position before moving on to The Philanthropy Roundtable and Cornell University. Also to former employees of my father throughout his four careers who contributed thoughts and anecdotes to this work. And to my fact-checker, Steve Magacs, as well as

Michelle Hemmingway and Jennifer Cottrell who between them typed and updated the pages of this book many times since its beginning some 18 years ago.

Finally, to my wife, Tetlow for her patience, and to my mother, Dorothy D. Park, who died in 2016 at the age of 103, for ably surviving her partnership with her quintessential and hyperactive spouse. God bless you all. And from all of us who wrote it, we hope you enjoy the story.

Roy H. Park giving his annual "State of Our Union" talk to Park television, radio and newspaper managers in Ithaca, NY, in 1979. Although he owned some 20 newspapers at the time, the name change to Park Communications did not take place until the company went public in 1983.

PREFACE

On the trail of another man, the biographer must put up with finding himself at every turn: any biography uneasily shelters an autobiography within it.

—Paul Murray Kendall

Tolstoy said all happy families resemble one another; every unhappy family is unhappy in its own way. This also can apply to family businesses, and if you're thinking of working in the family business, think twice. Those of you who are may already know why.

This is the story of an SOB in a family-owned enterprise. Not my father. Me, the *Son of the Boss*. It's also told by another son who worked closest to Roy Hampton Park—John B. Babcock, the son of the man who gave my father his first big break. With the exception of my mother, no one knew more about my father on a personal and social level and in a one-on-one working relationship than Johnnie Babcock and me. Both of us being sons of self-made men, we think it represents thousands of others living or working in the shadows of powerful fathers.

For Babcock, it was stressful to be second-in-command to a *Forbes 400* workaholic for almost two decades and to meet the high expectations demanded. As he points out, *his own* father enjoyed significant fame—but Johnnie never worked for him. He worked for my father—and lived a personal version of "the strenuous life."

For me, as the son of a self-made entrepreneur, I learned you can survive reasonably well if you maintain your independence. It's another scenario when you become an SOB. I had a normal childhood, a good education, and a strong and respectable independent advertising career going when I decided to accept my father's invitation to work for him. That's when the going really got tough.

In 1942, Johnnie's father, H.E. Babcock, an entrepreneur who founded the largest farm cooperative in the nation hired my father. My father, in turn, hired Johnnie to work for him for a few years in the late 1940's, and later to rejoin him in 1964.

When I left the advertising agency business to come to work for my father in 1971, I reported to Johnnie. Neither of us could have fully anticipated what "life with father" would be like. As his longest-lasting employee, after working for him for 19 years, Johnnie resigned in 1988. I lasted 17 years working in his communications businesses before buying the outdoor divisions I had been hired to run, and brought Johnnie back then as a director of Park Outdoor.

What it's like to be the offspring of self-made entrepreneurs may be familiar to sons and daughters of driven fathers whether they work for them or not. After finishing the first draft of this book, reading it for the first time, I suddenly realized what being a Son of the Boss really means. It means the possibility of massive war with your family, and I had to go to war twice. It was the only way I was able to keep the company I run and create the foundation we have. It is the reason I was in a position to write this book.

What I saw of my father as I grew up paled in comparison to the insights I acquired while working for him. Combined with Johnnie's view from the top, we think it's a story worth telling. It may even provide comfort for other SOBs or DOBs.

INTRODUCTION
IN THE BEGINNING

They're tearing down the street where I grew up,
Like pouring brandy in a Dixie cup.
They're paving concrete on a part of me,
No trial for killing off a memory.
Ashes to ashes, dust to dust
Can you find the Milky Way?
Long Tall Sally and Tin Pan Alley
Have seen their dying day.
Ashes to ashes, dust to dust
It'll never be the same.
But we're all forgiving,
We're only living,
To leave the way we came.

—From the song "Ashes to Ashes"
by Dennis Lambert and Brian Potter[1]

I first heard these words in the song from *The Fifth Dimension* in 1973. As far as I know, all the places where I lived growing up in Raleigh, Ithaca, Lawrenceville, Chapel Hill, Queens, Port Chester and Charlotte are still there. All except one. Possibly the house I rented for a year in Perrine, Florida, may have been destroyed by hurricane Hugo. But SW 184th Terrace is still there.

But now in my later years, I feel the concrete of my past beginning to pave over me, and there's much to remember. Some of those memories may or may not be of value to others. But they are of value to me.

So while I can, I remember.

There are many misconceptions about my father, wrong rumors I hear to this day. So I felt the need for a son's account, neither a tribute nor a condemnation, to set the record straight. He was a great man, though frequently hurtful to me, and it was instructive to take a journey down the hard road he took to build an estate worth close to a billion dollars—and realize his version of the American dream.

That dream probably didn't include being ranked in the top 140 of the *Forbes 400* richest Americans in 1993 when he died. Pretty good for someone who came off a farm to put himself through college, and whose first full-time job after graduation paid $100 a month.

Though not particularly notable in today's terms, back in 1993, only 15 percent of the *Forbes 400* were billionaires, compared to some 88 percent in 2005. Ten years later the price of admission was well over $1.5 billion and to even be included in the October 2017 *Forbes 400* you needed $2 billion. But for my father, building $1 billion in 62 years from his starting salary of $100 a month is not insignificant. And neither is a billion. A billion minutes ago, Jesus was alive, a billion hours ago our ancestors were in the Stone Age, and a billion days ago, nothing walked the earth on two legs, let alone had human dreams. Like a father, or a son.

"Any biography uneasily shelters an autobiography within it," Paul Kendall said, and shortly after I started writing this book about my father, I realized it was going to include a lot about me and his closest business associate, Johnnie Babcock. Because that was the only way my father's story, with the knowledge and anecdotes we bring to it, can be told.

My father didn't make his fortune through computer genius, promotion or ascension in a company, performance bonuses, family inheritance, technology or invention, gambling, market manipulation, entertainment, energy, the stock market or options, or through a dot.com. Instead he made it the slow, hard way, doggedly passing through four careers to achieve success. He started as a writer, editor and publisher, moved on to advertising and public relations, then into food marketing and franchising, and finally into broadcasting media which expanded into print through newspaper publishing, taking him full circle to his beginnings.

In an article in the fall 1979 issue of *Wachovia Magazine* Catherine Walker observed that he possessed "a special blend of talents including business acumen, a keen perception of ideas that sell, a razor-sharp memory and the persistence and drive to make it all work. In short, he is an entrepreneur of the first order and of the old school—an all too rare individual in American business today."

My father was an avid researcher, as am I. There were hundreds of articles written about him during his various careers, and as a journalist, and his son, I have read them all to sort out the truth. I have interviewed his remaining associates, and the research has been not only exhaustive, but exhausting. "It has been said that writing comes more easily if you have something to say," according to novelist Sholem Asch, and I hope I do. And to get to the truth and assemble the facts has been a long, time-consuming ordeal.

Oscar Wilde said, "Every great man has his disciples—and it is always Judas who writes the biography." I am no Judas, but I will tell the truth about my father, even when it is painful, and praise him when praise is due.

It was not an easy task being the son of an entrepreneurial father like mine, but I managed to survive in his shadow, absorb the best lessons to be learned from the way he ran a business and directed his life, and reject the worst. I have also learned from my own experience running a business that you can still accomplish your goals by trusting your associates and employees.

In the process I learned what it should be like to be a father to your children, and although I, too, was a workaholic while my kids were growing up, I tried to take time when I could, mostly later in life, to let them know I loved them, that I cared. I have also tried hard to avoid making the same mistakes my father made with me.

My father was manipulative and controlling and he knew

how to use charm to his advantage, but there was good mixed in with the bad in our relationship, and I have come away awed by my new discoveries about this straight-out-of-Horatio-Alger self-made man. The bottom line was always important to him. My bottom line is that I respect him more in death than I did in life.

Life is short, and I wish I could bring him back to tell him, for the first time, how much I miss him. But I can't, and though there was a time for many years when I thought we might not be meeting in the hereafter, I now feel that we will be together in the same place, at some time, again.

It is said that every man has a story, and it is through that story that we can live on. If the story may also be worth something to others, then that is the premise and the promise of this book.

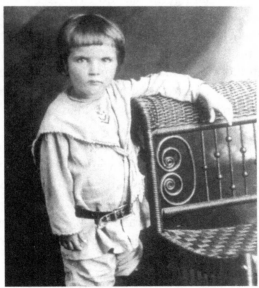

My father in 1915. Earnest and determined even at the tender age of five.

CHAPTER 1
HEARSAY AND HISTORY

I want to know what it says, the sea. What it is that it keeps on saying.

—Charles Dickens, Dombey and Son (1848)

To quote J.D. Salinger's narrator, Holden Caulfield, in the famous opening statement of the 1951 coming-of-age classic, *The Catcher in the Rye,* "If you really want to hear about it, the first thing you'll probably want to know is where I was born, what my lousy childhood was like, and how my parents were occupied and all before they had me, and all that David Copperfield kind of crap," and here Caulfield's quote ends with, "but I don't feel like going into it, if you want to know the truth."

Well, I feel like going into it. And I differ from Caulfield in that my childhood wasn't lousy; it was what came later that was. I started dictating my memories of my family relationship at the turn of the century in the summer of 2000 while on vacation on the Gulf of Mexico in Boca Grande, FL. I wasn't then, and still am not, into computers. Although everyone who works with me is computer literate from iPhones to mainframes, I still use a voice recorder for dictation. I feel that thoughts can be transmitted quicker through voice than through fingers on a keyboard. So, I continued dictating later the same year from the edge of the Atlantic Ocean in Pine Knoll Shores, N.C. Those vast, sighing, giving and taking seas that command almost three-fourths of our planet seemed to call to me and demand introspection, and once started, I found it hard to stop.

I was born on July 23, the beginning of Leo, in Rex Hospital in Raleigh to North Carolina parents in the Chinese Zodiac Year of the Tiger, 1938. As a Republican, as was my father before me, I find it ironic that the house that was my home for the first years of my life has become the Democratic headquarters in Raleigh. I don't remember much about the early years I lived in Raleigh. My memories really begin at age four, when my entire family moved to Ithaca, NY.

When I say the entire family, this included my father, my mother, my mother's mother, and my mother's grandmother. After my father and mother were married, he moved into her house. It was the middle of the Great Depression and times were tough enough to make ends meet for him to live in a house with his mother-in-law and grandmother-in-law, along with his wife. So I guess turnabout was fair play when he brought all of them with him when he moved to Ithaca.

After a short stay at the Ithaca Hotel, we crammed ourselves into a three-bedroom apartment in Belleayre, a building near Cornell University. My sister was not yet born, and I shared one of the bedrooms with "Muddie," my great-grandmother. (She was a dear soul, but the main thing that I remember about her was that she snored.)

BEFORE MY TIME

Where I was born and where and how I have lived is unimportant. It is what I have done with where I have been that should be of interest.

—Georgia O'Keeffe

My father was born in Dobson, North Carolina, on September 15, 1910. The youngest of four children and the second son of Laura Frances (Stone) and I. Arthur Park, Roy H. Park started life on a prosperous farm in Surry County near the Virginia border northwest of Winston-Salem, NC. This was unfortunate, since he detested farm life from an early age. I have heard that he did everything he could to avoid the labors involved with farming, even taking up reading the Bible before he reached his teens. This put him under the protection of his mother, the daughter of a Baptist preacher, and he was able to avoid much of the work in which his father and older brother were engaged that was required on a farm. Whenever his father commented on his absence in the field, his mother would tell her husband to leave their son alone because he was studying the "Good Book," and that was more important than pitching hay or shoveling manure.

My Grandparents on my father's side, Laura Frances and I. Arthur Park with some of their grandchildren (not including my sister or me) in the mid-1970s on grandmother Park's eighty-third birthday.

He was, therefore, highly motivated to leave farm life as soon as he could. It was said that he came down with pneumonia in December of his first year of high school and at age thirteen, spent the rest of the year in bed with what his doctor diagnosed as rheumatic fever. His mother, a former schoolteacher, believed that an idle mind was the devil's workshop, so she kept him busy with lessons sent from school. He returned to Dobson High School in the Surry County seat, some fourteen miles north of Elkin, the next fall. He took a test to see if he could rejoin his classmates and did so well that the school allowed him to skip a grade.

In high school he also delivered newspapers, and worked as a county correspondent for three weekly newspapers. His hustling drive, coupled with skipping a grade, enabled him to graduate from high school in 1926 at age sixteen. That same year, he headed "down east" to get a higher education, with the idea that he might become a physician. He first applied to Duke University, took the entrance exam, and was offered a scholarship.

But Duke lost a potential medical student when my father's brother, who by this time was a student at North Carolina State College in Raleigh, drove over to Durham to see him one day. He was driving a fairly new Chevrolet Roadster, and told my father if he transferred to State, he'd let him drive the car every now and then. So as one of the youngest students to attend NC State, at age sixteen he enrolled to study business and journalism, and worked, while attending classes, to put himself through.

"My father was a farmer, but my oldest brother graduated from State and my two sisters went to Woman's College [now The University of North Carolina at Greensboro]," my father recalled. "I knew that if I needed help from my family, it was there. But I always felt that if you could maintain your independence, you could take great pride in it." I was later to learn the truth in that.

There is one thing many people don't know about the journalism courses in which my father enrolled at NC State. I found it in my files among the many copies of my father's talks and speeches, some with his notes or alternate comments scribbled along the margins in his awful handwriting. It was part of his acceptance speech when he was inducted into the North Carolina Journalism Hall of Fame in 1990.

Stretching things just a bit, he called The University of North Carolina at Chapel Hill his alma mater, saying in a speech he gave many years after graduating that, "Of course I am a graduate of North Carolina State...but when I began college, this School of Journalism was on its campus over in Raleigh...and didn't move to Chapel Hill until after my senior year. "Although a coincidence, not a trade, when about the same time the Engineering School was moved from Chapel Hill to the Raleigh campus, my father went on to say:

"It was the kind of trade that makes both parties winners....I don't have to tell you that The University of North Carolina School of Journalism is among the best known journalism schools in the country...and I am proud to consider myself an alumnus of this School of Journalism." My father concluded his speech saying, "In fact, my son, Roy H. Park, Jr., and his son, Roy H. Park III, are both graduates of this School of Journalism." (In 1990 the president of The University of North Carolina, C.D. Spangler, Jr., wrote him a letter saying, "I am proud that two great universities within UNC can lay claim to you. Your comments about the Engineering School at UNC-Chapel Hill and the Journalism School at North Carolina State University convince me that I would benefit from a brush up on the history of the switch.")

Geography aside, at North Carolina State in 1926, even the $150 yearly tuition and $16.50 a month for food was a lot of money for someone who didn't have any, and I suspect that's when my father's real work ethic began. Although I share my father's passion to work hard, he was as true a workaholic as ever existed.

In his junior year, he was out driving with his friends one evening in the early spring and he ran into a parked car. He decided that rather than go home for the Easter break, he would get a job to pay to fix the car. I suspect that this reflected his penchant for work, and his decision not to spend the break at home also kept him off the farm.

One of the ways he earned a few bucks, along with a fellow

student with the unusual and unlikely moniker of "Pea Vine" Reynolds, was to sell magazine subscriptions. My father said many times the woman of the house would not come to the front door, but would call down from an upstairs window or porch to ask what they wanted when the door bell rang. My father's answer was "COD, lady," which would bring the prospect down to the front door. When they discovered a delivery was not being made, Pops would meekly say that COD meant, "come on down," and then go into his routine about being a poor student working his way through college by selling magazines. Most of the time it worked.

Reynolds, at age seventy-nine, said in a telephone interview from his Lumberton, NC, home, "Roy's got what you might call a broad view of the future. An' he figgers things better 'n any man I ever seen." Both Reynolds and Park must have done some fancy "figgering" because Reynolds says of their magazine hustling, "I started in [college] with two hundred dollars. I paid all the tuition myself, all the costs and finished with a new car, two thousand dollars in cash, and that was in the middle of the Depression." Pea Vine and Park went their separate ways after gradation in 1931, but kept in touch, and years later he would come back into my father's life.

Because my father had worked as a reporter for the campus publication the *Technician* since his freshman year, he was able to find a part-time job as an office boy with the Associated Press in Raleigh. He operated a mimeograph machine, stuffed envelopes, and ran errands for $4.50 per week, attending classes until noon and working afternoons for the AP.

He also wrote fillers for area newspapers (at 10¢ a column inch), and kept pestering the Raleigh bureau chief, W. Joynes McFarland, to "let me write some real stories." After he threatened to go home to Surry County "because I couldn't live in Raleigh on four dollars and fifty cents per week," McFarland found a spot for him on the AP staff.

Working with the Governor's Office, Raleigh newspaper publishers, the college extension editor, and others, his wages grew along with his responsibilities, including correspondence for two northwestern North Carolina newspapers. Another of his duties was covering executions by electrocution at Central Prison. "Nobody liked doing that," he said, "so we'd get ourselves a Coke with some ammonia in it before we went to the prison. And sometimes we'd put in something a little stronger. I thought it was very foolish at that time to sit there with a clock and see how long they struggled," he recalled. "It was pretty bad. It gave me nightmares."

By 1930, at age nineteen, my father had earned enough credits to graduate, and was making a stately $18 per week at the AP. He said the money was not as important as contacts with the influential people he got to know, but it helped pay for school. And these contacts were to prove helpful as graduation approached.

But he decided to enroll in graduate studies so he could serve as the *Technician*'s elected editor-in-chief. Jobs were scarce, and the position paid a salary of $37.50 a month plus one-fourth of the profits. "This, plus freelancing for out-of-town newspapers, paid better than the few dollars a week I would have received as a newspaper reporter in those days," he said.

I don't want to leave the impression that my father's college life was all work and no play, since he did take time to relax and have fun. He said he had two old cars. "That was so I'd be sure one was always running. I'd park them on a hill so I'd be sure I could get them started. One was a Willys-Overland—that was the fancy town car," he said.

In 1931, my father was honored by his senior classmates as "best writer." As one of 311 in his June graduating class, with a minor in journalism, he was among 37 to receive a BS in Business Administration from NC State. His college annual, *Agromeck*, predicted that he would be "a lord in the fourth estate." It was an oddly accurate prediction for a college annual, but in forty years it came true.

But back then it was the beginning of the Depression and jobs were scarce. Planning ahead, my father had been reading the want ads long before he graduated. As they say on the farm, timing has a lot to do with the outcome of a rain dance, and it makes sense to go after a job when one opens up that you might be able to get.

A TOUGH INTERVIEW

One day he saw a blind ad for a public relations job in the Raleigh *News & Observer.* It was signed Box 731, which was located in Raleigh's historic Century Station. Instead of mailing in his application, he hand-delivered his response to the postmaster in a colored envelope to make it stand out, then stationed himself in front of the box the next morning to wait for the person who came to pick up the mail.

Eventually a man came in to open the box, and my father eased over to introduce himself, pointed to the pink (sometimes he said it was blue) envelope, and asked if the owner of the box would kindly read his application first. The man turned out to be H.B. (Red) Trader, the secretary to Uria Benton Blalock, head of the Farmers Cooperative Exchange as well as the North Carolina Cotton Growers Association, one of the largest cotton marketing associations in the South.

Before the day was out, my father was able to call on his earlier contacts from the Governor's Office to the president of NC State to ask them to make calls on his behalf. Before the sun went down, Blalock had received telephone calls endorsing him from O. Max Gardner, governor of North Carolina; Josepheus Daniels, publisher of the *News & Observer*; John Park, publisher of the *Raleigh Times*; the NC State president; and three other influential local men. This made it difficult for Blalock to avoid asking my father to meet with him.

As my father later told an interviewer, "My letter got a favorable response. Anticipating that it would, I had bought myself a white cotton suit and showed up for the interview wearing it."

The job was director of public relations, which involved editing and publishing a newsletter, the *Carolina Cooperator*, for co-op members, and my father felt it was a perfect match. But the job offer was not immediately forthcoming.

At their meeting, Blalock said, "Look at all these letters. I've got letters from people with a lot more experience than you have. I'm going to hire another candidate, but I wanted to tell you that I was impressed by your initiative. If you keep going like this, maybe one of these days you'll amount to something." My father replied that he wanted to amount to something then, and Blalock did not immediately turn him down.

Instead, he took my father, who was still a student, along with him on a business trip to Kannapolis, NC. It was hot in Blalock's Lincoln limousine, and they would occasionally stop for a cold drink along the way. My father said Blalock would ask him to call the office and tell them to sell so many pounds of cotton, or buy so many. He'd write it all down and call it in, but thought it was one hell of a poor company to work for if they were spending money buying futures on this and that, with a fellow like him telling them what to buy. My father soon guessed, however, that Blalock was just finding out how many mistakes he would make.

A few days later, Blalock called my father into his office to repeat the bad news. He told him, "You're a pretty smart and resourceful young man, but you're too young. You ought to stay in touch, and after you learn something about journalism maybe we'll have a place for you."

But my father didn't give up. He told Blalock he'd saved some money and said, "I know I can do this job. I'll bring my own typewriter if you'll give me a place to put it and a lamp. You don't even have to give me an office. And I'll work for free for three months. If you don't ask me to stay, I'll come by and thank you for the experience I got and go on my way."

"We're a large organization and can't do that," Blalock told him. But then he thought for a moment and asked my father what he figured the job should pay. My father replied, "I think it's worth two hundred and fifty dollars a month."

To which Blalock said, "You're the damnedest young fellow I have ever seen. I'll give you a hundred dollars a month." My father responded, "You talked me into it."

Thus began my father's first business career, thirty days before his graduation. When he reported for work, his direct boss at Carolina Cotton was M.G. "Manley" Mann. My father credits him as one of the two people who gave him a role model for success, the other being his future partner Duncan Hines, who was internationally famous as an arbiter of taste. A tough taskmaster, Mann was another workaholic who expected work to be on time and done right. My father said Mann was good at business, but he liked him because he said he was also a dreamer, and that was something they both had in common. My father always felt it was OK to have dreams, as long as you were able to work hard enough to put a foundation under them. And he was good at that.

Mann to Man at Carolina Cotton in 1931. My father's boss in his first job, "Manley" Mann, was another workaholic who Pops credits as one of the two role models that shaped his life.

As director of public relations, my father stayed with the Cotton Association for eleven years in public relations, advertising and speech writing. He impressed his employees and their growing number of customers with his flair for creative editing and his skills in public relations and sales promotion. There was a lot of money in cotton in those days, and one of the more remarkable things he did was figure out a way to enhance the public image of cotton garments. As the traditional fabric of work clothing, being tough and comfortable, it was favored by the working class, and looked down upon by the socially elite and those who wanted to be. My father figured that if he could change that image he could substantially broaden the market.

He came up with the idea of holding Cotton Balls, highly publicized statewide affairs, which included parades and formal dances attended by the daughters of some of North Carolina's most prominent families. The promotion included "Maids of Cotton," young women dressed in all-cotton gowns. Park arranged for the manufacture of special gowns for the women and tuxedos for their escorts, and all in attendance wore cotton.

Including the lady who would become my mother, Dorothy Goodwin Dent.

MEETING MY MOTHER

Victory—a matter of staying power.

—Elbert Hubbard

A great many people thought that the first Cotton Ball was *where* he met my mother, but it wasn't. He met her earlier on a blind date.

My mother attended Peace and Meredith Colleges in Raleigh. My father first met her shortly after he graduated, while she was still a junior at Meredith. She was three years younger than he was. They met on a double blind date set up by her cousin—and my father was not intended to be her date. Yet somehow, my mother recalled, people got switched around, and he ended up in the backseat of the car with her. I suspect he had planned it that way all along.

My mother said she didn't really care for him from the start. She had seen him before the date as a student standing on the corner near her house, wearing a baseball cap and hitchhiking to school. I'm sure he had also seen her and had prevailed on her cousin to set things up with the girl he wanted to meet. Although this beautiful and effervescent young woman from Raleigh may have been a social level or two above him, he had already set his sights on her and began his courtship in earnest.

My mother loved to dance, and on their first date, she found out he couldn't. That was one negative. He wanted to sit out the entire dance in a secluded part of the combination basketball court and auditorium that had temporarily been converted into a ballroom, drinking Cokes and talking. My mother felt he was full of himself and quite pushy. Two more negatives. In fact, she said he told her on this first date that he intended to marry her.

He even embarrassed her when he was master of ceremonies at a dance she later attended, this time with *another* date. My father was with a woman who enjoyed drinking, and he had evidently enjoyed drinking along with her. My mother said he fell off the stage and landed flat on his face at one point while trying to introduce the next piece the band was preparing to play.

With all those negatives, he had to outfox his competitors, and he made a point of finding out who they were. Meredith was just down Hillsborough Street from NC State and its all-girl enrollment was an obvious target for the men at State, particularly the fraternity boys. Since my father had a car, one of his tricks, when he found out who the others were she was dating, was to pull up in front of their fraternities with her in the car and tell her that he had to run in and see somebody.

My mother said she wanted to crouch down on the floorboards until he came out of each house, and she suspected there was no one in there he needed to see, or even knew. But leaving her in his car in full view of the fraternity brothers on the porch each time was a clever way of staking his claim.

"Boy was he persistent," my mother remembered. He combined his strategy of eliminating his competition with a keen anticipation of what my mother liked and wanted. He showered her with baby chicks dyed purple and rabbits at Easter, and on special occasions, with other live creatures he knew she loved. He bought a Pomeranian for one of her birthdays and prevailed on his secretary to store it in her bathtub for the week before the date arrived. The secretary told my mother she couldn't sleep the entire period with the dog yipping in the bathtub, but my father had charmed her into it.

My father and mother in 1937, before I came along to spice up their life.

After my mother graduated from college, he continued his relentless pursuit, turning everyone who knew her into a supporter. She said her grandparents' cook and yardman loved him and told her what a dynamic go-getter he was. One could almost believe he paid them off. So using one strategy or another, he drove all other suitors away, and I think by default she accepted his proposal of marriage. His persistence won out and on October 3, 1936, they were married.

My mother was an only child, whereas my father had a brother and two sisters. As the saying goes, single children tend to be spoiled. My father certainly spoiled, or at least indulged, my mother not only during their courtship, but throughout their life together.

What other man would accept, after marriage, both his mother-in-law's and her mother's moving with him to another town, then living under the same roof in a small apartment? This may have been another reason he became a life-long workaholic—anything to get out of the house.

After I was born in 1938 and was barely old enough to start talking, I named my parents by mutual consent. My grandmother, Mildred Goodwin Dent, was trying to teach me to say "Daddy," and it came out "Dottie." But I could pronounce "Pops," so my father became Pops, and my mother became Dottie, which was close enough to Dorothy for her. She preferred that to "Mom," anyway, so the name took, and my father preferred "Pops" to Dad. My grandmother, by the way, became "Mimmie," as close as I could come to Mildred. Thus our communication links were established.

CHAPTER 2
BRANCHING OUT

Pops stayed with Carolina Cotton until 1942, but during this time he had also started to branch out into operations for himself. In 1937 he worked on the side for a year as senior editor for the Rural Electrification Administration of the U.S. Department of Agriculture in Washington, DC, and from 1938 to 1942 published their *Rural Electrification Guide*.

In 1939, he purchased an agricultural trade magazine, *Cooperative Digest and Farm Power*, directed to leaders of the state's farm cooperatives, and also published it on the side. This magazine, which he eventually took with him to Ithaca and published until 1966, as well as his successful promotions with Carolina Cotton, earned him a reputation that brought him to the attention of the head of what became known as Agway in New York State.

In fact, *Cooperative Digest* became so widely read among farm people that once, when it printed a story on farm co-ops that had run in the *Reader's Digest* and the *Saturday Evening Post*, its author received more mail from its readers than he had received from readers of both general-circulation magazines.

The author of that article was H.E. Babcock, in 1921 Cornell's first professor of farm marketing, who had resigned to raise the initial capital for, and to manage, the Grange League Federation. Known as the GLF, the organization became one of the largest farm producer and consumer cooperatives in the world. Ed Babcock also served for many years on the Cornell Board of Trustees, becoming chairman during the 1940s, including the World War II years. My father liked the one-man-one-vote philosophy of farm co-ops and was attracted to Babcock's dynamic leadership, writing skills, and his lifelong dedication to the welfare of the American farm family.

Babcock looked up my father during a farm co-op meeting in Atlanta and tried to hire him. My father told Babcock that if he left Raleigh, it could be only to run his own business. Babcock said, "Well, maybe you just bought your own business. We have an in-house advertising and research agency. You can buy it and have your own business."

My father told Babcock that he didn't know if he had enough money to buy it, and Babcock said, "I think you have. I'll lend it to you. In fact, I'll practically give it to you." And he did, through the arrangement of a friendly loan. H.E. Babcock was a hard man to say no to my father told me.

THE MOVE TO ITHACA

Nothing is too small to know, and nothing is too big to attempt.

—*William Van Horne*

So in 1942 my father was brought to Ithaca, the home of Cornell University, to take over the small GLF advertising agency, with the provision that as long as he handled the GLF advertising, he would be free to engage or solicit any other clients he wanted. He would also, with Babcock's help and no money up front, be able to buy the agency over time.

With a public relations career under his belt, he began one in advertising. He arrived in Ithaca, NY, with his extended family, including me, during a snowstorm on April Fool's Day in 1942. He abandoned his secure job of eleven years with the Cotton Growers Co-op, which had offered him both a pay raise and a promotion to stay, and in addition, he took a cut in pay. On top of that, the blizzard was so heavy he thought at the time we should turn around and head back south.

As he said in an interview with the *Ithaca Journal* reporter, Judith Horstman, "My wife and I and our young son were staying at the Old Ithaca Hotel, and as I looked out the window at all that snow and thought about the flowers that were blooming in Raleigh, I began to wonder if I'd made a good decision."

But later, he said the smartest thing he ever did was to see what he could do under his own steam, and my father began, at age thirty-two, his second career. This part, Johnnie Babcock, the son of the man who brought him to Ithaca, tells best:

"In the early 1940s, my father, H.E. Babcock, learned of Roy Park's exploits in promoting the North Carolina Cotton cooperative. It took more than a fair salary to persuade Park to leave his native state. Babcock offered the young southerner the opportunity to work out payments to buy the GLF's Ithaca ad agency. The chance to own his first real business brought Park a-running," Johnnie remembers.

"The ad agency, Agricultural Advertising and Research, Inc., or Ag Research, was located up some twenty linoleum-clad steps inside an ancient building on Ithaca's State Street. Park nailed down a spacious private office overlooking the busy street, though no one ever saw him raise the blinds to look out. His focus was on the business inside and the staff he assembled.

"People falling all over themselves in a rapidly expanding business? Hardly. Park maintained (as he would in every business he built or acquired) a minimal staff of multitask workers, preferably with a farm background and farmers' traditional ethic of hard work. Their humble upbringing also made farm-raised folks more affordable for Park.

"An outdoorsman, gifted creative artist and professional print executive, Bob Flannery answered as production manager, art director, print estimator, idea man, and staff coordinator. A retired newswoman, Grace Smiley wrote almost all the copy on her old L.C. Smith typewriter, dispensed editorial counseling, and got the morning coffee. Another mature lady, Louise Holcomb, kept the books and prepared the payroll. Roy himself retained a proficient secretary and trusted assistant. There were also less important employees: a receptionist, typist, and other clericals. Roy brought in a business manager with strong accounting credentials. Someone who you will understand is best left unnamed.

"A hands-on manager, Roy literally bounded up to the second-floor offices, two-steps-at-a-time strides belying the fact that he never observed an exercise regime. He was usually the first one to arrive. He dashed to his secure office, entered with his private key and took his commanding position behind a massive desk that was to become his office trademark. Park sensed that an appropriate space between employer communicating with employee was to his advantage, and a huge intervening desktop did the job perfectly.

"Though Park closely monitored the attendance and performance of each employee, the business manager had assumed a unique measure of independence. He picked up and emptied the contents of the post office box on the secretary's desk where Park opened most first-class mail personally. The business manager made the daily bank deposit of checks or cash received. Park personally initialed approval for payment of even the smallest trade expense and held unpaid bills to the last day they were due, and often a few days more. The business manager then wrote, signed and mailed the company checks.

"At night and on weekends, Roy studied the fundamentals of small business stewardship and bookkeeping, but in those early days relied heavily on his business manager.

"Few business owners personally reconcile the company's month-end bank statement and canceled checks with the books. But Park's confidence in his top man was replaced by suspicion when some questionable payments prompted Park to take the company records home one weekend to review every bill, payment, and canceled check and reconcile them with the bank statement. Bingo! Some payables were listed as made to a routine recipient, but the check for that amount was made out to the business manager.

"His key man glibly explained that a few people in a small town like Ithaca insisted on cash, and that he made those cash payments after paying the amount due to himself. That's all that savvy Park needed. Henceforth there would be no checks ever issued that he did not cosign.

"Park thought he had caught the manager red-handed. He took him to court, but sloppy preparation for the trial failed to yield a conviction. For the first time Roy H. Park had been taken to the cleaners. He vowed it would never happen again.

"This incident prompted revision of Ag Research's entire bookkeeping process. Park hastened to establish ironclad controls and authorized contacts. They became the disciplined framework for management, not to say micromanagement, of all his subsequent business ventures. As a result of his failure to catch the man in the act, Park assumed that people who worked for him might well be guilty until proven, over many years, innocent. This paranoia provided employment for a considerable number of internal and external auditors for years to come.

"Never straying far from his youthful passion for the printed word, Park's acquired agency continued to publish *Co-op Digest*, a trade publication focused on several farmer cooperatives. He opened offices in Albany, NY; Raleigh, NC; Richmond, VA; and, to promote potato farming and marketing in the east, set up a Washington, DC, office headed by lobbyist Whitney Blair.

"Flannery designed an attractive masthead that held up well over the years and saw to the printing of *Co-Op Digest*. Park micromanaged the magazine's content from a variety of contributors, making subtle and important editing changes that kept the magazine both appropriate to support of the farm co-op cause and a vehicle to expand his list of farm clients. It was well written and professional.

"New clients were brought aboard with carefully drafted contracts that called not only for routine trade commissions for the ad agency but for an annual prepaid service fee of several thousand dollars to cement Park's personal involvement and leadership. Ag Research had become a going concern, Park's flagship business. The agency provided services and placed advertising right up to Park's death.

"A boisterous, growing business required dedicated and skilled management. Park's evolving style required a high standard of staff accountability and hard work. To keep everyone at maximum output, he required frequent personal reports from those supervising employees. He rarely visited individual workspaces, relying instead on examining the end product or progress reports in his lair. He was a good listener and an incisive critic.

"When one of his most trusted employees was on the carpet, he would lean back in his high-back chair and gently twirl the plastic knob at the end of the control cords of the large Venetian blind behind him as he listened to the report. He never opened the blinds—the outside world was an unnecessary distraction. He took notes during each report and referred to them at the next session, reminding the employee of promises for improvement or change made at the last session, reiterating deadlines, and setting expanded work assignments.

"He did enjoy lunch meetings at the Dutch Kitchen restaurant in the regal Ithaca Hotel. The maitre d' always ushered Park and his guests to the same large round table in the rear of the restaurant. Once everyone was seated, Park put a written agenda on the table; it was the script that determined what would be discussed at lunch. He loved to have H.E. Babcock join him, but when my father was in town, he preferred to eat lunch at his Sunny Gables farm out in Inlet Valley. So Park's guests were usually officers of GLF, occasionally a Cornell farm economist, and when appropriate, a Park employee pertinent to the outside guests. Park was always a discerning and generous host, a practice he observed throughout his entire career.

"When Park left the downtown office for the day, he carried with him a briefcase bulging with financial reports, business publications and newspapers mailed to him from the southern markets he served. He read and studied every night and for the better part of Saturday and Sunday. He had a voracious appetite for almost everything in print, and a prodigious memory for facts. There was never a doubt that he worked longer hours than any of his employees or associates.

"Park was poised for greater things. As a brilliant business-man, he might well have invented the admonishment Buy Low, Sell High. But he practiced only the first part. He drove a hard bargain as a buyer because he always was better informed about the offering than even the seller. Park, as we will see, rarely sold anything, especially if it was profitable," Johnnie points out.

But there was a devastating exception to this, which we'll come to later. Johnnie continues:

"As a balance to their aggressive conduct of business, executives such as Roy Park proudly cited their rural roots as witness to love of nature, purity of heart, devotion to hard work, and thrifty family values. These attributes describe lots of farm folk, and they are guideposts to many business success stories. As a suitable preparation for acquiring business acumen, a solid farm background ranks right up there with the school of hard knocks. People from both backgrounds often claim that they are prerequisites for business success.

"Like Roy, I really did get my start on the farm, not just a homestead in the rural countryside or a small town, but a real working farm. My early memories are not of a poor lad scuffling barefoot down a dirt road to while away time fishing with a bamboo stick and bent pin.

"My boyhood years during the Great Depression had firm direction and called for hard work. I did not wear threadbare clothes and never missed a meal. My family lived in an 1851 Greek Revival house with eleven gables and nineteen rooms. And we got up when it was still dark to start a farmer's long day.

"We raised chickens, dairy cows, sheep and hogs. We owned or boarded saddle horses and broke-to-harness teams of draft horses that were sold or worked on our farm. My father had come from a hardscrabble farm, and as a teenager vowed to escape its squalor and devote his life to improving the lot of the Northeastern farm family.

"He purchased Sunnygables, the farm where I was raised, in 1921 and moved his own father from the stony hills above Gilbertsville, NY, to a small dairy farm near our Inlet Valley place. He did all of this on borrowed money. I have his tax returns recording negative net worth during the Depression years.

"We three kids, my brother, Howard, Jr.; sister, Barbara; and I, shared the tasks expected of children in farm families. Backbreaking chores and responsibilities, undertaken with plenty of help and encouragement from Mother and Dad, were the fabric of family well-being. Every meal was a family gathering and a forum to talk things over. Early to bed, early to rise was more than a saying—it was a way of life.

"Dad was a primary founder of the Grange League Federation in 1921. He took over as general manager when the new organization was about to fail. Widely known as "Ed" or "H.E.," Dad shaped the popular, member-owned production and marketing organization into the largest farm cooperative in the country.

"GLF was named for its founding agricultural groups: The National Grange, The Dairymen's League, and The Farm Bureau Federation. Other regional farm co-ops soon followed. One was the Carolina Cotton Growers Association, Roy Park's first full-time employer.

"Books were written to honor the exploits of Ed Babcock, and I wrote one myself called *Farmboy*. For now, however, I'll stick to the story of my own background prior to becoming Roy Park's number-two man.

"Dad worked us kids hard during harvest season, but about the time I got sick and tired of rising lame and sore in the morning from hard physical work the day before, he would perform a miracle. One memorable event when I was twelve was being spirited off with a hired-hand companion to the 1934 Chicago World's Fair. We country boys marveled at the plush accoutrements of our sleeping car, and the splendor of the Union League Club in the windy city. I loved the fair, and my older teenage chaperone bragged for decades about seeing the erotic moves of famous fan dancer Sally Rand.

"I had a choice of going away to boarding school during my high school years and then to attend Cornell or of finishing at

Ithaca High and going away for my college years. The family helped me decide to leave Ithaca High after my sophomore year, and benefit from the privilege, again arranged by Dad, of attending what was arguably the finest preparatory school in the country, Phillips Exeter Academy in New Hampshire.

"It was a humbling experience. After easing by with all As in my first year in high school, I was set back a year in New Hampshire and barely survived the cut after the first year at Exeter. I finally caught up with the program, graduated with respectable grades as an English major, and entered Cornell as a cocky freshman in the fall of 1941.

"At Cornell University's College of Agriculture, I completed the curriculum for acceptance to medical school and took courses in economics and animal husbandry. Since courses at Exeter covered material on a level of many college courses, I breezed through my classes, hardly cracking a book my freshman year. Life was easy, and beer was 10¢ a glass. My farm experience training horses helped me make the polo team. But by fall 1942, there wasn't much time for polo, since a gathering stream of students were called up or enlisted for service in World War II.

"I signed up in the enlisted reserves, and soon enough Uncle Sam invited me to join the Infantry in 1943. That was the time I should have asked Dad to intervene. He was in an influential position as chairman of the board at Cornell and could have arranged either a softer assignment or a transfer for me. I had passed up the opportunity to be an artillery officer after basic drill in the Reserve Officers Training Corps (ROTC). I heard that junior Artillery officers stood a good chance of being assigned as forward observers in combat zones, and that wasn't for me.

"Called to active duty, I spent months in basic infantry training and field maneuvers. I was sure the war would be long over before I made it overseas. Fate was not that kind. I found myself in an infantry division shipped out for the European Theater of Operations (ETO). Things moved rapidly, and suddenly in December 1944, there I was in a frozen foxhole on the front lines facing a bunch of snow-covered German pillboxes.

"That started 127 days of digging foxholes, artillery bombardments, shooting and getting shot at during the Battle of the Bulge, crossing the Rhine River over the Ludendorf Bridge at Remagen, and the final mopping up of the German army. A PFC (one stripe) in the States, I rose through the ranks to technical sergeant, earning three stripes and two rockers during combat. The fighting was desperate and the battlefield incredibly cold. My promotions in rank to platoon sergeant should have been based on bravery and ability. Fact is, I rose through the ranks in replacement of those who were struck down before me. World War II combat stands as the most draining and frightening experience of my life. My main achievement was survival. Fifty GIs in my rifle company, many of them barely eighteen, were not so lucky.

"I was busy studying and playing at college before the war when Roy Park came to the notice of my father as a replacement manager of the advertising agency employed by GLF, Agricultural Advertising and Research. Dad told me he had brought this bright young man in, and if he lasted, he might open up a writing opportunity for me after the war. It turned out to be just that.

"After combat, I was promoted to first sergeant (which added another rocker and star), and came back from Europe. After I was discharged, I returned to Cornell and studied English and literature in the Arts College. I met Roy and accepted a part-time copywriting job at the old offices on State Street. Most of my pieces dealt with co-op membership events and news reports on their one-man, one-vote meetings.

"Until then, I had known very little about his immediate family. His attractive and engaging wife, Dorothy, charmed me. Their two children—Roy, Jr., and his younger sister who was born in Ithaca, Adelaide—were seldom mentioned by him and very briefly acknowledged when I visited him at his home. I remember one evening before bedtime, little Roy (a denigrating southern appellation instead of Jr. for a son named after his father) timorously inquiring whether he could perform a magic show for his dad and me. His father granted permission but asked that the lad be brief.

"Young Roy mounted a few stairs toward the sleeping quarters. From that improvised stage, with various acquired aids, he performed a few sleight-of-hand tricks. While I applauded and encouraged him, his father, openly bored, asked him to wrap up his performance and get on up to bed. The dismissal had all the bonding and affection of a master telling his little dog to get lost.

"As the children grew, Roy provided plenty of discipline but not much rapport. It was hard to imagine that in an apparently normal family, the children were being raised in the shadow under a basket. There was no playing ball in the yard with Dad, no hikes with the kids, no family fishing trips. Roy was ill-suited for the rounded give and take of family life.

"My part-time work writing copy in Ithaca was good training. I quit school to open an Ag Research office for Park in Richmond, VA, to handle advertising for Southern States Cooperative, a mirror image of the GLF organization I knew so well. The pay was low even for those times, but sufficient for a single man living in a rented bedroom on a farm outside Richmond. I saw little of Roy. He not only failed to visit the Richmond office but also never asked me a question about my experiences in the military. I never volunteered a word myself."

Johnnie concludes that, "I realized that while Roy showed every sign of being an even more formidable businessman than my dad, he lacked Dad's warmer human attributes. In any case, my path would diverge from Roy Park's when the Richmond experience ended with my return to Ithaca after Dad's first heart attack in 1949."

CHAPTER 3
THE DUNCAN HINES CONNECTION

As time went by, Ag Research prospered and grew. When Pops first took over the agency, he inherited six employees on the third floor of the Tompkins County Trust Company building in downtown Ithaca. He said the agency was "pretty ratty" and didn't have many accounts. He hired some agriculture students from Cornell and said he taught them how to write and take pictures.

They took pictures of chickens and cows, which were numerous in upstate New York. My father told them that farmers are not interested in pretty pictures but in pictures that tell them something about the value of their animals. Thanks to this pragmatic approach, on such instruction the agency prospered, and in four or five years Pops had 125 employees and added an office in New York City to his branches in Albany, Washington, Raleigh, and Richmond, where Johnnie was working until 1949.

Another young man my father brought into the company was a graduate of the hotel school at Cornell University. While attending Cornell, he was the advertising manager, and later the business manager, of the *Cornell Daily Sun.* Stewart Underwood was hired as an account executive in my father's Raleigh, NC, Ag Research office in 1947 because of this experience, and was destined to work for Pops for the next sixteen years.

In the meantime, my father had moved his office to a building he bought in Ithaca in 1945, when he founded his real estate division, RHP Incorporated. The building also housed the printing plant for his two magazines.

His agency included Dairymen's League, American Cranberry Growers, Southern States Cooperative and the Philco Corporation among its clients, as well as Thomas E. Dewey during his political campaigns. Because of his reputation for successfully reaching a large segment of dairy farmers and the agricultural population, Pops directed the farm campaign for Thomas E. Dewey's 1946 successful run for governor of New York. When Dewey ran for president in 1948, he ran the advertising campaign for Dewey in the northeast. When he woke up on the morning after Election Day, Pops was as surprised as just about everyone else in the country when Harry Truman won. Most people had assumed that Dewey had it in the bag.

Flying High. Pops getting around in a helicopter during Dewey's campaigns.

If Dewey had won, Pops said he would have ended his career as a retired government bureaucrat. Fortunately, fate decided otherwise—and Pops knew that after Dewey lost he would be on the outside looking in, in terms of political pull or connections.

It meant he might not be able to do as much for his company's clients, so he told them that there wouldn't be any hard feelings if they wanted to move their accounts elsewhere. Some did.

"That was the year a piano-playing ex-haberdasher from Missouri showed Mr. Dewey a thing or two," he said. "Old Harry nearly wiped out my company because nobody loves a loser, and we had tied ourselves to one. 'Close' only counts in horseshoes." Most of the accounts that stayed with his agency were farmers' cooperatives.

But even before the election, his farm co-op clients had been talking to Pops about helping them develop a brand name. These producers of milk, fruit, honey, and other foods that were packaged and sold under other people's brands weren't doing especially well, and after the election, he turned to the project with renewed interest. Studies showed there was a clear need for the farmers' cooperative to increase revenue through franchising a name already established in the food field.

One of the early employees of Ag Research before my father took over was Monroe Babcock of Babcock Poultry, a friend of, but no relation to Johnnie's father, H.E. Babcock. Aside from his friendship with Ed, Monroe bought hatching eggs from him for many years. Referring to Ed as the man who made GLF at least the largest agricultural cooperative in the country, Monroe said, "Ed was one of the smartest men in America. Aside from being chairman of the Board of Trustees of Cornell University, he was a director of Avco Corporation, and he had fifty new ideas every day." Monroe said, for example, there were no freezers in American homes before Ed Babcock cooked up the idea and persuaded a company that made ice cream freezers to manufacture and sell them."

Ed had been talking to professors in the Cornell home economics department about formulating new, more nutritious foods, with his prime interest being a cake mix. My father and he agreed that if they could come up with a cake mix that was different from the rest, it could be one of the first products taken to market once they came up with the right name.

So in mid-1948 the search began for a brand name for GLF, and unbeknownst to my father, he was about to enter his third career, as one of the first franchisers in America.

A REVOLUTIONARY IDEA

Look for opportunity more than security and stability. Consider the breadth of an opportunity and do your best.

—*Roy H. Park*

After formal research and several weeks of old-fashioned brainstorming by Ag Research employees testing as many as 500 names, nothing seemed to stand out with the universal recognition they were looking for. As a last resort, Bob Flannery suggested maybe they should "bring in Duncan Hines." A lightning bolt struck, and my father instinctively knew that was the name that would work.

Pops decided that he might as well aim high. The man to go to was Duncan Hines. As the best-known food, restaurant, and lodging expert in the country in the late 1940s, his name was, in the minds of most Americans, synonymous with good food. The Bowling Green Jr. Women's Club said he was better known across America than the United States Vice President Alben Barkley, even in Kentucky, the home state of both.

Travelers didn't venture far from home without Hines' book of roadside restaurant reviews called *Adventures in Good Eating*, as well as guidebooks on lodging, resorts and cooking. Hines had helped millions of hungry Americans find good food, even in the least likely locations. My father was determined to get that name, and its seal of approval, on his products.

Hines had, of course, been approached time and time again by people promising to make this self-made man far richer than he ever dreamed, and time and time again he rejected their offers.

After all, he had a national reputation and was doing just fine on his own bottom line.

Born in Bowling Green, Kentucky, on March 26, 1880, Hines was the youngest of six siblings. His mother died when Duncan was four, and he and his youngest brother spent their summers at their grandparents' farm in the country. His grandmother was a wonderful cook who made full use of the farm's bounty of fresh and wholesome food: candied yams, sausage, country ham, turnip greens with fatback, beaten biscuits, cornbread, and pecan pie. Hines recalled that it was not "until after I came to live with Grandma Jane did I realize just how wonderful good cookery could be."

Duncan left home in 1898 to work as a clerk for Wells Fargo in Albuquerque, New Mexico, and a year later was assigned to their Cheyenne, WY, office, where he met Florence Chattin, his bride-to-be. His courtship was complicated by her family's opposition to their marriage for the next four years because his job level and bankroll did not make him a worthwhile suitor for their daughter's hand.

In 1902, he changed jobs, ending up in Mexico with a mining company, and worked hard to make money, establish a nest egg, and embellish his image. During his travels, with a palate accustomed to good food, he continued to find it a challenge to locate eateries good enough to accommodate his discriminating taste. Then, after her father passed away, Florence moved to New Rochelle, NY, and Duncan left the mining life to join her. They were married there in September 1905, and shortly after, he and his new bride moved to Chicago, where he worked for thirty-three years for the J.T.H. Mitchell company as a traveling salesman designing, writing, and producing corporate brochures.

As Pops told it, "Duncan was a specialty advertising and printing company salesman from Bowling Green, KY, who was also a freelance promotion man. He would go out and find a large company where—as he put it—the 'smoke was coming out of smokestack'—and he'd talk to the president about writing a book or a brochure." My father smiled at the recollection, "Most of the time they bought it."

Of all his accomplishments, Hines took the most pride in a book he did for Brink's Express. The manager he saw there said that most journalism was very poorly done, and that if Hines could produce a book without one typographical or grammatical error, he could set his price. But if there was only one error, he would be paid nothing. Hines accepted the challenge and pulled it off. He told my father that there was actually one error in the book, but they never found it at Brink's.

In the course of his work, Hines traveled a great deal, often taking Florence with him, and together they began to "collect" the names of restaurants and hotel dining rooms that consistently served excellent food. He would return home with fond memories of a certain deep-dish apple pie or the recollection of the taste and texture of a particular batch of buttermilk biscuits.

Hines's restaurant "collection" became a passion. People began to drop him notes about other good eating places, and he would advise his customers and good friends where to eat. In 1935, instead of a conventional Christmas card, the fifty-five-year-old Hines sent out a small brochure listing 167 superior eateries in thirty states and Washington, DC. He headed it "Adventures in Good Eating," and the response was overwhelming. Friends requested additional copies, as did strangers who had seen the list. Public relations was Hines' profession, eating merely his hobby, but in 1936, he realized that he could turn his hobby into a business and began publishing the book *Adventures in Good Eating*. The first edition was not an overnight success, selling 5,000 copies and netting a $1,500 loss. But by 1938, an article in the *Saturday Evening Post* and word-of-mouth put Hines firmly in the black, and he left sales and moved back to Bowling Green to review restaurants full-time, traveling up to 50,000 miles a year.

Hines' strategy of simply letting the public know where they might find quality food, carefully prepared by a competent chef in clean surroundings, answered a real need. In his many years on the road, he had visited his share of bad restaurants. Of one, Hines wrote, the gravy resembled "library paste." Another offered meals "as tasty as seasoned sawdust." Cleanliness was a problem, too. As he said about one greasy spoon, "If you get anything after the cockroaches are finished, you're lucky." Diner beware, Hines warned: "Usually the difference between the low-priced meal and the one that costs more is the amount you pay the doctor or the undertaker." Poor restaurants offended him personally, and he said he often expressed a wish to "padlock two-thirds of the places that call themselves cafes."

Fine restaurants were another story, and the places he liked best received enthusiastic, joyful write-ups. According to Hines, one Massachusetts institution made "a fellow wish he had hollow legs." One of his trademarks was to mention each restaurant's specialties.

A 1941 listing for a restaurant in Tampa, FL, read:

One of the most popular eating places in the South, four dining rooms, famous for its Spanish and French dishes. Marvelous sea food, especially their grilled Red Snapper steaks. Try their stuffed pompano, or crawfish, "Siboney style" or stone crabs, "Habanera" when in season. And to top all, have some "Espanol" or cocoanut cream dessert. Prices consistent with excellent quality.

Another in Central New York:

Watkins Glen State Park in the heart of the Finger Lakes region is said by many to be the Grand Canyon of the East. While here, you may put up at The Homestead, where "mother does the cooking." Chicken, steak or lake trout dinners their speciality. B., 35c up; L., 50c up; D., 50c to $1.

Newsweek magazine called him a "full-time eater-publisher," and the *Saturday Evening Post* called him "the country's champion diner-out."

This is the life of Duncan Hines in this picture from a 1945 *Life* magazine article by Phyllis Larsh titled HE IS THE TRAVELER'S AUTHORITY ON WHERE TO EAT.

With a second edition of critiques in mind, Hines sometimes grazed through six or seven restaurants a day and relied on a network of trusted volunteers to keep him up to date on those he couldn't reach. Their ranks included corporate chefs, bank and university presidents, and well-known personalities from cartoonist Gluyas Williams and travel lecturer Burton Holmes to radio commentator Mary Margaret McBride and Lawrence Tibbett, the opera singer. He was doing what Tim and Nina Zagat reinvented nearly fifty years later. Meanwhile, he branched out, publishing in 1938 the *Lodging for a Night* motel and hotel guidebook to help travelers find the best places to stay. "What do I care if Washington slept here?" Hines demanded, describing his reviewing philosophy. "Do they have a nice, clean bathroom and do the beds have box springs? That's what I want to know."

The same enthusiastic listing he used for the restaurants applied to lodging he liked. For example, a 1962 description for a motor hotel in Charlotte, NC, read:

156 rms. A.C., Ph., TV. Baby cribs, baby sitters. Sundeck, heated S.P., wading pool. Free ice. D.R., C.L. An outstanding new establishment. Airy units with dressing areas, some with studio arrangements, and a unique bubble enclosed pool for year-round swimming. Fine dining facilities. SWB $9-$12. 2WB $12-$15. Suites avail. No pets. Res. advis. Tel. ED 2-3121.

So the former traveling seller of advertising specialty items, brochures, and business pamphlets, in an era long before such establishments as McDonald's and Holiday Inn guaranteed uniform standards, became the source advising thousands of travelers on where to eat and sleep while on the road. By the end of 1939, his books sold 100,000 copies a year. Claiming there was "hardly a hamlet or crossroad" in the U.S. he had not visited, he also traveled to Canada, Mexico, and Hawaii and seven countries in Europe. Between his two books, more than 7,000 "recommendations" were listed. I should point out here that all of these listings were free. Other guidebooks were financed by the very establishments they purported to review, but Hines consistently refused all offers of advertising.

In 1939, Hines first published a book of his favorite recipes, *Adventures in Good Cooking*, and he had become virtually an institution, unique in the country. Perhaps no one, until the advent of Julia Child, had a comparable influence on American cuisine. By the time he was sixty-eight, he was internationally renowned for his ratings on eating places around the world and sales of his three guidebooks, including the *Duncan Hines Vacation Guide* published in 1948, rose to half million a year.

The Duncan Hines Guidebooks.

So here was my thirty-nine-year-old father with a lineup of food producers looking for a brand name after Duncan Hines, at age sixty-eight, had already become a household name. But as Leo Burnett, whose advertising agency handled Procter & Gamble products, and whom my father was later to meet and work with, said, "When you reach for the stars, you may not quite get one. But you won't come up with a handful of mud, either."

The challenge Pops faced, he said, "was how to tie the bell to the cat. I sent my people to the Cornell library and had them research everything they could find on Hines. Before I met him, I knew more about him than he did about himself, including his passion for watches."

Of course, Hines had no idea who Roy Park was, so he had no intention of granting him an audience. But the two self-starters who had come off a farm had a lot more in common than either one of them thought. After months of trying to get through the door, and thanks to his exhaustive research on the life and achievements of Duncan Hines, my father prevailed upon a prominent restaurant owner he knew in Raleigh to call a friend of Hines who was a restaurant owner in Virginia to arrange a meeting with him.

THE MEETING

Everyone lives by selling something.

—Robert Louis Stevenson

Hines was staying in the Waldorf Towers in Manhattan when my father finally got an appointment to see him in November 1948. Pops had Bob Flannery design a Duncan Hines logo and a number of food product labels for my father's presentation. The original logo changed little through the years, even under a succession of ownerships, and can still be recognized as similar to this day.

The original logo on the left as compared, despite three changes in ownership, to the logo that represents the Duncan Hines brand with over 80 baked-good mixes in stores today.

My father went into his meeting carrying the full-color labels that Flannery had designed and printed, affixed to dummy boxes, cans and jars. He felt sure it would show the world-renowned gourmet how well his name would look on products. "It's always an advantage to be better prepared than the other fellow," my father asserted; it was a credo he followed his entire life.

When Pops walked into Hines's suite, Hines was on the phone talking to someone from Ford Motor Co. who was apparently trying to persuade him to endorse one of its products (something

Hines had consistently refused to do for any product). My father overheard him saying, "I won't give you any endorsement for Ford. I had one when I was a young fellow, but it was such a rough ride it shook my liver." He hung up the phone and said to my father, "Well, I guess you're here to ask me to endorse something. I don't do that."

To which my father responded, "Mr. Hines. I know that. I want to name something in your *honor*." Not just something, he went on to say, but a whole line of fine food products, including a cake mix. "I plopped the displays on the coffee table and Hines picked one up. I put all the others away to prevent him the misery of choice." He assured Hines that all of these gourmet foods would be prepared under his guidelines, meet his high standards and "upgrade America's eating habits."

Nothing worthwhile comes easy. The meeting was inconclusive; my father left some material and asked for a breakfast meeting the next morning. "At breakfast, Duncan was very ornery," my father said. "He had spent the night out. I left some references and told him to call if he was interested and went home." My father concluded that his efforts had been in vain. "Then," he recalled, "in a couple of weeks, the people whose names I'd given Duncan started calling me, wanting to know what I was doing with Hines."

In what must have been his greatest salesmanship performance, my father had succeeded in convincing Hines to lend his name to an impressive line of foods. Part of his pitch was to set up a Duncan Hines Foundation to help pay scholarships for Cornell home economics and hotel students. So they got together and signed what Pops calls "a very one-sided contract in Hines' favor." Hines had the right to stop production with only thirty days notice if any product failed to measure up to his standards.

One of the intended financial backers of the venture was P&C, who had been helped and encouraged by GLF to find a niche in the growing supermarket grocery business to serve as a link between *producers and consumers*, hence the name. But at the last minute, just before the franchise program was launched, P&C Stores withdrew their financial support. To overcome his setback, and upon advice from H.E. Babcock, Pops borrowed the money himself. He set up Hines-Park Foods and took over a half-interest in the cake mix. Hines still agreed to a six-month trial period and helped to test several of the products himself. My father had some Duncan Hines products made up and got them into several stores. He didn't ask Hines to help him advertise, and that proved to be a mistake; at the end of the first six months, the launch without advertising was less than a success.

When the two met again, Pops brought Hines a certified check and asked for a six-month extension of the agreement. Hines said, "Roy, you haven't made any money on this thing yet?" "No, sir," my father admitted and was startled when Hines asked, "Why don't you ask me to help you?" "I didn't think I could afford you," my father said. "I think you can," Hines told him. "I like the idea, and all I want out of it is my expenses." Then he tore up the certified check.

Thus did Duncan Hines agree not only to lend his name but also actively participate in promoting the products bearing it. With what he described as grubstake, the only walking, talking trademark in the world, my father became one of the first franchisers in the nation.

And so just as he turned forty, as I said, my father's third career began.

THE OUTCOME

Nothing in the world can take the place of persistence. Talent will not; nothing is more common than unsuccessful men of talent. Genius will not; the world is full of educated derelicts. Persistence and determination alone are omnipotent.

—*Calvin Coolidge*

Pops started Hines-Park Foods, Inc. by selling shares of common and preferred stock but retaining for himself the controlling interest by a comfortable margin. The corporation was set up to license the Duncan Hines name to companies around the country. "We shipped the labels to the products, not the product to the labels," he said. Hines decided to stay out of the investment and instead received fees and royalties.

To test whether housewives would pay premium prices for a quality brand, my father, investing $50,000 of his own money, bought canned products from the S.S. Pierce company in Boston, slapped the Duncan Hines label on the cans, and put them out on shelves of upstate New York grocery stores. The products were also test-marketed in New England, Illinois and the place where I was to eventually end up as a student and to start my family—Chapel Hill, NC. This time, thanks to advertising and promotion in radio and newspapers, people looked for the products in their local stores and paid the higher prices, particularly for the new line of cake mixes that would revolutionize the food industry.

Among the first franchisers to step aboard was Nebraska Consolidated Mills, Inc. in Omaha, Nebraska, a manufacturer of flour, corn meal, and animal feed. Now known as ConAgra, Inc., the flour-milling company at that time had no previous experience with consumer products such as cake mixes. Under the able leadership of its thirty-two-year-old president, Allan Mactier, it worked out a franchise agreement with my father and launched production of the Duncan Hines cake mixes on June 26, 1951. The new line captured 48 percent of the market and the Midwestern grain company's cake mix sales quadrupled in a year.

The most interesting aspect of the success of the Duncan Hines cake mixes was that they were priced higher than the products of its competitors. The reason for the higher cost was that it was a much better-tasting cake because you had to add your own fresh eggs, milk and butter.

The product was launched after the war years when money was still very tight, and the best treat an average family could have was a great cake at the end of a weekend meal. Putting in fresh ingredients made the cake taste better than just adding water to a mix, and psychologically, it also made the housewife feel like she had created something special. She could see, feel and taste the difference.

The psychology offset the extra cost. Marketing also played a key role, and my father put his publicity genius to work in promoting the Duncan Hines brands. "We could never outspend the competitive giants like Pillsbury, Swansdown, Dromedary, Aunt Jemima and Betty Crocker, so we just tried to outthink them," he said.

"We were the first to sell cake mix on TV, with Mr. Hines himself doing the commercials. He was seen frosting beautiful cakes with chocolate-colored axle grease because it held up better than icing under the hot lights. We traveled extensively across the country conducting newspaper interviews and making radio and television commercials. We were the first to figure out that outdoor advertising was really 'outdoor TV,' so we used the same visual theme for both our TV and outdoor advertising, reminding

Venturing into billboards as early as 1953, Pops, Duncan and associates admire a standard 12' x 24' billboard welcoming Hines and his wife to Los Angeles during a Duncan Hines Day promotion.

the housewife on the way to the store of Duncan Hines and last night's TV commercial," Pops said.

The Hines-Park team was also first to use four-color ads in newspapers using comic presses for color, and Park also arranged "Duncan Hines Days" where Hines would receive a key to the city. Hines and my parents drove all over the nation for these promotional events, and sometimes I went with them. The travel schedule was exhausting, but Hines kept up the pace. His full story is told in a book by Louis Hatchett, published in 2001 by Mercer University Press entitled *Duncan Hines, The Man Behind the Cake Mix,* and Hatchett commented that Hines' "travels would make many men his age dizzy and exhausted, but surprisingly, he showed no sign of slowing down his hectic pace—or wanting to."

With the Duncan Hines cake mix line outselling its major competitors, it didn't take long for other major food producers, from bread and jam to canned mushrooms and peaches, to realize the potential of selling their products under the Duncan Hines name, and the idea caught hold immediately. A lot of companies were hungry for a recognized name for their products, and for a royalty on the sales, Park gave them one. As Hatchett reported "chicken from Washington, tomato juice from Ohio and New York, kidney beans from Ohio, coffee from Boston, pickles and relish from North Carolina, crab apples from Michigan."

Louis Hatchett reported in his book in 1949 my father's Ag Research budget was only $10,000 and in three years it climbed to over $1 million. The Duncan Hines brand entry into the food industry in August 1951 was covered in an article in *Tide* magazine entitled AN ADVENTURE IN FOOD MARKETING: A CASE STUDY OF A NEW ENTRANT IN AMERICA'S BIGGEST, FASTEST GROWING INDUSTRY.

Hatchett reported: "But advertising alone could not account for the firm's spectacular sales. This was proved when L.W. Hitchcock of the James H. Black Co. reported to Hines-Park executives of an experiment he conducted in Chicago. With the cooperation of a Chicago food distributor and several grocery stores it supplied, Hitchcock put Duncan Hines salad dressing on the supermarket shelves to see if people would buy it on the strength of Hines's name. For five weeks, there was no advertising, store signs, and no promotion of any kind. The results were phenomenal. The salad dressing was displayed, and supermarkets sold all available stock. When it was later advertised in Chicago, Milwaukee, and Minneapolis, supermarkets sold almost 9,000 cases in a few days."

It is interesting to note that the owner of this company, Jim Black, became one of my father's best friends, making many trips to Ithaca where I had the pleasure of meeting him and his young daughter when I was in my midteens. His daughter, Cathleen Black, former president of Hearst Magazines earlier worked for Al Neuharth (in later years another of my father's friends) as the president of *USA Today*.

By 1952, my father had licensed 124 companies to use the Duncan Hines label—twelve were bread bakers and eighty-three were ice cream makers. Another farm co-op, the Lehigh Valley Cooperative Farmers dairy in Allentown, PA, developed the rich-tasting ice cream, and in 1950 distributed a million cartons carrying the Duncan Hines name.

I don't think some of the unique ice cream flavors back then are offered to consumers today. One of my favorites was apple ice cream which contained chunks of cooked glazed apples, and this was one dessert where you could see, feel and taste the difference.

To go with the ice cream, Hines endorsed eleven ice cream toppings, and other licensees carried the Duncan Hines name on orange juice, salad dressings, chili con carne, fruit sherbet, spices, ketchup, steak and seafood sauces, and products from 20 jams and jellies to coffee and canned peas and mushrooms.

Every one of these food products was prepared under strict guidelines dictated by Mr. Hines through the Duncan Hines Institute, Inc., founded in 1949, and supervised by Pops as president of Hines-Park Foods, Inc. The name was not put on anything "unless you could see, feel, or taste a difference," Pops said. The Institute also carried on the "Recommended by Duncan Hines" tradition by publishing the books in which, by the way, the listing was free. The money was in the sale of the books and in leasing signs bearing the famous slogan to the listed eating and lodging establishments. It was said Park and Hines liberated America's homemakers from the drudgery of the kitchen and revolutionized the food industry.

By 1955, more than 250 products were carrying the Duncan Hines name, and these products were doing annual sales of $50 million.(Alas, even with all this exposure to gourmet food and travel with Duncan Hines, Pops still enjoyed onion and mayonnaise sandwiches and requested A-1 Sauce to pour over his steaks in restaurants.)

And aside from sauces, condiments and other fine food products through the Duncan Hines Institute, the licensing was eventually extended to manufacturing of electric coffeemakers, toasters, peppermills and outdoor barbeque grills. The Duncan Hines program was called "the last chance for the independents."The franchises even included a line of cookware, and up until a few years ago, I was still getting calls from people wanting to know where they could replace the worn-out Duncan Hines pots and pans they bought a half century earlier.

Through his corporation, Adventures in Good Eating, my father also took over writing and expanding the *Adventures in Good Eating, Lodging for a Night* and the *Duncan Hines Vacation Guide* and began writing recipe columns for newspapers as well.

Through the Duncan Hines Institute in 1955, he published Hines's *The Dessert Book* and the same year the *Duncan Hines Food Odyssey*, a 274-page book on a collection of Hines's recipes and traveling reviews.

Stewart Underwood recalls the effort he put into increasing the guidebook's circulation and sales. At first the books were sold only in the listed establishments, which restricted their circulation. His assignment was to find ways to expand distribution through other means. Underwood came up with the idea of approaching Standard Oil in Chicago with a proposal allowing Standard to put its logo on the front of the guidebooks if it would distribute them through its gas stations across the country. When he first walked into the marketing VP's office, the idea was rejected out of hand. But Underwood was persistent. As soon as he got down to the lobby, he told the receptionist to call the VP and tell him he was coming right back up for a second try.

When he walked into the office the second time, he received an apology from the VP, and with a fresh start, sold the idea. The agreement resulted in an initial order of 500,000 guidebooks to be displayed on cardboard racks in Standard Oil gas stations. The deal also led to Standard's competitor, Mobil Oil, moving into the guidebook business thorough their *Mobil Travel Guide*, which still exists today. Underwood also eventually got distribution for the guidebooks through bookstores that carried paperbacks, which vastly increased their circulation.

Utilizing the same art that appeared on the food packages and in advertisements, a distinctive sign was created and offered to restaurants and lodging places recommended by the guidebooks. This "Recommended by Duncan Hines" shingle, hanging in front of a restaurant, resort, or place of lodging, was to become a highly sought-after symbol of prestige. So much so that Hines had to take one con man to court for selling counterfeit signs. Duncan Hines, and later the cake mix, also became the subject of cartoons in magazines from the *New Yorker* to *Playboy*.

There was a second aspect of signage that Underwood recalls. Aside from supervising the five or so full-time salesmen on the road selling the shingles and guidebooks to listed restaurants, hotels, motels, and resorts, Underwood's job was to lease and erect billboards all over the country. The five-by-sixteen-foot signs displaying the "Recommended by Duncan Hines" message with the distinctive logo rising above the top of the billboard advertised listed establishments willing to pay the average charge of $85 a month.

At the time, the business was able to write off the entire cost of putting up the signs as a tax-deductible expense instead of capitalizing and depreciating the cost over seven years. This combined with the income, Underwood said, led to my father's realization of just how profitable the outdoor advertising business could be.

From this humble beginning, outdoor advertising was later to become an integral part of the relationship between my father and me. After returning from an independent career in 1971 to work for him managing his Outdoor advertising division until buying it in 1988.

CHAPTER 4
WHERE I CAME IN

Nothing takes as long as growing up. An hour is a hundred minutes, a day is a week, a week a month. And each month, waiting for the seasons to change, seems like two. A small house is huge, the front lawn a football field, a damned-up stream an Olympic swimming pool. Lightning bugs provide eternal fascination. Kick-the-can and hide-and-seek lasts all evening long. Fun goes on forever, but on our few bad days, the suffering does, too. And as the clock turns, we want to grow up faster. The process is far too slow. But the inevitable happens. An hour turns into thirty minutes. The days and weeks grow shorter. The months and years flash by. Things get smaller, nature gets overlooked, our calendars get crowded. Fun comes only in glimpses, no longer a day-long affair. The things we plan or anticipate too quickly come and go. Time rushes by, and we realize those long, long days we had growing up were simply not real. When we are old, the short, short days we know pale in comparison when we remember, in retrospect, that nothing goes by quicker than growing up.

—Roy H. Park, Jr. (2004)

While all this was going on, this transplanted southern-born kid was growing up a Yankee in Ithaca, NY. Although I remember aspects of my early years, they mostly come back as strobe-lighted flashbacks, like passages in a book highlighted by a magic marker.

At the age of four, I was hyperactive enough to drive my

mother crazy. Maybe all kids are. I know it applies to my grand-children. Looking back at the old movies my father took back then, I spent most of my time running around and making noise. Of course those old projectors did tend to make movement jerkier and faster than it actually was.

Shortly after we arrived in Ithaca, I am convinced, more to get rid of me than anything else, my mother enrolled me in an experimental Pre-K school at Cornell University. Back then the school was essentially carrying out experiments in educational methods, and we were the guinea pigs. I learned that they observed us through one-way glass, and they performed a lot of experiments to study the interaction among us four- and five-year olds.

While the other kids were scrambling around on the jungle gyms and swinging on swings, I developed a healthy, or some might call it *unhealthy*, interest in animal life. It included collecting every bug I could find on the playground. I guess that was regarded as an indication of a high IQ because they gave me a really fine score at the school. (Perhaps it is merely a coincidence, but Cornell is known to this day as the home of renowned entomologists, not to mention a certain amateur lepidopterist and author of *Lolita* named Vladimir Nabokov.)

My interest in living things sustained itself through the years. I raised orphaned robins, raccoons, opossums, and cottontail rabbits as well as baby chicks, turtles, alligators, and iguanas. I even built a homing pigeon coop in our backyard when I was twelve years old.

All this experience eventually led to extremely high marks in biology and science courses, but not so high marks in languages, history, and, particularly, math. This lack of interest in figures was to make my later education much more difficult.

When we finally moved out of our crowded apartment and into our first home, it was in a district that put me in the fairly elite Cayuga Heights School. I was enrolled along with a large number of Cornell professors' sons and daughters. It is interesting to note that our house on White Park Road was three houses down the street from the revered physicist and Nobel Laureate, Hans

Bethe, and I walked by his house each day to catch the school bus when I entered high school. The best memories I have are that we all kept our noses clean and got a good basic education. Many of us stuck together right through high school, and even college.

I remember my first girlfriend. I was about eight years old, when, as with young women, her growth spurt came early and she was taller than me. I had a bike. She didn't. She would follow me as I was riding along, and I felt guilty about her running along beside the bike on the way to school. But I got over it since being on the bike made me taller than she was.

Believe it or not, when we got a little older, most of my elementary school counterparts even attended dance classes. One of my mother's favorite memories is of a young lady a good foot taller than I was at the time who took a liking to me. She would always grab me as her partner. Since she developed early, and tended to hold me tightly behind my head while we were dancing, I came close to smothering on these occasions. My mother still reminds me of my attempts to come up for air on the gym dance floor.

I have fun kidding my grandsons about their possible girlfriends today, and until recently even the oldest before he reached fifteen, maintained he wasn't that interested in girls. When I was growing up, our crowd had plenty of interest in girls, and I had my first date at age eleven, and she was back at our fiftieth high school reunion in 2006.

My father drove us to a movie theater, and after we got a little ways into the picture, I put my arm around the back of her seat. She snuggled over toward me to the extent the seat would allow. I thought things were going pretty well. About fifteen minutes later, my arm began to feel numb, but I left it behind her anyway. I thought she would think I didn't like her if I moved it. When we finally left the theater, I had no feeling on my right side. Pops picked us up, and it took hours for my arm to regain circulation and be usable again.

Another not-so-favorite memory was of my mother's taking me shopping in downtown Ithaca. These shopping trips were always embarrassing because my mother, with her genteel Southern upbringing, never went anywhere without a hat. She had two she favored. Both made her stand out in our small town like a light-house during an eclipse. One had a bunch of red cherries off the side, the other a cluster of pheasant feathers that stood straight up. The good news was that I could always spot the hats above the counters and aisles of whatever store we were in. So I never got lost.

GROWING UP IN ITHACA

To paraphrase John Mellencamp reminiscing in his 1987 song "Cherry Bomb," when you think about those days, you just have to lean back and smile.[1a]

During these early years, while most kids were earning a few bucks with paper routes, tossing papers from baskets on their bikes, I was putting all my eggs in one basket with something unique: an egg route. At my father's instigation, I was talked into it by a local farmer, and I had to be careful riding my bike with such fragile cargo. I could deliver the cartons to only one or two customers at a time before reloading.

It went well for a while, but a problem arose when the customers (I had signed them on with advance payments of 12¢ a carton) ran out of eggs. And so did the farmer. In fact, he abruptly left town, so there was no way I could fill the advance orders. For a while I thought I would have to come up with the money myself. Fortunately, my customers were forgiving and I avoided filing bankruptcy at an early age.

After the eggs crossed the road with the chicken, I held an array of summer jobs through my teens and later during college. There was never a summer that I didn't work. I mowed lawns, weeded, and killed Japanese beetles eating the neighborhood's hollyhocks for a penny each by dropping them into a jar of kerosene. For a couple of years, I even tended an experimental iris farm. The owner was a Cornell professor, whose nephew, Anthony Perkins, later starred in *Psycho*. He was said to visit his uncle each summer, but I never saw him.

During my preteen years in Cayuga Heights, I also fell in with a group of neighborhood kids who mostly went to Cayuga Heights School, and who ran in age from seven to thirteen. We played games in every yard in the neighborhood, from hide-and-seek to kick-the-can to football. One yard was large enough to field a baseball diamond.

With my next-door neighbor, we put on our version of a carnival for a couple of years. It included a merry-go-round with pump handles (substituting for the wooden horses and other animals on the real thing), caged birds and animals, magic acts, horseshoe pitching, and other reasonably safe try-your-skill sideshows.

Our animal acts included white fantail pigeons, which lived in a coop but flew freely around the property. We safely colored them every shade of the rainbow with Easter-egg dye. We attracted quite a few kids. Most important was the admission charge, but in true carny spirit, we also charged separately for each exhibit, such as the *baby rattlers*, which were actually a couple of *baby rattles* in a toy crib, and it was too late to get your money back after discovering the hoax. Not only were the admissions nonrefundable, but we nicknamed one of the youngest marks "sugar bowl" because after he ran out of pennies for the exhibits, he would run home to get the coins his mother kept in a sugar bowl, assuring us that he would be right back.

As we grew older, the carnival attractions were replaced by riskier activities. In those days in New York you could buy cherry bombs that would disintegrate a mailbox like it was cardboard. We discovered another application for this firepower. If you lit a cherry bomb and put a coffee can over it, you could make the coffee can blast out of sight.

Predictably, the neighbors complained about the noise, and on one of our more active days, a patrol car came by just after I had put a cherry bomb under a can. The only thing I could think to do was to hold the can down with my foot, since we were in plain sight and couldn't run.

When the firecracker went off, the can lifted my leg about two feet in the air and numbed it for the rest of the day. It's a good thing I didn't stand with both feet on the can, not being able to fly. The police, of course, confiscated our firecrackers and threatened us with jail if we messed with fireworks again.

And, yeah, as I said, we played the real kick the can, and I still get goosebumps when I hear "Olley Olley in Free," or however it goes in a song or mentioned as in Rod Serling's Twilight Zone episode *Kick the Can*. We also did all the other usual things kids did back in the 1940s, too, playing in our own and invading our neighbor's lawns until we were exhausted, refreshed only by warm water from garden hoses.

Two sons who grew up in Ithaca, NY. Me, with son Trip (Roy H. Park, III) on the right, taking a break at the beach in Pine Knoll Shores, NC.

We played until the light gave out, climbed trees to the top, tunneled under the forsythia bushes, caught crawfish in the streams, kept garden snakes in the window wells, shot at each other with BB rifles, camped around fires in the woods, and built forts for protection during our snowball fights. We made piles of leaves in the fall, and when we got tired of jumping into them, we set them on fire without worrying about fire trucks coming by.

In the winter, we sledded down the middle of the road on the hill where we lived. In the summer, we used red Radio Flyer wagons, which had no brakes. We rode our bikes on sidewalks, in traffic, and through front lawns and woods without helmets. As summed up in Mellencamp's words in *"Cherry Bomb,"* "I'm surprised that we're still livin'."

But I also spent a lot of time alone, in safer pursuits, entertaining myself by reading, sculpting, drawing, painting, and collecting and keeping fish and animals. From these early days and throughout most of my life, I have been a naturalist, keeping and studying everything from praying mantises to alligators and iguanas, tree frogs to raccoons, even opossums. I've kept saltwater fish tanks for years, with corals, invertebrates, and fish including many versions of *Finding Nemo* clownfish. To this day I have dozens of descendents of the dinosaurs called birds flying around in a conservatory.

And along with birds' nemesis, cats, I have owned dogs from tiny Chihuahuas to Alaskan malamutes, mutts, and Russian wolfhounds, and from Rottweilers to Belgian, German and Australian shepherds.

My mother told me I even had a goat when I still lived in Raleigh, and it pulled me around in a little cart. I have seen pictures but don't remember it. My father did not share my indiscriminate passion for animal life. Depending on his mood, he ignored or was only vaguely aware of my menagerie. Occasionally he petted some of our dogs on their heads—and sometimes petted me on my head, too.

I also have fond memories during those early years in Ithaca of the many summers I spent with my maternal grandparents at Livingson Apartments in Allentown, PA, where Dent Hardware, the family business of my grandfather, Walter Reed Dent, was located. I watched many baseball games on TV with him, and made many visits to the Trexler animal preserve with my grandmother. I remember her allowing me to walk downtown to a pet shop, accompanied by my new friend, the janitor's son, whenever I visited, and bring back anything I wanted. One time when I brought back a white mouse, and my friend, who was black, brought back a black mouse, we laughed and kidded each other all the way home to the apartment over our respective choices.

My grandfather was a lot of fun to be with. We got along so well because to me he was young at heart and he knew how to talk to kids. He had a great sense of humor and a great exit line. When he got tired of playing with us, he'd ask if we'd like to see him walk like a duck. We'd say "Yes," and he'd exit the room and not come back.

When I later went away to Lawrenceville, he kept up a steady stream of correspondence. His letters were funny and clever. Occasionally he would call me on the phone. When we got together, he loved to play games. He watched games on television for hours, until glaucoma, which was difficult to treat at the time, took his sight. When he couldn't watch TV anymore, he gave in to old age and made his own exit proudly into the light, not walking like a duck.

After my grandfather passed away in Allentown, my grandmother came to live with us in Ithaca. I called my grandmother "Mimmie," since I couldn't pronounce "Mildred." She called me "Buddy," since she knew how much I disliked the "Junior" part of my name. When things were tough, her advice to me was that this, too, would pass. She told me that pain, whether physical or mental, does not last a fraction as long as the good things that happen to you, and when the pain is gone, you can't remember it. The few good things are the things that last, she said, and her beliefs would serve me well in dealing with my father in the future.

Sharing family photos with me, Tetlow and Mimmie. After seeing this photo, that's the first and last time I wore that suit!

As I mentioned, my great-grandmother, Love Caswell Houghton (who I called "Muddie," probably in another of my attempts to communicate at an early age, in this case to say "grandmudder") moved in with us when the family first came to Ithaca. She also came with us when we moved to our first house on White Park Road. When she began to fail she expressed a desire to return to her native Raleigh for her final years. My mother took her south on the train and found her a room in the Sir Walter Raleigh Hotel next to a longtime family friend, Margaret Hall, a resident of the hotel for years. Our friend, whom I knew as "Maggie," looked after her until my great-grandmother passed away in her beloved Raleigh.

My grandmother, "Mimmie," God rest her soul, died peacefully in my parents' house in Ithaca, in her sleep, at age 109. After a century of giving, this frail little lady had clung to life with tenacity. She was always cheerful and a good listener, and she made everyone feel like the most important person in the world. Her love of animals and her devotion to my mother and her grandchildren were evident to all who knew her.

She loved poetry and literature and wrote hundreds of poems throughout her life. This had an enduring influence on me. An avid student of the Bible, she knew the truth of Ecclesiastes that death is the destiny of every person, and that the living should take it to heart. One of the poems she wrote was read at her memorial service on February 21, 2001:

O God, in peace and tender love
Grant thou a soul's request
A body worn—a heart grown tired
Yearns for thine holy rest.

Fleet winged would I now embark
Into that joy-strewn past
Traversing e'en the dark unknown
To reach thy blessed heart.

And find my savior dwelling there
Within the far off gate
With only His sweet gracious love
Apart from bitter hate.

So Father from whom comes all good
Guide through our faltering light
Call Thou a vagrant spirit home
This pilgrim of the night

A body tired, a weary heart
Longs for the perfect rest
Against thy shelt'ring heart of love
Within thy holy breast.

—Mildred Goodwin Dent

I remember every Christmas that my grandparents would come to Ithaca. It was one of the few times that Pops would put aside his work in the evenings, or on a Sunday, for a game of Monopoly with my grandfather and me. It was my father's favorite game, but I was warned by my grandfather to keep an eye on the board. If both of us became distracted at the same time, Pops tended to make a few moves on the board that weren't the result of throwing the dice. He didn't look at it as cheating; he just wanted to win. And winning, in life as in Monopoly, was what mattered most to him.

CHRISTMAS SHOPPING

Another Christmas memory includes the last-minute shopping that Pops did for my mother. A day or two before Christmas, he would take me with him to the best women's store in town, Holley's, where he would invariably buy fancy negligees for my mother, ones which would embarrass even Victoria's Secret. My mother would immediately return them a few days after Christmas. Their taste in sleepwear ran in different directions, but the routine was always the same.

Sometimes when Pops ran out of time to shop for her, he would give her cash and ask me the morning of Christmas Eve to come up with a creative way to package it. I would quickly construct a cardboard house or something with nooks and crannies into which he could tuck money. On one occasion I was asked to find the unoriginal series of boxes that fit into each other. The payoff, of course, would be concealed in the smallest and last box she would open, but each box would have to be wrapped, and that was also delegated to me.

To be fair, my father was young and obsessively busy then, and as time went by he would plan ahead and pick out more substantial gifts for her, such as jewelry or cars.

The worst part was Christmas Eve, after he had purchased gifts for all his business associates, employees, and friends, including the maitre d' of the Dutch Kitchen in the old Ithaca Hotel, and we got in his car around 4:30 PM to deliver them. My job was to run up through slush and snow to each house or business he frequented and hand out the gifts while he waited in the warm car. This took place no matter how bad the weather, but it was one of the few occasions I could spend time with him. I figured it was one of the ways I earned my keep. But this circuit-riding gift-giving had another unfortunate aspect—it delayed the start of Christmas dinner each year, which in turn delayed the opening of family presents on Christmas Eve.

We opened gifts on Christmas Eve in our house. The arrival of Santa Claus, and our truly important presents were reserved for Christmas morning. Christmas was real family time—and there was precious little of that.

FAMILY TIME

When I was about ten years old, we were on a rare family outing, a two-week cruise through the Bahamas. My mother and Pops wanted me dressed for the part. They bought me a brilliant red jacket, which I thought made me look like an organ grinder's monkey. Plenty of girls my age were on board. That jacket stood out like a beacon, but their reaction to it was the opposite of attraction. After enough snickers from them, I discovered that the small public bathrooms had portholes just large enough to accommodate a red jacket.

Into the Atlantic it went. When my parents asked where it was, I said I must have left it in the room. When it wasn't in the room, I suggested that someone must have stolen it. My father spent the rest of the cruise looking for anyone my size wearing something red. Years later I told them what really happened. Pops thought that was clever of me and shared the story with his associates on many occasions.

Then there were the trips to Florida. To save money, my father would drive all the way from Ithaca to Fort Walton Beach and stay at Bacon's-by-the-Sea, a rustic motor inn on the Gulf of Mexico. It was in the top ten of Duncan Hines's favorite motels at the time, and Pops rented a two-bedroom unit with a kitchenette to save the cost of eating out. Not because my mother loved to cook.

But there was plenty of eating out on the way to Florida, alongside what used to be Route 1 and on side roads as well. Since it took several days to reach Florida, Pops's routine for sustenance was to stop at a country store for cans of sardines, saltine crackers, and sharp cheddar, what he called rat cheese. We ate the sardines right out of the can, and all through his life my father enjoyed sardine and onion sandwiches.

Hardly adventures in good eating. But because we were roughing it, it was an adventure.

When my sister was very young, she remained at home. But as we got older, we would both go along for the ride. I have to admit that I picked on her a lot. There was constant noise and action in the back of the car. I remember the many times my father's big arm would reach back over the seat with a rolled-up newspaper in hand, and try to swat me and my sister when we became unbearably obstreperous. We would both duck down on the floor of the car until the flailing tube of newsprint withdrew.

My sister and I squabbled plenty as all kids do, but our parents never taught us *time travel* by threatening to knock us into the middle of next week, or the concept of *justice,* pointing out that one day we would have kids of our own and they hoped they'd turn out just like us. But on an occasion or two I was taught the meaning of *anticipation* when my mother said "just wait until your father gets home."

In the normal course of things, particularly while I was still in elementary school and my father's business was growing exponentially, we seldom saw him at home at night or even during school breaks. He worked through every weekend and would close his den double doors after dinner and work far into the night. As my sister and I grew up, we saw little of either of our parents because they traveled a great deal. In fact, with the help of a nanny, we almost raised ourselves. My sister and I seldom ate with my parents. We took our meals with our nanny in a room off the kitchen my mother called the "breakfast nook." And in later years when we were both sent off to prep schools, and then college, we saw even less of them.

But before that there was one more instance of family time. As Pops became more successful, he decided to buy a boat. We lived adjacent to beautiful Cayuga Lake (the one celebrated in Cornell University's song, "Far Above Cayuga's Waters"). It is about a mile across at its widest point and some forty miles long and you can go through the locks at the end to access the Inland Waterway. You can pilot a boat from Cayuga Lake into the Atlantic Ocean and some pretty sizable boats have made their way back into our lake.

To most people, a sixteen- to twenty-three-foot boat would have been adequate, but my father went all out. He bought a thirty-six-foot Chris-Craft cruiser with a cabin area that would sleep four people and a dining area that would feed a small army.

My sister and I thought this was great when we were young. Our mother would pack lunches in an ice chest for the Sunday outings, her specialty being deviled eggs, which I still like today. My father's specialty was carrying as many newspapers and briefcases as he could put on board without sinking the ship.

I remember that after Pops first got the hang of piloting the boat, after backing it out of the dock and feeling the power of the prop, he felt his power as captain of the ship. As we neared the Ithaca Yacht Club, a sailing regatta was in full force. My father spotted the uniform line of white sails racing down the lake around the buoys that marked the course. He thought it would be fun to show off his new prize and stir things up, not realizing that sailboat competition was mighty serious on Cayuga Lake.

Our thirty-six-foot "stinkpot," as the sailing crowd calls anything with a motor, plowed into the racing sailors, cutting off wind and causing sails to droop and boats to topple. My father thought it was great fun. He interpreted the waving fists as friendly waving hands, having no idea that he had just blown out a championship race. He was blackballed from joining the Yacht Club for a year.

On a few occasions we spent the night on the yacht, and I remember one night Pops anchored too close to shore. I was the first to wake up the next morning to the sound of girls' voices and laughter. I pulled myself out of the bunk and went out on the back deck in my underwear to see what was going on. Standing in my jockey shorts, I realized that we had grounded at the Girl Scout camp and I was suddenly on stage in front of girls my age. While my father appealed to them to push the boat out enough from the shore so he could crank up the engine again, I retreated deep in the cabin, hoping none of them had recognized me.

Boating weekends were exciting enough while my sister and I were young. But after a couple of years both of us got tired of spending the whole day on the lake, sitting around while our father read newspapers and plowed through his work. The fun faded as we cruised the lake at low speeds while he worked, and we made up every kind of excuse not to go out with him on Sundays.

Father's unique use of newspapers did not add to the aesthetic aspects of voyages in the boat or travel by car. Aside from using a rolled-up newspaper as a swat, he was also an obsessive newspaper consumer, and once read, they were quickly disposed of, no matter where he happened to be. One of his acquaintances recalls a Sunday outing on the boat, by then piloted by a hired hand. "Park sat in the back taking the sun and reading his papers and throwing them over his shoulder. What he didn't realize was that the papers were going into the water. I mean he was throwing them all over the lake." The lake patrol noticed his papering of the lake and pulled up to the yacht and gave Pops a ticket. According to this friend's recollection, my father sold the boat the next day.

My father would have a good laugh at the story, saying, "Well, that's a good story, but that isn't exactly right." He said that the part about the newspapers going into the lake might be true. The truth is he sold the yacht after we all got tired of cruising around in his floating office.

A WIDER WORLD

I was twelve years old when I met the legendary Duncan Hines. My father described him as being like "the glamorous uncle a lot of families have. The uncle who would travel around the world and live the good life, go to all the best restaurants, and come home to tell the family how good it all was." I remember the first meal with Duncan and his wife, Clara, at our home in Ithaca. Hines' first wife of thirty-three years, Florence, passed away in 1938, and it wasn't until 1946 that Hines took a second bride. Clara was an effervescent conversationalist who, I felt in our first meeting, didn't particularly care for kids.

Aside from seeing Hines as the romantic, roving uncle, my father saw him as a personable, charismatic, and photogenic man who loved to travel, enjoyed eating, and was easy to like. Pops maintained that the large portrait of Duncan Hines that dominated his office captured the honesty, integrity, and ruggedness of the man. He said this man lived well and had, in turn, taught him how to live. "He had a flair for showmanship, and he had the brains to figure out a need and fill it."

At this first meeting, the Hines charisma had little effect on me. He struck me as a grandfatherly figure with an outwardly pleasant demeanor. But as I learned later, you didn't want to disappoint him or get him mad. When he started carving the turkey, the first thing he did was place one of the huge drumsticks on my plate. I'm sure he thought all children liked drumsticks, and that he was being kind by serving me first. I was horrified. I had always detested the dark meat of turkeys and chickens. When I looked at the dry, unappetizing leg on my plate and started to say something, I received a swift kick under the table from Pops. This meant shut up, eat it, and look like you're enjoying it. I ate it, but didn't enjoy it. That part was impossible to fake.

Duncan Hines on the road, and this time I was with him in 1954 during the filming of the movie *Prince Valiant.* Unfortunately, at 16, I wasn't old enough or important enough to get in the picture with Debra Paget and Janet Leigh so "Uncle" Duncan had them all to himself.

I got to know Hines a lot better later in, of all places, California. Travel during the years my sister and I were growing up was strenuous for all concerned, in part because of sibling rivalry. Our parents learned early on that traveling with two squabbling kids was not peaceful, so they would alternate us on their business trips. I remember one time my mother told me after they returned from a trip with my sister that she asked her, "Wasn't it wonderful to have such a peaceful time without your brother picking on you?"

To which my sister replied, "I kind of missed it."

For the next seven years, my parents took to the road with a vengeance, accompanying Duncan and Clara Hines to promote the food products. The quartet took their dog-and-pony show to hundreds of towns, going on radio and television, persuading mayors to proclaim a "Duncan Hines Day," and autographing the Hines books in Hines-recommended restaurants. Television was just starting up, and Hines was a natural entertainer, so he got a lot of airtime.

The "Day" concluded with a reception and sit-down dinner attended by governors, mayors (with keys to the city) other big-wigs and key chain-store buyers, all invited to bring their wives who received corsages and autographed Duncan Hines cook-books on arrival.

A Duncan Hines Day dinner with Duncan, Clara, and my parents on the dais.

Stewart Underwood was the point man in setting up the Duncan Hines Day promotions, and aside from his tours with Hines, my father spent time on the road with Underwood. Checking up on his employees, as he did all his life, Pops wanted to see how the guidebook sales and billboard advertising programs were going. Underwood said he will never forget the trip he took with Pops barreling down the road at eighty mph while looking over his shoulder to converse with another business associate in the backseat.

Nervous enough about the speed, Underwood said he looked over and saw my father was driving with his legs crossed. As soon as they made the next pit stop, he volunteered to drive so Pops "could more easily conduct business with the man in the back." Underwood said he made sure he drove the rest of the way to their destination, and stayed behind the wheel until they got back to their original point of departure.

There was another car story I remember vividly. The day had come when it was finally my turn to join my parents on a trip to the Golden State, while my sister stayed home. I can never forget what it was like to be part of a month-long Duncan Hines promotional safari in a Lincoln convertible. My mother did most of the driving because my father never took a break from his work. Part of his standard routine was to go through every newspaper he could buy during our travels, his favorites being the *Wall Street Journal* and the *New York Times*. As you know from the Cayuga Lake incident, he consumed papers voraciously and disposed of them in the most convenient way possible when he was done.

I remember we were driving down a country highway and my father, after reading each page, proceeded to throw the newspaper, section by section, into the surrounding countryside.

After the last newspaper section went over the side, a local sheriff pulled us over and gave us a simple alternative. Go back and pick up every piece of paper that had been thrown out of the car, or go to jail. I spent half the day chasing newspapers through three fenced-in cow pastures, and thanked God none of the pastures was home for a bull.

Later during the trip, Pops's incessant need to read newspapers almost killed my mother. She was driving along in the convertible while my father had the paper spread open on the passenger side and she couldn't see past it when she began pulling out into an intersection on a major highway.

A car barreling down the highway smashed head-on into our front end, which spun our convertible around three or four times in the intersection. The driver's door had swung open and Dottie was partially thrown out with one hand hanging on to the steering wheel. As the door swung back and forth, she was being dragged at an angle underneath the rotating car.

Because I had tired of being blasted by the wind in the back I had been sitting between my parents in the front seat. I quickly slid over behind the wheel and kept the heavy door propped open with both legs to keep it from slamming shut and severing her head and shoulder. But her foot didn't fare so well. The tip of one foot had been crushed under the tire and had to be put in a cast. Within a few days, when she could hobble with crutches, my father was raring to go again, my crippled mother was packed in with the baggage, and the safari continued. Dottie's foot took almost two years to heal properly; she was in and out of braces and casts, and she says it still gives her trouble.

When we arrived in California, I was always seated next to Duncan Hines during the dinners I attended. He insisted that I always sit to his left. I quickly discovered the reason wasn't his being grandfatherly when he placed me where I would be able to wolf down food that he didn't like. Each dish in these restaurants was usually presented with a flourish by the chef, who would disappear to prepare the next course. That was when Mr. Hines would transfer what he found undesirable to my plate. To this day I avoid escargots and drumsticks. As for Duncan Hines, he liked his bacon limp. His favorite food was a dollop of vanilla ice cream with cornflakes. I like my bacon crisp, but the cornflakes thing sounds like something I might want to try—someday.

WAKE-UP CALLS

The Duncan Hines food business Pops founded in 1949 was growing by leaps and bounds, but the stress of operating it, possibly combined with unconscious memories of covering executions when he worked for the AP, led to nightmares that literally jolted him out of the deepest sleep. I remember being awakened one night by a crash, followed by screaming and yelling like someone was being killed. The next morning I saw what had been my mother's glass whatnot, and all of her china collectibles, smashed on the floor by the bed. Dottie never understood why my father hadn't shredded his feet stomping on all of that glass during his nightmare, and frankly, she told me it annoyed her enough to wish that he had.

Another time, I was awakened by a shotgun blast and ran into my parents' bedroom to find my father, in the middle of winter, shooting through an open bedroom window. He had dreamed that someone was trying to get in the room, and after blowing up most of the snow on the lawn below the window, he finally woke up enough to realize he had been dreaming. Pops even had nightmares while traveling on trains. He frequently took the Lehigh Valley Railroad from Ithaca down to New York City and points south. When traveling with others, including Babcock, he often turned these railway journeys into his version of the movie *Murder on the Orient Express,* when his crying out during nightmares made passengers in sleeping cars nearby think someone had indeed been murdered during the night.

It was about this time, in 1950, that I entered junior high school, in downtown Ithaca. I continued to socialize with our Cayuga Heights crowd, which basically was a group of clean-living kids; there were no drugs involved, not a lot of alcohol, but a lot of parties. And because our group of about twenty didn't trash the houses of parents that hosted parties, there was a party almost every weekend during the summers. My parents hosted plenty in our basement playroom area, and most of the time our crowd did not get out of hand.

Throughout this time, I worked steady jobs every summer. As soon as I got my working papers, I graduated from mowing lawns. I went to work for my father. Years later, in 1981, I was quoted in the *Ithaca Journal* as saying, "When I was old enough for working papers, I did everything from sanding fire escapes to ceilings in my father's apartments. It taught me the meaning of a dollar—and the feeling of pain, if you've ever sanded a ceiling."

The most embarrassing job I had was holding ladders for my father's painters on his buildings in downtown Ithaca. I had to endure the sarcastic comments of my classmates wandering by. It was tough to explain that you are actually working when you are just standing at the bottom of a ladder, hour after hour, but I got paid to do it.

In junior high school, I became a friend of the friendless, always trying to help the underdog. There was one kid in the class who was pretty tough, and I figured that the best way to stay on his good side was to befriend him, which I did. When we played together at my house, and I use the word loosely, we averaged a couple of fights each time, but at least I didn't get the hell beat out of me in front of the other kids at school, some of whom he picked on without mercy.

I also learned that one had to be careful about one's choice of friends. There's an old Indian saying that when you save an Indian's life, you are responsible for him forever. For years to come, my friend would show up on my doorstep at the most inopportune times, dressed in his motorcycle jacket and boots. More than a few people raised eyebrows at the company I kept when we did the town together.

When I entered high school in 1952, my tendency to befriend the friendless came to the fore again. Jonathan Emerson, who has become a lifetime friend, transferred into our public school at the beginning of the freshman semester wearing a blue blazer and tie. To put it mildly, he didn't fit in and became an immediate target. He had gone to a prep school where students had to wear coats and ties, and old habits die hard. I befriended him and brought him into our crowd and Jon was gradually accepted, particularly when he stopped wearing jackets and ties to class.

Old Times Remembered – Jonathan and me in later years.

Ironically, about the time Jon was weaned from his dress code, I was forced to adopt it. Pops and Dottie were traveling a lot, and they thought I would get a better education, and stay out of trouble if I was shipped off to prep school. My grades were good enough for me to be admitted to the Lawrenceville School in Lawrenceville, New Jersey, in 1953 for my sophomore year. So after a brief shopping spree, off I went with a suitcase full of the blue blazers, white shirts, and ties I had persuaded my friend to abandon. As I departed for my new life, I carried with me a couple of valuable lessons learned growing up in Ithaca: humility helps keep things in proportion and a sense of humor keeps you from taking yourself too seriously. And both traits, for the most part, help to keep you out of trouble.

CHAPTER 5
TO FRESH WOODS AND PASTURES NEW

Tomorrow to fresh woods and pastures new.

—John Milton

To fully acknowledge John Milton, this chapter title would begin with "Tomorrow." For me it was yesterday. During the three years I spent in New Jersey at the Lawrenceville School (although the thought did occur to me it was a way to simply eliminate me as an encumbrance to my parent's travels), I did miss home. Having gone through the first year of high school in Ithaca, I missed my friends and my female counterparts at Ithaca High School, since Lawrenceville was not coeducational at the time.

The school did have a number of proms and other get-togethers, to which I invited some of my former Ithaca girlfriends. My Raymond housemates and I also watched the predecessor of MTV, *American Bandstand*, and since the high school girls who appeared on the show lived in nearby Trenton, New Jersey, we had a regular pen-pal party going. A number of them were invited to the Lawrenceville proms.

During this time, I lost track of what my parents were up to, but my mother and father kept close track of me. I had read J.D. Salinger's *The Catcher in the Rye*, which was published around the time I was in prep school, and I managed to prevail on my father to let me and two of my classmates spend a weekend in New York City. We stayed at the New York Athletic Club, which had for the first time decided to allow women in the dining room, but still not the rest of the areas in the club. My classmates saw the New York trip as an opportunity to smuggle any receptive woman they met on the street into the club, alas without success.

So we took this as an opportunity to kick off our drinking career. I remember the night after our healthy indulgence attending a first-run movie. Back then a "first-run" movie was equivalent to a Broadway show. It was a full house, and we had seats in the front row of the balcony. I was, unfortunately, more sick than drunk, and I finally lost my dinner over the side. The recipient below was smart enough to track me to the men's room after he found the seat empty directly above him, and went there to clean off the results of my evening. I have seen this in many movies since, and I'm sure I was not the first to close the stall door and stand on top of the toilet to avoid being spotted when he looked under each stall. That is where I heard, during his cleanup, most of the swear words that would stand me in good stead for the rest of my life.

I made the mistake, during a Thanksgiving break, of telling my mother about some of the things that happened in New York, and she started referring to *The Catcher in the Rye*. She asked me questions even the author hadn't thought about.

Assuring her that I avoided women of the night during this trip, I was also assured by my parents that it would be the last trip I would take to New York during the remainder of my Lawrenceville stay. My father had always feared a paternity suit, something that he might have to end up paying for. So he kept a watchful eye over my escapades even into my college years. This monetary concern kept my youth fairly tame, although I attracted and was attracted to some very good-looking and active women in the two colleges I would later attend.

Other than this, for the most part I stayed out of trouble at Lawrenceville. Back then (and still now), I did not go to bed before midnight. Late night was when I did most of my studying, and, I might add, my best work. Unfortunately the lights cut off in the dorm around 10:00 PM, and it's hard to sit at a desk and study while you're holding a flashlight. So I rigged up a device with an eight-volt battery wired to a light over the desk. The problem was to avoid being caught with a light on, so I wired the battery along the baseboard and the back of the door to the door latch so that when the knob turned, it broke the connection with the battery.

One night the dorm counselor spotted the light in my second-floor room from the ground outside and crept upstairs to check it out. When he quietly twisted the knob to the door, it cut off the light, leaving me sitting in the dark at my desk. I told him I had a waking dream and was sleepsitting.

At Lawrenceville, I met classmates with whom I have stayed in touch through the years. One was Doug Rowan, who later was in my class in what is now the Johnson Graduate School of Management at Cornell. We were both varsity wrestlers at Law-renceville, and some of my best memories are there. Wrestling creates ties that bind. During the season, we ran five miles a day, worked out in the gym, and practiced day after day and weekends. I represented the team in my weight class, but I wasn't the only one trying out. We all had backups in our weight class, and I had to wrestle off with mine before every match for the privilege of representing our team.

One of my opponents had both a psychological and a physical advantage over me, since he was born with only one arm. Now you might think that someone with two arms could easily beat someone with one, but it was not true in this case. At least not in collegiate wrestling which is quite different from *professional* wrestling.

In the mat position that starts a match, a right-handed competi-tor on top has his left arm around the opponent's waist, with his right gripping his opponent's right arm at the elbow. This guy's single arm was on the left side so there was nothing to grip. You were off balance to begin with, and during the match, he also had 25 percent less to hold on to. He was as quick as lightning, and to compound things, his left arm was the size of a leg. I managed to prevail once I got over my sympathy for him, and represented the team in most of the matches.

I'm not sure there are many sports that cause so much personal uneasiness and deprivation before the "game is on." In wrestling, you are part of a team but not part of a team effort. It is a distinctly individual sport. The team is dependent on each member's winning to raise its overall score, but no supporting teammate is there to compensate for your blunders. You are very much alone when you are out on the mat.

Most of us were a pound or two overweight for the class in which we wrestled, so the day before the match we smelled the food we couldn't eat while existing on concoctions of honey and orange juice to pull us through final weight-reducing exercises. As night approached I sat unfocused over my homework, accomplishing nothing, pacing the floor, or sweating in bed. Some of my teammates had enough confidence to go peacefully to sleep, but they were rare. Wrestlers have unpredictable ups and downs and a champ today can be pinned on his back looking up at the lights tomorrow. Most of us knew this only too well, and to the unfortunate roommate of some wrestlers the match was fought all through the night with groans and technicolor nightmares.

When the morning came our stomachs were as empty as a fraternity keg at midnight. We sat in the swaying bus headed toward our opponent's school, eating just enough chocolate to keep energy going. Some of us were convinced we were doomed to wrestle reincarnated Roman gladiators. We had been filled with propaganda about the crushing victories of our opponents. On arrival we would tumble off the bus and get into our uniforms. Before the matches began, the two teams would sit across from each other, each of us trying to ignore his opponent. Your weight class is announced, you step out on the mat, and though you may have aged a year in the last day, you could sometimes take comfort that maybe your opponent had, too. Contrary to popular belief, athletes who compete alone seldom hear the encouragement or advice from their teammates, particularly in wrestling with ear guards on. Had I heard my teammates' advice, I would have been the top dog in my weight class among the military and prep schools we competed against. In the final championship match, my opponent managed to pin me with five seconds left. My teammate, Doug, had shouted for me to simply roll off the mat to break my opponent's hold with ten seconds left. Had I done that, since I was ahead on points, a first-place medal could have been mine.

Overall, I won some and lost some, but the Lawrenceville wrestling team in its 1955–1956 season boasted the best record of any team in the previous ten years. We had six wins and two losses and retained our title as state champions for the fifth straight year.

VARSITY WRESTLING

Left to Right: Bottom Row: Losi, Rowan, Reynolds, R., Roskind, Barrett, R., Sylvester. *Top Row:* Mr. Delaney (coach), Van Vactor, Mills, D., Wight, J., Beebe (mgr.), Park, R., Green, R., Mr. Gaines (coach).

The Wrestling Team from the 1956 Lawrenceville yearbook where I also served on the Business Board. In the front row, second from left, is Doug Rowan, my classmate at Cornell as an undergraduate and later in the Johnson Graduate School of Management.

Aside from wrestling, I was a member of the Inquirers Club, on the Editorial Board of the school newspaper, the *Lawrence*, for which I reported and also contributed cartoons, and on the Business Board of the school yearbook, *Olla Podrida*. Looking back through some graduation comments from my classmates scrawled in the yearbook and addressed to some of my respective nicknames of "Royus," "Royondo," "Parkey," and "Roy-Boy," I note that one of them said, "I hope you will continue with your creative writing."

Among the notes I also saw was, "In spite of the fact that you referred to me as despicable, I still think you are a pretty good guy....Maybe when you look back at the past, you'll see that I'm not the bully you thought." I was a little guy and, understandably, not fond of bullies. In my senior year we moved off campus into The Lodge, and one of my housemates enjoyed picking on students smaller than he was. I was at the top of his list. About a month and a half into this, I got fed up and decided to go extracurricular with my wrestling abilities. I have my fair share of patience, but there comes a time when I just plain tire of taking crap. This was one of those times.

It is amazing how your adrenaline soars when you really get mad. He was unprepared for wrestling and was subjected to the best I could give in front of his classmates, and that was the end of his bullying me. Not only had I earned his respect but it also had an unanticipated impact on his general behavior—he stopped picking on the other small people he had formerly targeted as well. He could never be sure whether one of them might step up and repeat my performance.

My years at Lawrenceville gave me not only an excellent education, but something that lasted a lifetime—self-confidence. In years to come, I would need every bit of it, too.

Getting back to my father's business, by the mid-1950s despite distribution in only 23 states, the Duncan Hines cake mixes were number two among all brands in sales. Becoming a marketing force to be reckoned with led directly to a merger proposal from Procter & Gamble in 1956.

I was in my senior year in Lawrenceville when P&G approached my father and offered him a deal. Having abolished much of the drudgery in the laundry room, P&G decided that it was time to march into the kitchen. The Duncan Hines brand struck them as a useful wedge for breaking into that market. I didn't hear a lot about the behind-the-scenes negotiations, but my father said he had arrived at a figure that he would accept, and with a few refinements to be ironed out, told me he was going to hold to a "take it or leave it" deal.

I didn't learn until many years later that my father's Hines-Park Foods operation was under financial stress. The company was struggling because the costs of developing, packaging, advertising and distributing the product line were not yet being offset by anticipated revenues. Something not uncommon in a start-up business, and my father was not dealing from a strong position.

At the time, Stewart Underwood had become corporate secretary and general manager of the marketing division of the Duncan Hines Institute, and owned a fair amount of stock in Hines-Park Foods. Underwood was on his way to his honeymoon in Myrtle Beach, SC, when Pops had the state police pull him over and tell him to go to the nearest phone to call my father. Pops told him that P&G had made an offer and he wanted to know if Underwood was willing to sell his shares. Having worked for my father for sixteen years and knowing the state of business at that time, Underwood said he would be *more* than happy to sell. This allowed a P&G buyout to be made without any holdout shareholders.

I should mention here that while I was at Lawrenceville, shortly after Underwood's marriage, his young wife was asked by my father to drive me from Ithaca to Lawrenceville. Pulling up in her Chrysler convertible with a beautiful young woman made me an instant star at my Raymond House dorm.

At any rate, after the P&G offer we took another one of our few family vacations and went into the Laurentian Mountains in Quebec, Canada. It turned out to be an extended vacation. Pops had told the people at P&G that he was leaving town and could not be reached, and no one was to be told where he was. He said he would check with his secretary from time to time from various locations, and that he would return for the closing once P&G decided to accept his terms. We camped out in a resort completely removed from communications, and every morning my father would go down to the nearest village to check in with his office via the public phone. In a sense he was truthful in saying he was in a location where he could not be reached.

The days dragged into weeks and the numerous phone calls P&G made to my father's secretary were reported back to him verbatim. My father knew his terms would be nitpicked, and the P&G lawyers came up with every twist and turn on the deal that a magician could imagine. All of which were crisply turned down by my father's secretary, simply saying that she had no way to communicate these alternative offers to him.

Quebec is a French-speaking province, and although I took French at Lawrenceville, I disliked it intensely. My dislike of and lack of fluency in the language did not serve me well, since the girls who worked in the resort spoke only French, but I managed to find ways to communicate.

At first I felt isolated and bored, since we stayed longer than most guests, but I began to be welcomed at the nightly campfires for the staff after the day was over. Sometimes I snuck back into my room in the cottage we rented well after midnight. I was thankful my father was totally absorbed by his work; with his attention elsewhere, I was pretty much on my own.

I will never forget the night when one of the young waitresses took my French version of "See you later" to mean "See you now" and decided to follow me back to the room. Instead of a kiss good night at the door, she slid past me inside the room. Since my parents were sleeping next door, and my sister in the adjoining bed, I felt the visit would be inappropriate, but it took me quite a while to explain to the girl that she had to go. She left in a huff. Word spread among the young people I hung out with, and they came to the conclusion there was something wrong with me. Frankly, although I tried to explain the situation, I came to the conclusion that they were correct. Well into the second month of our stay, my father finally returned from his phone call in the village to say that his full terms were going to be accepted without change by P&G, and that we could return to the United States.

On the drive back home, I learned the price tag on the deal, which my father promised P&G he would not publicly disclose, but he did tell me that it would be enough to get him into whatever new career he wanted.

Although paltry compared to today's acquisition prices, back then it was a good piece of change. My father never told anyone what he sold the company for, and except to say he got 360,000 shares of tax-free P&G stock, I will keep his secret on the dollar value of the sale. The merger between Hines-Park foods and P&G was announced on August 17, 1956, and my father signed on as a consultant to P&G for the next six years. By the end of 1956, P&G had introduced twelve mixes into their new line of Duncan Hines baking products from flap jacks, muffins, and rolls to brownies, coffee, and sponge cakes. And I had graduated from Lawrenceville and was back in Ithaca as a freshman at Cornell.

TO THE (BIG) RED AND (SNOW) WHITE FIELDS OF CORNELL

One of the first things I did after arriving at Cornell was try out for the wrestling team which I made during the first half of my Freshman year. The opponent in my weight class had been a fellow student at Ithaca High who had gone on to become an Olympic champion. During tryouts I gave it my best shot and held my own without getting pinned, but in the long run, he solemnly assured me, putting aside any remnants of our high school friendship, "That will not continue to happen."

I took his word for it and along with being on a fast track for scholastic probation, bagged wrestling as a sport. Enrolling in the alterate standard physical education class required, I met with another champion in one-on-one sports when I took fencing during what proved to be the short time I survived at Cornell. My instructor was a world-class champion in this sport, and I would, ironically, end up traveling with him (I'll just call him "Mr. Raul") several years later while working in my father's business during a summer recess.

When I became a freshman at Cornell University, I went in with the largest class (thirty) of graduates ever from Ithaca High

School. We have a reunion every five years and almost everybody who's still alive shows up. I am not sure I want to go back for my fiftieth reunion because, at the last one, some of my classmates looked pretty old, a sad reminder of what I may look like when I grow up. On the other hand, I wouldn't want to risk reminding a long-lost classmate "you were in my class." I might be asked what I taught!

At the start of my freshman year at Cornell, I attended a then-compulsory summer retreat for freshmen. I spotted during this two-or three-day affair someone whose air of innocence and wholesomeness was magnetic. We started to date in the early part of our freshman year. It was like the courtship between a couple of fourteen-year-olds, and I treated her like she was the queen she was soon to become. That could have been my mistake because I felt she was untouched, if you know what I mean, certainly by me, but avidly sought after by others.

In those days at Cornell a Queen of the Freshman Class was crowned and the lovely young lady I considered my girl, was the one who was chosen. I got to escort her to the ball but, a few days later, when I called her for a date, I was unable to reach her. Every junior and senior male on the campus, of which there were thousands, zeroed in on my angelic freshman queen and the last time I ever dated her was the night of her inauguration. I can't blame her for passing me over, since she had her pick of 15,000 men at Cornell. Sometimes you get and sometimes you get got, and I did feel foolish thinking about the opportunity I may have missed.

Apart from being serious about her, during my freshman year at Cornell I did everything a freshman could humanly do to avoid getting serious about anything else. I cut classes, put my feet up, and took it easy. Why? Because the content of almost 90 percent of my freshman courses had been sufficiently covered, as I saw it, at Lawrenceville. In biology alone, I cut so many lectures (in those days you received a point off for each one cut) that my A+ at Lawrenceville turned into a barely passing 60 at Cornell.

The Epsilon Bulletin

VOLUME 28	ITHACA, N. Y., APRIL, 1957	NUMBER TWO

EPSILON PLEDGES TEN

Sitting (L-R): Leagans, Sparks, Thurlby, Tallman, Park. Standing: Mason, Bloom, Farley, Wynne, Sutherland.

Recommended by Duncan Hines. Shortly after pledging Sigma Phi, the famous connoisseur, as a favor to us, made the fraternity house the only one in the world to have this honor. Still a pledge when I busted Cornell in 1957, in a surprise event, I was initiated as a life member of the Epsilon Chapter of Sigma Phi in 2013.

It would never happen today, but I also had a car and a parking permit as a freshman at Cornell. Big mistake. I was also the Art Editor of "Sounds of Sixty," our class newsletter. I pledged Sigma Phi as a beginning sophomore, and my fraternity membership became another excuse to play instead of work. It wasn't long before I was on scholastic probation, shortly to be combined with social probation.

A number of people I had met during prep school who attended Cornell with me, some from Lawrenceville, formed a gang of hell-raisers to an extent unimaginable at Cornell. We pulled every stupid, mindless stunt in the books, from filling our two-story dormitory halls with straw from a construction site to putting work-site signs and flashing lights throughout the building. We stole toilet seats out of the dorm and put various objects in the beds of all of our classmates during the day while they were at classes.

That behavior, in addition to my visibly low grades (which are supposed to go up and not down when you are on scholastic probation) put me on the road to academic perdition. I busted out of Cornell at the end of the first semester of my sophomore year.

Needless to say, my father was not thrilled with this, but he did go to bat for me. He called his contacts in his home state to see if The University of North Carolina at Chapel Hill might give me a second chance. I went down, and as a favor to my father, I was given the following scenario:

If I took two courses in Cornell's Department of Communication Arts during what was left of the second sophomore semester after I busted out, as well as two correspondence courses from UNC and received at least a B average in all of these (step one), and if I attended a double summer school session at UNC—took four courses—and maintained this B average overall (step two), then (if I could maintain a B average in all eight courses across the board), I would be admitted as a sophomore at UNC. That meant I had lost a half-semester of college, which wasn't too bad, providing I was able to perform.

Extreme motivation is usually a product of extreme need. To redeem myself, and to redeem my father, as well, I pulled it off and entered the Journalism School at The University of North Carolina in 1958. Needless to say, the motivation that I generated did not leave me and has lasted throughout my life.

I moved in the direction of journalism because I truly liked to write and although I did have an above-average artistic talent, I knew I could never begin to make a living at it. Journalism was not a deliberate choice because my father started out in it, but I would have to think that genetics played a role. The apple doesn't fall far from the tree.

One of the courses I took at Cornell during this period was creative writing, and as a class assignment, I convinced my professor, William B. Ward, that I should write an article on why I busted Cornell. He was lukewarm to the idea, and after it was completed, it earned a C+. Fortunately, the rest of my articles were not affected by this low mark, and more as a challenge than anything else, I began to submit this article to magazines.

I will never forget when I received a call from one of the editors at *Seventeen* saying they liked the article and asked for my permission to run it when the magazine had a "hole." Without telling my professor, I gave the editor permission and kept my fingers crossed. About two months later I received another call saying they had a hole to fill, but they would have to "judiciously" edit my article to about half its length to fit, and said that if they couldn't do that I would have to wait until a bigger hole in a future edition. I took the chance, signed off on the release, and a month later the article appeared in the October, 1959 issue of *Seventeen*. As a feature in the issue, they even hired an artist to illustrate, cartoon style, the events that led up to my Cornell demise. I think one of the most satisfying things I have ever done was telling Professor Ward his low-graded article had been published.

Not only was the article a success, but the YOUR LETTERS section of the December issue of the magazine was dominated by letters from kids around the country praising the article. I also received several pounds of fan mail at The University of North Carolina from students simply addressed with my name at UNC. I later was told that the magazine, itself, had also directly received many letters that, regrettably, they had thrown away, so I never saw any of them.

Needless to say, this case history was used in the class taught by my professor at Cornell right up to his recent retirement, as an outstanding example of how to succeed in creative writing. It was headlined WHY I BUSTED COLLEGE. For those inclined to read this, my first major piece of confessional journalism, I have reprinted it, warts and all, but with enduring pride along with student comments in Appendix A in this book. As the saying goes, when you have a lemon, make lemonade.

Of special note was the letter published in the December issue of *Seventeen* from Cornell Associate Dean Rollin L. Perry, which read: "I want to say how much I enjoyed the article by Roy H. Park, Jr. I was very close to Roy and his situation here at Cornell and believe he has done a straightforward and sincere job of writing of his experience. Nothing but good can come from such honest reporting."

CHAPTER 6
A SECOND CHANCE

No question that 1957 was a memorable year in my life. After I busted out of Cornell, I buckled down at UNC to face the real world and started out on a hard-driving course that changed my life and times. While other teenagers, students and otherwise, were listening to music that led them in directions I began to dislike, I was listening to a different drummer and walking a narrow path of my own.

I arrived in Chapel Hill as a sophomore in 1958. I lost track of what my father was up to, since I was concentrating heavily on making my marks in college. And during this first year at UNC, my father was intent on making sure I had my nose to the grindstone. One of the ground rules that he laid down was that for that first year, to keep me away from roommates, fraternities, and the other temptations I experienced at Cornell, I was to be quartered in a small room at the Carolina Inn, a hotel smack in the middle of the campus.

To show good faith and gain experience, I wrote articles for the local newspaper, the *Chapel Hill Weekly*, the owner being a former professor in Cornell's Johnson Graduate School of Management. One of these was an interview with a man who started a pizza parlor in the heart of downtown Chapel Hill. He came to North Carolina from New York, telling me of his vision of serving the students and the community. I reported this in a beautifully sympathetic article, which made students flock to his door.

A month later, the pizzeria had been emptied of everything except the rats. The owner fled Chapel Hill with his belongings plus a lot that didn't belong to him, including all the kitchen equipment for which he had not paid. So much for being kind to people in articles, since that can come back to bite you on the backside. I took a lot of flack from townspeople and my fellow students on that one.

Aside from my studies, I had time on my hands, little to sidetrack me, and a lot to think about. Cloistered in a tiny room under a stairwell in which the only furnishings were a desk and a bed, I had plenty of time to turn my thoughts inward and learn about writing—by writing. I wrote occasional letters and stories for the *Chapel Hill Weekly,* the *Raleigh Times* and the *News of Orange County.* As I said, I enjoy putting words together, receiving my highest marks in writing courses from grade school on up, and with my coursework then concentrated in journalism, I also wrote for fun.

So along with articles, stories, and notes I made reflecting the things I remembered about my life, I tried my hand at my version of poetry. The oldest definition of poetry, from the Chinese, is that it is "the expression of earnest thought." Confucius said: "Who does not study poetry has no hold over words." I was going to deal with words in a big way for the rest of my life, so I figured it would be helpful to get an early hold on them.

"Poetry is the spontaneous overflow of powerful feelings," said William Wordsworth, and "it takes its origin from emotion recollected in tranquility." I certainly had plenty of tranquil time, so I expressed my emotions in a number of poems.

THAT (LONELY) LOVIN' FEELING

An Open Letter to a Girl

It will be a long time before I'm
With you again...perhaps never.
But the impact of what I left behind,
Will last.
It might have been an orchid in the
Cold heights of Everest,
Or a gardenia in the depths of Hell.
Most probably, it was just an angel

On earth.
Because of you, I know the old world
Is not black and Godless
As it often appears to be.
I know too, that the girl I shall
Someday search for, fight for,
And love,
Does now exist in more than
Imaginary terms.
You will be an inspiration to many,
Before you become an inspiration
To one.
Let no man break the stem which
Connects you to life in its real sense.
A blossom on the stem serves God's
Natural purpose before it dies;
One in the florist's window has only
A short moment of glory, and
Dies...
Purposeless.
Think in terms of eternity and
You shall become a part of it.
Think only in terms of this world,
And
You shall become a part of it, too.
But whereas eternity is endless, the
Dust of this small world cannot last
Forever...
Real love is immense: so great that it
May never be confined by any one
Aspect.
I only hope that someday we may
Both
Feel the pure happiness it can bring
Until then, stay just as you are...

The poems I wrote, like the one above, were published fairly regularly in the Raleigh *News & Observer* on the editorial page under the heading TODAY'S NC POEM. Some of them were about lost loves. I'd had a number of them during my summer breaks in Ithaca while I was at Lawrenceville, and a few more at Cornell. But none yet at Carolina.

Being pretty sequestered in the Carolina Inn, I hadn't met anyone. Besides, while I was at Carolina, the only girls on campus were graduate students or nurses. I was not old enough to easily capture a date with a grad student, and I thought not experienced enough to get a date with a nurse.

But things worked out and improved in 1959 on at least one memorable occasion. I ushered for a wedding in Grosse Pointe, Michigan. Henry Ford II's mother, Eleanor Ford, was a close friend of the bride's mother who arranged for me to be a guest at Charlotte Ford's coming-out party.

And then there was my encounter with the formidable mother of a future president of the United States.

AN INTERVIEW WITH ROSE KENNEDY

It was my father's idea to interview Rose Kennedy when she swung through Chapel Hill, campaigning for her son. She was headquartered at the Carolina Inn, and, of course, she also campaigned in Raleigh and Durham, NC. Pops, who was in Raleigh on business at NC State at the time, heard she was staying in "my" hotel, and thought it would be a coup for me. The staff was secretive about her schedule, and I explained the difficulty of getting through to her with her unknown schedule and my full class load. Pops thought about that and developed a strategy.

His idea was a twist on his application for his first job in Raleigh. He suggested that I write down on a notepad all the questions I wanted to ask her, leaving space under each for her to handwrite her reply. He felt that I could persuade the desk clerk I knew at the Carolina Inn to put this in her box along with my room number in case she decided to respond.

I took this a step further. I called her on the phone in her room when the desk clerk informed me she had returned around 10 PM. I told her what I planned to do, and since she seemed to be in a receptive mood, I asked her if she could talk for a minute and was able to carry on a phone interview for the next half hour. She also had a copy of her speech that day sent down to my box.

After our conversation, I wrote her a note confirming that I was a student in the journalism school also staying at the inn. My note said:

Dear Mrs. Kennedy,

Thank you for allowing me to look over your speech.

I don't know if you saw my list of questions, but if you don't have time to look them over, perhaps your maid could leave them in Box 1017 when you check out. If you did have the time to go through them, you could leave both the questions and answers in the same box, or at the Carolina Inn desk in Chapel Hill.

There are many students, as you know, in the area who will be voting for the first time and would like to know about Kennedy when he was their age. I am sure this would be of interest to them.

Enjoyed talking with you over the phone last night, and am sorry I did not get the chance to meet you.

Very sincerely, Roy H. Park, Jr., University of NC

I picked up the written interview she left in my box the next morning, along with her handwritten note which said: *Thank you for your interest. While awaiting the car I have tried to help. Rose Kennedy.* Combined with the notes I took during our phone conversation, I had an article ready to go before noon.

Calling the major newspapers in the area, I found the *Durham Morning Herald* to be immediately receptive, drove over, and handed the article to them, and was delighted to see it featured at the top page of the second section on October 3, 1960, the next morning:

Mom Tells of Kennedy's College Life, Childhood
by Roy H. Park, Jr.
(Durham Hill Company Inc. Reprinted with permission from the *Durham Morning Herald*, October 3, 1960.)

UNC Journalism student Roy H. Park, Jr., taking advantage of a visit Mrs. Rose Kennedy paid to Chapel Hill during the weekend, came up with a bevy of questions which the famous mother hadn't faced in thousands of previous interviews.

Mrs. Rose Kennedy, who rested this weekend in Chapel Hill, took time out to answer questions about her son that only a mother could answer. "Was Jack a good student in college?" Her answer, "Good at school, but not brilliant. He did not make all A's."

The Democratic presidential aspirant graduated at 22 from Harvard, class of 1940. Mrs. Kennedy said Jack "was probably one of the best informed college graduates of 1940." One thing that most moms invariably complain about is the lack of correspondence originating from their sons or daughters away at college. Jack, however, wrote his mother "weekly," and as an afterthought, "usually" was added. It is true his father gave him $1 million when he was 21. Mrs. Kennedy also named his favorite sport as sailing.

"Jack was a prodigious reader when he was young. He was particularly fond of adventure, history and biographies." Mrs. Kennedy said, "Boston abounded in monuments of this country and Jack heard about them and viewed them when he was knee high and then, when he would return home, he would read books which I had bought for him to supplement his knowledge. And we would discuss these stories at family meals.

"In those days there was no radio or television. And he grew to know and love the great heroes and American history, much the way some boys today know and love their wild West heroes on television. That love and knowledge of history that increased over the years went on until as a teenager he could answer almost any question on American history."

In a telephone conversation, Mrs. Kennedy said, "We used to play games where one person described a famous person and the rest tried to guess who it was. Jack always won." Did Mrs. Kennedy ever think that her son might someday be a presidential candidate? "Every mother has that privilege," she said. At one time, however, she felt her eldest son would be the politician in the family, but he was killed in World War II.

Mrs. Kennedy herself went to the Boston public schools, Dorchester High School, Convent of the Sacred Heart, Aix-la-Chapelle in Germany and New York. She also "had been in a German convent and had visited Germany, Poland and the Soviet Union."

"As a little girl," Mrs. Kennedy went on, "I lived on a farm in New England about 25 miles outside of Boston. Those were the days when we slept in feather beds and read by the light of a kerosene lamp and our milk came in a five-gallon can. But I was happy and contented helping my grandmother in the garden and riding home proudly with my grandfather on a load of hay after the men had piled it high and packed it down in the old farm wagon which was drawn by the farm horse."

Were these trips she is taking her own idea or Jack's? "I started the idea," she replied.

In a telephone interview, Mrs. Kennedy expressed some slight concern over the religious feeling in the South. The following morning she called it "a pity to waste time on it when there are so many issues of worldwide importance. France and Germany both have Catholic leaders, and there is no interference from Rome, which is an idea of the middle ages."

How does she think Jack's chances would have been if he were not backed by the Kennedy wealth? "Excellent. He has the family tradition, tenacity, personality, intelligence and interest in world affairs." Mrs. Kennedy added that "As a baby Jack was practically rocked in his cradle to the sound of political lullabies."

Why did not Jack's father give him more public support? "It's easier for a son if a famous father gives him the complete stage."

The complete stage? I didn't need that, but this stuck with me for life, because once I went to work for him, my father seldom gave me any part of the stage, even a corner behind the curtain.

He did, however, like another poem I wrote that appeared in the *News & Observer* in July, 1961. Since I was a student in the journalism school, I decided it was appropriate to write it:

Credo for a Journal

If this journal can
Bring to just one person,
As well as to many,
A single slender ray of
The sharp, cleansing beam
Of Wisdom,
If it can help us here
To pass on a small fragment
Of Faith in the good,
And the clean,

And the pure,
Or to touch one lonely,
Unnoticed heart
With a tiny crystal of
Laughter,
If it can represent Courage
That holds up in the face of
Pain and evil and death,
Clean Moral defiance at
Corruption and fraud,
And the concealed Beauty of
The tiniest things...
If it can project one sharp,
White,
Thunder-bolt
Of unprejudiced, clarifying
Truth
Into the world around us,
Unblind one eye,
Or unlock one heart,
Anywhere,
Then it has done its job.

Later, much later, when I was working for my father and he got into the newspaper business, he asked me to share this piece with all of his publishers.

KEEPING IT PLATONIC

As I said earlier, the reader should bear in mind that my father's greatest fear was a paternity suit, and my greatest fear was providing grounds for one. Three occasions come to mind:

At Cornell, after bombing out with the Freshman Queen, I struck up a close relationship with another very popular and attractive coed who had a great sense of humor. I had pledged

Sigma Phi, one of the Union Triad, the first three to found the fraternity system in the nation, and my nine freshman fraternity brothers were intrigued by our relationship. Particularly when they learned that the two of us were going to my home in Ithaca, a short distance from campus, to study together in the evenings. They were convinced that we studied a lot more than books, although that was not the case.

Telling them nothing only fired their imaginations. We could have made speculation reality, but our friendship was more important, and we thrived on what became our campus-wide notoriety.

In 1959, the summer before I transferred as a sophomore to UNC, my date and two other couples (one of them bringing along a male white rabbit they carried everywhere) went to the Newport Jazz Festival. I was dating the same girl who followed my bike back in elementary school, and I had finally caught up to her height. We had rented space in advance in a boardinghouse in Newport, Rhode Island, and when we got there discovered there were only two rooms: a front room with two single beds and a back room closed off by a curtain with a double bed. The arrangement made it impossible to split up with guys in one room, girls in another. One of the couples was engaged, so no problem. My date, said she had no intention of sharing one of the smaller beds, but the third couple thought it was fine. So we ended up in the "private" room with the double bed.

But I had to promise her I would stay on my side of the bed. Keeping my father's fear in mind, I promised, and it was not hard to fall off to sleep since I'd had plenty to drink. When I woke up and said "Good morning," I was greeted with silence. I asked her what was the matter and her response was, "You just don't understand women." The white rabbit nodded in agreement. I understood then, too late, and I never got another date with her. But I'm glad we went to the Festival that year, though, because riots caused performance cancellations the following year.

During my junior year at UNC, I was attracted to a cheerleader I had seen riding around town in convertibles with members of the football team. I found out she was from the New York City

area, and being from New York myself, I made the Yankee connection work and stole her away from the team.

She invited me to go home with her on one of our breaks, and
her parents appropriately separated our sleeping quarters. Her
bedroom was upstairs, and mine was a sofa bed directly behind the
glass doors of their study at the base of the second-floor stairway.
After her parents went to sleep, she slipped downstairs, and all
they had to do was look down the steps to find us together. The
sound of my heartbeat alone would have been enough to wake
them. I could feel a paternity suit hovering, and both a father and
a potential father-in-law on my back. It was a short visit, and all
this caution was of no benefit to me. But it did honor my father's
wishes, and I figured I was saving him money. Of course any
appreciation he might have shown could not offset my sacrifice,
and he didn't show any, anyway.

NOSE TO THE GRINDSTONE

I got through my first year with high marks, and at the beginning of my junior year, I moved out of the Carolina Inn into an
off-campus boardinghouse. All of the rooms were either doubles
or triples, so I moved in with a student I knew. Another friend,
Jim Frazier, whom I met when he was a student working tables at
the Carolina Inn (and who was taking some of the same courses I
was), also moved into the house. There were four other students in
the various combinations in the house, and we all got along well.

This time, I didn't have a car and the walk to campus along
the unpaved red Carolina clay paths was messy. You looked like
an advertisement for the "Red Shoe Diaries" by the time you arrived on campus. The journalism school was on the same side of
the campus as the rooming house. That was good since I spent
a lot of late nights in the library researching articles we had to
write. I even made a run for student council as an Independent,
which was a futile effort since the fraternity guys had the candi-
dacies sewed up. It did give me a taste of what you have to do in

politics, which permanently inoculated me against ever running for public office again.

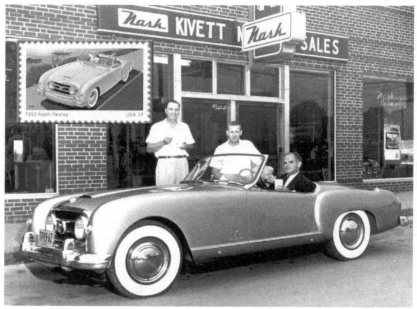

Courting Car I drove as a student at Chapel Hill while courting my wife. Stewart Underwood said he was there when Pops picked up the car from the dealership in 1952, but he's not in this picture. The Nash-Healey was one of the eight classic "sporty cars" of the 1950s featured in 2004 on U.S. Postal Service stamps (see insert).

Along about the second semester of my junior year, I persuaded Pops to let me have a car again, one from his antique car collection in Ithaca—a 1952 Nash-Healey sports car. It is interesting that this same car was featured in 2004 on stamps as one of eight classic *America on the Move* "Sporty Cars" of the 1950s issued by the United States Postal Service.

This time I used the car sensibly because I didn't want to lose it—as well as my ability to date off-campus. Since Carolina was not truly coeducational at the time, the best place to find girls was at the Women's College, nicknamed "WC," in Greensboro. It is now known as The University of North Carolina at Greensboro. It was a good hour's drive over there, but the guys said that all you had to do was to drive through the campus in a convertible and the girls would pour out of the dorms and jump into your car. That was not true, but it sounded good, and it was as close to a smorgasbord as you could get for those of us who had a tough time getting dates on the Chapel Hill campus.

I made a number of new friends during the year, and a bunch of us decided to make another move our senior year, even farther off campus. By that time, we all had cars, so six of us rented an entire two-story house in Carborro and made it our home. It had four double bedrooms with kitchens. When we rented the house, one bedroom was already occupied by two nurses. Occasionally we needed them, and it made it even more like home.

The floors in the old Carborro house were tilted. The beds leaned downhill or sideways, depending on how you placed them, and you had to turn them every so often to sleep in the opposite direction to even out whatever circulates in your brain.

My housemates, some of whom I still keep in touch with, also remember the many parties we had there, with streamers and balloons all over to dress the decrepit old place up. Even the water in the tropical fish tank was safely colored *Carolina Blue* with vegetable dye.

A month or so into my senior year, my father came down to Raleigh for a business meeting, accompanied by my mother, and invited me to come over to his hotel and have dinner. Of course he asked me if I wanted to bring along any of my friends and their dates since this would be a special occasion. I wasn't dating anyone seriously at the time and wanted to find somebody special. One of the guys in the house was going steady with a girl at WC, and I asked him if he could help me line up an attractive blind date. I told him the circumstances and promised him and his girl a fine dinner with my parents, as well, if they came through.

Party in Carborro. There would have been all six of us guys in this photo, but I was the one taking the picture shortly after I met my future wife (center) on a blind date.

I had double-dated with them on several occasions and his girl was attractive and personable, so I thought she would do well by me. I learned later she carefully picked a blind date for me with someone she felt had no interest in finding a boyfriend, or in getting tied down, and the date was set up.

MEETING MY FUTURE WIFE

I think it is unusual for parents to meet their future daughter-in-law on their son's first date with her, but that's what happened. She was well-known as the granddaughter of John Oliver Newell, the only doctor for miles around Franklinton, NC, where I drove to pick her up on a Friday during Thanksgiving break.

I remember her later telling me when she looked out of the louvered front door before she opened it, all she could see was my shoes. They happened to be Italian loafers with a snakelike twirl stitched on the top, and her first thought was that she was going to kill her friend who had set up the blind date.

When she opened the door, I was blown away. I knew I owed her friend big-time for her choice. I made a great impression on her right from the start, as well, when her father, William Brooks Parham, asked me what I would like to drink. I told him Scotch, and he disappeared into the kitchen. I later learned that he asked his daughter what kind of jerk she was dating that would ask for Scotch in Bourbon country. I settled for Bourbon, but he never forgot it.

We joined my mother and father for dinner at the Sir Walter Raleigh Hotel, and we all had a lot of fun that evening. At the time, none of us knew this match would take, and that Elizabeth Tetlow Parham would become my wife a few years later. Her nickname was Tet, and when I asked her how she got that name, she said her mother didn't feel Elizabeth suited her, so she called her by her middle name, which her friends naturally shortened.

I drove her home and asked if I could pick her up on Sunday to take her back to school. She was a little miffed that I didn't make a date the following day on Saturday, which left her wondering if I was going out with someone else. The jealousy factor helped, although I didn't learn about it until later.

Tet told me that when she got back to the dorm Sunday night, her friend asked her how she liked dating me. Tet said she thought it was fine and that I was going to ask her out again. That was when her friend burst into tears, and when she stopped crying she said she hadn't expected Tet to get involved with anyone. She had picked her for that reason, and that's when Tetlow learned her friend had set her own sights on me. But her friend got over it, and our blind date led to our going steady.

I spent a lot of time driving to Greensboro to pick her up, or to Franklinton, where Tet spent her weekends. Although I am not a slow driver, and during my seventy-six years I've driven hundreds of thousands of miles, I've only had one speeding ticket in my lifetime. A second I should have gotten, but didn't, showed me how much pull Tetlow and her family had in their small town.

While dating, I drove to Franklinton from Chapel Hill on many Sundays to take Tet back to Greensboro. I made it a point of arriving by 11 AM to go to church with the family. Once you got off the major highway, on the last stretch to Franklinton, the road went up and down like a roller coaster and had plenty of curves. One particular morning I was late and was roaring along at eighty-five mph to make up the time. I could handle this in my sports car, although it was a dangerous speed. But there were no radar detectors back then.

I realized that I had flown by a sheriff's car when I saw the flashing lights in my rear-view mirror. I was more afraid of being late for church than I was of getting a ticket, so I nudged the accelerator up to ninety-five and saw the flashing lights disappear behind me on the winding road. I had pulled up in front of the church and was on my way in when the sheriff caught up to me with his siren wailing. He had had no trouble finding me, since the car was distinctive, and the church was in the center of town.

"Son, I don't know how fast you were going," he told me, "but you gave me a run for my money. What's your rush?" I explained that I was late for church with the Parhams, and I couldn't believe it when he smiled and gave me a pass with the warning that if I ever did that again, he would throw me in jail.

Of course, the siren just outside the church doors had interrupted the service, and when I entered the building the entire congregation turned to look at me. I just slipped into the pew beside the family with an angelic expression on my face and didn't admit "nothin'" until the service was over. In the interim, I sang my praises to the Lord along with the best of them.

When our relationship became comfortable enough to feel secure, I branched out a bit and acquired a dog. The Russian wolfhound was a beautiful animal with a brain that did not match its size. When he rode with me in the car, the dog was so big that he took up all the passenger side and a good portion of my side, as well.

The Russian Wolfhound that happily took over the single front seat of the Nash-Healey during my courtship with Tetlow.

I named him Sabre and took the wolfhound along on our dates, which Tet tolerated—barely. That type of tolerance is to be commended since she had a choice of either having the dog's drooling head or its back end in her lap when we drove around. Encounters like this also brought out her sense of humor, which was a match for mine. So we laughed a lot and dated steadily through my senior year, going to discos and restaurants within an hour's drive from Chapel Hill.

I liked her father, too, who did not suffer fools gladly, and we had that in common. We both liked boating and fishing and generally keeping things stirred up. He also had a great sense of humor, so the time we spent together was lively and entertaining. I learned the invaluable lesson—you don't just marry the girl, you marry her family, as it were, so good relations with your in-laws are not just a luxury, it's a necessity for a happy and lasting marriage. Fortunately my future in-laws not only seemed to like me at the time, they liked (I thought) my oversized hound. But they did learn that when you get to thinking you might be a person of some influence, it doesn't extend to ordering someone else's dog around.

But Sabre had a sad end. When I flew home for Christmas break, no one in Chapel Hill had a crate large enough to ship the Russian wolfhound on a plane so I built a huge carrying case out of plywood. I drilled sufficient air holes, I thought, and put a rope handle on each end since it needed two people to carry it. The crate was put aboard at the same time I boarded, and carried, believe it or not, into the pilots' cockpit instead of being placed in the baggage area. I was assured my dog would be OK. Unfortunately, the plane was grounded in Atlanta for two hours with engine trouble and everyone left the plane while repairs were being made. The temperature in the cockpit rose to ninety-plus degrees, and when I arrived at my home airport and opened the crate, I found my dog dead from suffocation.

I think one of the toughest things a person can experience is losing a dog. As Will Rogers said, "If there are no dogs in Heaven... then when I die, I want to go where they went." The oldest fossil evidence shows that dogs and humans started a relationship some 20,000 years ago. It's still an open question if humans adopted dogs or dogs adopted humans, but the relationship is long-standing, dynamic, and deep, and the loss of a dog is devastating. As someone who has observed dogs for a long time, M. Acklam, said, "We give dogs time we can spare, space we can spare, and love we can spare. And in return, dogs give us their all. It's the best deal man has ever made."

I love dogs, and if you feel the same way, check out Appendix I: Dog Story.

As Dean Koontz perceptively wrote in his heart-gripping 2007 book, *The Darkest Evening of the Year,* "If you are a dog lover...and not just one who sees them as pets or animals, but...perhaps being but a step or two down the species ladder from humankind...you watch them differently from the way other people watch them, with a respect for their born dignity, with a recognition of their capacity to know joy and to suffer melancholy....

"If you watch them with this heightened perception...you see a remarkable complexity in each dog's personality, an individualism, uncannily human in its refinement, though with none of the worst of human faults. You see an intelligence and fundamental ability to reason that sometimes can take your breath away."[2]

I've had many dogs since Sabre, and have them now. But back then it was a long time before I could muster up the will to think about replacing Sabre with another dog. In the meantime, I had plenty of other family things to think about.

A FATHER'S LETTER: MY FIRST DEGREE

> *Entrepreneur: A person who organizes, operates and assumes the risk for a business venture.*

Tetlow was two classes behind me when I graduated from UNC and came back to the graduate school of management at Cornell. Pops was about to negotiate the purchase of his first two radio stations at the same time he was running the Duncan Hines guidebooks, then owned by Procter & Gamble. I promised Tet I would try to stay in close touch, and we corresponded regularly.

All in all, my three years at The University of North Carolina had been everything you thought college should be. Having avoided fraternity partying, sports, student activism, and hell-raising in general, and living with conservative roommates on scholarships for whom an education meant everything, I developed a lasting positive outlook on life when I graduated in 1961.

I had found the girl I expected to settle down with when I finished graduate school. To round it all off, I also received a letter from my father on my twenty-first birthday. It was a letter a son could be proud to receive from a father in his third career and three years away from launching his fourth. It did not appear to be meant as a lecture and clearly advanced his own image of farm-bred sincerity and good old-fashioned work ethic. The thing my father really sold best was himself.

As an entrepreneur, Pops was as good an organizer, operator, and planner as a business person can be, and although he assumed risk, he was not a consummate risk-taker. He never set out to be rich. It was a by-product of his hard work and entrepreneurship. But once he made money he knew how to hold on to it.

"Mortgage the limbs, but never the trunk," was his prime philosophy and it worked. So regardless of any self-serving elements and at what I now consider to be the tender age of forty-nine, he passed his personal wisdom and business philosophy along to me in a letter dated July 22, 1959. It began, "Happy 21st Birthday":

> Tomorrow you will have reached that magic milestone of twenty-one. You are now legally a man with all the rights and responsibilities that go with having come of age.

> For twenty-one years you have been a great joy to us…with just enough disappointment and sadness at times to make us fully appreciate your good points which predominate. I look back over the past twenty-one years and can follow clearly your progress from your first squall of life…your first toddle…your first day in school and your days in Lawrenceville and Cornell…right on to your present status at The University of North Carolina. You—and we—were blessed in that you have always been a person of unique ability and distinctive character. It is not often that one person is endowed with the abilities to express himself in words and colors, to have a winning personality, and to have a great appreciation of the beauties of nature which so often are taken for granted.

> I'm sure, Roy, that we have made mistakes—many a time—in bringing you up over the past twenty-one

years, just as you have made them along the way, but they were honest mistakes of the heart and not of the head. Sometimes I think that our disagreements and occasional flares of temper tended to weld us together just as blue heat welds the finest steel.

At least these have been twenty-one eventful years, never boring for long and usually bringing a new challenge. It is good that we are generally happy with these years, for nothing we could do now could change them. I hope that you will often look back over your first twenty-one years and that you can use them as a guide— on what to do and what not to do—for the future, both for your own life and for that family of your own that you will have.

And you have a full life ahead—as full as you want to make it. Your insurance man will tell you that you have forty-six more years if you are average. If you watch your sleep, your smoking, your diet, and your dissipation, and use care and caution in your driving, you can exceed that figure substantially. You came from a healthy strain of "long-livers," and you may easily look forward to at least sixty more years of Life, Fun, Creation, and Service. Perhaps even longer based on the strides medical science is now making.

As you enter your new status of legal independence, you will be making more and more of your own decisions. Eventually you and members of your new family will be making all of them. If these decisions are right, you will benefit. If they are wrong, you will suffer. That is the price and the reward of being on your own.

For what they may be worth, I am listing below a few suggestions that may be of some help to you in planning your life and making your day-to-day decisions. I take no pride of authorship, these are things that I have learned the hard way. Doubtless they were told to me many, many times but they became ingrained in my mind only when I learned them through experience. I hope you may keep this letter around and refer to it occasionally—and I also hope that I may be around to discuss the following points with you when your own son reaches twenty-one.

A. TIME—Of all things at your disposal, the most important and the most precious is *time*. Each of us has a given amount—and it is never quite enough. In youth, time moves too slowly. In later life, it speeds by and we know we will reach our final destination too soon for us. How you use that time, how you arrange it to take full advantage of every minute, is one of the most important arts you can master. And I do not mean that you should use all of your time in work and in self-improvement. You should take some of your time and use it for the fun of living. Do just what you want to do for the joy of doing it. But you don't "kill time" by indecision or waste. In fact, you cannot kill time, it moves on constantly. All you can do is move forward with it or stand still while time marches on.

B. HEALTH—If you are going to make the most of your time, then you must be in good *health*, eager to enjoy the fullness of life. Most of us start out as reasonably healthy individuals. Some remain that way for the most of their lives. Others never fully enjoy the hours that God has given to them because they are sleepy, they feel bad, or they are physically or mentally upset. I believe any doctor would tell you that the key to good health is moderation in eating, in exercise, in drinking, in work, and in pleasure. No one has yet found a substitute for a regularity in meals, in sleep, and in rest, and in work.

Witness the way winning football teams have their schedules regimented during training. Here's to your health. May you not only preserve it, but up-build it to the end you are able to enjoy fully all the good things in life.

C. CHARACTER—What you do with your time here on earth will depend on your *character*. Here you have always excelled. You have been honest, generally forthright, and considerate—sometimes too considerate of some and not enough of others. I do not hold that character is molded fast in the early period of life. It changes as we go along, for good or bad, and it is the responsibility of the individual to make constructive changes as he develops.

Character is a lot of things. It is the ability to be right and say NO when it would be easier and more pleasant to say yes. It is the willingness to hold fast to your beliefs when they are not popular with the crowd. This does not mean that you have to impose your philosophy or creed on others. That can be boring. It does mean that you should not be swayed by popular acclaim.

Character is the desire to be self-reliant, pay your own way to individuals and to society as a whole. It is dependability. It is that force that keeps you going when weaker souls give up the cause.

A strong character is the Automatic Pilot that can keep you on course when the going is tough. It is the most personal thing you own. Character is made up of heart, head, and of experience and judgment. Strong character is based on reason and not emotion. Sometimes it is best to use your head rather than your heart in making a decision.

D. FRIENDS—They used to say, "A man is known by the company he keeps." A smart advertising man recently paraphrased this as an institutional ad to read, "A company is known by the men it keeps." At any rate, until you prove yourself in a community, you will often be judged by your *friends* and by their deeds and by the impressions others have of them. This is a reasonably accurate criterion for in a free and mobile society, we usually are drawn to people who have similar tastes and desires.

You will, as time goes on, make relatively few deep and lasting friendships. They will last only if they are based on mutual respect and understanding. Friendship is something that can never be bought. It must be earned and earned constantly through consideration, sincere interest, and the giving of yourself oftentimes at personal sacrifice. In friendship, dependability takes precedence over ability.

In a democracy you pick your own friends. That is as it should be. You should, however, take time to choose wisely, and I should hope that you could contribute something to the well being and pleasure of your friends and that they could reciprocate.

E. YOUR FINANCES—Generally speaking, in our country, a man to be self-respecting, must be self-supporting. There is no freedom without responsibility and that applies to economics as well as political doctrine.

What we want out of life in the way of material or psychic pleasures and what we are willing to pay for them are often two different things. I have seen happy people who had very little more than the bare necessities of life, materially speaking. They got their pleasures from the application of their time to projects other than earning money. I have also seen unhappy people who had accumulated great wealth. But I have never seen a happy person, be he rich or poor, who had a champagne appetite and a beer income. Such people are hounded by creditors, frustrated and harried, and are prone to tell you what they could have done had they been able to take advantage of an opportunity.

It is not enough to say, "I want this or I want that." At the same time, you must say to yourself "Is it worth the price? Am I willing to sacrifice the time and effort to buy and take care of it?" There is an axiom that adults learn— but often too late—and that is it may be good business to go in debt to buy things with a permanent value, such as land, houses, or securities; and, of course, education falls into this category, not just for the amount of money that is represented, but also for the time that you spend in developing your mind either formally in school or in your spare time later. It is almost always *bad business* to go in debt for things that are fleeting and once consumed have no further value. This is a hard lesson to learn but we all learn it at some time in our life.

Once you have correlated your desires with your willingness to pay for them, you should then plan your *personal finances* in such a way that you live within your income and save a reasonable amount of what you earn. If you were to start now putting aside 10 percent of your income or allowance and invest it in good stocks, such as you already own, you would be surprised at the way your estate would grow. If you adopt this 10 percent rule and keep it inviolate, you will have a comforting reserve when hard times come, and believe me they come to us all at one time or another.

Sometimes we take poetic liberties and try to think that only the poor are good. Outstanding religious authorities have long ago disproved that idea for they will tell you openly that before you can convert an infidel race, you must first satisfy their bodily needs. Judges will tell you that most embezzlement results not from some master mind wanting to take advantage of other people, but rather from some poor soul who has gotten himself in hock to the point where he sees no other way out. Succinctly stated, an economically successful man is the man who has a comfortable margin between *what he owns and what he owes*. And, of course, what is a comfortable margin depends on what his income is and what his desires are.

F. PLANNING AHEAD—They used to say circumstances make the man. Today the word is Men Make Circumstances. You now have your goal and feel you know what you wish to do in life. This, however, is a good time to question that goal while you are still in school. And if you waiver or doubt you have chosen correctly, then do not be afraid to change your course.

Once you are sure of what you wish to do, then you should go resolutely forward in that direction. Remember that the way you walk a mile is to take a required number of steps. Greatest Progress comes not from spurts and stops but rather from steady, consistent effort.

The only way you can make steady, consistent progress is to plan ahead, not just day by day, but year by year. Modern businesses, for example, require their executives to plan at least five years ahead, and to make such a plan each year. This establishes the goals and also drives home the point that it takes consistent, steady effort to attain those goals.

How each of us plan our work and use our time is a fairly personal matter. Some do it with elaborate systems of notes or card files and record books. Others do it on pieces of scratch paper or almost entirely in their own mind. How you do it is not nearly as important as that you do it. And once you have made your plan, then make the plan work for you.

In such planning, you must be realistic and not lay out a program that is so ambitious it cannot be accomplished. Such a plan can only result in frustration. Furthermore, if once the plan is made, you take it lightly, then it is of no benefit to you.

Finally, in *planning ahead* we must keep in mind that it is a human failing that we all like to anticipate success, acclaim and leadership. We do not look forward with the same zest to the work and the effort that has to go in attaining these goals. The weak point of most plans is the tendency to wait until tomorrow to put the unpleasant part of the plan into effect and to be impatient for the benefit to descend upon us.

So ends my letter to you on your twenty-first birthday. Let me add that you have not only our love and affection, but our sincere wish that you may get out of your life as many of the things you want as it's possible for anyone to achieve. And it is our wish to help you toward this accomplishment and toward your personal happiness in any way we can that is sound and right and reasonable.

Twelve years later I went to work for my father and found that some of the philosophy he expressed in this letter did not quite apply. At least where it concerned me. When it concerned salaries and raises, there was little local autonomy in the companies he owned, and all of his business practices did not reflect the humble, sincere and positive qualities he voiced in this beautifully crafted letter. But many of them did, and those are the ones I learned from.

As Johnnie Babcock later put it, a public relations genius, which my father was, clearly relishes the opportunity to crown a prince or king, providing it is he who also is feted. In later years, my father's relations with the public occasionally approached what Alice Roosevelt Longworth said of her father, Theodore Roosevelt. That he was so bent on being the center of attention he wanted to be the bride and groom at every wedding and the corpse at every funeral.

By an extraordinary coincidence, my mother was going through her papers while I was writing this book and sent me a paper I had written for a creative writing course at UNC that she kept. It's the next chapter, and may have been written in response to my father's letter to me since it dealt with my relationship with him.

After what I was to experience in my version of *Life with Father* in subsequent years, it sounds rather Pollyanna-ish to me now, and its tone is reminiscent of the plucky togetherness of a once popular television series, *The Waltons*. But I can promise you we didn't go through the "Good night, John-Boy" or "Roy-Boy" routine in our family when we bedded down.

As an exercise, however, in that ancient Roman virtue, filial piety, it can't be faulted!

CHAPTER 7
REVERSE JUDGMENT— MY FIRST
TWENTY-ONE YEARS

There are few successful adults who were not first successful children.

—*Alexander Chase*

As a student at UNC, I wrote about my path to adulthood being the result of the way I was raised and of the way I responded to my parents during my first twenty-one years.

When I was about six we still lived in an apartment building. I had a couple of friends and without a real lawn or woods to explore, collecting bugs around the building and parking lot was one of our pastimes. With tin cans clutched in our fists we searched the grounds for anything we could catch. I always wanted to use a glass jar to be able to see what we caught, since watching praying mantises and lightning bugs in a tin can just didn't cut it. But my mother warned that a jar could break and cut me. The first day I snuck one out I fell and broke the jar, nearly losing the tip of a finger on my right hand. I ran back to the apartment, blood making a trail up the sidewalk, stairs, and hallway into the apartment. I was not quiet about the pain, and my mother piled me into the car and headed for the doctor. On the way she made sure to remind me of her earlier warnings, and of course later called my father at his office.

It was one of those, "wait until your father gets home" moments, and I expected to be punished. But when Pops came home, he just asked if it hurt, and that was it. They both told me that I would know better next time, and I agreed I sure would. The scar is still there to remind me, and I see it every day.

As Will Rogers said, if good judgment comes from experience, then a lot of that comes from bad judgment. Incidents like this proved my parents knew what they were talking about. They would warn me not to do something, I would go ahead and do it and suffer any consequences. Punishment came only when the consequences of my error didn't come naturally. That didn't happen often because life had plenty of punishment in store for me whenever I tempted it. So at an early age, I developed an inner discipline, and instead of resenting their guidance, I mostly appreciated my parents' advice.

When I was a little older, we moved into a house and I developed a new group of friends. The antics of our small gang were mostly harmless, but when some of them tried their hand at stealing, I wanted no part of it. The few who stole usually got caught, and when I stop to think about it, I remember one of them spent a stretch in reform school.

I had no brother, but my closest friend growing up took the place of one. He was an only child and his home wasn't a happy one. He spent most of his time at our house. He told me his parents would argue a lot and had a way of catching him in the middle. I tried to help him through the tough spots. One year his mother didn't give him a birthday party. I told my mother about it and we had a party for him at our house the next day. My parents were always willing to help somebody out who needed it, and it rubbed off on me.

My friend went away to preparatory school when I did, but he flunked out. He went to another and flunked out of that, too. He was an outstanding artist and at a young age fled to New York and was famous for a while in the art community. Then he got involved with drugs and flunked out of life as well. Seeing things like this helped keep me straight early on.

As I said, Pops traveled a lot in his work, and sometimes we would all go with him. Before I was fifteen, I'd been in every state in the country except four and in a few countries outside. These family trips were fun and brought us together despite the fact that Pops always worked hard. His work came first, and that left no time to play. He apologized to me for not being more of a companion when I was young. He explained he had to get his work done so that he could do things for us. I didn't like it, but that was the way it was. But his hard work did set an example for me.

Always working, even at his grandson's graduation from the School of Journalism at UNC-Chapel Hill. Here we were keeping an eye on the ceremony through the box window at the stadium, with Tetlow using binoculars next to Dottie and my daughter watching intently at the end.

During this time, Dottie became more than just a mother. She was a friend and companion. Often we would travel together and meet Pops at the other end. She put herself out, and when we were too young to drive, she did more than her share of taking groups of us to movies and parties and retrieving us afterward.

There's no question that when my parents laid down rules sometimes I broke them. But they said the rules were because they loved me. "Someday you'll have a boy of your own, Son, and you'll feel the same way," Pops would say. "You may not like this now, but wait a few years and you'll see what I mean. When we ask you to do this, or tell you not to do that, we're doing it for your own good, and not to hurt you. And maybe we're a little selfish about it now, and you probably think we are, but we don't want anything to happen to you."

I didn't want anything to happen to my younger sister, either, and as she was growing up she went through the same stages I had. I felt I helped to raise her right along with my parents. I could get through to her and she would listen to me. As an older brother, I gave her the benefit of what experience I had and began to experience what my parents meant about having children of my own.

When I was about thirteen, I remember my parents had a fight. My father was at a crisis point in his business. Because he worked constantly, my mother threatened to leave him. I wasn't going to stand by, so I played the role of mediator. I told them I loved them both and didn't intend to spend the rest of my life visiting one and then the other. Something that foolish just wasn't going to happen to our family. My sister backed me up on everything I said.

We all ended up in the living room talking it out, and when I could tell things were getting better, I quietly exited with my sister. After a while we could hear them laughing, and they came out and thanked us for being great kids. We all went out to dinner together that night.

Except for incidents like this, we shared a sense of humor and knew how to make each other laugh. Problems were settled through discussion. I can't remember a disagreement we had that didn't end in apologies and a better understanding of each other. We could always tell when one of us was bothered by something, and we'd bring it out and resolve it then and there.

Coming from a large North Carolina farm family, my father did what he had to do on his own—putting himself through college, becoming the student editor, and winning every honorary key on campus. Dottie was proud of a charm bracelet made from them. I respected Pops's opinion, but more importantly, I felt he respected mine. Enough to back down if he saw I was on the right track. He would refer to his wealth of experience, apply it to me, and I would sometimes get angry and say, "Times have changed, Pops." He would tell me that times really hadn't changed, that basic things were always basic, and that I would eventually find out what he meant.

(And I did. I came to understand that children only begin to realize the value of their parent's advice when they have kids of their own. Unfortunately, then it's too late for a grandparent to give advice on how to raise them.)

When I was twelve, my mother began to let me join them drinking wine at supper. Whenever they ordered a bottle of Champagne when we ate out, I'd have a glass, too. When I reached sixteen, they began to let me drink Scotch. That way I began to accept alcohol in a natural way, and as I grew older, with some notable exceptions, I didn't think it was all that smart to drink to excess.

The same principle applied to smoking. When I began to think it was smart to smoke, Pops saw it coming, and gave me a cigar one day. It cured me for a while, but unfortunately, I picked up smoking again. It started my first year at Cornell when the going got rough and I was under pressure. Dottie didn't like it, but Pops didn't say anything. He told me that it wasn't a good habit to start, but I'd have to decide on my own. When things got better, I quit for a while, and then I took it up again. But that was my decision, too.

My father set an example for me to live up to but left the choices and decisions up to me. If I knew I was right, he would back me up. Sometimes, if he tried to push me into some things against my will, my mother would intervene. As I grew older, I became more and more independent. They let me choose my friends, my education, and my career. They loved me as a son, but I think they respected me as a person. Mutual respect was a great force behind my development.

Pops wasn't blind to my faults, and he pointed them out in a gentle way. And I appreciated this. We were close and would talk freely about everything. I never held anything back, and my parents didn't either. They were reasonably open discussing sex with me at an early age. I learned about it on my own, but they confirmed my discoveries without embarrassment when I brought them up. Out in the open, sex became a natural part of life, put in its proper place. I noticed the guys who boasted the most about their conquests always had the most complexes.

Pops admitted that he was pretty active in this area when he was young, and the one thing he warned me about was getting involved in a paternity suit, or what he called a "shotgun wedding." Dottie and Pops even made a bet when I was sixteen. They bet I'd lose my virginity before I was eighteen. I won't tell you who won, or whether I already had, but it shows their attitude about the subject.

My grandmother was religious, and when I was young, I'd often ask her questions about the Bible. She had a clear sense of right and wrong. She helped me believe in a being greater than us poor humans before I ever went to church, and I developed a religious outlook on life at an early age. Pop was a God-fearing Baptist before he became a God-fearing Presbyterian, but for a long period he never had time to go to church. He'd work all day Sunday from morning to late at night. My mother wanted to go but didn't go without him. I didn't feel the need since my grandmother said I could reach Him from wherever I was. So though we kept God close, we didn't always go to church to stay in touch. When my father had more free time, he made up for it by becoming an elder in Ithaca's First Presbyterian Church.

My mother and father made sacrifices for us along the way, some that I never knew about. When they sent me away to the Lawrenceville School, they bought this old Packard. Pops had explained he got it as a collector's item, and they drove it for three years. When he sold it my first year of college, I asked him why. He said he was going to get a better car and that was all.

He later said in one of our talks that they had driven the car because it was all they could afford and put me through an expensive prep school at the same time. Pops said he had my college education paid for through an insurance policy even before

I was born.

I point all this out because an old farmer's advice is to live a good, honorable life so when you get older you can think back and enjoy it a second time. Judgment doesn't wait at the end of the line. In our generation, in these days and times, every day is judgment day.

Overall, I had good parents, and their parenting allowed me to emerge from childhood with plenty of hope for the future. My father's letter to me on my twenty-first birthday had spelled out the principles he (mostly) lived by, and his attitude toward me.

But things were later to change when I entered his business world in 1971 to run his Park Outdoor billboard companies. But I'm getting ahead of myself, and will come to this later.

PARK OUTDOOR ADVERTISING at its full complement covered 45 counties in Upstate New York and Northern Pennsylvania, serving an area populated with some 3 million people.

CHAPTER 8
THE GUIDEBOOKS END

In 1956, after his sale to Procter & Gamble, my father was retained for the next three years by P&G as vice president and director of Hines-Park Foods, Inc and for the next seven, as a consultant, without competing. But he was also allowed to conduct his own business 50 percent and he became a director of ConAgra Foods, Inc. in Omaha, NE, shortly after the sale. He also became a director and member of the executive committee of the First National Bank and Trust Company and a director of the Ithaca Gun Company, both in Ithaca. All in all, he became a director of some eight other corporations from Florida to New York during this six-year period, all the while casting around for a new career.

My father *hated* being a part of corporate life, and with his P&G stock as collateral, he was keeping his eyes open for a new opportunity. He was in a position to choose any number of different directions—and he knew that fortune favors the prepared. He already had publishing, public relations, promotion advertising, and franchising under his belt. He wanted to call his own shots, again. In the meantime, he endured and despised the corporate world with its schedules, meetings and rules.

There was, however, one part of the job that I could tell my father enjoyed, because he frequently talked to us about meeting and working with Leo Burnett, P&G's Chicago advertising agency handling the Duncan Hines cake mix line. I could tell he identified completely with Mr. Burnett, its founder and CEO, who he said was one of the hardest working people he'd ever met. He told me that even when Burnett was walking from one office to another, he had papers he was reading in his hands, and was intent every minute on his work. I am not sure if Leo Burnett, himself, told him the story where late one night he was so involved with the papers in his hands that he opened the door of what he thought was the men's room and ended up in the janitors' closet.

According to the story, the door locked from the outside before he realized where he was, so Burnett spent the night with the mops, brooms and washtub sink until he could get an employee's attention the next morning by banging on the door. My father said he told him he had a light and enough work he carried with him to keep him from being entirely bored during his imprisonment.

During this time, Pops continued to publish and print the Duncan Hines guidebooks at his press in Ithaca. By the end of 1956, *Adventures in Good Eating* was in its forty-ninth printing, *Lodging for a Night* was in its thirty-ninth, *Adventures in Good Cooking* was about to come out for its twenty-sixth publication and *Duncan Hines Vacation Guide* was going into its eleventh revision.

If you never heard about or saw one of these guidebooks, the write-ups, as illustrated in Chapter 3, gave a comprehensive overview of each establishment that was fun to read. There were detailed recommendations on the specialties restaurants were famous for, the range of prices, the dress code and ambiance, and whether children were welcomed. The resort and lodging guidebooks even rated the number and quality of bath towels and washcloths, the way the beds were made up, and what perks came with your stay.

Right after Procter & Gamble purchased the Duncan Hines business, my father learned that all of the big shots at P&G took their vacations in New England, many at Cape Cod. He was determined, therefore, to make sure the Duncan Hines–recommended restaurants and resorts were highly reputable. Not only did he want to drop listings of places that weren't up to the Hines standard, he also planned to add as many new places with outstanding reputations as possible.

During the summer of 1960, going into my senior year at Carolina, I was hired as a New England field inspector for the Duncan Hines guidebooks. I was actually a Procter & Gamble employee since the company now owned the Duncan Hines Institute, but I reported to my father, which afforded me additional insights into "family business." I had wanted to go to Alaska, where the guidebooks were making inroads. I even bought and had sawed-off a 30-30 rifle for the expedition. (I considered the rifle a necessity because I was warned that during the summers when bull moose are in rut they could charge cars intruding into the back roads of their territory.)

I was just one of dozens of inspectors hired all over the country. The summer job did not pay well, but room and board were covered. We worked on a draw where we were paid $10 to inspect each restaurant, and had to inspect between five and eight a day just to make ends meet. My father was not the most generous person when it came to compensation, and he expected everyone who worked for him to really earn it.

I didn't do what Duncan Hines had done, which would be to head for the back of the restaurant to detect odors from the kitchen, condition of the refuse and garbage cans, and presence of cats or other scavengers.

I went in the front door, and these inspections were intensive and thorough. From measuring the temperature in the meat lockers to removing the vents over the stoves to checking for grease accumulation to checking out the laundry facilities in hotels and resorts, they were, in fact, as rigorous as a health department inspector would conduct. Many times our investigations upset both the chefs and the owners of the restaurants. I remember being chased around the kitchen by a Chinese chef with a chopping knife when I made a comment about the way he was storing food. I was lucky to emerge with my head.

Our inspections were not only to see if a restaurant qualified for a Duncan Hines listing, but also for those already in the book that didn't measure up, we had to remove the signs hanging in front of their establishment. And they definitely didn't like that. We were paid $5 for each "Recommended by Duncan Hines" sign we took down from restaurants that failed the inspection. There were times when I had to come back at night and stand on the hood of my car with wire cutters to take down a sign in order to avoid a confrontation with the chef or restaurant owner.

As David M. Schwartz wrote in his article entitled DUNCAN HINES: HE MADE GASTRONOMES OUT OF MOTORISTS, in the November 1984 issue of the *Smithsonian* magazine, "Hines was not the only one to profit from the success of his guides. Mere mention was enough to save an innkeeper from a break-even existence or outright bankruptcy. With each revision, restaurant owners dreaded the possibility of being dropped from the 'Duncan Hines Family' the way society women feared omission from the latest *Social Register.* The pressure to get in—and stay in—exerted in oft-mentioned influence of the quality of road food." Even long after the guidebooks ceased publication, nobody ever wanted to give up the signs.

The sad part of the job was that none of us were allowed to eat in the restaurants that we inspected. It was too expensive. We submitted expense accounts for overnights in low-budget motels, as well as whatever we could grab in the way of meals at a fast-food or family diner in each area. I can tell you that these expense accounts were very carefully scrutinized and a thorough comparison was made on the expenses filed by each representative on a division-by-division basis.

As I mentioned earlier, I had taken up fencing at Cornell my freshman year. The person who became my supervisor that summer was none other than my fencing coach, since he had worked in Europe as an inspector for the Michelin Guide Books. He only traveled with me two or three times during the entire summer, and during those times I knew I was safe from harm, since he was an established kick-boxer as well. When we overnighted together, he would exercise by keeping a sofa pillow in the air continuously with his feet, with his hands behind his back, without letting it hit the floor. In the heat of the New England summer he wore a wool sport coat at all times. We were required to be well-dressed and I wore a shirt and tie but without a coat until I entered a restaurant or resort.

I finally asked him how he could stand to keep that wool coat on at all times since there were always drops of sweat pouring down his forehead and below his ears. He took the coat off to show me his shirt had only a front. It was backless, and he explained to me that it was cool under the wool coat, which he said insulated him from the heat. While I appreciated his theory, the results were not quite what he maintained, since he always looked like he had just emerged, dripping from the surf on Cape Cod.

After covering every restaurant from Connecticut to New Hampshire, I worked my way to the real objective, Massachusetts, and in particular, Cape Cod. After I covered the listings and tried to bring in a number of new resorts along the Massachusetts coast, I settled in on Cape Cod for the last month of my tour of duty. I picked the elbow of the Cape, Chatham, as a hub and was able to get a weekly rate to keep expenses down on a room in a boardinghouse close to what became my favorite hangout, the Christopher Ryder House.

Since our food costs were limited by an allowance, I paid the extra bucks to have dinner there at least two or three nights a week. The food was great, along with the scenery. The scenery included a dozen waitresses from various universities, mostly from Cornell.

The Christopher Ryder House was fun because it had a huge

circus tent in the back, and around 10 PM each night they brought in a band. I hung out with the young people who worked at the restaurant, and toward the end of the evenings, we were able to take advantage of the dance floor.

About two weeks into my stay in Chatham, I passed an Indian reservation and spotted a young boy with a baby raccoon on a chain. I also spotted the FOR SALE sign. Being an animal lover, I couldn't resist. For 20 bucks, I had the raccoon in my car. He was a cute little fellow and would sit on the back of the seat with his paws holding on to my neck while I was driving and he didn't seem to mind staying in the car when I made my inspections.

However, after about a week the landlady discovered the raccoon in my room, and I was told to get rid of it or get out. Four of the gals who worked in the restaurant roomed together in a house they rented for the summer, and I prevailed upon them to keep the raccoon, which they thought was adorable, in their basement.

Later that summer, Tetlow was traveling in New England with her parents, and since they were staying in Boston, I drove over and picked her up one night. I made the mistake of taking her to the Christopher Ryder House for dinner. The girls were surprised to see me with a date, and when she went to powder her nose, I learned later, they paid her a visit en masse. I guess she was pretty ticked when the questions got around to "How well do you know Roy?"

After dinner we danced and I drove her back to Boston, never suspecting a thing. The next night when I tried to find a dance partner at the restaurant, I was shut down. For the rest of the summer, not one girl would speak to me. I learned later what had transpired in the ladies room. Tetlow used a variation of the technique my father had employed when he was courting my mother, and told the girls we were secretly married.

At the end of the summer, I collected my raccoon from the not-so-friendly coeds and brought it home with me. He lasted in my upstairs study until he pulled all of the books out of my bookshelf, and I took him to a place that rehabilitated raccoons so he could be released in the wild.

It was at the end of the summer, just before I was to become a graduate student at Cornell, when it became clear that Procter & Gamble wanted to keep only the best-selling Duncan Hines products, the cake mix line. Procter & Gamble is known as a company that does its homework. It was not about to run a widespread food-licensing operation when the money was in the mix. All the other licensing arrangements went by the board—and the product that had enabled a small company to hold its own against the giants ended up in the hands of the largest advertiser in the country.

P&G's strategy required phasing out all the other product lines, and included on the hit list were the Duncan Hines guidebooks. The guidebooks had annual sales of a half-million dollars, but that was chicken-feed to P&G, and they wanted no part of it. After my summer as a field inspector, I could understand why they didn't want to be involved in the intensive, continuous inspections that needed to be done to keep the guidebooks going, and the national staff that had to be hired and trained to do this.

I remember when my father called me into his study to explain an opportunity that P&G had offered, to see if I had any interest in it. They had given my father the opportunity to continue the publication of these books, which, at the time, were the American equivalent to the Michelin Guides in Europe. Procter & Gamble told my father they would allow him to maintain publication of these four books, as long as the Duncan Hines name was dropped and changed to a name of his choice. He was given three years to make the transition. Bottom line was P&G granted my father the opportunity to hold on to the best guidebooks in the nation, but they wanted the exclusive use of the Duncan Hines name for their cake mix.

My father and I both came up with an appropriate transition name at the same time. Our middle name was Hampton, which had more class than "Roy." It had a distinguished quality that we thought could possibly work: *Hampton Park Adventures in Good Eating.*

My father had other fish to fry, so the offer was dumped in my lap. The question became whether or not *I* wanted to spend the rest of my life as a plump gourmet driving around the country, as the celebrity behind the new Hampton Park guidebooks. This did not appeal to me, since it would have been a lifetime commitment. My desire was to build a career in the advertising business. It may have been a missed opportunity, but I didn't regret that decision. It led to the end of the most personalized guidebooks America ever had.

Stewart Underwood recalls the massive effort and complexity of dismantling the guidebook program by Procter & Gamble. Leases had to be broken, over 185 billboards around the country torn down, and hundreds of Duncan Hines shingles in front of establishments returned. I remember how hard it was for me to remove just one sign when a restaurant was de-listed. It was a full-time effort for well over a year, and P&G made sure this was done expeditiously, installing a personal representative in Ithaca to monitor the entire procedure.

Duncan Hines had gone into semiretirement at age seventy-six. He died two years later in 1959, by which time five million copies of *Adventures in Good Eating* had been sold. The knowledge that a listing could mean the difference between success and bankruptcy motivated many restaurants to improve their menus and clean their kitchens. Hotels, diners, and inns across the country proudly displayed RECOMMENDED BY DUNCAN HINES signs. The popularity of his name was so widespread it was part of the song, "If I Were a Bell" in the Broadway musical *Guys & Dolls*, and a small diner in the Ithaca countryside displayed a parody of his sign in its window that read: DRUNKEN HINES COOKS HERE. With all the time he spent on the road, it was fitting that, according to Wikipedia, after his death a portion of U.S. Highway 31W north of Bowling Green was named Duncan Hines Highway.

One chef concluded in 1961 that Hines had "done more in four years to lift the standard of the American cuisine than all the cooks had done in the previous forty." In his 1984 article in *Smithsonian*, David Schwartz also said the *Adventures in Good Eating* guidebooks "became a fixture in automobile glove compartments, and when wartime gas rationing was lifted, bookstores nationwide were swamped with requests for the latest edition of the little red paperback. For two decades, the name of the author, Duncan Hines, was etched on the biting edge of the American appetite."

And even as recently as 2005, renowned gossip columnist Liz Smith, in her book *Dishing* ("on great dish and dishes") opened her first chapter "Food, Glorious Food!" with a quote from Duncan Hines. It read *"Nearly everyone wants at least one outstanding meal a day,"* and Mr. Hines dealt in good eating every day of his life.

The Duncan Hines portrait that hung over the fireplace mantle in my father's office for more than three decades.

In the meantime, with the guidebooks gone, my father , while still consulting with P&G, entered his fourth career, founding Park Broadcasting, Inc. in 1961 with the purchase of two radio stations in Greenville, NC. The same year I reentered Cornell, this time seeking a master's degree from the Johnson Graduate School of Management.

CHAPTER 9
GRADUATING INTO LIFE

I was fortunate enough to be accepted in midterm as a graduate student at Cornell in 1961, immediately after receiving an undergraduate degree in journalism from The University of North Carolina. With my BA in Journalism from Carolina, combined with an MBA from Cornell, I felt assured my education would be perfect for a career with an advertising agency.

I was never around for graduation ceremonies at either college, because of the timing of my degrees. As soon as I learned a Carolina diploma was forthcoming, I returned to an Ithaca winter. The business school, then known as the Graduate School of Business and Public Administration, was later renamed the Johnson Graduate School of Management in honor of its major benefactor, the philanthropist Sam Johnson, president of S.C. Johnson Co., and one of my father's friends. Getting back into the same university I busted out of redeemed my earlier failure. It was pleasing vindication, but I had no idea what I was getting into.

At Carolina, I had concentrated on marketing courses. Needless to say, my undergraduate courses were not heavy in statistics, finance, economics, accounting, or math of any sort. I was prepared as a writer and creative thinker, and quite unprepared to handle statistical formulas that would take up a paragraph in a *New York Times* editorial.

When I first set foot in the building, I found myself surrounded by students carrying around what I thought at first were little white "sticks." It took me a while to realize that they had movable parts, that I was surrounded by engineering graduates, and that I was more than somewhat out of my league. These slide rule predecessors of today's computers were, in the hands of the engineers, quicker than the eye could follow, and they were used to solve all the test problems in courses that dealt with figures, while I was still trying to decipher numbers in my head. I never did learn how to use a slide rule, and the courses in accounting and statistics just about did me in.

My struggle with accounting reminds me of the story about the time a Chief Financial Officer (CFO) of a huge company was honored in front of all the employees at a dinner party. He had taken the giant corporation from red ink to solid black, and the CEO, at the end of his speech, asked him his secret to success. He said he had noticed the CFO opened and closed his top desk drawer quickly first thing every morning, and wondered what was there he had been referring to. The CFO said, "Debit to the left, credit to the right." I had a tough time in accounting even keeping that much in mind.

At the Johnson School my major, once again, was marketing, and I also got high marks in the business administration, business law, advertising, public relations, personnel, political, and production courses. I enjoyed solving the case history problems, but I never would have survived statistics and finance without the help of a friend. He was a wrestling teammate back at Lawrenceville, and Doug Rowan came back into my life again for the third time.

We had both entered Cornell as undergraduates and had spent much of our first year together before I busted out. Later, when I came back to business school, Doug was there again. He was a genius with figures; for him, statistics was a walk in the park. With his help, I was able to keep up my grades in those courses without pulling down the high marks I got in the rest of them.

It's an understatement to say my first semester in the business school was hard work. I was living with my parents on a third floor, lonely as hell, and spending a lot of time missing Tetlow and writing letters to her. The second semester was even worse. During Christmas break I made a decision that would change my life forever—and much for the better.

VOWS TAKEN

That Irrepressible Dawn

To many, Love may appear
As the coming of Spring
Waking up from the icy
Unfamiliarity of Winter,
Uncontrolled, and as the
Spring, not be governed
By the calendar.
And as the Spring, it may
Take the path of deliberate
Gradualness,
Or the highway of suddenness
And surprise.
But then one morning we
Wake up with the fervor of
Fascination in our heart
And the shine of wondrous
Recognition in our eyes,
And we throw up the window
And behold the change in
The World outside:
The infant softness of
Green trees, the fragrance
Of undiscovered blossoms,
The radiant, glowing warmth
Of a New Sun.
And we know that soon our
World will open into the
Richness of Summer.
Not without its periods
Of storm, but then,
What is Love without
Some Darkness? Or
Summer without its rain?
Yes, our Spring has come
And with it a New Life;
And in chorus to the
Music in the air,
We shout it to the world.

—Roy H. Park, Jr.

My poem in the Raleigh *News & Observer* said it all.

I scraped together enough money to buy an engagement ring, jumped in the Nash-Healey one night and drove 16 hours straight through to North Carolina. When I crossed the state line, I got out of the car and in thanks touched my forehead to the ground. About 7 a.m., I arrived at Tetlow's front door, much to her surprise. Although welcomed, I spent the rest of the morning sleeping to recover, and she had no idea what my spontaneous visit was all about.

That night I proposed and gave her the ring. I even had a camera with me to record her expression when she opened the box.

By the time I got through my first year at Cornell in 1961, I had interviewed for and been given a salaried position for the summer, as director of public relations for the United Way of Raleigh, so I wouldn't be separated from my fiancée during those months. The United Way campaign included a full-length movie I wrote and directed *Of Money and Miracles*, highlighting each one of the agency's recipients. Our slogan, on bumper stickers and posted throughout the Raleigh area on billboards, was "Somebody Loves You!"

Just married. Part of the wedding party with Minister Charles Hubbard, center, in front of the church on Franklin Street in Chapel Hill, NC.

It was becoming clearer and clearer that my parents wanted me to wait until I graduated before I got married, and that her parents (who seemed to like me well enough when I was just the boy friend) didn't want her marrying me, being a Yankee, at all. That would mean they would rarely see her when I took her away. Defying negative pressure from both sets of parents, we planned a July wedding at the small Methodist church on Main Street in Chapel Hill. Our parents were not invited, but my best man, Jon Emerson, traveled all the way from the Naval Academy in Annapolis and did his duty in his dress white uniform. Tet's roommate was the maid of honor.

It was a memorable wedding with maybe twenty good friends. Since we both had jobs, we slipped away for a short three-day honeymoon at The Cloister in Sea island, Georgia. From there we each called our parents and gave them the news.

On the return from our honeymoon, I spotted something along the road that interested me and pulled off, claiming that I needed to make a pit stop. I returned to the car with what looked like a flower box containing my purchase. I handed her the box and got behind the wheel of the car while she opened the lid. Instead of flowers, she was shocked to see the mouths of two baby alligators gaping up at her. She married and was stuck with a husband who liked animals, and I give her credit for her tolerance through the years. The Russian wolfhound was only the beginning!

We returned to a furnished basement apartment I rented, if you could call it furnished. The mattress on the bed had been well used and had a depression in the center where a meteorite appeared to have crashed. For the short time we were there we didn't have to worry about falling out of bed.

Honeymooners. Taken on our brief stay at Sea Island, GA.

BACK TO CORNELL

At the end of the summer, Tetlow and I returned to Ithaca together, me for my second year in the MBA program, and Tet to work as a medical receptionist for a group of obstetricians in order to help put me through college. I dropped her off at work each morning on my way to classes. I should mention that my father refused to cover my tuition, now that I was married. I had gone against his wishes and was ignored for doing it. So to make ends meet, I also found a job with a local advertising agency in the afternoons when classes were over. Laux

Advertising turned out to be a great experience, confirming that advertising was the field I wanted to go into when I graduated.

On our return to Ithaca, I had rented a one-bedroom apartment on the second floor of a building overlooking Cayuga Lake above the Yacht Club. The location was on the opposite side of the lake from Cornell. The drive to get to campus took twenty minutes. During the winter with the wind coming off the lake, it was bitterly cold. We burned candles inside the convertible to try to heat the car up when we started out each morning. Each weekend we had to wash the soot off the inside of the windshield.

Our first child, a daughter, was born in Ithaca in late 1962, and we moved into slightly larger quarters with two bedrooms. I enjoyed my job at Laux as research director and senior writer part-time, then full-time during the summer between Cornell semesters. While I was there, working with the president, J.D. Laux, we brought in several new clients, including Schweizer Aircraft, a manufacturer of gliders in Central New York, and the hybrid seed company, Robson Quality. I worked on other local accounts including a manufacturer of snow cream shake syrup, a seafood distributor in Elmira, an optical service and even something called Unique Products Manufacturing Company. On the environmental side, Robson Quality even came up with a wildlife corn that could be planted as survival food for pheasant, quail, duck and geese when all other wild foods were inaccessible in the northern winters.

My father had given me, as well as my sister, some P&G stock a few years earlier, and I used that as collateral to borrow from a local bank. My debt was nothing like the debt piled up by student loans today, but $10,000 back then was pretty substantial. My father finally relented and told me that if I managed to graduate

Clara Hines (left), who I first met when I was twelve, visiting with Dottie and Tetlow in Ithaca in 1962 the summer before our daughter was born.

(unlikely, he thought, because I was married, which he felt would distract me, or even cause me to drop out), he would reimburse me for the tuition I paid. This turned out to be $10,000, although my total loan ended up being $13,000. I finished up in Ithaca in 1963, and when I graduated, I went on to start my advertising career only $3,000 in debt.

By this time, my father had added, in 1962, a television station to his two radio holdings in Greenville, NC, and in 1963, in Tennessee, a TV station in Johnson City and another TV and two more radio stations in Chattanooga. While his business was taking him in a southerly direction, mine kept me in the north — heading to New York City.

And so began my careers.

First Union National Bancorp, Inc.

KINCAID ADVERTISING AGENCY, INC.

PARK OUTDOOR

Park
BROADCASTING

AgResearch

Park
COMMUNICATIONS, INC.

Triad Foundation

CHAPTER 10
"MADISON AVENUE, HERE I COME!"

*If I were starting life over again, I am inclined to think that
I would go into the advertising business in preference to any
other. The general standards of modern civilization among
all groups of people during the past half-century would have
been impossible without spreading the knowledge of higher
standards by means of advertising.*
—Franklin D. Roosevelt

"Madison Avenue, here I come!" Well, actually not Madison,
Lexington Avenue, but I was going to the largest advertising
agency in the world at the time

In 1958 I had come across Martin Mayer's, *Madison Avenue,
USA.* It was a reporter's book about advertising and the people
who work from their "rising in the morning to their falling down
at night." Of the 19 chapters in the book, two were solely on the
J. Walter Thompson Co.

The book pointed out that its elaborate offices occupied at
least three floors of the enormous Graybar Building beside Grand
Central Station on Lexington Avenue, with each floor representing
more than an acre of space. It had no organization table, no
flowcharts, no fixed system of work, yet only four agencies
had billing figures of more than $200 million. With billing of
$300 million, J. Walter Thompson (also known as JWT), led the
pack: with three-fourths of it in North America, and the rest in
34 offices in 19 countries on the other four inhabited continents.
Ownership of the agency stock was held by people who worked

at the company and was spread throughout every executive level.

Suffice it to say that I fell in love with the agency through the book, and it was the only place I wanted to work.

In 1963 J. Walter Thompson's New York Graybar Building headquarters, alone, housed 3,000 people. In addition to Ford, Pan Am, RCA and Lever Brothers, JWT accounts ran the gamut from Kodak to Kraft, Mennen to Oscar Mayer, *Reader's Digest* to Rolex and Scott to Squibb. Products advertised went through the alphabet from Beachnut to Brillo, Fleischmann's to French's, Planters to Ponds and Quaker Oats to 7-Up.

To be hired by JWT required passing a series of stringent tests. After I applied, I was mailed three case histories of products for which I was required to create marketing and advertising campaigns. In one case it was a mythical new product that had not even been named.

While writing was my training and my trade, my avocation was art, so I put my best foot forward. The marketing plan for each product was a snap, and I was able to create some clever approaches for ads. But the highlight was my ability to illustrate what a final print ad might look like. I may have done myself a disservice because I was hired not in management or marketing but for $5,000 as a writer in the creative department.

An MBA was a relatively new degree when I graduated, and although big corporations such as P&G caught on to the value of this degree in their management and marketing departments, the advertising industry had not. I was told a couple of weeks after I was hired that as far as the personnel department knew, I was the first MBA hired by a major New York ad agency. With its worldwide clout, Thompson had no problem recruiting successful advertising people away from their jobs. They were staffed with professionals from other ad agencies, and since my experience was limited to the University of Learning, they really didn't know what to do with me.

What they did see was my creative flair, so they put me in creative. Ironically, my first assignment was creating billboard copy for the Ford Motor Dealers Association, among others. I learned at the outset the magic rule for outdoor advertising copy: say whatever it is you have to say in seven words or less, or your message isn't worth conveying, let alone being a message people have time to read. The general philosophy at J. Walter Thompson was that if you couldn't come up with your key selling point, the message you wanted to drive home in a headline or a TV or radio commercial in seven words or less, you didn't have a handle on what you were trying to sell.

In 1963 LeFrak City was in its second year of construction of a 20-tower housing complex for middle income New Yorkers and I was one of the first tenants of the first completed tower in the development. Well outside of Manhattan, the $200 a month rent was the only thing I could afford which was half of my roughly $400 a month income after deductions and taxes. Today, a similar apartment rents for roughly $2,000 in this mega-complex covering 40 connected acres. At the time, I was impressed that you could see the New York skyline from the roof of our top 16th floor apartment. My wife was not happy that with only one other tenant on our entire floor, it was a scary experience with me two subway rides away in Manhattan each day.

J. Walter Thompson was everything I had hoped it would be. It was hard work, but exciting and fun. But not so much fun for my family. There was little time left for family life when you left for work at 7 a.m. and didn't get home until 7 p.m. Mayer's book warned ad people don't want a phone at home since just as you were dropping off to bed, it would ring at 1 a.m. from someone at the agency "wanting to check something with you."

Two months after arriving at JWT, I got a call from the personnel office. They had already adjusted my meager salary up to $7,500 since I seemed to fit in, and they had an unusual assignment for me. It seemed that Unilever, which was handled by our Canadian branch, had developed a new sunflower oil product and they were having trouble getting our Canadian office to develop a marketing-advertising approach to launch it. That branch was basically creative, and the marketing people at headquarters in New York, who had responsibility for Lever

Bros. in the states but not the more international Unilever, had little time and no intent to do the job for them.

I was told JWT could lose the account unless we came up with a complete campaign from scratch in one week. They wanted to know if I was willing to apply my MBA training to the project.

I was told if I could pull off something to save the account, the reward would be substantial. The catch was that if I failed, I would be the scapegoat. They made it clear that, in all probability, I would lose my job. They put all their eggs in my basket instead of pulling together a team in New York to work on the project. It was a gamble, and I was given a chance to decline. I said "yes" after explaining the situation to my wife. She felt we had nothing to lose, living as we were at a subsistence level on the fringes of New York City in a complex still under construction.

The Park Family in New York City in the 60s. When I joined J. Walter Thompson we were able to have an occasional dinner with the family during their frequent trips to the City. Along with Pops, my sister, me, Tetlow, and Dottie, the waiter wanted to be part of the picture, too.

I took on the assignment with a vengeance. Reading all the background sent down from Canada, I immersed myself in the project, staying up all hours of the night to get it done. This was my one chance to prove myself, as well as demonstrate how useful someone with an MBA could be in an ad agency. My wife would wander into the living room, which served as my study, at 4 a.m. to find me still at it. My sleep was confined to my two subway commute where an annoyed passenger would push me away when I nodded off on their shoulder.

I had to come up with a name for the product, a logo, product packaging and design, and that is where my creative ability came in. I had to develop a marketing campaign defining the target audience, and a media plan and budget and, finally, design the TV commercial storyboards, billboard copy, magazine and newspaper ads. The project included direct mail and brochures describing the benefits of the product.

By the end of the week, I had completed the entire assignment and turned it in to my agency for review. With a few minor adjustments, which were done in the office on Monday, the campaign was hand-carried across the Canadian border by courier and delivered to our Canadian office for presentation to Unilever the next day. Two days later I got word the client was pleased with the entire presentation, and that the company had saved the account.

I breathed a sigh of relief, at least knowing I had held onto my job. The reward came along shortly, and it was hard to believe. It was an opportunity to be interviewed by JWT's office in Coral Gables, FL, for the position of writer and account executive for Pan

America's Latin-American division. Pan Am, which flew to 114 cities in 86 countries, had been a JWT account since 1942, and this was a job many people of those in our New York headquarters—who had been with the company much longer than me—were vying for. A number had already been interviewed for the position, which was coming open because it was held by John Minahan, author of *The Sudden Silence*, who had asked for a leave of absence to write a second book. He went on to write another 18 or so after that.

When my wife and I were flown into Coral Gables, I thought I had died and gone to Heaven. The manager of the office, Joe Kelleher, picked us up at the airport and drove us to a beautiful hotel, with reflecting ponds full of flamingos in the front. I always loved tropical plants and climates, and this was beyond belief. The next day I interviewed everyone in the office and a day later we were flown back to New York to await the decision.

ESCAPE FROM QUEENS

It came within a week, and the answer was positive. I had the job and a lot of senior JWT people who had their eyes on this assignment were, to say the least, upset. The company wanted me to leave immediately, and that's when a hitch developed in the plans. The lease I signed with LeFrak was for three years, and being one of a handful of tenants in the first completed 16-story building, there was no leniency in breaking the lease. That wouldn't have been a problem today with its $70 million dollar upgrade resulting in a 98 percent occupancy by young, employed middle class families and professionals.

I told our JWT personnel department about the problem, thinking that would be the end of it. I couldn't imagine the company being willing to pay thousands for the term of the lease in order to send me to Coral Gables. But they told me to go back to find out on what terms I could accomplish this.

The following day, I discussed my situation with the various managers of the complex, explaining that I was being relocated by my company, and returning to Thompson the next day told them the amount. The agency didn't bat an eye, and I took the subway home that night with cash in my briefcase worth what would be the equivalent of over $20,000 today. Considering the two subway rides, and the empty field I had to cross in Queens where the next tower complex was scheduled to go up, I was nervous as a cat. Had I been held up, and lived, it would have been tough to explain, and I certainly couldn't ask for more cash for a second try.

The next day the lease was released and my company informed. They scheduled the following week in September 1963 for the move and set up the movers.

We began packing.

INTO THE EVERGLADES

Arriving in Florida, there were no floodlighted pools with wading pink flamingoes for us. I finally found a house we could afford to rent in Perrine, about a 30-minute commute to Coral Gables. It had a screened-in swimming pool in a peaceful community on the edge of the Everglades. Being a solid ground floor versus a high-rise, it looked beautiful to us. Since we lived in in the Everglades and only a couple of blocks from the Atlantic Ocean, I thought it was a great idea to have a Jeep. You know, driving on the beach, jungle safaris and all. Back then shock absorbers on Jeeps had yet to be invented and after the third time her head hit the canvas top when I took Tetlow for a cruise, I knew I would be trading in the Jeep in the next day. I did and we ended up with a second-hand Nash Rambler. Far from the most macho car in the world, but survivable enough for the commute to Coral Gables.

By this time, we were finally ready for another dog and adopted a Belgian Shepherd. Actually, it simply turned up and never left, so it adopted us. It was the only animal we were happy to have, but living in Everglades we got gratis many more.

The treasured swimming pool turned out to be a good early lesson, and I've never had one since. Aside from the bobcats that came down our neighborhood chimneys, scorpions in our child's crib, and alligators in our garages when it flooded, snakes often swam in the pool. Spiders, wasps, and mice floated on top, and scum clogged the skimmer. To keep the pool clean, it would have had to be filled with sulfuric acid. After I gave up wearing out skimmer nets sweeping the accumulated live and dead bodies from the pool, I hired a service and quickly found out that it cost me more than I was paying in rent.

We also put up with termites, ants, spiders, and land crabs. Our small community was tucked off a major highway running along the coast. When the land crabs invaded, they poured into our garage and carpeted the ground outside the house. They also carpeted the highway. We learned to drive slowly through them, and they would part like the Red Sea. Many drivers thought it was fun to run over them. But the land crab's sharp, tough claws wreaked their revenge. We could hear the tires being blown out on the highway from our house and felt good that the speeders were receiving poetic justice.

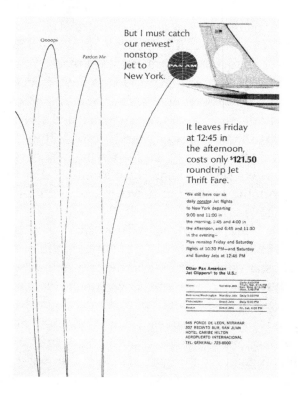

As creative and account executive for Pan American, I was responsible for all Latin American Division advertising, including television, radio, cinema, newspaper, and magazine advertising and publicity. Our Coral Gables office worked with senior Pan Am management, including Pan Am President Juan Trippe. He allowed me to do some pretty creative things with Pan Am's sacrosanct world globe logo, even picturing it bouncing along on the tarmac behind a departing jet with the logo missing from its tail. Announcing new flights, the advertising copy read, "Oops!

Almost missed our newest 12:45 AM flight to New York" or San Juan or wherever.

The huge Pan Am headquarters of the thirty-seven-year-old company in Miami was set behind a block-long reflecting pool lined with the flags of every country Pan Am served in the Islands and South America. It was a dramatic setting for the Latin-American division of the "World's Most Experienced Airline," as its slogan proclaimed.

The division's advertising was directed, in all languages, to vacationers' dreams: the islands of Antigua, Barbados, Curacao, Guadeloupe, Jamaica, Martinique, Puerto Rico, St. Croix, St. Lucia, St. Maarten, Haiti and the Dominican Republic, Trinidad, Nassau, and destinations such as Mexico, Panama, Surinam, British and French Guiana, Honduras, Brazil, and all of South America. Even Aruba, if tourists still want to go there.

We placed ads throughout its service area, and advertised flights from Miami to the New York World's Fair headlined SEE TOMORROW TODAY, and to Rome, Italy, headlined, SEE YESTERDAY TOMORROW. We also advertised flights to the Middle and Far East. Our color magazine centerspreads appeared in Latin-American

editions of *Time*, *Life*, and *Reader's Digest*. One of my ads under the headline Look Closely. This Happens Every Dawn, pictured two jet vapor trails reflected in the pool of the Taj Mahal. These, as the copy read, marked "the swift passage of two Pan American Jet Clippers©—one heading east, the other west—six miles high in the Indian sky." Airlines flew mostly on time back then.

I was also assigned to creative development for Outboard Marine Corp, the New Jersey and Florida Ford Dealers Associations, and Florida National Bank, which were all handled out of our Coral Gables office.

In mid-1964, Pan Am's famous headquarters building straddling Park Avenue, and looming over Grand Central Station in New York City was completed, and the Miami headquarters was closed. President Juan Trippe was named chairman of Pan Am, and out of twenty-two people in our Coral Gables office, four were moved back to New York: my boss, Joe Kelleher, our Spanish-language writer, Alfredo Jarrin, our media buyer, Ruth Williams, and me.

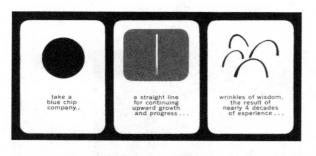

CHAPTER 11
RETURN TO NEW YORK

When we moved back to New York, dog and all, JWT put my family up in a hotel in White Plains, NY. They had a lot of patience, since it took me a month and a half to find a place to live. I was looking for an apartment that would allow dogs, and I finally gave up. He was adopted by a nice family that gave him a good home.

During this time, while the company was covering our living expenses, I remember we went into New York. Not knowing much about New York restaurants, we wandered into the Four Seasons for dinner. When I put in the expense account for that, along with other expenses, the company suggested that I might want to tone down the places I chose to dine. The bill was only $50 for the two of us, but that was a lot of money back then.

Most advertising people lived in the Westchester suburbs, and almost nobody drove to work since the highways were packed tight and Grand Central Station was around the corner from the office. In fact, the railroad terminal was like a private reserve, with one entrance leading directly into the Graybar Building. You could go almost anywhere in New York from the underground Grand Central tunnels without ever seeing the light of day, and return home through its secret portholes, as Martin Mayer said, "uncontaminated from the herd in the Station Concourse."

We finally located a two-bedroom, first-floor corner apartment in Westchester County on the fringes of Rye, NY, and my routine commuting into the City began.

I was assigned to administrative duties at our New York headquarters, and shortly after my return, named secretary of the Review Boards for the New York office. I served for the next five years with the senior corporate executives on the boards that reviewed and approved the marketing and creative proposals for all U.S. accounts. I was there when a Lark Cigarette was filtered over a mountain of charcoal and Walter Mitty drove his first Ford Mustang. I sat in with well-known advertising legends like Dan Seymour, Henry Schachte, Ted Wilson, Don Armstrong, Paul Gerhold, Larry D'Aloise, Ed Robinson, Rud McKee, Allan Sacks, Nancy Stephenson, Bob Colwell, Harry Treleaven, Chip Meads, Ruth Downing, O'Neill Ryan, Jack Devine, Philip Mygatt, John Monsarrat, Stever Aubrey, and of course, Chairman of the Board Norman Strouse.

BRILLO REVIEW BOARD—Shown l. to r. are Roy Park, Nancy Stephenson, Allan Sacks, Ruth Downing, O'Neill Ryan, Ed Robinson, John Monsarrat, Rud McKee.

The marketing and creative reviews assured all JWT clients that their advertising plans represented broad agency experience that met the standards of the agency as a whole. I reported directly to John Monsarrat who was appointed overall chairman of the Review Boards.

During this time, management determined that the company also needed to revise its corporate marketing and Creative Review Board procedures, and I was named Advertising Planning Director and assigned this task, along with other responsibilities. As the ad planning director, I teamed up with Director of Research Paul Gerhold, who later became president of the Advertising Research Foundation. Among our accomplishments was a white paper on corporate name changing, which resulted in National Dairy Products changing its name to Kraftco, product planning for Oscar Mayer, and a significant revision of JWT New York office management systems. I also served as an advisor to the New York new-business team.

The Atlanta Film Festival awarded the first-place Golden Eagle for our TV commercials for Kodak in the late 1960s, and as Awards Chairman, I accepted it on behalf of J. Walter Thompson. The trophy was too large to pack in a suitcase, and in those days I was allowed to carry it on the plane where the eagle and I both received a great deal of attention.

In 1965, I was also asked to help JWT win more creative awards and was named chairman of the New York Awards Committee. The assignment overlapped with the others. I kicked it off as a screening judge for the Advertising Club of New York's Andy Awards. By the end of 1968, the program I started led to JWT's winning more awards than any other U.S. agency. One hundred and seventy to be exact, of which one hundred and nineteen, an increase of 400 percent, were for the New York office alone. Among the coups, we took the top Golden Eagle award for Kodak at the Atlanta Film Festival. The two-foot-high statuette of an eagle with open wings wasn't about to fit into my suitcase, and when I carried it back from Atlanta on the plane, the flight attendants thought I was a movie star who won something large enough to eat the Oscars.

It was JWT's long-standing point of view that no attempt was ever made to create a specific look for a Thompson ad. Never creative for creative's sake. David Ogilvy of Ogilvy & Mather, said, "If it doesn't sell, it isn't creative." JWT's advertising was created to solve specific client problems and to increase a company's sales. But as Awards Chairman, I was quoted in our company's JWT newsletter saying, "If in the process, we are honored by our industry, we are pleased."

In 1965 I was asked to introduce an internal luncheon speakers program. REP Information Exchange allowed account representatives to share information between their management of the JWT client accounts. With all of this going on, to the best of my knowledge, I was the only employee at JWT, aside from the chairman, to have two full-time secretaries.

Then, in 1966, still on the Review Board, I was assigned as an account executive on the Office of Information of the U.S. Department of Defense special task force on drug information, which helped change the approach on drug communications to the Armed Forces. I was also named account executive on the Institute of Life Insurance, I suspect because I had worked so closely with Chairman Strouse, since this agency client had his full attention because he had founded the Institute, and kept a close eye on its advertising programs.

We had a hit with our print campaign, for which I signed a release on one ad because the headline (using my daughter's name) read: SOMETIME SOON LIZ PARK'S DAD WILL ASK HIMSELF IF HE HAS ENOUGH LIFE INSURANCE. (AND HOW MUCH IS ENOUGH, ANYWAY?) Our television commercials were soon to win awards, as well.

THE POLITICAL GUILLOTINE

I can understand why my father didn't like the politics of large corporations such as P&G. Plenty of politics took place in his own company, but he didn't have to worry about it. He owned the company. I did have to worry about it, however, at J. Walter Thompson, although there was probably less political maneuvering there than in the hierarchy of our large client corporations.

But, inevitably I ran afoul of politics, and almost lost my job.

On behalf of our client, the Institute of Life Insurance, our group pioneered the effort to sell insurance not only to male heads of household but also to married and single women. We had just finished a couple of highly creative commercials (of which one later won a first prize in its category in the International Advertising Film Festival in Venice), and I received a call from the production company that the first prints were done and ready to be picked up.

I came back into the Graybar Building with the reels under my arm and walked into a crowded elevator to get to the seventh floor to deliver them to my management supervisor. That's when I heard, from the back of the elevator, the distinctive voice of Chairman Strouse say, "Hi, Roy, those wouldn't happen to be the prints of our Institute commercials, would they?"

A hot-flash went through me when I told him they were, immediately alarmed that the next thing he might say was to get them to the screening room so we could look at them. That's exactly what he said.

As soon as I got back to my office, I contacted my account supervisor and told him what happened. He warned we had better get in touch with our management supervisor before we set up the screening. It was then about 2:30 PM and our top boss was nowhere to be found. He had a long business lunch with a client and couldn't be reached. All of us were used to taking fairly long lunches when clients were involved, but knowing the client he was lunching with, I thought this one might be longer than usual.

About 2:45 PM I received a call from the chairman's office

wanting to know which screening room had been set up. I stalled a little longer and then at 3 PM I received a second call from his office. Not daring to wait any longer, I booked a screening room and paced the hall until the third call came at 3:15. In the meantime my management supervisors' secretary sent scouts to our frequented restaurants in New York City looking for him, without success. I stalled as long as I dared, and when 3:30 came, the chairman joined us to screen the commercials without our leader.

That's what you really call being caught between a rock and a hard place. To put it mildly, I caught hell when my boss returned at 4:30 that afternoon. The next day I found myself off the account. I thought about going to Mr. Strouse to let him know the result of the position I had been put in, but that could have had some far-reaching repercussions, so I didn't.

Within a few days, I was moved to the fourteenth floor of the Graybar Building into a massive wood-paneled, high-ceilinged corner office with two windows and its own private bathroom. Anyone entering the office would have thought I was running the company. But I was waiting for the axe to fall. The fourteenth floor, if you weren't in media buying, was the floor to which you were temporarily exiled when you were unassigned, retired early, or fired. The benevolent nature of the J. Walter Thompson Company gave everyone in that position an office to work out of and plenty of time to locate another job before being removed from the payroll.

In 1967 I was still on the Review Board, but all of the other jobs I created had been reassigned. I had been removed from a key account, and I felt the way I did when I busted out of Cornell. I contacted friends I had in head-hunting businesses in the City to help me start looking for another job, and I had a number of successful interviews in New York during the next few weeks. Among them was Grey Advertising and BBD&O, which was also located over Grand Central Station. But decisions to hire at my level depended on openings, so there was no quick promise of a job.

Continuing on the Review Boards with top executives such as Don Armstrong, Larry D'Aloise, Ted Wilson and Stever Aubrey.

To my surprise, my exile turned out not to be the end of the line. It didn't take long for a memo to go out from Philip Mygatt, the personnel director of JWT's creative department. "All of you know Roy Park through assignments...with the Review Boards and Research Groups. I have asked Roy Park to join me in various aspects of the administration of the department. I know you find he will carry out his duties with his customary effectiveness and good spirit," it read.

Among other things, working together we developed an information-sharing program similar to the one I put in place for account management through an initiative we called the Creative Forum Papers.

I was also asked to coordinate the JWT Luncheon Speakers Program and was able to attract speakers such as author Walter Lord; William Emerson, editor of *Saturday Evening Post*; Art Buchwald; researcher and public opinion pollster Elmo Roper; *Harper's* magazine editor-in-chief John Fischer; John Scott, editor-in-chief of *Time, Inc.*; Chancellor Dean E. McHenry, University of California, Santa Cruz; and Albert Parry, chairman of the Department of Russian Studies at Colgate University.

In 1968, this experience led to my assignment as a personnel group head, working directly with Bob Hawes, head of the JWT personnel department. In his memo to senior management, he said, "About a month ago, we tapped Roy Park for this assignment because he has certain characteristics one finds in good intelligence men, and we discovered he could handle this assignment in addition to his other duties." I was put in charge of a sophisticated new national program directed at recruiting senior management and top creative people, and was able, in that capacity, to bring in some high profile talent.

During this time, I also did some writing on the side. An article I wrote entitled, WHERE DOES ALL THE BEST MEAT GO?, published in the *American Way* magazine in 1968 led to an offer of a public relations position from the meat packing industry. Of course I turned it down. Now, if that offer had crossed my path in 1967, I might have taken it.

In 1969, J. Walter Thompson was about to go public, and in every press release the company put out, the RCA account was always mentioned. Thompson was the company handling accounts such as "Kodak, RCA and Ford," or "Lever Bros., Standard Brands and RCA," or "RCA, Liggett & Myers and Pan Am." In all cases, RCA was one of the top clients mentioned, and for one reason or another, at this sensitive time, the company was in trouble with the account. The last thing it needed was to lose RCA just before its public offering, so every effort was made to save it.

To do this, they started at the top, bringing back Jack Morrissey, a top manager from another agency who had worked with RCA in the past, and whom RCA respected as brilliant. They then began recruiting top people from within the agency to bring together an entirely new creative and marketing team to handle the account. Luckily, I made the list and was chosen as senior account executive on RCA's consumer audio products and black-and-white television lines. Our group also was to handle all of RCA's trade, premium and military service campaigns as well as its international advertising.

JWT Admen on the RCA consumer audio account management team. Left to right: Fred Kingman, account executive; Chuck Roedema, account supervisor; and me, senior account executive.

RCA required frequent trips to Indianapolis, which brought me back full circle because we flew back and forth on Pan Am.

My teammates were dynamic, energetic and creative—and sometimes off-the-wall. Our job was to come up with a whole new image for RCA's consumer products. We not only came up with a new image, we actually came up with ideas for new products that ultimately were manufactured and successfully sold, particularly to young adults.

Under the theme "New vibrations from an old master," our advertising in magazines including *Life, Look, Time, Esquire, Sports Illustrated, Playboy, Saturday Review, House Beautiful,* and *House and Garden* announced "We've come a long way from the little dog and his horn." The cassette tape line was featured with headlines such as FROM STEVIE'S FIRST BIRTHDAY TO BEETHOVEN'S NINTH, wall clock radios were "Stick 'em up," one-and-a-half-inch-wide radios from the Indianapolis Company were "Indiana Slims." Products from the military market were "Our new recruits," and we bragged for the RCA sound systems:

"These speakers can blow out a match."

It felt great to help breathe new life into one of the oldest companies in America, and the account was saved. J. Walter Thompson's public offering came off without a hitch.

WE'VE COME A LONG WAY FROM THE LITTLE DOG AND HIS HORN.

A long way since 1906 when the Victrola® phonograph was introduced. And Nipper heard His Master's Voice.

Now it's the 70's and we haven't even stopped for breath. Our latest milestone is Dimensia III stereo. A complete audio center for the home. Stereo phonograph, AM/FM stereo radio, and tape cassette player/recorder. All in one.

You've never seen anything like it before. As for Nipper, he'd never have thought of it in his wildest dreams.

New vibrations from an old master.

RCA

Shortly after we got going on the RCA account, the company was the first advertising agency to be hit with the government's Affirmative Action program. The agency was a test case and we knew we were on the line. We had plenty of women in high positions in the agency at that time, so the emphasis was on recruiting minorities. One of the young people recruited was assigned to me as an account executive on RCA. His credentials were impeccable. He had graduated from an Ivy League college with an MBA. He was hired at more than I was making at the time. But once he got the job, he became quite laid-back, and his cavalier attitude gave me fits.

One instance of his fecklessness came when our full team flew to Las Vegas in preparation for a week of presentations to key RCA personnel. Thousands of national and international RCA sales and management people from all over the world were being flown in for the event, which was the first screening of the consumer campaign for all RCA products for the coming year. We left our apprentice account executive behind in New York to fly out with the final creative material while we traveled in advance of the meeting to set things up. He was scheduled to come in with the material the day before the sessions were to begin, and two of us met him at the airport. He came off the plane whistling, and we went with him to the baggage-claim area to pick up the presentation material. A single bag came around the conveyor belt, which he picked up, saying he was all set to go. We looked around and asked him where the creative material was for the presentation. There was a moment of silence. He had forgotten to bring it with him. Needless to say, we booked him on a turnaround flight to New York to get it back on the red-eye that same night. Bottom line, the next day, the presentation went fine. I had an interesting time in Vegas, didn't lose any money at the tables and recovered nicely when I arrived back in New York.

Jerry Della Femina said, "Advertising is the most fun you can have with your clothes on," and I'm inclined to agree. Another way of putting it, to keep it in the "G-rated" category, was the advice of Foote, Cone & Belding's Fairfax Cone. "Advertising," he maintained, "is what you do when you can't go to see somebody. That's all it is." And I like David Ogilvy's advice to copywriters; "The consumer is no moron. She's your wife."

All in all, I loved every year, every day, and every minute working for J. Walter Thompson. In 1970 its worldwide billing was $774 million, with its closest competitors being McCann Erickson with $543.9 million, Y&R: $503.5 million, Ted Bates: $424.8 million, and Leo Burnett with $422.7 million.

My experience at JWT was more than I had hoped for. It combined all of the things I had been taught at two great universities. It gave me a great opportunity to practice my inclination for political peacemaking, taught me how to work as part of a team, improved my writing style, creative thinking, presentation and sales approach, and sharply honed my ability to survive.

But the time had come to be thinking along new paths. My family was growing and the commuting ate into the little time that I had to spend with them. The decision was forced sooner than I had planned. A devastating family health crisis required my family's immediate return to the South. I'll come to this later, but in 1970 when I notified J. Walter Thompson I would be leaving, I received a letter from RCA's vice president of advertising services, John Anderson, saying:

> "Jack Morrissey tells me that you decided to drop out of the New York rat race. I doubt you will ever regret it. This is just to say that your efforts will be deeply missed on the RCA account. In the rush of everyday business, particularly in the last chaotic year, we may have given you the impression that your conscientiousness has gone unnoticed. Believe me, that was never the case. Our very best wishes for your continued success in your new position, and thanks again for your many contributions to our advertising in recent months."

Last year marked the 150th anniversary of the J. Walter Thompson Co. The John W. Hartman Center at Duke University, which is the repository of its history, wrote JWT "is the oldest enduring advertising agency in the United States and one of the largest and most successful in the world," and named five JWT clients whose "products and services became part of the fabric of American culture: Ford, Kraft, Ponds, Kodak and Pan American." I worked on Ford and Pan Am and was involved in changing National Dairy Products' name to Kraft.

I left the "If I can make it there, I'll make it anywhere" City feeling pretty good and I look back on JWT with affection. And during my time there my father brought his broadcasting holding up to 14 stations with help from John Babcock, whose path led him back to my father in 1964 as related in the next chapter.

CHAPTER 12
ONE-ON-ONE
by John B. Babcock

There remains only one person who worked one-on-one with the late Roy H. Park, and that has to be me, John B. Babcock. As I said, I was acquainted with Roy back in the early '40s when he often sought advice from my father, H.E. "Ed" Babcock, out at our Inlet Valley farm, Sunnygables. He hired me to write copy at the State Street offices of Agricultural Advertising and Research for a few months before leaving for WWII, and I started working there again after finishing my studies in English and literature at Cornell after the war. My duties included projects for the successful agricultural campaign during Thomas E. Dewey's 1948 quest for the presidency which Park headed with help from my father, Ed Babcock. Park proved that he had learned to communicate with farmers, studied how they thought, and knew what was needed to motivate them.

When I was sent south to manage his Richmond, VA, Ag Research ad agency office, for a year or so, my specialty there was ad ideas, copy and effective communication with top management of our client, Southern States Cooperative. That co-op was so similar to GLF with which I had grown up, that I found it easy to carry out my duties. I had little to do with Park personally except on visits back to Ithaca, when he would regale me with his growing list of accomplishments. During this time, Southern States' marketing manager, T.K Wolfe, whose son Tom was later the celebrated journalist and novelist in the white suit, gave me some lessons about writing.

I left my Richmond position with Park when I returned to

Ithaca in 1949 after my dad's first heart attack. Famous for his writing and farm economics expertise, Ed Babcock was serving on Avco Corporation's Board at the invitation of Victor Emanuel. Emanuel in turn provided solid support during Dad's chairmanship of the Cornell Board of Trustees. A business magnate in his own right, Emanuel took charge of the finance committee of Cornell's board.

Emanuel introduced me to the intriguing world of broadcast communications. In 1949, I left Park to take a much better paying job at Avco's Crosley Broadcasting Division. I spent fifteen years with various divisions of Avco Corporation, starting as a farm announcer at WLW radio in Cincinnati. From there, I was promoted to construct and manage the last Midwest TV station owned by Crosley, WLWI, Indianapolis.

Convinced that I was bright and capable, Emanuel opened up the corporate world for me. I was inundated with copies of Avco interdivisional office correspondence as Emanuel sought to give me what he called "exposure" to the real fabric of corporate management. He was grooming me for additional responsibilities within Avco. The early wet, chemical copy machines produced copies of documents that he mailed to me almost daily. They were brittle, brown, hard to read, and very confidential.

During this time, I dropped in to see Roy whenever I visited Ithaca, including several times over the untimely death of my father in 1950. In 1956 Roy had taken an advisory position with Procter & Gamble, which had absorbed his Duncan Hines brand. Despite spectacular success and recognition, Roy was restless and ambitious to get into newspapering and broadcasting. I boasted about the fat profit margins in television, and he vowed to be part of that emerging industry despite his admitted first love for small-town newspapers.

That brings me to my path back to Park. Roy phoned me regularly in Indianapolis to talk about broadcasting and how licensees were governed and regulated by the Federal Communications Commission. He loved the potential operating profit and asked me if I would join him as operations manager to seek out and acquire a group of broadcast stations. He was persuasive, promising eventual stock participation and a retirement plan.

I took him up on his offer early in 1964, resigning a promising and remunerative career as a corporate VP in the Midwest. I happily moved my wife, Nancy, and three little daughters to my old stamping grounds, Ithaca, NY. I was an early victim of what will be pointed out later as the "Ithaca Trap," Park's practice of persuading new employees to buy an expensive home that would keep them tied close to the job as continuing payments came due. I cashed in my Avco retirement program equity for the down payment on my Ithaca house, confident that it would be replaced and improved on by Park's promised but never fulfilled retirement program.

Roy, Jr., then twenty-six, had graduated from the Johnson School and was working with J. Walter Thompson in New York City and Miami when I joined his father's company for a second time. I was forty-two and aware that I was entering those prime years of executive productivity that contribute most to a successful business career. Roy Park lured me away from vice presidency at a major broadcast corporation with the charm and wiles that made him a great salesman.

Looking back, I realized that Park's personal courtship had been persistent and deliberate. He never remained long out of touch, and when I was available, he was a gracious host in his comfortable Cayuga Heights home. He performed at home just as he did at the office, burrowing immediately into his business affairs and exploits, the atmosphere somewhat softened by a taste or two of excellent cognac. His wife, Dorothy, was always warm and cordial but quick to leave us alone in his well-appointed home office to pursue business.

I was soon to find out that my employer rarely took a vacation. When he did, his office and daily regime hit the road with him. When others in the company took vacations, he referred belittlingly to the absent staff member as "being on holiday." I learned soon that even hard-earned vacations were so frowned upon as to discourage even trying to plan for them.

Family Portrait. Johnnie Babcock and wife Nancy, center, with daughters, left to right, Susan, Jeannie, Nancy and not to be left out, their beloved dog Brownie.

So there I was in 1964 headed for another tour of duty for the next nineteen years as Roy H. Park's vice president for operations. I brought to the table years of experience in broadcast management and the maturity imparted by effective big business performance. I was the perfect age to assume top executive responsibilities and brought along a tolerance for hard work. I was to spend more time personally with Roy than any of his associates or family.

CHAPTER 13
BUILDING A BUSINESS EMPIRE

The world is all gates, all opportunities, strings of tension
waiting to be struck.

—Ralph Waldo Emerson

While I was in my first year in business school in 1961, and three years before Johnnie Babcock joined him, as I said, my father had moved into his fourth career in broadcasting. Consulting with Procter & Gamble under a non-compete contract as the vice president and director of Duncan Hines foods, he was able to watch one of the world's great merchandisers at close hand. It became evident to him that if P&G knew one thing to do well, it was to advertise. The company had the money to do it on a large and highly effective scale, and one of the reasons my father sold the Hines operation to P&G was that he knew he didn't. P&G took Duncan Hines cake mixes into the food business big-time—via television.

I remember all the Christmases growing up in Ithaca when my grandparents and family would gather around the black-and-white television to watch talent shows and comedies, and the last thing you would want to do was to advertise food products on TV. The only foods that might look OK in black and white would be a bowl of rice or black olives. Then television made its debut in color, and P&G began shifting ad dollars away from magazines and into television. The cakes looked great, and color TV put the eye appeal back into food. My father was sitting on top of

360,000 shares of P&G stock, and he couldn't think of a better way to use this collateral than to break into the broadcast business. Companies were now pouring money into television advertising.

Working with P&G, Pops realized the full marketing power and potential of television. He was impressed at the way the Cincinnati marketing power bought up hours of radio and television time to promote their many brands. The P&G stock gave him the financial collateral he needed to borrow at low rates, move to the media side of the equation, and begin buying broadcast properties.

Johnnie Babcock remembers that in the early stages of building his broadcast empire my father had him accompany him on visits to large banks, where he aspired to secure credit and negotiate loans. He had long ago exceeded the loan capabilities of the Ithaca area banks. Babcock referred to his ability in this area and his technique as "Banker Up."

I'll let Johnnie take it from here.

BANKER UP

"Shortly before my arrival in 1964, Roy's first broadcast investment was funded by Wachovia, with help from the Society Bank of Cleveland," Babcock recalls. "Roy had applied at Society for a loan to pay cash for his first TV and radio stations in Greenville, NC. His research revealed that Society Bank was uniquely experienced in broadcast financing, and at first it was the only major bank Park dealt with. The people there welcomed him and his balance sheet. With the anticipated loan, Roy eventually reached the maximum dollar limit allowed a single client by even that large bank. The ever-strong attraction of his home state, North Carolina, was to lead him to Wachovia Bank's Raleigh office, where he was taken in practically as a favorite son. A large regional money center, Wachovia eventually became his lead bank. Contact with bank officers became so frequent as to make the bank's senior loan officer a virtual partner in his holdings.

"But before he reached his limit with Society Bank, when he was ready to buy his second and third TV stations in Chattanooga and Johnson City, Tennessee, he asked me to take a break from my job and the two of us took a charter flight to Cleveland. He liked the idea of my participation in the negotiation because I was conversant with broadcast management terminology and was deeply involved in fashioning the pro forma operating budgets for the stations we sought. His trusted senior financial officer, Kenneth B. Skinner, prepared the business plan, filling in the below-the-line items of debt, amortization, depreciation, and taxes. This is where Park shone, and he gave Ken close scrutiny and guidance. He had become adept at scanning a balance sheet and immediately flagging any incorrect or weak entries," Babcock remembers.

"To lighten things up on this particular mission, as our cab made its way to downtown Cleveland, I asked if it was true that the senior bank officer at a prestigious place like this would have one glass eye. 'No,' Park replied. "A really top banker has two glass eyes.' When we finally met with the senior loan officer, Park was a humble but chatty new client, doffing his Chesterfield velvet-collared coat and homburg hat, and settling in a high-backed leather chair. He sported solid gold cuff links, and a gold chain coursed across his middle to the watch pocket of his crisp Sulka black suit. Roy had fine, soft hands with tapered fingers that suggested artistic capabilities. In addition to a couple of heavy ornate rings, he wore a wristwatch that fairly shouted of opulence and good taste. As for our host, he was polite, not much for small talk, and whether they were glass or not, he had a steady eye that hinted of inherent distrust.

"The talk turned quickly to business. Park knew financing and how to focus attention on his own personal account. Stepping up to the plate as 'banker up,' he conceded that the bank officer knew salient facts about him from his first loan, but to spare the gentleman the gesture of opening his own client file folder, Park laid an updated balance sheet that could be quickly and easily scanned on the adjacent coffee table. He then went on to explain the amount of the credit line he wanted to establish at the bank.

He said that in his practice of cash acquisitions of businesses, he made it a condition to withhold 10 percent of the purchase price for at least a year—longer if he could persuade the seller—as a reserve against any claims of unforeseen liability. He wanted to protect himself from defending possible claims with his own money. Bankers seemed to like that feature.

"Confident that his portfolio of Procter & Gamble stock easily collateralized the loan he sought, he opened the point of compensating balances. More often than not, big banks liked to have their borrowers keep a percentage of their line of credit as cash in the bank as a key condition of the loan. This was negotiable, replied the banker, and something that he would review with the bank's loan committee. Park did not imply that the amount of the compensating balance could be a deal breaker, but he made no concessions on the spot. The banker needed two good eyes, not glass, to size up this potential client.

"Park's negotiating skills were super smooth, always just a bit vague and underplayed. He was tough to size up. In a few minutes, he stood up and suggested that he and I head out to our charter plane. With appropriate exchange of good will signaling end of the meeting, we were alone in the elevator with Park wearing a big smile," Johnnie recalls.

"It was evident that Park was fascinated with the big regional banks and their management. Those banks had the one single commodity that topped his wish list: money! Building a bankroll for expansion was his obsession, and doing it with no financial or equity partners his unwavering method. No trusted employee ever shared in his ownership, and he was painstakingly careful in his prime motivation that no relative or family member had even a small piece of his growing fortune.

"Park did have oft-repeated advice for anyone dealing with a bank. Never surprise your banker. If you are in or foresee trouble with your account, tell the banker up front. When the bank discovers bad news as a result of an audit or just plain snooping, it goes much harder. His final word was a good maxim: Never try to fool your banker. Give him hard facts and let him come to his own conclusions.

"When Park finally signed the loan agreement a few days later with its negotiated compensating balance, he leaned back, smiled and said: 'Thanks a million!' He had his money and a track record of how to get more. Profits from present holdings built reserves and gave him even greater leverage," Babcock points out.

SETTING A FAST PACE

Make no little plans; they have no magic to stir men's blood...make big plans, aim high in hope and work.

—Daniel H. Burnham

I am picking up the story again at this point, and as his son, I can tell you that my father's "Thanks a million" was hardly the simple expression it seemed to be. Interestingly enough, Pops financed his first broadcasting properties with help from a $1 million loan from an insurance company whose president he happened to know, along with loans from Society Bank.

On September 26, 1961, at age fifty-one, he founded what would become Park Broadcasting, Inc., a Delaware corporation, with the purchase of two radio stations, WNCT AM/FM, in Greenville, NC.

Early in the following year in February, driving his 1961 Lincoln Continental convertible from Ithaca to Greenville, he purchased WNCT TV, his first television station there. He said he arranged the loan thirty minutes before the deal closed by walking into a branch of Wachovia Bank and Trust Co. in Raleigh with "the country-boy approach" and asking "to borrow a few million dollars." With Procter & Gamble stock as collateral, of course, which he said allowed him to borrow at low rates. The price tag was $2.5 million, and WNCT TV boasted that its facilities covered eastern North Carolina "from the capital to the coast."

This was followed in rapid succession by the purchase of a

television and two radio stations in Chattanooga, TN, in 1963 for $2.5 million, and a television station in Johnson City, TN, in 1964 for another $2.5 million. He never returned to the friendly insurance company for these acquisitions once he learned that banks lend up to 80 percent on such purchases, while insurance companies lend only 30 percent. Financing these purchases was not a problem, since he said he had "ample" lines of credit at Wachovia and Society Bank.

It was after the purchase of the Johnson City television station in 1964 that my father hired H.E. Babcock's son, Johnnie, bringing his career experience in broadcast media to manage this first group of TV stations. "Food was interesting," Pops told an interviewer about the industry he left in 1962 to start a new career at the age of fifty-two, "but media work is exciting."

Reflecting on Pops' meteoric rise in the broadcast industry, *Broadcasting Magazine*, in its issue of February 3, 1964, said: "If reverse logic can be applied to the maxim that idle hands are the Devil's tools, then Roy H. Park is one of the purest men beneath the firmament. A relentlessly energetic businessman, his every step from the North Carolina farm of his birth to his present prominence has been marked by a stubborn will to succeed and a sure instinct for dealing with his fellow man."

Working together, my father and Babcock began to rapidly expand Park Broadcasting with the strategy of acquiring stations in the top 100 markets. Other purchases from 1965 through 1969 included a television station in Richmond, VA, for $5 million, then radio stations serving Minneapolis, MN, and Yankton, SD. The signal for WNAX, in Yankton, served four states. Paying $7 million for another TV station in Roanoke, VA, in 1969, Pops noticed that the prices were going up, so that same year he decided to build his own tower and start a UHF television station in Utica, NY.

It is interesting to note that his Utica start-up took far longer for payback on the investment than the acquisitions he made. It goes to show that it's a lot easier to buy an ongoing business than it is to start one successfully. Contrary to the old farmer's advice, sometimes life is not easier when you try to plow around the stump. Trying to save money on another acquisition, my father put a stump in the ground.

At some point, also, during the period between 1966 and 1969, when the word was out in the general community that my father was acquiring things, Pops received a call from the visionary Robert Arthur Moog, the inventor of the first modular synthesizer, who lived in nearby Trumansburg, NY, at the time. Mr. Moog received a PhD in engineering physics from Cornell in Ithaca, and his musical invention, which received a patent in 1969, was ready for expansion and he offered my father the opportunity to invest in his venture.

There are opportunities that come along during every person's lifetime, and this may have been a big one. I was working at J. Walter Thompson when my father told me about it, and although I had a short run with piano lessons as a kid and at my fraternity took a crack at drums, I could hardly qualify as a musician. I could not envision the breakthrough role the Moog synthesizer would play in the music world in the future including being used by The Beatles, Donna Summer and in Michael Jackson's "Thriller." My father was not a musical guy, either, so we passed on what could have been a truly great opportunity.

But as I was to learn later in life, maybe this missed opportunity was for the best. I remember in the far future being sidetracked from my full-time job to try to help market an environmentally friendly retail product which I thought might set the world on fire. I'll never forget the advice I received at the time from a client and a friend, John Miller, who was then the media director of Y&R in New York. He simply said, "Stick with what you know." As tempting as it has been to disregard over the years, as so many of us know, it was good advice, and I took it. I'm glad that I did.

But it's interesting that one of Moog's daughters, Michelle Moog-Koussa, a native of the Ithaca area, at the age of four moved with her family to North Carolina. She was the same age I was when my family did the opposite, moving from North Carolina to Ithaca.

When Michelle contacted me in 2007 to help in honoring her father's legacy our Triad Foundation helped her fund the Bob Moog Memorial Foundation for Electronic Music in North Carolina. Sadly, in 2013 the decision was made to move his personal archives out of North Carolina, but at least they found a much appreciated home in Ithaca at Cornell University.

In any event, after a short pause, my father's acquisitions continued in 1973 and 1974 with the purchase of radio stations in Portland, OR, Eden Prairie, MN, and a TV station in Birmingham, AL. In a special feature, NBC Radio's *Monitor* program reported that Park Broadcasting, Inc., "operates eighteen radio and television stations, the largest broadcast group wholly owned by one man." The group covered nine cities in six different states. In 1975 and 1976, he bought more radio stations in Seattle, WA, and Syracuse, NY.

Through all of these purchases, my father had a nose for profitable properties. As reported in the July 25, 1977 issue of *Business Week,*

> His country music radio station in Yankton, South Dakota, for example, might seem too small for the owner of seven costly TV stations to bother with, but it reaches five populous farm states with radio's strongest daytime signal. Park recalls adding his first FM stations in the mid-1960's even though profits then were almost nonexistent. "I carried them along because I knew they were going to make it sooner or later," he said.[3]

Cecil L. Richards, a broker in Falls Church, VA, confirmed that the two Virginia TV stations my father bought at an average of $6 million were each worth in excess of $10 million by 1977.

Along the way, my father was also asked if he thought about investing in cable. He said cable was not his style. "It's highly capital-intensive, and it's going to wind up in the hands of a few large companies," he said. He was right. At the time he also said the problem with the cable networks and the independent stations was that they failed to cover local news. His stations took pains to cover things such as the local Rotary Club and high school football games. "It may not be CBS Sports," he said, "but if your kid is playing, you're going to watch it."

As Pops was nearing his legal ownership limit of twenty-one broadcasting stations, seven each of television, AM and FM radio stations, he realized that at this time, in order to continue to grow, he would have to move to other media acquisitions. As reported in the *Winston-Salem Journal*, "Like Alexander the Great, he had run out of worlds to conquer. But instead of sitting down to weep, he did what he said he had wanted to do at the beginning. He bought his first newspaper at the age of 62—41 years after his college paper and AP days."

While he was still buying broadcasting stations, he entered the newspaper field in 1972, and by 1977, he owned forty newspapers in nine states. They comprised one-third of his wealth. His media acquisitions through the years are far too complex to follow in the pages of this book. He moved through radio, television, outdoor advertising, and, finally, newspapers. His holdings are summarized in Appendix B, Building a Media Empire.

In an interview with Virgil Gaither in the August 22, 1979, issue of the *Tulsa Tribune*, my father expressed his desire to get into the newspaper business, and why he started with broadcasting:

> I developed some trade publications [right after leaving the Associated Press], and always wanted to get into the [newspaper] business. When I could, I got the television business because at the time—back in the 1960s—I thought the newspaper business was a dying business.
>
> I picked a market area and over a period of time bought television stations in North Carolina, Tennessee, Virginia and Alabama. I also built a station in Utica, New York, but it is helpful if you can buy in one general

area because you keep up with the economics and politics of the region. When I got into radio, I had to buy where stations were available. I have stations in Seattle, Portland, Minneapolis, Syracuse, South Dakota, Greenville, Chattanooga and Richmond.

After we generated some cash, I moved over to my first love and bought newspapers.[4]

REACHING THE LIMIT

In June of 1977, Johnnie and my father agreed to purchase WONO FM in Syracuse, NY, for $340,000. In so doing, he became the first broadcaster to reach the Federal Communications Commission's then-legal-limit of twenty-one broadcasting stations. At the time, not even communications giants such as CBS, ABC, RKO, Westinghouse and Metromedia, with seventeen or eighteen each, had reached the twenty-one-station ceiling. By this time, his broadcasting group reached 25 million people or 12 percent of the total population of the United States.

There was another area of new electronic technology that interested my father after he reached the ceiling in broadcast ownership. That was the new low-power television stations the federal government had begun accepting applications for in the early 1980s. The stations would have a range of about ten miles from the broadcasting tower, and he applied for forty such stations, mostly in areas where he already owned a publication. He didn't expect to get many of them approved, but he felt by using some staff from the publications, such as the bookkeeping department, he could begin operation with the addition of little more than a "couple of guys with cameras." But he never followed through on this because his focus shifted to newspapers.

RESTRICTION LIFTED

During the years 1983 and 1984, the "7 Station" rule became the subject of FCC review. It took some time, however, before the rules were changed, and when they were, it was in piecemeal form. My father, who was a member of the Broadcast Regulatory Review Committee, which met regularly with the FCC to discuss deregulation of the broadcast industry, said, "I figured something was going to happen down the road, so we've been saving our cash."

Some Congressmen called for hearings on the matter, among them U.S. Rep. Matthew F. McHugh (D-28th District, where Park Broadcasting was located), who said the FCC decision raised a serious policy question, and that Congress should hold hearings and make policy judgments on it. "The real issue is whether the decision by the FCC will have the effect of a major concentration of ownership in the hands of a few large media conglomerates," he said.

As reported by Helen Mundell of the *Ithaca Journal*,

McHugh said he's not as concerned about the rule change allowing one owner to have 36 stations as he is about another FCC decision which would remove the limits altogether in 1990. If Congress doesn't act, the FCC rule change will become law 30 days after the decision is published in the Federal Registry.

Her article, reprinted with permission from the *Ithaca Journal*, also engaged in a little political criticism, pointing out that:

Park recently contributed $1,000 to McHugh's campaign for re-election. McHugh is running against Republican Constance E. Cook, a former Assemblywoman from Ithaca. McHugh said he thinks it is the first time Park has contributed to his campaign. But Park said he thinks he gave once before.

Asked why he contributed to a Democrat's campaign when it is assumed he's a Republican, Park said he doesn't always vote a straight ticket. Park said he thinks McHugh "is doing a very good job. I supported his opponents three or four times, and he always won, so I decided I might just as well support the guy who's doing the job." Asked if there is any connection between the contribution and possible hearings on the FCC decision, McHugh laughed. "His $1,000 won't buy my vote."[5]

But the rules did change, and the limits on the television stations that could be owned came to be based on size of audience. An owner could acquire a TV station if the acquisition, when combined with other stations owned, did not reach, on a combined basis, more than 35 percent of the total national audience.

The rules on the limits on ownership of radio stations were also relaxed, then relaxed again. Now the rules focus not on the number of stations owned but on the size of the markets and the audience reached. Radio limits depend on how many other stations are in the market. It is difficult to explain how this evolved in a simple way but, for example, in a market with at least forty-five stations, one owner can own as many as eight stations; in a market with thirty to forty-four stations, one owner can own up to seven stations, and the FCC formula goes on.

When the restrictions loosened, my father had $100 million earmarked for expansion, but no intention to rush out to try to find stations, since he knew the prices paid by the major broadcast networks and larger corporations would be astronomical.

He did, however, buy one more radio station about ten years after his penultimate purchase of WONO FM, the radio station that made him first to reach the old FCC limit. All of my father's TV stations were CBS affiliates except the UHF in Utica, which was ABC, and WSLS in Roanoke, which was NBC. The majority of his radio stations were ABC affiliates. He crowned his broadcast group in 1986 with the purchase of KWLD AM / KFMW FM in Waterloo, IA and the popular WPAT AM/FM, which covered New York City from Clifton, NJ. This brought his final broadcasting tally to seven television and, because he sold four radio stations in Duluth and Roanoke between 1977 and 1985, back up to twenty-one radio stations, and ended his expansion in the broadcasting field.

Photo by Joe Rosenberg, John Blair & Co.

This "21" Plaque presented to my father and Johnnie by the president of Blair Television's Market Division, Harry B. Smart, left, and John Blair & Co. President Jack W. Fritz, far right, reads "America's First Maximum Station Broadcaster." Park Broadcasting was the industry's first broadcaster to reach the Federal Communication Commission's 21 station limit.

And while all this was taking place, from 1964 on, Johnnie Babcock, when he wasn't traveling, was sitting across from my father's big desk. Johnnie describes his experiences during those years of rapid expansion.

CHAPTER 14
THE BIG DESK

In Johnnie Babcock's colorful recollection: "If credit hours were logged for the time I sat across the desk from Roy H. Park in the manner logged as flying time for an airline pilot, I'd have a very full book. To match it, a pilot would have to be maybe 113 years old.

"I had observed Roy at his desk as a casual employee, but reporting to him personally changed things. My first summons in 1964 came on the interoffice phone. My private office was around the corner from his in a building that had been Duncan Hines foods headquarters before P&G took over. Roy was comfortably ensconced behind the big desk that had adorned his now-vacated Ag Research office. He was still on State Street in Ithaca, just a few steps up the hill.

"My private office fell a little short of privileged. It was the former test kitchen for Duncan Hines foods. My desk chair straddled a sunken drain in the tiled floor. My veneered desk looked like it came from a minimally furnished Cornell student rental room. When I moved my chair even an inch, it became as unbalanced as a milking stool, one or two legs grasping air instead of the floor. I was busy marking up a map showing home totals delivered by a TV station in each county of its coverage. I rattled my chair around to unseat myself and headed for Roy's office.

"As I rounded the bend to his office door, he came striding out to meet me face on. Apparently I had not been quick enough to answer his summons. I was taken aback but still mellow at being back in my hometown. I went in without comment and accepted the chair he pointed to across the polished surface of his desk. He handed me a yellow pad and suggested in the future that I bring one with me when we were to be together. There was no small talk about the long trip to Ithaca with my family from Indianapolis. His only personal inquiry was where my family was living and when I would be buying a house. I replied that I was comfortably installed in a rental unit in Lansing, and that I wanted to study the community before choosing a permanent home. I had to close first on sale of my home in Indiana. Roy offered help in locating a nice place and promised to get me hooked up with the right people at the bank.

"Then we talked about pricing broadcast stations either by multiples of sales or operating profit. I said both were important, but that sales growth and totals were the better indicator of potential. We could use our own devices to control expenses. Sales momentum was harder to build and maintain. I returned to my office feeling that we were off on the right foot.

"I was to learn and remember that he tried to get every key employee to commit to a home purchase, and the more expensive, the better. A man saddled with house payments was more likely to remain a loyal employee than someone who could relocate on short notice. If you had a big mortgage, you tended to stick. The inventory of big homes tallied by executives hired and moved to Ithaca indicated that Park's advice was often followed, and that included the substantial house I eventually chose.

"Park had made detailed plans to install me in far better quarters, and soon the entire broadcast operation took up residency next door in what had been the Ithaca Post Office in the nineteenth century. I had a roomy ground-floor accommodation that had lots of windows, cheerful lighting, and a decent view. I was assigned space in the covered garage that served the building, right next to Park's reserved slot. Again, Roy's office was handy to mine, though I cannot recall that he ever entered it. We spent our days at his desk. He had windows that remained perpetually hidden behind Venetian blinds. It was as if he wanted to eliminate any distractions from the world outside.

"My most frequent engagement with Roy, usually bright and early, was to devise what he called "talk sheets" to guide him in his phone calls to prospective sellers. He never had to think of what he would say next. It was right there before him and thus gave him time to be an attentive listener. We would word-smith these scripts, right down to the introductory remarks asking of the health of the wife and family. Then it was down to business. Instead of bluntly asking how sales were going, he would slide into the topic by commenting on how business was faring, and the state of the economy. This usually produced an outpouring of the prospect's sales problems, staffing decisions, and negative observations about the general business. Park carefully took notes and listened, making sympathetic and helpful responses.

"If serious negotiations were indicated, he would ask for operating reports and make a tentative date for a visit to the man's station(s). If the conversation went as he had hoped, his final words on the phone were always: Thanks a million!

"Observing Park in action over many years, the generous phrase "Thanks a million" often meant that the fish was hooked, and on Park's terms. He'd hang up with a broad smile, intense eyes under his bushy eyebrows sparkling with anticipation. The call often culminated a period of intense digging and research by Park that gave him insight into the personality and vulnerabilities of his quarry. When he was on the cusp of a major acquisition, he knew his seller better than the seller knew himself.

"The homework he had done before approaching and selling Duncan Hines the idea of having Park license his name became the model for winning over other acquisition candidates. Park could be tough with his own staff, his lawyers or his accountants. With prospective sellers, his manner was shaggy dog softy—and deceptive. There was, I soon learned, nothing soft about Roy."

MORE THAN A BUSINESS

While Johnnie was sitting across from the "big desk," Pops, through his company, cosponsored a series of lectures on communications at Cornell. Bill Ward, my earlier professor and by then head of the Department of Communication Arts at Cornell University, introduced the address my father gave to his students on December 10, 1971, and it should be noted that Johnnie said he wrote 95 percent of my father's speeches.

In his introduction, Professor Ward said: "No one in America is more qualified to discuss communication media as a business—and more than a business—than Roy H. Park, president of Park Broadcasting, Inc. A man with his long and broad experience in all forms of mass media wouldn't be himself if he didn't stress the vital importance of black rather than red ink on a ledger and what must be done to make a profit and stay in business. 'There's very little glamour in working for a bankrupt company.'

"At the same time, Mr. Park 'humanizes' the media, especially radio and television, where his main interests are now centered. He shares with us an inside view of management and the criteria he used to build his group of eighteen television and radio stations," Ward said, expressing his appreciation to Mr. Park and his company for being a cosponsor of our Cornell communication seminars during the 1971–72 academic year. One of these addresses given by my father was entitled COMMUNICATIONS MEDIA: MORE THAN A BUSINESS.

Although he said it was *more* than a business, it was all business, and a profitable one, to him. Just how much it was "all business" I would soon learn—the hard way. As Johnnie tells it now, he learned the lesson the same way—quick and hard.

MANAGING BROADCAST AS PROFIT CENTERS
by John B. Babcock

While young Roy was busy attending the Johnson Graduate School of Management, and recently married, living in his own apartment in Ithaca, his father was snapping up broadcasting stations. By 1971, when he joined his father's company, Park had already accumulated eighteen stations, and I was into the throes of managing all of them.

Park saw gold in owning broadcast stations. They are reasonably invulnerable to competition, not overburdened with depreciable assets, high profile in their community, and while regulated by the government, the franchise for the assigned frequency on the airwaves is protected by Uncle Sam. The end product is what goes out over the air each day. At the end of day, there is no inventory remaining. Direct costs are for energy and equipment to send the signal out over the airwaves, programming, and payroll for sales and operating people. The difference each day between those costs and advertising time sold is operating profit.

Other than acquiring detailed knowledge of the dynamics of the industry—how TV and radio work—Roy cared about the details of station operation about as much as he sought to understand how his mechanic kept his cars running. He didn't care to look in the toolbox. He focused on the operating profit that a broadcast station produced every day. Park regarded all of his businesses as money machines. A TV station stood out like a foolproof slot machine. You pulled the handle to start the broadcast day, and by sign-off each night, the station returned in cash in the tray as much as two times what you paid to play that day.

My job was to produce those operating margins. I targeted 45 percent for our broadcast group, and looked to our most successful CBS station to throw off well over 50 percent in operating profit. Radio was expected to produce in the high 30s, outdoor billboards in the low 30s, newspapers in the mid to high 20s. A big grocery retailer does well to turn a profit of 2–3 percent; industrial concerns score success if they exceed 10 percent operating profit. Broadcasting was pretty fat cat.

The term operating profit, as it is calculated in broadcasting, does not account for all the costs. Referred to as "above the line" charges, it contains all those elements needed to air the programs, and the cost of selling them. Profit is sales income less out-of-pocket costs (direct expense), before interest, depreciation, and taxes. Below-the-line items include the cost and repayment of loans, federal income tax provisions, interest charges, depreciation of equipment and long-term amortization.

That's where Park's trusted financial advisor, Kenneth B. Skinner, came in. A retired financial officer with the Ithaca facility of National Cash Register, Ken agreed to help Park and me develop a business plan for each of the stations considered acquisition candidates. Ken oversaw other accounting people, but he was most comfortable hunched over a big, green accounting form, plying his Cross pencil and pink eraser.

After studying operating statements of the target company, I would suggest budget goals for sales by months from the principal sources: local, regional, national, political, and production. I worked with Ken toward totals about 10 percent higher than most recent results, taking into account variances such as anticipated political campaigns, special events, and sports coverage rights. After we had massaged income figures, I went entry by entry into expense categories with the goal of a 5 to 10 percent overall reduction. Salaries were reviewed and adjusted to numbers I thought we could achieve, usually less than the present owner had paid. Of course we eliminated top management and owner salaries, substituting what we felt would attract competent hired management. I always included liberal amounts to promote higher viewing levels, confident that Park might reduce these numbers when he reviewed our work, but hoping he might give less scrutiny to items that I felt more important to the station's growth and welfare.

We extended the month-by-month financial plan for the station to three years, by adjusting annual totals by a modest 5 percent increase in expenses, a 10 to 15 percent increase in revenues. That produced attractive annual growth in profitability including resources to pay off the loan.

Skinner worked directly with Park to schedule the below-the-line entries. Depreciation was applied to the assets provided by the seller, and Ken made monthly entries on his green analysis tablet that rounded out the business projection for the foreseeable future. By the time he had provided for the new depreciation for assets to be acquired and interest payments, taxable income had been shrunk considerably. Now Park had the hard information to finalize the price he would offer in cash, and how much he would need to borrow.

I was left with one remaining assignment: to fulfill the business plan and provide Roy Park with the promised profits.

A Profitable Venture by 1981, 17 years after Johnnie joined the company to manage the Park Broadcasting stations including the television team here photographed during a sales strategy meeting on the lawn behind the Terrace Hill headquarters building in Ithaca, NY. Pops wanted visitors to know the flag on the headquarters roof had flown over the White House.

CHAPTER 15
THE "ITHACA TRAP"

As his son living in Ithaca, a lot of people have asked me over the years why my father continued to headquarter in this small town. While I was mobile and moving around, I wondered, too. I know why he originally moved to Ithaca, and how he went through his earlier careers there. But when he started building a media empire, access to financial institutions and ease of travel for prospects, employees and others with whom his business was involved would have been better situated in a place like New York City.

After he concluded the sale of the Duncan Hines Institute to Procter & Gamble, my father could afford better housing. Once his business was sold, he was free to go anywhere, and I suspect my mother may have been having some thoughts about returning to the South. At the time, both my sister and I were away at school so the extra room wasn't needed, but the purchase of a larger home was an incentive for my mother to stay in Ithaca where my father already had investments in real estate.

As was his style, Pops had already started exploring the possible purchase of an estate in the Ithaca area, regardless of the fact that none were for sale at the time. He had approached people and families that owned the kind of property he was looking for, and, in particular, became friends with one older gentleman which assured, when the gentleman died in the mid-1950s, that a first right of refusal had been made part of his will.

The house, situated on seven acres in the Village of Cayuga Heights, was a stone mansion built by stonemasons brought over from Italy, many of whom remained in Ithaca after the project was completed. I am sure it wasn't the weather that kept my father here, since he wouldn't know a snow shovel from a walking cane, but with the nature of this commitment, it was difficult for my mother to push for a move elsewhere. At any rate, to keep her happy, Pops gave my mother carte blanche with interior decorators and furnishings. Not only was the house splendidly fitted out, it also served as a refuge and fortification in which my father could retreat from what in many ways for him was a hostile world out there.

As you know from my childhood, my mother loved animals, and my father's estate provided ample room for dogs and peacocks. The original peacocks were loud, but eventually, to keep peace in the neighborhood, another species of peacock was found with a quieter call.

But despite this settling in, it is interesting that over the years my parents did little shopping in Ithaca, preferring New York City for purchases and medical care. But the Ithaca trap had firmly snapped shut on my mother, and to an extent on my sister and me. It also afforded an excellent snare for my father's headquarter employees.

I learned over the years Ithaca was the ideal environment from which my father could run his company. First, its location is "centrally isolated," which gives Cornell University fits when it comes to attracting recruiters, even from New York City, for its graduating students. Rail service ended forty years ago. The airline schedules are abysmal, and getting worse. No recruiter can get in to conduct a meaningful interview schedule and back out in a day. And no disgruntled Park employee could go across the street to find a new job, with no other jobs in their specialized categories of expertise available in Ithaca, NY.

Other escape routes were also sealed. My father told me he did not believe in sending his executives to association meetings or business conventions, feeling it too easy to have employees recruited away at these affairs. He belonged to all the right associations, but if anyone from headquarters attended the meetings, it was usually my father and Johnnie Babcock.

The other part of the trap was that Ithaca offered readily available housing in a country setting, ideal for enticing people from higher-cost-of-living areas around big cities. My father made a point of meeting the wives of prospective employees, hiring those with the most aggressive wives. He knew when a wife was ensconced in an expensive house, and had a liking for expensive trappings and a high style of living, they would encourage their husbands to make more money. And they would tolerate the extensive travel necessary to their husbands' job.

Park Wives, not *Stepford Wives*, but some in this picture and others over the years succumbed to the "Ithaca Trap." My mother heads the row on the left, Johnnie's wife, Nancy, anchors the far right end and Tetlow is six up from Nancy.

The only exception to this rule was me. When I moved to Ithaca, Pops insisted I *rent* a house for a year, even though by that time I had enough money to buy one from the proceeds of my first house. Before I made a commitment, he made sure it was *my* toe that was put in the water, not his. At that time, Ithaca did not offer many houses to rent, but with a dog and two kids we could not have existed again in a condo or an apartment. The only house for rent I was able to find was so small that we used the dining room for a third bedroom and ate in the kitchen. Shades of my sister and me growing up. The yard was so small that our dog didn't like it either. The Malamute ran away every chance he got.

But I'm getting ahead of myself. Ithaca was not yet a gleam in my eye. While the Upstate New York atmosphere was working for my father, the bright Big Apple lights I commuted to from cramped quarters in Westchester County were beginning to dim.

ESCAPE FROM THE CITY

You're the keeper of the castle,
So be a good man to your babies,
The creator of the sunshine in their day,
In the garden that you've seeded,
Be a friend when a friend is needed.
You won't have to look the other way.

You're the keeper of the castle,
Be the father to your children,
The provider of all their daily needs.
Like a sovereign Lord protector,
Be their best of needs director.
They'll do well to follow where you lead.

—From the song "Keeper of the Castle"
by Dennis Lambert and Brian Potter[6]

I was reminded of my responsibility as my children's "best needs director" by *The Four Tops* in this song in 1971. Weekend mornings were noisy at our Rye Ridge apartment complex. Our corner apartment, around which the lawn wrapped, was staked out by every kid in the complex as the best place to play. Starting around 6:30 AM I'm not sure which commuting parents got up that early on a Saturday morning, but I'm pretty sure they put the kids out like cats and then went back to bed.

Aside from living with the noise, there were too many kids on not enough lawn, and my daughter was growing up.

By 1970, our second child, a son born on a Friday the

thirteenth in 1967 in the United Hospital in Port Chester, had reached the "terrible threes." Fortunately, he was not terrible at all, but after commuting back and forth to New York City for some six years, and with our growing family, the living conditions were wearing on all of us. My wife began thinking it was time to give our family some space and a better environment...as well as a father who had some time for them to grow up with. As Tetlow had reminded me, she only saw me from 8:00 to 11:00 PM before collapsing from exhaustion from raising our children alone and sometimes only one full day out of my working week.

As I said, the final decision was made for us. Tetlow's mother, Jeannie Williams Newell, known as "Billy," had developed an incurable brain tumor, and we needed to be near to her for the short time she had left to live.

I researched agencies located as close as possible to Franklinton, including my place of birth, Raleigh, and interviewed with two or three agencies there without immediate success. I expanded my search to other North Carolina cities in the geographic area, and the research pinpointed a small in-house agency in Charlotte, NC, owned by First Union National Bancorp.

THE CHARLOTTE EXPERIENCE

The philosophy behind much advertising is based on the old observation that every man is really two men—the man he is and the man he wants to be.

—*William Feather*

Charles A. Kincaid, who had been operating successfully with a small staff and minimal billings, founded Kincaid Advertising Agency, Inc. in 1954. After it became Kincaid's largest account, First Union National Bank, Inc. bought the agency in 1965. The agency had won a number of top awards in local, regional, and national competition and its ads scored big in advertising club contests in Charlotte. Overall, it had picked up more than forty awards during the '60s, including an "ADDY" from the American Advertising Federation.

After positive response to my application, I was flown to Charlotte for an interview that went well. I joined the agency in 1970, being impressed with its atmosphere and creativity. At that time Kincaid billed a little over a million dollars. As a subsidiary of First Union Bancorp, a $2.2 billion holding company, First Union National Bank, the third largest in North Carolina, as I said was its largest account. Another Bancorp subsidiary and Kincaid account, Cameron-Brown Company, was the eleventh largest mortgage bank in the nation.

Other accounts included Belk Stores Service in New York; Buena Vista, a Walt Disney Productions distributor; and Hunter Jersey Farms, a dairy products marketer.

The agency also handled Public Service Company of North Carolina, a natural gas utility covering twenty-six counties; Jefferson Standard Broadcasting Company; Harris Teeter Supermarkets; projects for the Research Triangle Institute; and Holly-Farms Poultry Industries, the largest processor of poultry in the world.

Although it didn't occur to me at the time, it is ironic that I had honed in on an advertising agency situation that was almost identical to the one that had brought my father to Ithaca and led to his first big break. It was an in-house agency and as long as it did a first-class advertising job for its owner and subsidiaries, it was given carte blanche to pursue other clients and sources of revenue.

I was brought in as vice president of marketing and account management, and the job included media management, so I had six people reporting to me. I was also put in charge of new business. As such, I worked under Charlie with my creative director partner, Jim Pringle, to come up with a mission statement that would separate us from the crowded agency field in this rapidly growing state. When it was finished, it said, in part:

We believe a creative idea that does not lock securely into a client marketing problem is mere invention, novelty or difference, because our basic test of success is the degree to which we can help our accounts grow and profit.

We challenge ourselves to create a total personality that is uniquely right for a given product or service. We believe a good ad is one person talking to another and saying the most meaningful thing in the most positive way at the most appropriate time.

If we speak singularly, our customer listens. Otherwise, he doesn't. That's why we understand the person we are talking directly to before trying to impress him with our own or the company's views about a product.

We believe that it's important to remember that everyday people go out to buy products because they like the style of the advertiser.

And believe what he has to say. To make them feel we offer something they have wanted all their lives. But just never heard of before.

Our small agency was loaded with professionals, and we even recruited talented people away from other prestigious agencies including Cargill, Wilson & Acree in Richmond and Charlotte; Doyle Dane Bernbach in New York; McCann-Erickson in Atlanta; and Foote, Cone & Belding in Chicago. Within a year, we brought in six new accounts and increased our billing by 20 percent.

One of the new accounts was First Mortgage Insurance Co, in Greensboro, NC, licensed in twenty-one states and the fourth-largest underwriter of mortgage guarantee insurance in the country. Others were Triton Investment Corp, a McDonald's franchisee, and Gaston County Dyeing Machine Co. in Mt. Holly, NC, a manufacturer of textile dyeing, bleaching, extracting and drying machinery in eighty countries around the world.

Our television commercials for Hunter Dairy and Holly Farms and our "Let's Make Tomorrow Together" campaign for First Union, including a song recorded by The Young Carolinians and a version sung by Harry Belafonte, won top national awards. We combined broadcasting with a massive billboard buy (my second outdoor advertising encounter after creating billboards for the Ford Motor Dealers Association at JWT) with our "Tomorrow Together" message covering every highway leading into North Carolina. The song also became the theme song of many North Carolina high school proms, and I was told the campaign gave our competitor, North Carolina National Bank, fits.

This was confirmed when I met the former VP and director of public policy for NationsBank in Charlotte, who worked for North Carolina National Bank at the time before it became NationsBank. He remembered the campaign and told me he hated it. When my daughter graduated from The University of North Carolina at Chapel Hill, she joined NationsBank before it became Bank of America, so she ended up "working for the enemy." This is ironic because First Union, where I was employed, ended up merging with Wachovia, my father's primary bank throughout his media business career before becoming Wells Fargo.

While in Charlotte, I also served on the public relations committee of the Charlotte Chamber of Commerce, and working at Kincaid was great, continuing the satisfaction I felt during my seven years at JWT. During my time at the agency, I was fortunate to meet and work with prominent North Carolina businessmen such as Dan Cameron, Hargrove "Skipper" Bowles, and Ed Crutchfield.

When I had come to Charlotte, we bought our first house with my profit sharing from JWT in a place called Robinson Woods. It had a small stream in the woods behind the house, and my young son was as attracted to the water as he was growing up. It may have been overkill, but to keep him from toddling near the stream alone, particularly after a heavy rain, I told him there were packs of wild animals in the woods. At night, when we would tuck him into bed, he would look at us wide-eyed, mumbling, "Dere woofs in duh woods," but at least he slept well and it didn't translate into nightmares.

But a nightmare was pending for me and fate set me up for perhaps the most momentous decision of my life. It led to my leaving Kincaid Advertising in 1971, and shortly after Jim Pringle, who I knew had been planning it, also left to start his own agency in Atlanta. A year later, Kincaid was bought by Cargill Wilson & Acree, then the South's largest ad agency and a subsidiary of Doyle Dane Bernbach.

In 1973, Ed Crutchfield, First Union's marketing director and primary contact with our agency, became, at the age of thirty-two, its president. At that time he was the youngest president of a major bank in the United States. Crutchfield took the assets of the bank from $5 billion to over $250 billion, retiring the year before First Union merged with Wachovia in 2001 and before it became Wells Fargo.

A REQUEST TO RETURN

The act of writing is the act of discovering what you believe.

—David Hare

As much as I was enjoying my first year at Kincaid, the offer from my father to come to work for him couldn't have come at a worse time.

His first call took me by surprise, and it conveyed a mixed message. It seemed he was trying to lure me to Ithaca and at the same time talk me out of making the move. He offered me the role of his administrative assistant, and while he was describing the job, he was also deprecating it. There was no question that a position was open, and that he had been looking for someone to fill it. But because of his aversion to nepotism, he made it clear he had a concern about the reactions from his business associates, particularly Johnnie Babcock, whom I liked and respected.

He told me that he couldn't put me in a line position without some working experience in his business, and he laid down the rules if I took the job. He said I would have to keep my reserve up, my mouth shut, and my emotions down. He warned me that I'd have to work long hours and earn my own respect. I was already doing the former, and had already earned the latter, and as we talked, I could tell both of us felt this job relationship, and its ramifications, would be a difficult path to set out upon.

How much respect can you earn as the son of, and an errand boy for, the boss, doing his every bidding, without the freedom to do anything on your own? I suspected my mother might have been behind the offer. But here I was with two hard-earned university degrees and successful management experience with two fine advertising agencies. I told him I would think about it. I had been discussing the possibility of moving to Atlanta with my creative counterpart at Kincaid to start our own agency. We had earned the reputation in the South by that time to be able to do it. I had no intention of taking the job my father had described.

Before I entertained any further thought about it, he called back a week later with a second offer—the job as general manager of his outdoor division, a spot where I would be running a business, not just a member of his staff.

For a brief period I struggled with the idea of returning to Ithaca. I decided to sit down and list the pros and cons of joining my father. Of course, back then I did not know as much about the difficulty of being the Son of a Boss in general so I was not fully aware of what things might be like in a long-term business relationship with a father, mine in particular.

I started with salary, which was to be only a couple of hundred dollars a year more than I was already making. No huge incentive there, but I considered the trade adequate since I really wasn't motivated by money. Looking at overall compensation, I was told there would be an incentive of 1 percent of the gross operating profit increase, but no profit-sharing, and was told that there would be no salary review for one year from the end of the year in which I joined, when it would start on an annual basis. I had a company car with Kincaid and was to be provided with one with Park Outdoor, so that was a wash.

On insurance, Kincaid provided me with a $100,000 life insurance policy; Park Outdoor would provide only $5,000, which would cost me 65¢ a month per $1,000. The medical insurance was provided by both jobs but totally paid for at Kincaid. At Park, it would cost $18.50 a month. A negative there.

The fact that I would be returning to the town I grew up in was not that appealing, and I was told I would be doing so without being able to buy a house for a trial period of at least a year. I had a house in Charlotte and the tax deduction that went along with owning it. A move to Ithaca would also put me into a higher cost of living, renting a house with two kids, two cats, and one dog. I was also faced with the time pressure of selling the house I had. He said he would pay for the move.

My father, encouragingly, said the job would put me into a management position, but I was already in one. I had worked for years to earn it and I already had people reporting to me. He said it would heavily involve sales. I was never a high-pressure salesman, although I could put together blow-out sales pitches when I had something to sell, and I had been selling advertising campaigns for years.

In my advertising field I was working with people who were as bright, or brighter than me, and I loved the give-and-take. My father said I would have to remain aloof, as the officer in charge, from people who reported to me. No socializing with the troops. That was not my style. There was very little in his job description that fit my lifestyle and the way I enjoyed working with people.

My father argued that it was a chance to learn the realistic side of business, but I don't know what he thought I'd been doing for the past seven years. In outdoor, I would be competing with experts in their own field. I would be out of mine, and I didn't need a failure on my record. It was a big risk with no guarantee. I held the cards in the advertising field, and I would be going into a new field with a lot of cards stacked against me. As a novice in outdoor, I would be under tremendous pressure to perform, as my father made sure to point out.

I also knew, having worked with him before, that he was strongly bottom-line oriented, and from his experience rightfully so. He said he kept score by the money, whereas I was more creatively and socially motivated and people-oriented. I saw where that could be a problem. He said creative was to be secondary to management, and people were secondary to profit. My father had already told me he thought by his standards I was not as logical or realistic as I should be, and he felt I was too emotional. I was more human than automaton, and I couldn't change that, at least not at that stage of my life. I remembered how tough he had been to me in the past, and I had the right to be gun-shy.

I had always lived my own life, and I had reached the point where I didn't need anybody telling me what to do. I could honestly not feel I would be comfortable in the job, performing under my father's standards, especially when I was at the peak of my current career. I had learned too much in the business world to not try to apply it in Ithaca, and I knew that could be a problem. In the job I had, I at least had a final say.

He wanted me to try it for a year, but I felt one year would not be long enough to make it work. I also knew that one year could disrupt my current career, remembering that he criticized the campaign Kincaid had done for First Union, which had increased loans by 30 percent to young Carolinians, and profits in the bank by 80 percent in six months. It also won one of the top eight Bank Marketing Association awards in the nation, and this, plus the success of other campaigns we had done, filled me with pride and satisfaction.

I also remembered that when I worked for my father, there was little rapport. It was a mechanical relationship that held a degree of criticism on almost everything I did. This continued in both my personal and business life for the seven years I was out on my own. I remembered that during the years I lived in Rye, he was in New York City constantly but never once came to visit. When I lived in Charlotte, in my first home, although he was frequently in Raleigh, he also opted not to take time for a visit.

He said I would be expected to be the first to arrive and the last to leave, to take short lunches, to spend two or three days and one or two nights a week on the road. In regard to this travel, he also said he expected me to be very "circumspect" on expense accounts. He also said he expected me to keep a Dictaphone with me at all times and to work around the clock.

I was already working long hours into the night, and sometimes I was tired the next day and I knew that wouldn't go over well with him. Overall, the fit just wasn't right. My father told me not to come if I had any doubts, and I had plenty of them. They were justifiable at the time, and I could honestly say that I felt it would be an uncomfortable situation. I had doubts I could do things by his standards, and I told him so.

One of the things that disturbed me the most was that he said my relationship with him and my mother would have to be cold and impersonal—like ice. It was to be a clear *separation of power*; only later would I fully appreciate the consequences. But the fact that he pointed this out so clearly made me think, again, that perhaps he *was* feeling some pressure from my mother.

He went on to say there would be business problems to solve but that I would have to solve any personal problems on my own. Otherwise, he said I would be "involving him" outside of the job. I didn't have any personal problems at the time, but where do you turn to for help, except to your parents, when you need it? I liked the relationship the way it was then. I certainly had not received any personal help, but at least I had a father and he had a son, and I felt it might not be that way if we worked together.

Having been the object most of my life of my father's "talk sheets," I prepared my own answer to him. I had learned very well how to work up a talk sheet and had used them effectively during my business career.

I called him on the phone and this is what I said:

"I've not had much sleep. You've given me an extremely difficult choice.

"In weighing alternatives, what came to forefront was my need to leave J. Walter Thompson to further my career at a higher level, not as somebody whose career peaked out after seven years in the business.

"The opportunity you offer me is challenging, but I want to dedicate my efforts in a field I know and continue my all-out exploration of every opportunity the advertising agency business may offer.

"It may not work, but I can never say I didn't try.

"In a year or two, Kincaid will be on the map or it won't. Whatever is accomplished will be significantly attributable to my efforts.

"The management experience you offer could be valuable and maturing. In working with you, I am as convinced as you are about the danger of nepotism. I know I would report to Johnnie Babcock, not you, and agree with Johnnie that working for my father could result in an arbitrary and necessarily low salary. I'm worth what Kincaid is paying me now and may not be worth that to you for several years.

"In outdoor, I think I could be a good salesman, but I might not be. I know I can sell corporate images, marketing plans, and creative ideas to advertising clients who hired us for our advice, but maybe not billboards to new customers through cold calls.

"In my field I am already a competent and proven manager. I would rather learn and develop my capabilities in a situation that puts no pressure on the two of us. If I don't make it here, neither of us will be embarrassed. We would be if I failed working for you in the job you offer.

"I know what it took you to offer me this spot. I'm deeply moved that you think enough of me to do it. My major concern is that my refusal will lead you to shut the door on the possibility of working together in the future. I hope this won't happen. I'm sure you can understand."

And so I turned down a second, but this time upgraded, offer from my father.

CHAPTER 16
BACK TO ITHACA

Lemme down,
There's a lot of us been pushed around,
Red, yellow, black, white and brown,
With a tear their own.
Oh, can't you see,
While you're picking on society,
That the leaves on your family tree
Are calling you to come home?

In your head,
You don't believe what the Good Book said,
You're gonna strike out now instead.
'Cause the world's been unkind,
But through thick and thin,
Whatever shape your heart is in,
You only have one next of kin.
Better keep 'em in mind.

—From the song "Keeper of the Castle"
by Dennis Lambert and Brian Potter[7]

"Better keep 'em in mind" came to mind from *The Four Tops* again in this song a year after I moved to Charlotte. My earlier premonition that my mother's role behind the scenes of my father's offer was confirmed when a letter came from her saying that if I did not take the offer, I would be passing up a great opportunity to return to the family.

I was thirty-two going into the 1970s and I joined my father the following year. The music of the '70s, still popular today, will always be in my blood, and as the song said, family is family, and kin are kin. Considering my mother's veiled invitation, the leaves of my family tree were calling me to come home.

There were several reasons I changed my mind and decided to make the move, among which was knowing it looked like Kincaid agency would be losing our creative director. I also wanted to see if I could try bringing the now three generations of our Park family together. And, I also was determined to prove to my father that I had enough practical business sense to handle anything that was thrown at me. I never anticipated what he would throw at me to make the job almost impossible, and to say my wife was apprehensive about the move was an understatement. Tetlow's premonitions would prove to be correct.

But after long days of agonizing, and to the chagrin of my family, I decided to give it a try. Some anonymous person wrote "What happens first is easy. It's what comes later that's much harder." Amen to that observation.

When I came back to Ithaca at age thirty-three, I had already lived in sixteen different houses, apartments, boarding rooms, inns, hotels, and dorms up and down the East Coast. Four in Chapel Hill, two in Raleigh, and one in Charlotte, NC, one each in Queens, White Plains and Port Chester, NY, along with Perrine, FL, Lawrenceville, NJ, and four earlier in Ithaca before my final return. This did not include another three moves to be made in Ithaca *after* my return, but it was good to think about settling in one place for a while.

Now I was about to take on a significant position in one of my father's core businesses. In 1963, in the midst of his broadcasting expansion, my father's real estate division, RHP Incorporated, began the acquisition of some 3,000 outdoor billboards, under companies he named Park Outdoor Advertising and Park Displays. He felt outdoor, being an out-of-home medium, reinforced and served as a perfect complement to television, and outdoor was an attractive investment due to its depreciation contribution to cash flow.

Park Outdoor Advertising, Inc., owned outdoor posters and painted boards in dozens of cities in New York and Pennsylvania; Park Displays also owned outdoor posters and painted boards in other New York and Pennsylvania counties. In 1969 he bought more billboards and formed Park Outdoor Advertising, Inc. of Scranton–Wilkes-Barre, Inc., based in Scranton, PA. These were the earlier three companies Pops brought me back to Ithaca to manage, the survivors of which I own today.

When I came back to Ithaca to take over the outdoor division, with 3,000 billboards it was among the top twenty in the United States. I never had to ask the question that our friend, Sam Johnson, found most difficult to ask in *Carnauba,* his brilliant and moving movie tribute to his father: "Does my father love his business more than he loves me?"

I knew that answer from the get-go, and it didn't bother me. I knew very little about managing an outdoor business but just wanted to work hard and do a good job to continue the success I had in the jobs I held during my advertising career. With the kind of work ethic ingrained in me after seven years in advertising, I figured that handling a new challenge would be a piece of cake.

Among other things, I was buoyed up by a letter my father shared with me from then North Carolina Senator Hargrove "Skipper" Bowles, Jr. dated November 1, 1971, which read, "My good friend, Dan Cameron, told me about seeing you in New York. He also gave me the news about Roy, Jr., having joined your firm in the outdoor advertising division. I had the opportunity to see Roy, Jr., when he worked for Kincaid and the quality was evident. He was the best thing in the agency...I know it makes you mighty proud he was successful on his own and has now decided to join your organization."

But again, I had no idea of what I was getting into. Johnnie Babcock's following account about life with my father is, if anything, more objective than mine:

TASKMASTER

"Roy Park was a tireless worker who drove his executives hard. He was a very tough man to work for.

"Proceedings at a typical Monday morning management meeting at the height of his business career describe how he directed his men and illuminate facets of Park's complex personal profile. To neighbors and casual acquaintances, he was simply Ithaca's wealthiest and most enigmatic citizen. To those who worked for him, he was a hard-driving taskmaster. Described by the local newspaper at this stage of his career as a media mogul, this owner and chief executive was in absolute control. No operating detail escaped him. Nor was there any doubt as to who was in charge. The weekly 8 AM management meeting got his key people to the big board table in his office a half-hour before normal business hours. A printed agenda covered reports to be made and left plenty of room for Park's directives and criticism. Earlier, each person attending the meeting had received detailed minutes of the last management meeting detailing various accomplishments, failures and statistics about a TV or radio station, a newspaper or an outdoor billboard location.

"The atmosphere in the room? Uneasy apprehension by some, tension for all. Monday meetings took place during the height of Park's media-acquisition drive. To put to rest any hopes that his quest for more wealth might dilute his ardor for micromanagement, he preceded the agenda with pointed personal remarks.

"While his staff indulged in family life over the weekend, Roy spent his time hard at work in his sequestered office in his Cayuga Heights home. On Saturday his administrative assistant, Ben Williams, watched him open the mail carried to his house from the company post office box by staff aide Oscar Harrell. Ben took notes for Park's use during the upcoming week. On Sundays, Park emptied the box himself, making it risky for company employees to use the mail for personal correspondence between them, or company postage. He opened every envelope, marked personal or not. He savored letters of complaint, sensing that they might never have come to light had he not intercepted them.

"Roy would take up a letter to one of his department heads who had yet to see the new mail, and if it was a complaint, read it aloud to the group. More often than not, the intended recipient was summarily dismissed from the meeting to go to his office and return immediately with an answer that would satisfy the writer, or him.

"Remember Park's student partner in the magazine business at NC State? Signing his letters "Pea Vine," he often criticized the program content of a Park TV station. Park took pains to answer him personally but not until there was an exhaustive investigation into the circumstances. This personal gesture as an entrepreneur was meant to show clearly that he was the in-charge owner-manager. His reaction nonetheless demoralized the involved department head and left him with a headache or worse.

"Now ready for the agenda, Park would address the remaining management staff: Johnnie Babcock, broadcasting division; at the time, Conrad Fink, newspapers; Bob Burns, real estate, Tommy Thomas, chief financial officer; Roger Turner, radio; Roy Park, Jr., (after he joined the company in outdoor); Dave Feldman, outdoor and real estate financial director; and his personal assistant, Ben Williams, who kept detailed minutes.

"Park should have invented the PC and the Internet, but it was way before Al Gore was around to claim that honor. Anyway, his mechanical aptitude was limited to his cigar clipper and winding watches from his antique wristwatch collection. He rarely typed anything and had such a whispery vocal delivery to his dictating machine that only his personal secretary could understand and reproduce the words on paper.

"Park wanted, demanded, and received hard-copy information about each of his properties. Many of the reports now available through sophisticated electronic gear were gathered the old-fashioned way for the boss. Park's accountability device: the teletype that Park had familiarized himself with during his early newspaper and publishing experiences. The home office machine chattered day and night, feeding the owner concise data from each of his far-flung businesses. Unless attended to hourly, the scroll of paper cranked out would flood the entire hallway off the elevator to his fourth floor office.

"Over the noon hour was an especially busy time in the tele-type room. Park wanted reports by midday to assure him that the key people were hard at work at each place of business. Bank deposits for the day were included, as were disbursements. The bank balance was compared to the day before. As cash built up at a location, Tommy Thomas swept the account and transferred balances judged beyond immediate need to the corporate account at Wachovia Bank in Raleigh. Park's ambitious purchase of broadcast stations and newspapers was accomplished with what proved to be a very acceptable asset: cash. As explained earlier, when Park merged his Duncan Hines business with Procter & Gamble on a tax-free exchange of stock, he became a very large holder of the company's stock. Those shares were the leverage to secure large cash commitments from big banks to make his cash acquisitions. Large loan balances were whittled away by the positive cash flow from owned properties.

"After summarizing daily the teletype cash reports, Ben Williams gathered each location's sales report. The various sources of revenue were reported and compared to budget for like categories. As the month advanced, sales booked were expressed as a percentage of the budget for the current and two advanced months, and same period a year earlier. If on the twentieth, sales were 60 percent of budget for the current month, Park demanded to know why and to challenge whether the shortfall could be sold in the few remaining days. Many of my station visits were to address and help repair such shortfalls. The target percentage of operating profit in television before amortization, depreciation and interest was 45 percent. Some of his larger network affiliated TV stations returned more than 50 percent of their net sales as operating profit.

"After cash and sales, Park placed great reliance on his own invention, the head count report. It was summarized for him from each property compared to budget. If raises had been granted since the last report, they were individually reviewed and usually roundly criticized even though listed as budget-approved actions. As he repeatedly admonished, even a five-dollar weekly increase adds up to a $520 additional cost after two years. An unauthorized raise, perhaps to save a resignation of a popular newscaster, resulted in an order for the Ithaca supervisor to travel to the location immediately to upbraid the general manager and possibly reverse that action. There was little wiggle room when it came to employee compensation. Park rarely examined in detail the professional credentials of a station supervisor. His evaluation relied on two prime conditions: that the prospect was available and affordable. That left plenty of room to let some bums and thieves slip in.

"A strict lecture closed most management meetings, with advice to respond quickly and positively to the various actions agreed on by him at the meeting. Minutes circulated that same day underscored commitments for action that would be grist for the next regular meeting. Monday was not a happy day at Park Broadcasting."

MY FIRST WARNING

I think one of the most amusing stories involved in my coming back to work for my father is the saga of my company car. Because of his antipathy to "nepotism" but knowing the spread-out territory I would be required to cover, he reluctantly came to the realization that I would need a company car. But he didn't want it to appear ostentatious, and he worried about what his other executives would think. None of them had company cars since their travel was all by air.

As I have said all along, I had no problem with keeping a low profile but the extent to which my father went was a monument to obscurity. In order to achieve the desired effect, he called on his friend Bill Zikakis, one of the largest car dealers in Ithaca at the time. As Bill tells it, his first prerequisite was that the car be midsized, low-priced and of a subdued coloration, in this case black.

Pops's second requirement to eliminate ostentatious show was that the tires not look expensive. Therefore he requested black walls. Keep in mind my father went through the generation where white walls cost a handsome premium, and he was apparently unaware that they were now standard equipment, and that black wall tires not only had to be special-ordered, but cost more. Bill says he tried to explain this to him, but to no avail. So, in order to diminish the appearance of my company automobile, my father paid a handsome premium for four black wall tires.

Then he asked Bill to equip the car with an AM radio only, preferably one that broadcast nothing but news. Zikakis again explained that all cars then came equipped with AM/FM radios and that it would be an extra cost, and almost impossible, to locate and install an AM-only radio. It was obvious my father didn't want me tooling around New York State and Pennsylvania listening to music, and aside from listening solely to news on the hour, he apparently didn't want me to have the radio on at all. It was his preference I be occupied on my Dictaphone or driving in silent contemplation of ways to increase the outdoor bottom line.

His fourth requirement was that the car have a manual transmission. I would have had no problem with that, having driven a stick shift car all through my college days, but the model he ordered only came with an automatic transmission. Manual shifts mostly came in high-priced sports cars, and it took some time for Bill to point out that all American cars at that time came off the assembly line with automatic transmissions.

At any rate, when the special order car finally arrived, I had trouble finding it in the parking lot since it was so cloaked with invisibility. The good news, surprising as it was, was that my father *did* provide me with a parking place for the car adjacent to our offices. At one point I was pretty sure that he would want me to park the car on the outskirts of the city so no one could see that I had a company car, and walk back and forth to work from some remote location.

STEPPING INTO THE OUTDOOR QUAGMIRE

I knew outdoor was a time-tested, powerful, strong and creative advertising medium. I wrote plenty of outdoor copy for Ford and Pan Am at JWT, and we bought it as well for First Union at Kincaid. But I knew nothing about the technicalities of how the boards got there in the first place: the aspects of leasing and zoning approvals, state licensing, construction, maintenance, production, etc. The closest I'd been to that was the Burma Shave signs of my youth spaced evenly along a farm roadside or highway, for which the owner probably picked up a couple of bills a year, and at a time zoning and DOT restrictions didn't exist.

Even back then, Burma Shave conveyed traffic safety and DWI messages, to wit: "At Intersections/Look Each Way/A Harp Sounds Nice/But Is Hard to Play." I also remember, "The Midnight Ride/Of Paul For Beer/Led To A Warmer/Hemisphere" and "Car In Ditch/Driver In Tree/The Moon Was Full/And So Was He." Burma Shave even snuck in a little self-promotion along with their safety messages as in: "Passing School Zone/Take It Slow/ Let Your Little/Shavers Grow."

I soon learned there are a lot of easier things to do than to run an outdoor advertising company in New York Sate. Despite the fact that tourism is one of the state's key industries, and billboards are essential for travelers to find where to eat, sleep, shop and look, government regulations and zoning in New York were, and still are, extraordinarily strict.

At the time I took over, the outdoor division had lost or was on the verge of losing some 600 boards to neglect, competitive lease jumping, zoning changes, and government condemnation. The federal government still had funding under the 1965 Highway Beautification Act known as Lady Bird's Bill to pay for the removal of billboards, so condemnation proceedings were taking boards left and right. It was almost impossible to replace units that were removed because of the strict zoning in most of the territories where we operated, and the state of New York was loaded with environmentalists who were pushing for even stricter zoning against billboards. We had our problems with college and activist environmental vandalism as well.

At the time, there was adequate Department of Transportation funding to build new roads, and this continued over the next twenty years. The board takedowns caused by road construction created further losses, and changing traffic patterns made delivering accurate traffic counts more difficult. Upstate New York's five months of severe weather is hardly conducive to maintaining and servicing the units, inflicting wind and storm damage to the boards along with freezing temperatures on the men. Other natural disasters had contributed to the condition with the floods in Wilkes-Barre, Binghamton, and Elmira, which put much of our inventory under water. The managers informed me that six more boards had just fallen down from neglect the month before I joined the company. In addition, under New York State law, a nonconforming board, which most of our inventory was, could not be repaired or refurbished for more than 15% of the value of the board. Since the value of these old boards was so low, repairing or upgrading anything became a difficult logistical problem.

These were some of the long-term uncontrollable problems when I took over, on top of the entire outdoor division being in poor shape to begin with, having been assembled mainly through the acquisition of antique billboards from a variety of companies and had never been upgraded or repaired. The age of the boards was a major problem. When I took over, the Park Outdoor plant consisted of boards purchased at various times by my father from Donnelly, General Outdoor, and Max Andrews. The Max Andrews boards were more than forty years old when we bought them, and the others weren't much younger.

Except for the Elmira division, where some minimum maintenance had taken place over the past few years, hardly anything had been done, and most of the boards were built on telephone poles with green latticework underneath. In addition, I inherited untrained manpower and was faced with no reserve of professional billposters, construction people, or painters. New production, sales, and management people had to be hired, and they all had to be trained.

I remember riding the boards (in outdoor lingo, the "plant") in what we called our *Western Division,* headquartered in Jamestown. I saw flagging paper, rusted panels, and leaning billboards. I saw that even if the space on these old structures could be sold to advertisers, many couldn't be posted with paper since they were in such bad shape.

One board I photographed during that trip foreshadowed doom. It was back from the highway behind a rise in the ground, and it had begun to sink behind the edge of the ravine. It bore a Ford advertising message with a doomsday bearded messenger holding a sign reading THE END IS HERE.

The condition of the plant still wasn't the worst of it. When I began looking into the management of the company, I found there were uncollectibles on the books, in addition to receivables that were three to four years old that had not been written off. The inventories of existing signs had also been understated, with only one inventory report that had been spot-checked in recent months.

The shape of our inventory had caused business from national advertisers to plummet, with all of the major liquor and tobacco companies abandoning Park. We also had no demographic information or traffic audit verification for the boards. At that time, we didn't belong to the Traffic Audit Bureau (TAB) and, in fact, had no association memberships at all. I urged that we hire KLAD, key sales rep firm at the time for outdoor located in New York City, but the decision was pushed off for three months.

I also found that the past managers had not reported boards that had come down. One of my first projects was to see how many we had lost in the past year. In addition, many of the old land leases, which had not been properly negotiated or monitored, were expiring or coming up for renewal. We discovered also that some former managers had given away our boards to property owners, although we couldn't prove it because the leasing and inventory records were so inaccurate. They also were selling by making deals, some of the trades benefiting them personally, misusing petty cash and postponing maintenance and repair.

The decline in national business had also resulted in manpower cuts, which had an immediate effect on the condition of the billboards. All of this added up to a steady decline in our capacity, the number of outdoor units we had left to sell.

Riding the markets took several days, from one end to the other. While riding, I realized how labor-intensive the division was going to be to run. The same inventory concentrated in one market, or in a smaller geographic area, would have required far less manpower and brought in much more profit.

In short, my timing for taking over the outdoor operation was just plain bad. The "beautification" money from the government that was forcing us to remove our most productive billboards should have been used to upgrade the boards. But my father was putting it into his real estate parent company below the operating profit line, while maintenance costs continued and were included as operating expenses, thereby reducing an already sparse operating profit.

The outdoor division was also being charged with "management fees" and rent, with little legitimate basis and no explanation offered on the way these amounts were calculated. It was just another way to pull money out of the outdoor division into the parent real estate company. Seeing the way it had been run, I began to realize the future for the outdoor division, squeezed as it was, was mainly a tax advantage. As a poor sister of the RHP Incorporated real estate division, it also provided active income versus the real estate's passive income, which kept the real estate holding company from being declared a personal holding company. The passive income from the stock portfolio and real estate, which made up most of RHP Incorporated had to be offset with active income from outdoor advertising. The only other "active" income was minimal and came from my father's orange groves and timberland.

Back to the farm. Of sorts. Pops visiting one of his Florida orange groves.

It was evident that the job would make it difficult for me to function professionally, let alone succeed. The challenges were massive, and having worked with my father before, I knew that I would be swimming upstream. This made it easy for my father not only to keep me under his thumb but also to thwart any attempts I could make to explain the difficulty of my position to my mother.

Of course, the dark picture he painted of me to her was further motivated by our differing philosophies, the natural result of my trying to run the outdoor division at more than a survival level.

Little did I expect to step into an atmosphere where what I did was nitpicked and put down. As I said, my father claimed a strong view against nepotism, which prevailed in his dealings with me, even though I made every attempt to keep a low profile and mind my own business. He deliberately went out of his way to try to make me look like something to simply be tolerated. The implication was that I couldn't get a job anywhere else.

Worst of all, the harder I tried to do the job that *needed* to be done, the more we fought. And the more we fought, the easier it was for him to justify painting me to my mother with a black brush. It would have been a shock to anyone's ego, and as the attacks continued in daily doses, I began to feel like a voodoo doll. His implication that I was a creative type lacking in financial ability gave him an excuse to use the pins. His invitation to join the company resulted in a trap that snapped shut when I lost my independence.

He interpreted attempts at rational discussion as arguing, and any disagreements were treated as rebellious. In time, I found myself subject to what I despised as much as anyone—short emotional outbursts—which only reinforced his subjective judgment of me. This did not happen all at once, but slowly, over time. Since my father despised nepotism so much, I wondered, why had he brought me into his business? It may have been my mother's influence, but it was a debilitating change in the career path on which I had started. While my father's nightmares during my youth woke him up, I couldn't awaken from mine. My nightmares continued sporadically throughout the next seventeen years.

FIRST ASSIGNMENTS

When I was hired, Pops was having problems with the person who was his CFO at the time. Pops preferred a CFO who would nod his head up and down, not back and forth, and this CFO did not hesitate to argue with him. The individual also combined his work-hard with a play-hard lifestyle, which my father found distasteful.

The CFO's second in command, Dave Feldman, was to be my teammate in the outdoor division, in addition to his responsibilities for my father's real estate holdings. The first morning I reported for work, my father told me to pay a visit to Mr. Feldman's office and "establish control." In effect, I was to go down and blow him out, since Pops felt he was too close to the CFO who had hired him. It was the first time I had ever been told to blow out someone I hadn't even met. But, I gave it a shot, and as Dave Feldman reports:

"My first anticipated meeting with Roy was with a guarded sense that as the only son of the owner, he was brought back to Ithaca to eventually take over for his father. Although I had a great feeling of loyalty to the CFO who hired me, I realized that if I was going to work together with Roy in the outdoor division, I needed to dispel any trepidation or feeling of a lack of cooperation that Roy might have with me.

"Roy quickly learned that by working together we could overcome any negative aspects of the poorest part of his father's holdings. Despite his father's continual portrayal of Roy as merely a 'creative, dreamer type,' with no financial awareness, I quickly found that Roy indeed had a good feel for business and financial planning, as well as for organization. In fact, his creative ability combined with his business knowledge was a great combination, one that I envied and still do to this day.

"We made an excellent team, and I feel that we learned from each other. I also had learned that the best way to address his father's timetable for delivering reports, budgets, and other operational demands was to politely, but firmly, tell him that we can't have an answer on a request until we had time to *research and then deliver*. This was unlike other people on his management team, who out of fear promised that they could deliver right away, hoping Mr. Park would forget. That was their biggest mistake, since he forgot nothing."

A second assignment I was given was longer-term: to learn as much as I could from the man who was supervising the outdoor division, and then to fire him when I was ready. That put me in a Judas position, knowing that the closer we worked together, and the quicker I learned, the sooner my teacher would lose his job.

The person I was to work with was a sly old fox. He was the only man I knew who could get credit four times for selling a single contract. Here's how it worked. First he would get a call from longtime cronies in the advertising agencies and buying services in New York such as the National Outdoor Advertising Bureau saying they were about to issue some contracts for Park Outdoor.

Next he would tell the management committee that he needed to go down to New York City to see if he could bring in some national business. Already knowing what it entailed, he would spell out the contract dollars he "hoped" he could sell and bring back home. In the meantime, the contracts were already signed, but his buddies delayed mailing them so he could hand-carry them back to Ithaca and take full credit.

Later he would call from New York and say he was about to lock up the business after his sales presentation, that everything looked good and with some luck he would have the contracts in hand in a day or two. After a suitable interval, he would finally present the contracts at the management meeting, peeling them off one by one and laying them on the table to earn that fourth (self-satisfying) pat on the back. Despite everything, when I retired him, I felt terrible. The old fox got his gold watch, but I never collected my thirty pieces of silver.

CONTINUING THE CLEANUP

When I took over outdoor, it employed sixty-two people in two states, and I was on the road four out of five days for years. I recruited, hired, and trained personnel, made sales calls and collections, and met the principals of all the major accounts. I brought in national business from Ford, Kodak, Seagram's, the Army and Marines, Alka-Seltzer, Black Velvet, Chevrolet, Corby's, Delta Airlines, 7-Up, National Distillers, Christian Brothers, Fleischmann, Heublein, Genesee, and Rolling Rock, as well as all the tobacco brands: R.J. Reynolds, Philip Morris, Lorillard, American Tobacco, and Brown &Williamson. I took local sales up 30 percent, held expenses down, and raised our conversion ratio: the amount carried down to the operating profit line out of each dollar of sales.

My father, who had seen fairly steady operating profit under my management from 1971 to 1975, watched it drop to $250,000 in 1976. He was aware that the increased maintenance expense caused the drop. I had tried to clean up a tragically neglected plant, and since we didn't have money left over to put into capital improvement, the expense for cosmetic cleanup added to our overhead.

When I took over, there had been little effort to obtain leases from new locations, and certainly none to install new structures at better locations. Why put up new boards when you couldn't sell the ones that were already there? Adding to other problems, the company had a dearth of sales and promotional material. The maps showing our billboards' locations were literally hand-drawn, with no attention to scale, and locations were noted along the sketched roads with circles or dots. There was no indication whether the board was illuminated and which way it faced along the road. Our rate structure was loosely and unprofessionally defined, and barely adhered to as long as a sale could be made.

As I said, one of the first things I did after I was hired was to ride the 3,000 boards that my father owned, spread out in a 25,000-square-mile area. It was a depressing job that took about two months. At that time, my sales manager was a former pilot, and he drove the car like he was flying a plane. I made a point of taking a photo of every board we owned, and he would slow down from cruising at 60 mph to a well-crafted landing alongside the road just long enough for me to snap a picture, and then would effortlessly blend back into traffic again.

After I had pictures of all the boards, most of which were built in the 1940s, I issued instructions to remove the old-fashioned latticework that hid the telephone pole uprights. My second instruction was to paint all the uprights black. If they were black I felt they would fade into the scenery. Artists tell me the predominant color on earth is black. Any time you doubt it, look into the woods, the buildings around you or anything else in your line of sight. Squint your eyes and you will see that most areas surrounding the things that stand out fade to black. It's the shadow effect, and I knew a lot about that.

At the time I took over the outdoor operation also, few signs carried our Park Outdoor logo. Later the logo IDs became required by New York state law. My photographic portfolio covering every board we owned included instructions pasted under each billboard on what needed to improve its appearance and salability. Showing it to my father and pointing out the poor condition along with the missing logos, I could tell what he was thinking. I give him credit for an ironic sense of humor when he said, "I think that might be a good thing."

One of the worst problems was flagging paper on neglected boards that hadn't been sold and couldn't be sold in the condition they were in. Forty-year-old rusted faces that wouldn't hold paper were replaced with new faces, brush was trimmed, lights were fixed. All of this was a heavy drain on the bottom line, but the plant was slowly becoming more presentable, even if most of the upgrading was cosmetic.

About this time, I got a hand-written letter from my mother telling me that she had never seen Park Outdoor signs look so bad. Coming back from New York City, between Greene, NY, and Ithaca, she said she didn't see "one in the bunch that wasn't peeling." Her letter gave me insight into my father's modus operandi. "Get people in my organization who will work…work hard…or you'll have to make other arrangements" her letter said. "It can be done and is done all up and down the highways with other peoples' signs," she wrote. She was not telling me anything new. But the limited number of workers I inherited made only slightly more than minimum wage, and the inventory was so old and rusty it wouldn't hold the paper. The board faces needed to be replaced, not the men who posted them.

Her letter continued with her advising me to "get a chip on your shoulder with every workman you have and keep it there." She warned me not to smile or get friendly. Be an "old stone face" and "put on a hard exterior," which she said would be hard for me to do because I probably wanted them to like me. She said they must "have a fear of losing their job if it is not done well."

All this advice clearly echoed my father's thinking in his conversations with my mother, and whether she was aware of being manipulated or not, it added to my burden. Particularly coming at the same time both my father and Babcock said my *first* job was to prevent the two outdoor divisions that served this area from being *unionized*. My mother's meant-to-be-helpful advice was to "keep my distance, get out after I have had my few words, and let them know they would have to tow the mark," or I would be the one who would be blamed. But I was getting the blame already, and I knew that counter to my mother's advice, I had to work *with* the men to persuade them to vote against unionization.

My mother insisted that they must fear and respect me, but fear would drive them to unionize. I had to substitute the word "trust" for "fear," so I could begin to build a team and establish mutual respect. I also had to get some capital-improvement money so our products could be posted and sold.

The Scranton plant, consisting of roughly 1,000 12'-x-24' poster billboards and many large 14'-x-48' painted bulletins, had already been unionized by a branch of the AFL-CIO. The Teamsters out of Buffalo were trying to unionize the Binghamton and Utica operations. How could I prevent this, since it was obvious the employees held no trust in management? There was no leadership and little professionalism among the workers, with low wages and no benefits.

Plato said, "Be kind, for everyone you meet is fighting a hard battle." So while the union was spreading its propaganda in preparation for a vote, I sat down and talked to each employee, one-on-one. And I learned about the battle each was fighting and began to win their trust. They began to realize I intended to bring in a new way of doing business and a caring management that they and their families could count on in the future. Where my father welcomed turnover because it kept wages and salaries low, I wanted to build a loyal, well-cared-for cadre of employees.

This approach succeeded. When the vote was taken in each of the two operations, the unions were rejected. Now I had my hands full trying to convince my father that we had to set up a system of scheduled reviews and raises.

But though unionization failed in Utica and Binghamton, I was left with a union in the Scranton division. It had been in place for some time and was a subsidiary of the AFL-CIO. In 1973, a union contract was coming up for renewal, and by my father's standards the wage and benefit demands were excessive. After a period of negotiation and attempts to settle, the workers went on strike.

We brought in our billposters from Binghamton, Elmira, and Utica to keep the contracts posted on time and assigned our managers and sales personnel to patrol the boards to protect our billposters from threats by striking workers. The strikers followed them around with balloons filled with paint and weapons, including machetes and guns they would occasionally fire off into the air. During this perilous time, we interviewed replacement workers at a motel that served as our headquarters during the strike. As people were hired, they were trained by experienced billposters from our other divisions.

As time passed, strikers realized they were getting no pay or benefits from their union, so they voted to disband. When some of them decided to come back to work, we made a point of not firing the new workers we had hired and trained. We had promised them full-time employment when they were recruited, and we did not go back on our word. In the meantime, a number of our former employees had found other jobs, so between the new and returning employees, we ended up with a balanced and motivated workforce in Scranton. Things were looking up.

Then I had the first and one of my last management mishaps in Scranton. The general manager I inherited decided to retire. He urged me to replace him with a much younger employee he had hired in sales.

My father had a flair for sales contests, especially in outdoor, since the operation wasn't spread all over the country as his other holdings were. Pops thought sales contests got the juices flowing. Keep in mind that the majority of our business was national, so to give local a boost, the prize was a briefcase full of money to the person who brought in the most local sales. The briefcase was full, all right, but with crumpled, brand-new dollar bills packed in so tight that they would fly out and hit you in the face when the case was opened. The bills amounted to only $400 or $500.

The contest lasted a month. After three weeks, one contract after another flooded in from my newly appointed general manager in Scranton. They were long-term contracts for large painted bulletins advertising various resorts in the Poconos. They were dutifully processed by bookkeeping and the tally for the Scranton manager kept growing. When the contest ended, he won the briefcase hands down. It wasn't until then that we realized that the locations for these contracts didn't exist, or the locations were where zoning would prevent the construction of new units.

The manager already had the prize money, and other things began to pop up that didn't look right. We received late-payment notices on a car phone that had not been approved, and calls began coming in from production companies wanting to know where to send the manager's money. He had set up trade agreements with our advertisers and kickback arrangements with our suppliers.

This person was also smart enough to have an inside track: my secretary, who, unknown to me, he had been dating. So the morning Dave and I set out for Scranton to fire him, he was tipped off and waiting. I thought he was mighty casual about it after we took away the keys to his company car and called him a taxi. He said he already had a friend waiting for him, picked up his brief-case and headed for the door. But before he got out, I told him to open the briefcase. It contained copies of all our leases and sales contracts, and we confiscated everything from the briefcase that belonged to the company. Apparently he had no long-term hard feelings because ten years later he called me and asked if I wanted to get into business with him on taxicab signs.

During the first years that I ran the outdoor division, annual sales averaged $1,700,000 and operating profit ranged from $400,000 to the low of $250,000 I mentioned earlier in 1975 because of the continuing and accelerated cost of maintenance and repairs. The task was not easy. The fortune cookie I opened in a Chinese restaurant in Ithaca in 1975 reading, "Nothing seems impossible to you," hardly buoyed my spirits. You will note I quote a number of these sayings in this book, but before you think I put a lot of weight on them, it's not that. I have lunch in Chinese restaurants a lot to keep the weight off of me, and the cookies are free with the meal. Sometimes the fortunes are fun and appropriately on target, but the timing was poor on this one.

Even a vacation was hard to take. In mid-December 1975, for example, I received a note from my father saying, "Since you are in New York today and won't be back until Friday, and I'll be away on Friday, I want to tell you I am rather concerned about you taking vacations just before Christmas and just before the New Year.

"As you know, in the broadcast and newspaper business we have to work every day of the year and we have a general policy of minimizing vacations around key holidays because if the man-agement group does it, then the rest of the employees feel it's all right and they will want to do it, too," he wrote.

This prompted me to take a look at the vacation days I had taken since I joined the company in 1971, keeping in mind that I had three weeks of vacation each year at the previous agencies I had worked with. To my chagrin, I found that I had averaged a little over one week of vacation a year for the past four years. So I wrote back to my father that I had taken only five days so far in 1975 and had hoped to take the remaining two days before the end of the year, only two weeks away. I pointed out that after checking the calendars for the rest of the executives in Ithaca, they all had managed to get in two weeks each year, with the head of newspapers taking two straight weeks in September and October in addition to a trip he took to Europe earlier in the year.

ITHACA JOURNAL

ROY H. PARK JR.

United Way Taps Park

Roy H. Park Jr., vice president of RHP Inc., has been named chairman of the public relations committee for the Tompkins County United Way's 1973-74 campaign. He served previously as public relations director of the United Fund of Raleigh, N.C.

Truth be told, my father didn't like employees taking vacation, even the minimal two weeks he afforded them. He never referred to days taken as vacation, and when a person took *any of it*, he referred to that daring soul as *"being on holiday."*

Unbeknownst to me, the stage was being set for my move into another arena. As the outdoor clean-up process continued, Pops thought it would be a good idea if I also began to get more involved in the community. Although I had my hands full, I didn't disagree. In 1973, I was appointed chairman of the public relations committee of the United Way of Tompkins County.

In this capacity I worked with the campaign chairman, Paul Miller II, who was Gannett's publisher of *The Ithaca Journal* at the time. He was the son of the late Paul Miller, former president and CEO of the Gannett Corporation for 21 years and president and chairman of the Associated Press for 14, who was also my father's good friend. It was interesting that the two of us also became good friends, and it was through him that I also met and had dinner with another son of a powerful father, Steve Forbes. At any rate, we borrowed, with permission, parts of the "Let's Make Tomorrow" campaign theme I used at Kincaid for First Union in North Carolina, and it was equally successful in Ithaca.

I also joined the Tompkins County Chamber of Commerce and in that capacity found myself with a daunting task. As a

Second Generation Sons: Paul Miller II and I have continued over the years the lasting friendship our fathers had before us.

member of its public relations committee in 1975, I was named bid chairman and publicity director, heading the project of bringing the Junior Olympics to Ithaca. We were successful, and with the help of Cornell University and Ithaca College, Ithaca hosted the Junior Olympics the following year, for which I was given the Chamber of Commerce's Project of the Year Award.

NATIONAL
AAU JUNIOR
OLYMPIC MULTISPORT
CHAMPIONSHIPS

ITHACA

1975
AUGUST 8-11

COME LIVE THE GOOD LIFE!

TOMPKINS COUNTY CHAMBER OF COMMERCE / CO-SPONSOR / 122 W. COURT ST. / ITHACA, N.Y. 14850 / PHONE: (607) 273-7080
COOPERATING SPONSORS: CITY OF ITHACA / CORNELL UNIVERSITY / COUNTY OF TOMPKINS / ITHACA COLLEGE

```
Dear Roy:              I want you to know how much I appreciate
your untiring efforts and your skillful arrangements as Director
of Public Relations & Publicity of all of the intricate details
of providing the NJO with superb press coverage, advertising
and public relations, your close liaison and working arrangements
with AAU and your unique ability to anticipate areas of need
and to get things done were remarkable.  I still don't know
how you did it, but I can say that of the numberless things that
could have gone wrong, very few did.

     I am satisfied that we put on one of the greatest spectacles
this community has ever seen, thanks to you and the other members
of your committee.  The people of Ithaca and Tompkins County
should be forever grateful for your outstanding work in making
this wholesome event one of the most memorable in local history.
```

Robert J. Kane
Honorary Chairman
Richard H. Comstock
General Chairman
Roy E. Staley
Assoc. General Chairman
Donald J. Culligan
Competition Director
Patrick J. Filey
Support Director
Richard L. Jewett
Special Events Director
Roy H. Park, Jr.
Publicity Director
Hanley W. Staley
Resources Director
Ray Van Houtte
Finance Director

CHAPTER 17
WORK AND MANAGEMENT STYLE

Aside from the thoughts my father put in his letter to me on my twenty-first birthday, he established early in his career some specific guidelines and work habits, many of which serve me well today.

Right up to the end, my father worked ten- and twelve-hour days for seven days a week. But he felt he really never *worked* a day in his life. Work to him was a pleasure, a joy, a bold adventure, a vacation. Every day was a holiday. As former U.S. Sen. Sam Ervin, when he was a director of Pops' paper in Morganton, NC, said, "Work is his recreation, not just his job." And Pops summed up his passion for work, the only one he had, by saying, "You have to give to get...and whatever the job takes you give." He said, "When things are running smoothly, I get bored."

My father said he had never been in a business he didn't like. That might have been one of the things that helped build his empire. He never did anything or got involved in any field that he didn't find interesting. "I don't think I ever sat down and said I want to get into this business because I can make a lot of money," he said. "You plan ahead, but you travel mile by mile to get there." On his seventy-first birthday, he said, "If you're looking backward, you're not looking forward," and he was still going strong.

One of his two most important rules was never to touch the same piece of paper twice, or move anything to the bottom of the pile that you face each morning. He maintained that nothing should ever be put in a desk drawer, or be filed before it's resolved, because it will slip through the cracks. The one exception to this, however, was the drawer full of talk sheets that he kept on each of his key employees. He added to the stack of sheets on each person periodically in anticipation of performance reviews, which were tied in with budgeted payroll raises. If anyone wanted to know his true misgivings about employees, his notes were all there.

His other discipline was to carry home unfinished work from the office, and complete it so he could start with a relatively clean in-box the next day before the mail and memos arrived. When it came to taking work home, one of the two managers who ran the outdoor division when I transferred into broadcasting for five years had his own rule, which ran counter to my father's. He told his associates that he might carry a briefcase out of the office, but he always left it on the front step until Monday morning. He lasted about three years before he resigned.

The business side of my father was methodical and organized. Since he personally opened each communication or piece of mail, made a decision on its contents and disposed of it, his desk was always clear. A mail drop twice a day from his home office to wherever he was when he was traveling kept him up to date and well informed. He would open each piece of mail, or read each memo as it came through, and immediately dictate his response to be attached to the material and sent to the appropriate employee before moving to the next item in the pile.

In an interview with my father, staff writer Jim Dumbell of the *Charlotte Observer* reported in 1982: "He takes telephone-equipped Lear jets on frequent visits to his properties. His punctuality is assured by the two or three wristwatches he wears, 'to exercise them.' In his pockets are two small tape recorders which he uses in car, plane, or wherever, so no fleeting thought will escape, no waking moment be wasted."

It should be noted that once he concluded an acquisition, after one first-time trip to the property, he seldom returned to the so-to-speak, "scene of the crime." As Dumbell reported, "In fact, Park is better known in the executive offices of many banks and national corporations than in the newsrooms of his own papers in the communities they serve."[8]

But when he was away from the office visiting any of his properties, or negotiating to buy more, he always carried his

Dictaphone. He had a rule that the sun doesn't set on an unanswered piece of correspondence. He was fanatical about it. One of his managers recalled that once my father's secretary was typing letters from his tapes, when suddenly a pause interrupted the dictation and there was someone else's voice: "Pass the cranberry sauce, please." Apparently someone at the Thanksgiving table passed the sauce, and he resumed his dictation. That must have been a Thanksgiving I missed, but my father liked the story.

Speaking of Thanksgiving, I've already pointed out how difficult it was for employees to take allotted vacations. My father's deliberate scheduling prevented taking long weekends, too, especially if they were adjacent to paid holidays. Since Thanksgiving always falls on Thursday, he made sure he scheduled a management meeting on Friday morning beginning at 7:30 to prevent anyone in Ithaca from taking a long weekend to be with family or friends.

Another thing I learned working with my father was to tackle the toughest, most apparently unsolvable problems first. I now firmly believe that for every problem there is *always* a solution. The fortune cookie prediction that "nothing is impossible" turned out to be right. It may take time to find it, but if you keep it gnawing at the back of your mind, different ideas emerge in your head over time. If you track them, they begin to fit together. The pieces eventually fall into place until the puzzle is solved. My father often said, "I enjoy solving a problem. I view each problem as a great opportunity. Meeting a challenge and resolving it is to me the best part of a good day's work." I learned never to postpone, bury or put any problem back in the closet. It will always stay there to fall out on your head, sooner rather than later.

Johnnie Babcock, who supervised hundreds of Park employees, put up with managers contacting him each day with problems they would try to lay on his desk. His standard response was to ask how they propose to resolve it, and if they didn't have a resolution, he would say, "You don't have a problem. You have given your problem to me. Therefore, how can you ask me to resolve a problem that you no longer have?"

My father had strict rules for running a successful business. As already pointed out, he believed in *doing things on time*. Answering mail the same day it's received it, taking work home, starting the next day with a clean agenda. An extension of this was *taking action* to quickly resolve problems that come up. If you have the facts and common sense, you move. You have, he claimed, better than a 50 percent chance of being right.

My father also claimed he believed in *delegating responsibility*. But only, he added, to the degree that he felt that someone could handle something as well, or better, than he could. But of course, no one could, so he always kept his finger in every pie and maintained his authority to change the rules on a whim despite his delegation. Though he theoretically had a chain of command, he never made an apology for overriding it. He would upbraid or direct anyone regardless of whom the person reported to, and he had the urge to do this often. As Johnnie Babcock can attest, although Pops had great confidence in Johnnie's management skills, Pops never hesitated a minute to overreach him, intervene and take control of my supervising functions. After all, I was family!

He also believed in *paying attention to details*, and most of the people to whom he "delegated" authority found out in a hurry what he meant. He second-guessed them frequently on details, and in some cases they personally became the *detail* he paid attention to.

Another one of his principles was to *reinvest cash flow* and always keep a liquid position. It was always Pops' policy to promote growth by reinvesting the company earnings back into the company. Park Broadcasting and later Park Communications never paid cash dividends on its stock, to him or any other shareholders. Instead, profits were used to fund new acquisitions. He always maintained that "we use the money to improve the properties, acquire additional properties and retire bank debt."

Although consistently listed year after year in the *Forbes 400* list of wealthiest Americans, my father never talked about his wealth. He said the money wasn't what mattered. He took little out in salary considering the size of his company; his salary never exceeded $600,000 per year. Of course, since practically everything he did involved business, most of his expenses were paid for, anyway.

He would advise people to "mortgage the limbs but never the trunk." Personal guarantees on loans were taboo, and he always used only a portion of his business or stock to secure and guarantee a loan.

My father was smart enough to listen and learn from his elders. "I feel that successful older people always have time for ambitious younger people who are willing to work," he told Jim Dumbell, staff writer with the *Charlotte Observer*. "You've got to learn. I want to learn from somebody else without having to discover it all myself. I found I could save time if I got advice from someone older. It was not mandatory that I take it all."[9]

My father, of course, firmly believed in *showmanship*, and his sales ability was legend. If he had stayed on the farm and was told by his father to haul away a dead mule, he would have auctioned it off to 100 people at $5 each. When the winner took delivery of a dead mule and asked what he was going to do with it, my father would have said, "You're right, here is your money back," and he would come out $495 ahead. Of course, he wouldn't take the dead mule back to the farm. He'd leave it along the road somewhere for someone else to clean up, along with his newspapers.

He also believed in *homework*, and he excelled at research and preparation. All through his advertising and promotion days, he used extensive research and analysis, and with each new area of endeavor he moved slowly at first until he had a "formula" for a successful operation. He said, "I never bought a property I didn't study carefully, and I knew more about it than the man who owned it."

His penchant for research found its peak and maximum use, as I mentioned earlier, in the ever-present *talk sheet,* my father's principal tool of communication, which Johnnie Babcock describes in detail:

"Almost every word heard on a home television set is read aloud by the performer from a screen of enlarged type that scrolls by at a comfortable speed as words are delivered. While the words are being read and delivered, the teleprompter gives the news anchor, politician or comedian the luxury of staying on track.

"Long before this performer's crutch was invented, Roy Park carefully followed a printed memo dictated by him to guide his many phone conversations, and sometimes face-to-face situations. Just as with Park's speeches, they were meticulously phrased, edited and reedited before they were delivered. I know. I wrote the first drafts of his speeches for him.

"In the first few days of my service as operations vice president, a detail arose about my supervisory functions. As we talked, Roy rummaged about in the generous top drawer of his desk and came up with a neatly typed page that had guided him through that final negotiation session that resulted in my being hired. Referring to what he had covered during that meeting, he made it plain that he was absolutely sure of the understanding we reached then, confirmed by his memo. So what became known as a "talk sheet" was not an innovation for my convenience, but Park's patented, regular business discipline.

"At our typical private, early morning meeting, we talked about phone calls that Park wanted to make that day. We reviewed points to be covered that had been typed up the previous afternoon; or if that chore had not already been done, we worked up a talk sheet on the spot, dictating it to his secretary for immediate transcription. His clerical help had to be both accurate and very fast. If a stenographer was not handy, I repaired to my office and typed it up on my error-prone Underwood.

"After completion of a phone call guided by our talk sheet, Park dictated a cover memo into a recording device, urging my input as he did so. There were not many changes. That report went in the files. Very confidential or highly important talk sheets were secreted permanently in his top drawer, a practice that was to prove material to me years later.

"On the credenza behind his desk, Park kept a shelf from which he could readily select a named folder. The folder names were key Ithaca staff members, his wife, each of his children, and usually one or two trusted confidants, including a banker or two.

If a talk sheet had found use for one of these people, it went in his or her folder, which also contained one-word memo reminders dropped in by Park to bring up topics important to him the next time they met.

"The talk sheets and our name on a folder invited close and persistent follow-up by Roy Park. While I traveled to a different operating venue almost every week, I could be sure that on my distant arrival, a call back to Roy was expected, and during my visit progress phone calls to his office were also expected. Infrequent vacations drove him crazy. I attempted to escape completely by going so far into nature's preserves that I could not be reached. One such place was a fishing spot in Canada owned by a large lumber company. No electricity and no phones. No road access, either.

"I went there after recalling that Roy once took one of his very rare vacations with a friend at this remote site. No electricity, newspapers or phone, and no American radio signals. After a single day of recreation, Park extracted from a largely French-speaking fishing guide that the lumber company did have a telephone some miles down a logging road and across a stretch of lake. Roy persuaded, or possibly bribed, the guide to take him to that nearest phone. His friend reported that he returned tired and grumpy, the country phone line so bad that he couldn't even get stock quotations from his office. Never again Canada for Roy, despite his earlier seclusion from P&G. But it did suggest an escape that worked out for me a time or two."

MEETINGS, BUT NOT OF THE MIND

As Johnnie mentioned talk sheets were used to guide Pops through many phone conversations, but while he was using them with acquisition prospects, a secretary skilled in shorthand was frequently on another line making notes on exactly what was said for careful analysis at the conclusion of each call. The notes were critical to developing a *second* talk sheet zeroing in on any weaknesses detected in reasons given for the prospect's hesitancy to sell. Or for that matter, any thoughts that could be countermanded and overcome with a new approach and a new, improved offer to go along with it. Knowing the details and every nuance of how the conversation went gave Pops the advantage going into the second round.

But talk sheets, as Johnnie Babcock recalls vividly, were just the first step in my father's elaborate "command and control" management of *his* managers. Johnnie paints this picture of the dreaded 8 AM management meetings:

"I remember, as his second in command, we would gather at the heavy oak conference table with no more than peremptory morning greetings. The profound dread of some of the members relentlessly pervaded the rest of the group. Meetings were never relaxed or chatty. As soon as we were settled, Roy would stalk from behind his desk, walk toward the large oil painting of Duncan Hines at the end of his great office until he reached his seat at the head of the table. He carried a large stack of folders with our names on the tabs, and several bulky reports. The agenda before each of us was based on the meeting a week earlier and demanded verbal accountability by whoever was on the carpet. But before tackling the agenda, we received a little lecture from our chief.

"Whatever broad subject his opening speech covered was focused narrowly on our management group. If it was government threat of wage controls, he'd admonish all to be prepared for a round of wage belt tightening. If it was a tax issue, he would remind us of towering corporate debt and our individual responsibility to improve profits. If there had been news of a drought in an area served by our group, he'd emphasize the need in that troubled economy for a more effective local sales force, not only on that spot on earth but throughout the company. Then he'd sweep the table with his eyes beneath his trademark bushy eye brows. Although the cast of characters changed over time, here's a sample of who he would see:

"First, his trusted operations vice president and *torpedo*, me. I say torpedo because Roy never fired anyone. He'd direct me, or sometimes another department head, to get rid of an employee he considered undesirable. The reason could be as minor as a crank letter from a viewer or negative vibes from an advertiser. He had his own way of personally separating people he didn't want or like. He simply made life at work so unbearable that they'd resign. I never came in for abuse at the meeting.

"Next, his vice president of finance. This gentlemen sat near Roy so he could observe and confirm figures that Roy recited. Whether or not the numbers were correct, if Park challenged them, he was expected to be right there to agree. Roy could insist that two plus two was other than four and not expect an argument from his financial person.

"Then, the manager of real estate for RHP Incorporated. The son of a popular and revered real estate principal, he was recruited from the family business to be Roy's real estate professional. He had the family charm and affability but no head for figures. He was the deer frozen in the headlights at every meeting, scolded by Roy for his late performance. Often Roy would request that he leave the gathering to write up rental payment delinquents or to make a personal collection call. He took his beating placidly, then resumed his routine, leaving behind word that he was out of the office on collection calls and hence unavailable. His travel was frequent and confusing. Roy might ask him to go by Ogdensburg, NY, on his way to Brooksville, FL. Trips were scheduled on the spur of the moment, with no time to plan ahead.

"Another was Park's administrative assistant. His job was to produce minutes of the meeting and at the meeting to produce the folder Roy would need for the next subject. He had come by his skill at this function after working in the same capacity for a retired president of a major university, who was a taskmaster, too, but one who assigned tasks with equanimity and humor. Roy leaned hard on him, including a requirement that he deliver mail from the box on Saturdays and wait at the Park home for Roy to process and give him instructions for Monday dissemination of the packet.

"Then there was the vice president of newspapers. Having

reached initial goals of broadcast acquisition, Park applied himself with the same energy to procure small daily and weekly newspapers. One person who held this title was hired from a highly responsible post with a major press syndicate to seek out and evaluate prospective sellers. He came to meetings with a high stack of folders, prepared to answer each and every question. Roy just plain didn't like his style and was irritated by the depth of knowledge he articulated and his broad range of top industry contacts. This gentleman's reports were always crisp and to the point, but often in part refuted in response from Roy. This was the classic example of Park making his life so miserable that he'd go away. A direct and painfully honest man, leave he did, becoming a professor and author at a major university.

"Next, Dave Feldman, treasurer of Park Outdoor and Roy's real estate holdings. He attended meetings to report the financial information on Park Outdoor, managed by Roy's son. Dave's job was to present the financial reports and forecasts. Though the most tenured of Park's financial staff, it was obvious that he would not be first choice as chief financial officer (CFO), because he would dispute inaccurate data and statements. Instead the post was conferred on another who was expected to agree with everything Park said.

"I was made aware that one year, Feldman, during his review, was told by Park's finance vice-president he wasn't getting any increase, and when he asked why, he was told, 'Because you don't smile enough in the meetings.'

"Finally, Roy H. Park, Jr., general manager of Park Outdoor. A meeting attendee who had served in several posts for his father and who had acquired advertising expertise both through a Cornell MBA and as an executive of a nationally ranked ad agency. Pops, as Roy, Jr. called him, gloried in saving from the weekend mail a complaint not yet seen by Roy, Jr., Dave Feldman or me (the executive through whom Roy, Jr. reported to his father). Roy verbally accused his son for whatever deficiency had been reported in the letter he intercepted, regardless of whether it was valid or not, inferring that it might have gone unremedied had his vigilance not brought it to light.

"The abuse of some of the other officers was accepted or seemingly fell on partially deaf ears. Not so with young Roy. He stood his ground, despite knowing who held the winning hand. When Pops objected to a $5-a-week raise for a secretary who had been with the company for 40 years and hadn't had a raise in the last five, young Roy said she was doing a good job and deserved one. His father said she didn't because she had protected past managers, covering up any transgressions by not reporting them. Sometimes silence is the best answer, but not this time. When his son asked, 'Then why did *you* keep her?' his father moved quickly to another subject.

"I could see and feel Roy, Jr.'s foot suspended in air by his crossed legs under the conference table, vibrating as it oscillated in a tapping motion of frustration and anger. His father's dictatorial and unfeeling conduct with his own family planted seeds of doubt as to the eventual treatment of me as well, a 'non–family member.'"

Pops and me at a WNCT-TV client barbeque, one of our many PR trips when I was named VP Advertising and Promotion for Park Broadcasting, as covered in the next chapter.

CHAPTER 18
THE BOSS AND THE SOB

In early 1975, my fourth year of managing the outdoor division, my mother sent me an article in the *Wall Street Journal* entitled, You Have Problems? Consider the Plight of the Nation's SOBs.[10]

The outdoor division was looking much better, the inventory had improved, and we had made some productive acquisitions. We had a stable workforce, competent management in the field, a good working relationship with all of the employees and a growing national business, accounting for 80 percent or more of our billing. But my father was still picking at every detail, finding fault without recognizing accomplishments, ignoring what the plant was like in the past while criticizing the present, and offering no hope for a better future.

The article, by staff reporter Everett Groseclose, was dated March 20, 1975, and helped me realize what was going on was really not unusual. A lot of SOBs *(Sons of Bosses)* were, like me, between a rock and a hard place.

The subhead flagged how wretched their lives could be, and provided insight on this "hypersensitive, emotion-filled world of conflicting wills, bruised egos and rivalries."

Groseclose pointed out that "most men that run their own firms are intensely competitive entrepreneurs as opposed to professional managers who can run any number of companies without becoming emotionally involved." I'm not making the call that any particular finding applied to me, but Harry Levinson, a psychologist who has studied father-son relationships in family-held firms, said, "For the entrepreneur, the business comes to define his position in life, thus when a son comes into the firm an entrepreneur may view his offspring as a threat, a potential embarrasment or merely someone to be tolerated to keep peace in the family. Only rarely is a son welcomed and given free-rein."The *Wall Street Journal* article pointed out that in 1969 an organization known as Sons of Bosses International was founded with chapters in twelve states. The group was made up of young men who had either taken control of the family business or were in line to get the job. I knew I was not in line to take over the family business, having been hired to run one of its divisions, so I didn't seek out membership in this group. The core of the organization is the father-son relationship. As Groseclose said, "There is still a lot of mourning because, to hear SOBs tell it, the life of an SOB is anything but easy."

Groseclose went on to say, "Most SOBs agree that once they have decided to go into the family business, the most difficult problem revolves around how much authority, if any, the father is willing to yield. In many cases where the answer is none, a parting of the ways is sometimes inevitable. SOBs note, however, that it is usually the son who departs."

As Groseclose noted, the founder of SOBs, Gerald D. Slavin, said, "The key thing all SOBs have in common is that we're all trying to solve the problem that we have working with and for our fathers. Believe me, that's not easy."

Therefore, "for many SOBs it is a question of biding their time, behaving themselves while the father continues to run the show," Groseclose said. And with the outdoor operation, alone, that's exactly where I was.

It was a combination of my father's feeling that since all the major problems in the outdoor division had been solved, and because the plant looked respectable and had a solid base of national and local clients, it might be time to improve the bottom line. That, plus what I believe was a desire to expand an audience for his ego, led to a change in his career plans for me. He felt it was time to step up the promotion of his media companies as well as "step up" the outdoor bottom line by turning the outdoor companies over to professional outdoor managers.

THE FIRST PARK COMMUNICATIONS

In 1976 I was shifted from the outdoor division to become vice president, advertising and promotion for Park Broadcasting, Inc., which included advertising and promotion for fourteen radio and seven TV stations, plus thirty-nine newspapers, the outdoor divisions and real estate in eighteen states. But my father's main purpose in this move was to have me create *Park Communications,* an eight-page monthly tabloid newspaper for our then more than 2,500 employees.

In preparation, my father asked me, at age thirty-eight, to go back to being a student taking a graduate news writing course in the Department of Communication Arts at Cornell. I was by far the oldest student in the class and sat in the back of the room. My professor was the publisher of the *Ithaca Journal* at the time, which put him well to the left of center. My first reports received C+'s and low Bs with a massive amount of commentary in the margins. Sometimes I thought he was writing more in the margins than I was writing in the article. His comments were all slanted toward moving what I prided as my objectivity to a more liberal viewpoint. I adapted to this without changing my philosophy, and when I finished the course, I got one of six As in the class out of thirty-six in the graduate student body. I went on to publish *Park Communications* and my former professor went on to become a government press secretary.

My father's formula for the newspaper was simple: include something about every division he owned in each issue: a picture, announcement of a new employee, a birth, marriage, news or feature article. As its managing editor, I had to become involved in what was happening in every one of the roughly 100 different subsidiaries my father owned, spread from the West Coast to South Florida. Aside from our employees, the newspaper also went to network executives, outside suppliers and advisors, and potential media he targeted for purchase.

In those days we had progressed past carbon paper but were a long way away from computers. Every article, caption, and headline was hand-typed and subject to Pops' approval. In those days before computers there were not even memory banks on our electric typewriters. To avoid every article from being completely retyped after he revised it, I made heavy use of White-Out and corrective tape. We'd patch in the changes the best we could and send it back up for final approval, only to have it come back looking like Attila the Hun had savaged it. The corrective tape would be peeled up on every page, making each sheet look like the floor after New Year's Eve. He wanted to see what had been under the tape before he gave his approval.

Every month, like clockwork, regardless of bad weather, I drove 150 miles to Ogdensburg, NY, and worked with our general manager, Chuck Kelly, to supervise the printing and folding of the newsletters, which I took back to Ithaca the next day.

The articles were sent up as they were approved, typeset at the newspaper and sent back to me in Ithaca for paste-up. I would arrive in Ogdensburg, NY, around 11 PM, grab subs from a place that was open late, and stay up all night with the blank tabloid pages, scissors and hot wax to finalize the layout. This included juggling headlines, photos, captions, articles, announcements and artwork, if a map updating his holdings was shown. Bleary-eyed, I would drive the paste-up to the newspaper at dawn the next day for final photographing and printing.

I remember on more than one occasion Route I-81 from Syracuse to Watertown was completely closed off, blocked by at least two feet of snow. I knew that if I slowed the car for a moment, I couldn't break free, so to keep the car's momentum, I white-knuckled the normal four-hour trip in six hours, being the only car on the road.

Then the publications had to be mailed to each employee, not to their business offices but to their homes. Keeping track of thousands of employees with constant turnover and movement with updated addresses each month was a nightmare in itself. Again, we did this without computers.

My job also included writing press releases, developing slogans and logo changes for the stations, and attending public relations events on the launching of new programming for the three networks around the country. This part of the job entailed attending the annual kick-off celebrations of the new network shows and sitcoms, and I had dinners and hobnobbed with sitcom and movie stars from Jack Lemmon to Bernadette Peters.

You may remember some of the old network programming. I met with Mary McDonough of *The Waltons*, Bess Armstrong of *On Our Own*, Christopher Norris of *Trapper John, M.D.*, Candice Earley of *All My Children*, Sharon Lovejoy of *Magazine*, Connie Sellecca of *Flying High*, Tony Randall of *The Tony Randall Show*, and Bernadette Peters of *All's Fair*.

I remember a joke I played on the former president of the Ithaca Gun Company, John Park. He had moved to Nashville, TN, to start another business after the gun company declared bankruptcy in 1979. He found out I was coming to town and he asked me to come over for dinner at his home. I approached Connie Selleca, who was staying in the same hotel for the CBS kick-off, and she agreed to help me play a joke on him.

Connie Selleca – the TV star who didn't come to dinner in 1978.

When he came to the lobby of the hotel, I walked arm in arm with her and after introductions, told him that she would be with me for the evening. He didn't bat an eye but simply described what we were going to have for dinner. At that point, she said it sounded great, and would rather go for a home-cooked meal with us than stay at the celebration banquet. I reminded her that the actor she was being seen with who played a diver in one of the new shows would probably not think her leaving would be a good idea. I knew she probably was putting me on anyway, and she agreed.

When we got out to the car, I said, "Good Lord, John you didn't even bat an eye." He said, "You had me going all right, but in case you were serious, I didn't want to show it."

The job also included supervising the advertising for all of our companies and I developed a corporate advertising campaign. While doing all this, I continued to attend each of my father's weekly meetings and was responsible for developing the visuals for his annual address, which covered every property with graphs and charts showing each company's progress on national and local sales, expenses and operating profit. All these slides were hand-done, with the individual bar charts pasted up by a professional at Cornell and then photographed for slides. No PowerPoint back then.

In 1976, I was also named managing director of Ag Research, my father's *Redbook*-listed advertising agency founded in 1952 that created the Duncan Hines brand. I redesigned nine company logos and came up with new call letters when radio stations changed formats. For example, when Pops changed his station in Syracuse from classical music to country, he asked me to come up with a new name. I suggested something with his initials, WRHP, telling him that sounded like country to me. He agreed.

The agency also handled all promotional advertising done by the company's newspapers and broadcast properties. From 1976 to 1978, the agency's operating profit increased 300 percent.

In addition, I accelerated involvement in community affairs. In 1976, I joined the public relations council of the Tompkins County

Chamber of Commerce. I served as the public relations director of the Tompkins County Conference and Tourist Council and as chairman of the sign ordinance committee and legislative action committee and acting chairman of the nominating committee. I also served on the Board of Directors of the Tompkins County Council of the Arts. In 1977 I was a guest publicity executive to the United Way of Tompkins County; and in 1979 on the finance committee of the Special Children's Center. Finally, I served on the board of the Ithaca Assembly, becoming chairman in 1978 for three years.

You would think with this kind of workload I would be assigned secretarial help. But I was given only part-time help by whoever the receptionist-switchboard operator happened to be at the time. The job required her to answer all phone calls to headquarters from hundreds of employees, suppliers and related business contacts to greet people coming off the elevator, make coffee and run errands. I was dictating all of my material, and every time she would put the earphones on to type my dictation, the phone would ring.

So there I was, the person who always had full-time secretaries at the companies I worked for before joining my father, trying to keep things going with sporadic part-time help. What I had gone through earlier as general manager of the outdoor division wasn't looking so bad.

QUIRKS AND CHARACTERISTICS

There was another side of my father, not often shown, but he could be sentimental and at times prone to whims. These inconsistencies could confuse people making it difficult for them to categorize the man.

When he was decorating his office at Terrace Hill, which overlooked the city, for example, he moved part of a wall back about three feet "at considerable expense and effort" because he didn't like square rooms. He brought the black marble fireplace from the old mansion at 408 East State, site of his former offices, to Terrace Hill and installed it prominently. But he did not hook it up to a chimney. He also brought a chandelier from an old mansion, as well as some massive paneled doors. The huge office was furnished with leather and fruitwood French provincial furniture to make it look like an elegant living room. My father felt that if you spent so much time in a place you needed an atmosphere conducive to doing your best work.

His office was described by reporter Floyd Rogers of the *Winston-Salem Journal* in May 1988 as "a roomy, walnut-paneled office on the fifth floor of his gracefully aging office building on Terrace Hill here. But it is not a lavish office." In truth, having a comfortable office was practical—God knows he spent enough time there. In any case, what most people simply don't understand is that my father, and people like him, work for the sheer joy of it and probably would *pay* money to work if that was the only way they could do it. My father said in the *Charlotte Observer*, "You must remember, a person's worth is not the amount of his assets. It's the amount of his assets minus his liabilities."

In minimizing his liabilities, where most people avoid it, my father welcomed turnover. He felt it kept payroll costs down. I feel exactly the opposite. The cost of the search and recruiting, interviewing, training and payroll setup, on top of moving costs and the long-term costs of losing trust and loyalty, make turnover an anathema to me. Dave Feldman and I have worked together for thirty-five years through thick and thin. Many employees average twenty years with the company. We even brought some back after they left for a period of time for other reasons.

My father was frugal, but he wasn't cheap. Except for the limited salaries he paid employees, he was generous with friends and colleagues and to those whose companies he had targeted for purchase.

But anyone you know who went through the Great Depression was changed. You never forget what it was like. If you started without money, there was no way to get it, and if you started with it, you could end up with nothing. Few had money, and it affected everyone who went through it for the rest of their lives. After all, Pops started with nothing. Add his experience during the Depression to that. So he was frugal with me, and this really applied while I was in college. I was chained to a strict budget for essentials of rent, food, laundry, clothing, textbooks, etc. and it kept me from being spoiled.

Roy H. Park – This picture by Fabian Bachrach highlights his trademark eyebrows.

My father also had another distinguishing feature: bushy eyebrows, very bushy. Woe to the barber with any gardening experience who sought to take a brush cutter to those bushes. In fact, his eyebrows, like misplaced mustaches, were so unique that a feature writer for the *Ithaca Journal*, Franklin Crawford, in his "Frankly Speaking" column, wrote in 1991: "One of the punishments for mocking or making funny names about the City of Ithaca's new Chevy Caprice cars, if made among two or more persons and one of those persons is wearing Birkenstock sandals, $1,000, 30 days in jail, or 250 hours of community service including the grooming and maintenance of Roy Park's eyebrows."

A reporter for the *Ithaca Journal*, Judith Horstman, in a 1972 article headlined, ITHACA'S ROY PARK: A MAN OF MANY CAREERS, described him as a dapper dresser, with a soft-spoken and gentlemanly manner; she said he was "a person who retains a southern charm and reminds you he was born and educated in North Carolina."

She said that on the day of the interview:

> Park was wearing a subdued plaid suit and I noticed two watches. "Duncan Hines rather liked watches," Park explained. "So I used to search out all the unique watches I could, and give them to him. In the process I got a little hung-up on it myself, and now I must have, oh, I expect 40 watches now."

> He also has an antique Packard and Duesenberg that are in prize-winning condition. "I don't drive them much," Park said wistfully. "It's a lot more fun before you get them in show condition. Then you start worrying about a pebble flying up or something, and damaging the finish."

> In contrast to these possessions are some others he appears to value almost as much and which he keeps in his office: copies of the guidebooks he wrote for Duncan Hines; empty cake mix boxes with the Duncan Hines label; and some cast-iron toys his wife's father made in his manufacturing business at the turn of the century.[11]

Keeping all of these things in mind, I wasn't too surprised to hear an anecdote that probably sums up Pops's personality. A Cornell student who spent some time interviewing my father and watching him work was awed and exasperated by his methodical, organized approach to everything. As he finished his interviews, the student somewhat sarcastically asked Park's administrative secretary, Jean Ballard, "Mr. Park certainly does everything in an organized manner. I'm curious, did he meet his wife that way?"

"I really don't know, so the next day I asked Mr. Park," said Mrs. Ballard, "and he burst into laughter."

"Good grief, no," he said. "I met her on a blind date."

In his interview with Dumbell in the *Charlotte Observer,* my father was described in this way:

> On the terrace outside, a gale wind swirled the remains of a 10-inch snow that had fallen the day before. The wind's howl could be heard inside over the indignant squawk of a small caged parrot. Park released the bird, smiled as he stroked its colored plumage, then replaced it in the cage, and now the bird was affronted. [What Dumbell didn't know was that my father usually shared his Rice Krispies with the bird.]

> [The interview continued] Park wore a brownish, chalk-striped suit. A small diamond stickpin held his patterned tie in place. Sideburns reached below his ears and his hair grew long on the back of his neck. Long, thick eyebrows climbed up and outward over deep-set eyes. There was a resemblance to Jimmy Cagney, the actor.

> The only obvious throwback to his North Carolina upbringing is the way he says "can't"—a word he doesn't use often. When he does, he says, "cain't."

> Park said he is looking for more small newspapers, particularly in North Carolina—"a part of my heart is in North Carolina—but it's awfully hard to find any good newspapers for sale there."[12]

The reference to newspapers in hand reminds me of another story about my father's voracious newspaper consumption, told to me by Stewart Underwood years after my father passed away. The question arises as to what to do with all that newsprint once you are done with it with no wastebasket handy. My father's simple solution, as you have heard, was to get rid of it wherever he was, whether into lakes, pastures, under restaurant tables or, in this case, out of the windows of a private airplane. Underwood told me when my father chartered short business trips on small planes, where he had to sit in the cockpit beside the pilot, the windows could be opened since they were flying low. Out went the newspapers into the air until the pilot, after it happened a third time, pointed out that the plane could crash since they could end up catching on the rudders.

Later, I remember flying with him on larger charters where there were so many slippery sections of newsprint on the floor you had to hold on to the back of the seats or whatever you could when you were leaving the plane to keep your feet from sliding out from under you.

Being intent, focused and demanding, my father was under continuous stress. But he thrived on it. He told the Cornell graduate business students, "The number one thing is to be honest. And you have to learn how to handle pressure. You're not going to get anywhere unless you can deal with stress. But stress can be the greatest thing in the world. It can make you do things you didn't think you could do."

I don't think I need to point out that his stress was also imposed on others, and he did a good job of keeping us under it. He even installed a buzzer, connected to his desk, in his secretary's bathroom. The buzzer would go off just about every time his secretary disappeared from her desk.

In social situations, my father had a great sense of humor. He allowed himself to loosen up. Sometimes too much. He enjoyed that first drink, and the second, and if my mother didn't catch him, a third or more. Al Neuharth said, "It was a delight to be with him socially. He remembers the little niceties, [and] when it's appropriate to…say nice things, to offer congratulations."

Happy Days. Cross section of a combined summer management meeting and party with Ithaca friends in 1976 included from left to right: Johnnie Babcock, towering over me; Ellen Broome (who married my cousin Hoyle); Hank Tribley, general manager WNCT-TV; Bob Patterson, Park Broadcasting CFO; Tetlow; Pops; and John Park, president of Ithaca Gun Co. In the center looking down: my mother, left, and Nancy Babcock, right, and crouching left to right: Bob Burns; John Clark, WNCT-TV sales manager; and Pops' secretary, Jean Ballard.

But sometimes his kidding meant trouble for others. There were times you couldn't get him to give a straight answer. I remember when my wife and I were invited to a dinner party at his house on a cold November evening in the early 1970s. Tetlow called him and asked what she should wear. He told her it would be a churchy-type group, so she dressed in staid, tweedy attire. We arrived before most of the guests, expecting the group to be dressed as my father indicated.

She remembers sitting on the piano bench with a clear view of the front door. As guests arrived she noticed their attire was much more glamorous. Then a beautiful blonde apparition came through the door dressed to the nines, and she thought how much she looked like Ginger Rogers.

Mingling with the stars. Pops came in contact with many celebrities during his careers, from Mary Tyler Moore to Joan Crawford, to picture a few.

One of my father's guests ran Ithaca Industries, at the time the nation's largest private-label manufacturer of pantyhose. He was the supplier for J.C. Penney, which in 1972 signed a seven-year deal with a celebrity to act as a traveling fashion consultant. The vision at the party was, indeed, the lovely Ginger Rogers, and Tetlow vowed never to take fashion advice from Pops again.

It should be noted that Ginger was a lot tougher than she looked since Johnnie took her skeet shooting with the good old boys the next day. It wasn't only her looks that left them with their mouths hanging open. Johnnie said she was a crack shot.

I suspect that it was my father's keen, and sometimes warped, sense of humor that helped sustain him because, although he loved what he did, he took over far too many responsibilities at any given time. Of course we know, as J.J. Procter said, "There are things of deadly earnest that can only be safely mentioned under cover of a joke," but I think his sense of humor carried him through. He once jokingly told the NC State student body that friends at the college said that after he left North Carolina on April Fools Day in 1942 "North Carolina really started to move."

His last assistant, Jack Claiborne, said that along with his love for work, Pops had "a dry and droll wit." Claiborne remembered when he hadn't got the seating arrangements made in time for the company's management meeting one January in Raleigh, NC, so there was some confusion. Everybody got to sit where they wanted and some people liked that. At the end, Roy glossed it all over by saying, "We had a good time this year. Next year we'll mess it all up by being organized."

It was seldom that Pops was at a loss for words, but there were exceptions. One day our fourth floor receptionist came to work dressed in a cowboy outfit complete with boots, bandana and hat. On his way up to his office, the elevator stopped at the fourth floor to let off a passenger and my father's mouth fell open at her unusual, eye-catching apparel. For a moment people say he was speechless, but as the elevator doors slowly closed, he was heard to say "Howdy."

Another story he told on himself was wanting an expensive computer watch when digital watches were first introduced. For some time, he had his eye on one at Tiffany's in New York City. "My wife thought it was too expensive so I bought it for myself and had it engraved: 'To RHP from RHP, Christmas 1975.'" Later, Pops said, Dottie told him the message should have read: "To RHP from your closest friend."

Which brings me to a new story I heard about my mother this year. As you can well imagine, with all of the Park Communications employees coming into Ithaca for business meetings along with other business associates and community friends, my parents presided over many parties and after my father died she continued this practice. Dottie's sense of humor equaled her husband's and preparing for one of these parties, she turned to an arborist who worked with both of our families over the years. He told me this story because it was the day after 9/11 and he felt at first it all seemed so strange to be continuing with plans for a party at that time. But then he said he felt it was the right thing to do since we all needed to carry on and it showed the resilience of my 88-year-old mother.

What my mother had asked Jack to do was to install in the trees above the place for the party fake rope vines and a life-sized stuffed monkey. He was twenty feet above ground when my mother came out of the house to yell up to him in her southern accent "Mr. Simrell, do you like Tequila?"

In response to his puzzled "yes" she disappeared into the house

The Monkey before its treetop ascension posing with Joanne Florino.

while he continued his work and shortly reappeared carrying a silver tray with two silver goblets. He said he has never forgotten her asking: "Mr. Simrell, would you care to come down and join me for a Margarita?"

Aside from being one of the best bartenders going, Dottie was a good match for my father since neither were the most patient of people. Jack told me another time my mother responded to a job she asked him to do that he couldn't schedule immediately, "Mr. Simrell, I don't wait well."

When asked what it was like living with Pops, my mother said "life with Roy has been fun, hard and breathless."

Yes—and I could add a word or two to that.

EXPRESSIONS AND IMPRESSIONS

Without knowing the force of words, it is impossible to know the man.

—Confucius

Along with reading newspapers, his own included, my father would occasionally browse through a political book "to find out what politicians are good and which are bad," he said. He added dryly, "The ones who are good, of course, are generally the ones who wrote the book."

There were a number of expressions that my father used with consistency. When he was nearing the close of a deal, he would allude to "getting down to the short rows," a farm expression about plowing a field.

Another favorite expression was a result of my stint as a wrestler. Since I frequently practiced without earguards, I developed a minor case of cauliflower ears and went to the hospital to have it corrected. For months afterward, my mother told her friends the details of the operation as if it were a big deal, and whenever she got to talking too much to other people about anything my father would say, "Now tell them about the ears."

My father did not like words that ended in "ism." He told the Johnson School graduates, "There are some 'isms' you should avoid like the plague: favoritism, cronyism and nepotism." I doubt if Pops would have liked *unchecked environmentalism* and *rabid anticapitalism* much either.

He referred to gossip and chatter when the talk became less rational, more emotional or anything he did not want to hear as "Dickey-Bird" talk.

And lawyers will tell you the commonly used, two-word legal phrases applied to claims considered excessive or frivolous are "arbitrary and capricious," for which they are "shocked and appalled." I remember the day my father looked up what to him was a new word under the *C*'s in the dictionary. From then on his favorite two-word expression for someone who argued with or opposed his views was that they were "surly and *churlish*." I heard that a lot.

Like me, my father tried to avoid trouble, and I heard him frequently say to Babcock, "We don't need to be pioneers, do we, Johnnie?" Avoiding trouble meant being cautious on anything that might cost money unless it was absolutely necessary.

Another of my father's favorite expressions was "bug-dust" when he thought something was cheaply priced. But it wasn't "bug-dust" whenever it was time to give an employee a raise. When he went through my outdoor budgets, the first page he always turned to were the proposed raises. When it came to raises, or anything to do with wage or salary overhead, my father was not into largesse.

He also used the expression, "I wash my hands of it," which signaled end-of-the-round finality. Once he encountered something he didn't like, be it a conversation, argument or situation, he turned away and seldom looked back.

His tendency to move on when he was through with you, or hoped you were through with him, was capped with, "Is that it!" If he received the hoped-for "Yes," he would clap his hands together and move on to the next thing on his mind, to the next plane of existence, and whether you were standing there or not, you ceased to exist.

But his most ominous phrase was *"Thanks a million,"* particularly if you were the one hearing it. This generous sentiment generally meant that the deal you just concluded with him had worked out, as Johnnie Babcock said, "One hundred percent to him, twenty percent to you."

POPS'S HOBBIES

As for hobbies, Dumbell reported in the *Charlotte Observer* that he "voraciously reads fiction and nonfiction, magazines, newspapers and technical journals, shows his cars, enjoys deep-sea fishing and raises peacocks and dogs at home." Actually he read very little fiction. He was an avid reader, however, of business magazines, and you already know how he devoured newspapers. He did enjoy deep-sea fishing; I went fishing with him in the Gulf Stream off Florida, as well as in lakes in Canada on a few rare occasions.

When it came to his raising dogs, he just collected them, telling Dumbell, "Some are Bedlingtons, and some are just mutts we picked up off the street." As far as raising peacocks, it was mainly my mother's interest, not his. There was nothing wrong with peacocks wandering around the yard, but he took little interest, other than visual, in the birds.

Other collections were a different story. As Treva Jones reported in the *News & Observer* in 1997, in addition to radio, television stations and newspapers, Park collected watches, reported as "fine gold watches," as well as antique cars. The paper said he had "more than half a hundred watches and more than a dozen classic cars."

Business reporter John Byrd wrote in the *Winston-Salem Journal* in 1983 that during his interview,

> Roy Park sat on the edge of the sofa, gold cuff links in his sleeves and a diamond pin in his tie. On his right

wrist Park wore a watch with twin dials, a Christmas gift from his wife, Dorothy, that helps him keep up with time zones when he travels.

On his left wrist was a gold watch-calculator that, conceivably, he could use to calculate his fortune or figure the worth of a newspaper he'd like to buy. He bought the watch at Tiffany's in New York, after Dorothy had seen it but, quite inconceivably, told him she couldn't afford it. From his pocket he pulled an English-made watch disguised as a cigarette lighter, another Christmas gift. And in the desk drawer was a chiming watch that he had used as an alarm that morning.[13]

As for cars, actually, he had 16 vintage cars and some weren't so vintage. Reposing under individually tailored dust covers in his garage, among others, was a 1940 Packard Darrin convertible, a ten-year-old Lincoln Continental, a Nash Healey, a boat-tailed Auburn which was a replica formerly owned by Rod Serling and two Jaguars which were certainly vintage, but not antique.

His search for cars even went global. One of the Jaguars was a Mark X Sedan he tracked down in Paris. He also had a Bentley that he picked up at the factory in London along with a supercharged 1936 Cord "and a few others." "With fewer than 2,000 miles on it, the Bentley was, "for all practical purposes, brand new" he said.

But his favorite was a 1929 Duesenberg Model J roadster, one of only 480 built. That automobile almost invariably took first place in every show it entered. It was judged the most popular of 90 entries in the Grand Prix Concours D'Elegance at Watkins Glen and was judged the best of 152 shown at the New York State Fair. He enjoyed an occasional ride in this car which according to a brass medal in the car was capable of cruising at over 100 miles per hour, "If you could find a good smooth road," my father said.

John Watlington, Jr., former chairman of Wachovia Bank and Trust Company's executive committee, was an old friend of Pops. He told about the time he drove the Duesenberg, "Roy asked me if I wanted to drive it. I had no idea at that time what it was worth and I said sure. I noticed Roy didn't seem very enthusiastic, but I drove it around the block. When I got back, he walked all around the car and carefully checked it out. When he saw I hadn't put a scratch on it, he sighed and relaxed. When I found what that car was worth—one hundred thousand dollars!—I nearly died!"

The Duesenberg brings back happy memories of an auction my father went to in northern New York attended by 200 to 300 people. It's ironic that I went with Pops when he bought it, which was the only occasion I was with him where he pulled off one of his many deals. He bought a car for $5,300 in 1961, and Skip Marketti, executive director of the Auburn-Cord-Duesenberg Museum in Auburn, IN, valued the car at up to $250,000 some twenty years later. Right after I attended the auction with Pops, a story appeared under the headline, DUESENBERG ROADSTER BRINGS $5,300 AT SALE in the *Watertown Daily Times* on Friday, October 27, 1961. The subhead said, ROY H. PARK, ITHACA, PURCHASES CAR—300 ATTEND AUCTION AT CARTHAGE.

Black Gold from the north country was this 1929 Duesenberg bought at auction for $5,300. This picture of the two of us taken in October 1961 by the Watertown Daily Times. The car was eventually valued from between $100,000 up to $250,000.

Staff writer John W. Overacker started the article with,

"Sold to that gentleman for $5,300." So Auctioneer Edward J. Madden, trust officer, Watertown National Bank, announced the sale of the 1929 J Model Duesenberg roadster to Roy H. Park of Ithaca, head of Duncan Hines Institute, at the auction conducted Thursday afternoon on the island of Carthage.

Approximately 300 persons crowded on the island for the sale. They were from all over New York State, from Connecticut, New Jersey, Ohio, Pennsylvania and Michigan. And those interested were principally Cord and Duesenberg "buffs," here to again witness that a "classic" car's appeal never dies.

When a J Model Duesenberg on its 142-inch or 153.50-inch chassis went quietly down the road, all of its 300-odd horsepower purring like a kitten, handling like a racing car, something happened to each person who saw it. It was a car designed for the "big rich" and the "big rich" bought it. The chassis alone of these cars went for something like $8,500 to $9,500 and when personal body designs were added the total tab often hits as high as $20,000.

One of the most interested persons to attend this auction was Gordon M. Buehrig, who designed the original Cord automobile, who was with Cord when he purchased Duesenberg and designed several J models, and SJ models, including one for Gary Cooper. Mr. Buehrig was later with the engineering and research staff of the Ford Motor Company, Detroit, Michigan.

Mr. Buehrig had come to Carthage to bid on the Cord, a car which he had not owned for 20 years. He decided not to bid on it, feeling that the auction was "a bit too rich for my blood. I knew this when the J Duesenberg went for $5,300. And I have my eye on a Duesenberg which I may buy at some future date."

As for my father's purchase, Overacker reported,

It was the consensus of the Duesenberg buffs that Mr. Park *had not overpaid*. Asked how much more money would be needed to put the roadster into good condition, several answers were given but they averaged out between $3,000 to $5,000. All insisted that six whitewall tires would have to be purchased, and that would run approximately $750. A valve job by Hoe would run $400 more. Some thought that as much as $2,000 would be needed to do a good chrome job and then there were additional odds and ends, such as upholstery, paint, dashboard, etc.[14]

All the work was done in short order by Phil Soyring, my father's auto mechanic, and the car won award after award, year after year. When Pops died, he left it in his will to Soyring, who had taken care of all his antique cars, and the rest of the cars in his collection were sold or given away. Only one or two remain with the family today. The one I kept for our foundation is not even an antique but has an interesting history. It's the boattailed Auburn replica that was custom-built for Rod Serling, who had a home in Ithaca and whom I got to know quite well. I was, and as you can guess by my familiarity with his TV episodes, still am a fan of Serling's *Twilight Zone*.

He and his wife, Carol, came to my house for a cocktail party and I attended a number of other parties with them. After he died, Carol called me to say she had received offers for the car in California and asked me to check with my father to see if the offers were fair. I suspect she knew my father would personally be interested because of her husband's connection with Ithaca College, and of course Pops ended up buying it.

Rod Serling's Boattailed Auburn that Pops bought from Serling's wife, Carol. This is the only one of the 16 antique cars in his collection that has been retained to honor his legacy and is now a part of our Triad Foundation in Ithaca.

NEGOTIATING AN AUTOMOBILE

Just watch out if you hear somebody say "please don't throw me in that briar patch."

—John Dartnon, from the book Neanderthal

Aside from the Duesenberg, I was told about another time where my father clearly did not overpay for an antique car. He had his eye on one, and Phil Soyring was invited to go with him to drive it back if he could work out a deal. The price on the car was more than Pops was willing to pay, but they took the two-hour drive to see what he could negotiate, anyway.

When they got there, the owner of the automobile stuck to his price, and Pops said it was beyond his reach. After some haggling my father invited him for lunch. During this time, Pops offered a figure $3,000 below the asking price and was still turned down.

Toward the end of the meal, my father said he'd done his research on the fair value of the car, and he just didn't have enough available cash to pay what the owner was asking. He restated his offer, saying that he felt what he was offering was still too much and it was going to be a stretch to pay it.

After a second refusal, my father said, "I'll tell you what, let's split the difference. I will understand if you don't take the offer, and I'll walk away without the car. I'll almost be glad if you turn me down." Finally the owner, softened up by the lunch, agreed to go along with it.

Pops then named the new price at $1,000 more than his first offer, wrote the check, shook hands with the former owner, and the two men left. When they arrived at my father's home, Soyring said he noticed when he named the price, the $3,000 difference hadn't been split evenly, and that Pops had paid only $1,000 more. He pointed out that the owner had been shorted by $500 and my father said, "Well, he didn't catch it, did he?"

Another "vintage" car that was part of my father's collection was this 1937 Supercharged Cord Phaeton. The picture, taken in 1979, shows CBS Vice President Affiliate Relations, Tony Malara, in the driver's seat, while Pops plays the role of a valet parking attendant at the door. The car was shown at the New York State Fair that year.

As Pop's collection expanded, he started using his cars for his Christmas cards saying *"Merry Christmas. Take time to look backward to pleasant memories and forward to new hope."* signed Roy H. Park.

Note that one of the cards as featured below was the Nash Healey I drove as a student at the University of North Carolina, also pictured on page 110.

CHAPTER 19
THE CIVIC SOLDIER

As Johnnie Babcock points out, "While he valued privacy in his home, Roy was active and maintained a high profile in civic affairs. He was as much a joiner as the insurance and real estate agents who dominate most service club memberships." His civic and business activity earned him many honors and awards.

As Babcock said, "A loyal Rotarian, Roy rose through official chairs but never accepted its presidency. For many years he was instrumental in securing top-drawer speakers for their Wednesday noon meetings. It proved unlikely that anyone would refuse Park's invitation to address the organization. He was a faithful Presbyterian, not only as a ruling elder, but also an usher, frequently passing the collection plate. He even found time to take responsibility to oversee and supervise the minister."

Tony DiGiacomo, former president of First National Bank, on which board Roy served, was quoted in the *Ithaca Journal* when he was running area United Way operations in the 1950s. Roy was chairman of the United Way's fund drive, the economy wasn't good, and the drive was faltering. DiGiacomo said, "I called a board meeting on a Sunday night when you wouldn't kick a dog out of bed. Roy appeared in a smoking jacket, casual as you please, and gave everybody a pat on the back. It was much needed, much appreciated, and that's typical of Park's community involvement."

As reported in the *NCSU Alumni News* in 1971, "Roy's kindness, thoughtfulness and generosity captivate those with whom he comes in contact. Despite his sometimes frantic schedule and worldwide travels, Roy finds time to lend a helping hand to many in both his professional and personal life."

"One of Roy's last significant community gestures was to establish at the Cornell Graduate School of Business an annual lecture series by nationally renowned business executives to honor the late Lewis H. Durland, retired treasurer of Cornell University. Roy regarded Lew as his best friend. He relied on Durland's advice about investments and interest rates, and greatly admired his business acumen," Johnnie remembers.

A BUSY MAN

Contrary to H.D. Thoreau's philosophy, "If you give money, spend yourself with it," my father always said, "Give of your money or your time, but never both." Well, he mostly hung on to his money, but he sure gave of his time.

While he was still consulting with P&G in 1956, about the time I graduated from Lawrenceville to become a freshman at Cornell, he was elected a director of ConAgra in Omaha, NE, becoming chairman of the executive committee in 1975. In 1957, he became a director of Molinos de Puerto Rico, Inc., an egg-production business in Santurce, Puerto Rico, and in 1958, a director of the Fosgate Citrus Cooperative.

In his hometown, Pops became a director of the internationally famous Ithaca Gun Company in 1959, serving for eight years until it ran into business problems and was sold in 1967. Before it was sold, he was involved in making sure the Smiths, his long-term friends and members of the family that owned the company, got the best deal on the sale. He told me that without his involvement, they could have been taken to the cleaners.

It is interesting to note that the first-time buyers used Ithaca Gun as a cash cow, overextended themselves in the recreation business, and reorganized under Federal bankruptcy laws in 1979. The company that put Ithaca on the international map was brought out of bankruptcy by new owners in 1987, but financial failure again led to liquidation in 1996. After a third change of hands, facing debt, competition and different market conditions, the last owners of the 125-year-old company were forced to sell its equipment at auction and sadly closed the doors on Ithaca Gun a final time in 2005.

In 1961, Pops became a director of Atlantic Telecasting Corporation of Wilmington, NC, the Pepsi-Cola Bottling Company of Wilmington, NC, and the South Carolina Bottling Corporation of Columbia. He also started buying orange groves through the Avalon Citrus Association, Inc., in the Orlando, FL, area, and became president and director of the association in 1962. Then he got into timberland in North Carolina, calling it great business since "You just buy it, and it grows, and after a while, you cut some, and plant some and go away, and it does the same thing all over again."

In 1965 my father became a director of the Variable Annuity Life Insurance Company. In 1966 he became a director of the First National Bank and Trust Company in Ithaca, and then a director of Security of New York State Corporation in Rochester, NY, in 1974, when it took over the bank. He was a member of the trust committee when it became Security-Norstar until 1984, before it became Fleet Norstar Bank.

During this same period Pops became involved in the Tompkins County Area Development Corporation, the First Research Development Corporation in Ithaca, and from 1960 to 1966, was president and director of both the Upstate Small Business Investment Company and Great American Investors.

In 1966, he founded and funded the Park Foundation, Inc., based in Ithaca. In 1968 he became a director of the Occidental Life Insurance Company of Raleigh. Pops also retained his Agricultural Advertising & Research agency, which became a division of RHP Incorporated, and continued to create and place advertising for a few outside clients but mostly for the Park Companies. He held the position of president and director of Ag Research until he turned it over to me to run when I was named VP, Advertising and Promotion of Park Broadcasting in 1976.

In 1972, he became a director of the Raymond Corp., a manufacturer of fork lifts and other material handling equipment, and that same year, a director of Wachovia Bank and Trust Company in Raleigh, NC.

In 1984 he became a director of the Boyce Thompson Institute, a private research laboratory for agriculture and forestry that had moved from Yonkers to the Cornell Campus in Ithaca. Serving on its audit committee and the investment committee, he remained a director of the Institute until his death in 1993.

This was the tip of the iceberg. He was an officer or board member of some twenty other corporations, churches, hospitals, councils, committees and associations and a member of some forty professional, social and honorary organizations. The dozens of awards and citations during his business career are summarized in Appendix C, Memberships and Honors. But what mattered to him most was what he had struggled successfully to get for himself—education.

In 1973 he became a trustee of Ithaca College and in 1977 a trustee of his alma mater, NC State. That same year, he was named to the Advisory Council of the Johnson Graduate School of Management at Cornell University, and in 1989 became a member of the Board of Advisers of the School of Media and Journalism at The University of North Carolina at Chapel Hill.

His responsibilities meant a lot of travel for my father, a lot of it trips to New York City. I remember one of the affairs we attended in New York when my mother and father were seated at the table with Walter Cronkite and his wife, Betsy. It happened to be both my parents' and the Cronkites' fiftieth anniversary. My mother remembers Cronkite asking her what Pops had given her for the special occasion. Dottie proudly replied, "$50,000! A thousand dollars for each year we've been married." Cronkite said, "That's all he gave you? That's awful. If you figure it out, it comes to only $2.74 a day."

When my mother asked him what his wife had given him, she remembers he said, "A stack of arrows and a bow in my front lawn, along with an effigy of me." He said his wife explained it was so his neighbors would finally have a chance to take a shot at him.

My father also met Gen. Alexander Haig in New York City

when he invited and introduced Haig at another affair. My mother and father liked the way Haig's chauffeur handled the limousine and later got in touch with him. Matthew Miele became our family chauffeur in the City from that day on. Mr. Matty, as we call him, could declare fame in his own right. He was the steady driver for Frank Sinatra and the frequent chauffeur for Elvis Presley, the Beatles, Dolly Parton, Chicago, the Beach Boys, Burt Reynolds, the Moody Blues, Rod Serling, Crosby, Stills & Nash, Led Zeppelin, Sharon Stone, John Denver and Eric Clapton, not to mention Mr. Rogers and Alan Shepard of Apollo 14.

When my granddaughters asked him for his autograph after hearing only part of this list, Mr. Matty sent them each a letter listing his famous passengers and ending with the note, "Last But Not Least, My Favorite, THE PARK FAMILY."

COMMITMENTS TO HIGHER EDUCATION

Throughout his career, expanding educational opportunities for others was his highest nonbusiness priority. He spent an enormous amount of time to achieve that goal. As the chancellor of NC State University said in 1978, my father "emerged as one of the nation's most articulate spokesman on the important role of private support for public higher education." And William C. Friday, former president of The University of North Carolina, hailed his contribution: "Among North Carolina's illustrious achievers during this half century, none stands taller than Roy Park. Always of good humor and with a generous heart, he moved among his peers sharing of himself gladly in the service of others."

Over the years, Pops served in many capacities at NC State, including president and chairman of the board of the University Alumni Association, chairman of the public relations committee of the Development Council, and chairman of the Board of Trustees in 1977.

He also became chairman of the NC State University Development Council. His efforts helped propel the university into the top ten universities in the nation in terms of corporate support. "For seven years," said Rudy Pate, who was State's vice chancellor at the time, "he headed our development council. He has one of the greatest organizational minds I've ever encountered. Roy had been a generous and major contributor. He raised literally millions of dollars."

In recognition of his interest, he was honored in 1970 by the NC State Alumni Association with its Meritorious Service Award. In 1975, he received one of one NCSU's first three Watagua Medals, the university's highest nonacademic award.

In 1985 he was inducted into The Order of Walter Hines Page at State, and the same year, he became a Distinguished Alumni Fellow of the NC State University Center for Economic and Business Studies. In early 1992, Pops received the Centennial Award from his alma mater.

Pops's association with Cornell University went back to the beginning of his third career with Hines-Park Foods. He engaged Cornell to research American eating habits before launching his food enterprises, and after his food research in the Cornell labs, Pops made his link with Duncan Hines. Through Cornell he was named a member of the Advisory Council of the New York State College of Agriculture and the Agricultural Experiment Stations at Cornell University, serving from 1965 to 1969.

In November 1976 my father spoke to Cornell MBA students through the Cornell Executive Forum, a program launched by what is now the Samuel C. Johnson Graduate School of Management. He was one of 12 top executive speakers including the chairmen of P&G, Citicorp, Coopers and Lybrand and Morgan Guaranty and the presidents of Chase Bank and Eastern Airlines. In his introduction, Dean H. Justin Davidson said an entrepreneur is a special person who has opted for the excitement and risks of independent businessman rather than the comforts and security of corporate life. He said Roy H. Park is such a man and called him "a uniquely American phenomenon."

In July 1977, Pops became a member of the Advisory Council of the Johnson Graduate School of Management and in one of his talks, he told its graduating class, "Finally, as night comes after day, you'll have your ups and downs. Don't gloat over your success, for it may be only a hair's breadth from a failure. And if you fail don't whimper or give up. Pick up your shield and your sword and go into battle with renewed purpose."

As Johnnie mentioned earlier, in 1983 Pops was instrumental in creating the Lewis H. Durland Memorial Lecture Series which continues to this day. He and a group of supporters endowed the Durland Memorial Fund in honor of the former treasurer of Cornell University. Before Mr. Durland's retirement in 1973, he spent twenty-five years directing Cornell's financial life. While he was treasurer, Cornell's investment portfolio grew from $45.2 million to $322 million.

Lewis H. Durland, right, former treasurer of Cornell University with Tony DiGiacomo, former president of First National Bank and Trust Co.

In 1971, my father began a long-term relationship with The University of North Carolina at Chapel Hill. Chancellor J. Carlyle Sitterson announced the establishment of the Roy H. Park Scholarship and said the first award for the 1971–72 school year would support major expenses of one student a year in the Department of Radio, Television, and Motion Pictures in the University at Chapel Hill.

In 1980, Pops became a trustee of The University of North Carolina's School of Journalism Foundation. In 1982, he was inducted into the NC Broadcasters Hall of Fame. In 1989, he became a member of the Board of Advisers of the School of Media and Journalism at UNC. And on April 8, 1990, he was inducted into the North Carolina Journalism Hall of Fame at The University of

North Carolina at Chapel Hill.

Pops once said, "I love North Carolina. I've known all the governors since O. Max Gardner (from 1929-1933) and I can't remember one that was anything but a fine gentleman."

Richard Cole, the former dean of the School of Journalism and Mass Communication, worked with my father for over 15 years and was the featured speaker at his last Park Communications managers' meeting, in 1992. He called my father "a giant in mass communications, and a self-made man," and Pops was one of his strongest supporters. Our family goes back three generations with Richard, and in April 2005 I spoke at his retirement dinner.

If my father were still alive, I said, "he would be here with bells & whistles, and I'm sure he is looking down on us now."

In commending Richard and lamenting the loss of his leadership, I shared with him one of my father's favorite quotes, the words of the late Peter Kiewit, entrepreneur and former owner of the *Omaha World-Herald* (now the largest employee-employer owned newspaper in the United States), because they so perfectly fit Dean Cole:

> *"I do not choose to be a common man. It is my right to be uncommon if I can. I seek opportunity, not security. I want to take the calculated risk; to dream and to build; to fail and to succeed. I prefer the challenges of life to the calm state of Utopia. I will never cower before any master nor bend to any threat It is my heritage to stand erect, proud, unafraid, to think and act for myself, to enjoy the benefit of my creation, and to face the world boldly and say, 'This I have done."*

Cole put the UNC Journalism School on top and I concluded, "This you have done, Richard Cole, and for this you should be proud. I know all of us are proud of you."

Because of his devotion to education, it was a given that my father would be pursued by other colleges and universities, including another in his hometown, Ithaca College. Pops became a member of the Ithaca College Board of Trustees in 1973 and was elected chairman in 1982.

Johnnie Babcock recalls why he decided to immerse himself in the nitty-gritty of education funding and management at Ithaca College, a highly regarded liberal arts school:

"The local college turned out exceptionally qualified musicians, theatrical professionals, athletic coaches and health-care practitioners. It began to offer courses leading to an undergraduate business management degree after Roy joined them as a trustee."

"He was particularly interested in the college's communications programs in broadcasting and journalism. When he advanced to chairman of the board, he planned and guided the construction of a brand new building for those specialties and saw to it that they were equipped with state-of-the-art equipment. He helped raise funds and New York State money to pay for the school. The handsome new facility began to be identified with Roy H. Park or referred to as the Park Building. Roy did not give the building, to the disappointment and consternation of many on campus and in the community. But he did contribute significant cash even though only a small portion of the total cost. He was proud of the building but to name it he felt would look like a payoff...

James J. Whalen, president of Ithaca College, felt that Roy's enduring commitment to the school came directly from his appreciation for what the school was trying to accomplish. 'I think Roy, to some degree, looked at this and said there are some people up there trying. I think Roy has an appreciation for people that struggle, and I think he helps the struggler. And he has a big impact on this school.'"

Johnnie said, "Park's involvement as a trustee and chairman of the Board at Ithaca College involved working with many Ithaca-based businessmen, many of whom were IC graduates, few of whom had accumulated anywhere near Park's resources. The relatively new and young president of the college had distinguished academic credentials but little hands-on experience with the general management and affairs of an institution of higher learning. He was an attentive student of Chairman Park, who treated him to additional lessons in financial management by making him a director of his local bank, and then chairman of the bank's advisory body, a position the educator held until the bank was relegated to a branch by its final owner. The local advisors were given a commemorative clock and disbanded.

"The president of the college pursued the stewardship of his college much as I did Park's communications businesses. His authority was as absolute as Park wished it to be, and he had almost daily guidance, as did I. If there was any doubt of his loyalty to Park, it was obviated by extra cash Park paid him in addition to a salary that rose in concert with the success of the school. The docile Board ratified quickly Park's agenda, except in real estate and facility management, where some members had definite ideas of their own and plenty of expertise," Johnnie said.

My father was also a member of the Friends of Ithaca College and received an honorary Doctor of Laws degree at the College's 1985 Commencement when he delivered the main address. His outlook on life was exemplified by the conclusion of his speech to the graduating seniors.

He said, "Finally, and I think most important, be honest in your heart, your soul, and your mind. Integrity will help you move forward, and the lack of it will topple you from the perch of whatever success you may achieve."

Many have heard a variation on how nice it is to be remembered, but how much less expensive it is to be forgotten. Not necessarily my father's thoughts, but as far as naming a building or a school I know how he thought. Funding for a named program can be terminated. The name on a building or for a school cannot.

Despite this, on September 15, 1989, Ithaca College in recognition of his efforts on behalf of the College and his accomplishments in the field of communications, named the three-story building the Roy H. Park School of Communications and its home, the Roy H. Park Hall. Housing approximately $2.5 million worth of equipment—was described by its former dean,

Thomas W. Bohn, as "one of the finest, if not the finest, and most complete schools of communication in the country."

In 1991, the Ithaca College Alumni Association also presented him with the highest award given by the college, the Meritorious Service Award.

My father's pride in his close association with both Cornell and Ithaca College became clear to a visitor from N.C. State. As reported by Rudolph Pate in the *NCSU Alumni News* in 1971, the North Carolinian accompanied him from his breakfast on a typical day in July 1970 to his office, where my father "worked through a busy morning of correspondence, telephone calls, staff conferences, then attended lunch with his fellow Rotarians to hear a talk by a university professor on Cornell's plantations.

"After the Rotary Club luncheon," Pate said, "Roy conferred with his assistant, Jean Ballard, put in a heavy schedule of office work, and headed home. On the way, he made a point of taking time to show me the modern campus of Ithaca College and the sprawling grounds of world-renowned Cornell University."[15]

Pops didn't limit his involvement in education to North Carolina and Ithaca-based centers of higher education. He was a trustee and member of the Board of Associates, Meredith College; and a member of the Board of Trustees of Keuka College, Keuka Park, NY, 1967 to 1972, from which he received a Doctorate of Humane Letters in 1967. In 1981, he was named to the Deans Advisory Council of the Newhouse School of Communication at Syracuse University. In 1985, Wake Forest University awarded him an honorary doctorate of laws degree.

In 1990, Shenandoah College and Conservatory in Winchester, VA, calling him a man who could write a book on entrepreneurial spirit, awarded him in 1990 the Free Enterprise medal and named him Entrepreneur of the Year. In his remarks, my father paid tribute to his longtime friend, former U.S. Senator Harry F. Byrd, Jr.

"Senator Byrd, as a fellow newspaper publisher, a fellow farmer, he grows apples, and I grow oranges, and a gentleman of exceptional intelligence and ability, has long been among my most valued advisors," he said.

At age 80, after 60 years in four business careers culminating in a media empire, Pops never forgot his farm roots. It is said, "Take a country boy to the city and they never go back," and my father never went back to the farm. Although he didn't like farm *life*, the farm was in him, and his interest in farming continued throughout his life. Farming and food products gave him his start in public relations, promotion, advertising, franchising, citrus grove and timberland ownership, real estate and investments. Even the majority of his broadcast stations and newspapers were located in farming areas, from North Dakota to North Carolina.

He also never forgot the value of a good education, which was what gave him his start in life, or his home state of North Carolina. His connections to North Carolina State, Cornell and Ithaca College were even more extensive than can be covered in the pages of this book and can be found in Appendix D, *Deeper Connections to Education.* Johnnie Babcock refers to him as the "Teacher of Teachers."

TEACHER OF TEACHERS
by John B. Babcock

"Whether he was involved with N.C. State, Chapel Hill, Cornell or Ithaca College, I have always thought of Roy as the teacher of teachers and remember his growing interest and involvement in education. After the sale of the Hines operation to Procter & Gamble, while he was serving as a consultant to the corporation, he weighed Cornell's offer to lecture and teach. That seemed too tame. He told me that if he were not busy and involved in a variety of projects, he might become just another rich drunk. He resigned his P&G position and set out to conquer the field of communications, and I came aboard to help him.

His new-won fame and growing fortune were a natural attraction to educational institutions. They always need more money. He ignored those simply seeking a handout, but established a close relationship with North Carolina State, his alma mater, and the North Carolina University system in general. He became an advisor to Cornell's new Graduate School of Business, and a trustee at struggling Ithaca College, where he helped with finances and expansion. For a while he also served as a trustee of Keuka College in New York's Finger Lakes region.

Whether it was a dollar-a-holler radio station in a broadcast group, the huge P&G Corporation, a small college or a major university, Park examined and evaluated its operating statement and balance sheet with equal intensity and thoroughness. He was a master at glancing at an analysis sheet that covered most of a large table and pointing out a discrepancy, inconsistency or outright error. He had specific questions that often the chief operating officer being interviewed was unprepared to handle. The embarrassed executive would have to summon staff to come up with a satisfactory answer. Once Park found an anomaly, he often sped through the other figures in the report, sometimes deliberately dismissing the credibility of the report and the business, and always to the distress of the author.

He liked colleges and college people. At N.C. State, before he made any financial gifts of support, he met with officials regularly and devised campaigns to raise money from other alumni. It was said he raised so much money for State over the years that development officials there speak of him in tones of hushed reverence.

He elected the N.C. State president to the board of directors of his Greenville, NC, broadcast stations. To accommodate the educator's attendance at periodic meetings, he held them right in Raleigh. He'd hole up at the Velvet Cloak Inn just off campus and entertain various university officers and state politicos. He made a point also of being seen around lunchtime in the lobby of the old downtown Sir Walter Raleigh Hotel. There he was greeted and glad-handed at noontime by the politicos and old-timers who hung out in that historic watering spot. He was their famed native son.

Park held back no details from his board of the business figures for his stations, saw that I kept accurate minutes of the meetings, which would be signed by the secretary of his companies, his wife

Dorothy. She was usually present by the end of each meeting and tickled to accept her $100 director's fee, a check also given to the university president participant. We'd usually dine that evening with N.C. State officials and discuss everything from finances to the fortunes of the then-seasonal N.C. State athletic team, often a national contender. Roy valued the school's CEO as a business associate and close personal friend.

Despite heavy civic and educational commitments, Pops kept both his Board of Directors and his $100 director's fees small. The Park Broadcasting board in 1981, two years before going public as Park Communications, included John B. Babcock, executive vice president, my father, Lewis H. Durland, my mother, who served as secretary, and Kenneth B. Skinner.

If there was an important public event at Cornell or Ithaca College, Roy was near the top of the list of those invited. He retained a prominent box at the football stadium and could talk in general terms about the prowess of the Ivy League Cornell football team. If he attended part or all of a game, he schmoozed with prominent alumni or political guests. Come bitter weather in November, he'd fill the box with local social friends and neighbors and stay home, not bothering to listen to a radio account of the game.

His focus on education did not distract him from his focus on the many business operations he owned. When it came to his real estate activities, Park had his own ideas and domain. Not really a slumlord, he nonetheless owned several old residences that yielded handsome return as student off-campus rooming houses for Cornell and Ithaca College. He owned and occupied choice space in the office complex that once was headquarters for GLF (later Agway). He bought the First National Bank building, which housed his local bank.

He bargained for parcels of open land that could be developed or become sites for the billboard company he later sold to his son. His real estate manager served as the rent collector for the Ithaca domain but was also called on to inspect and report to Roy on hundreds of acres of tobacco and pulpwood acreage in North Carolina and on large holdings of orange groves in Florida. Sometimes luck can play as big a role as entrepreneurship in a successful venture. Hard work isn't always the answer. But even with luck, nothing ever comes for free (the closest thing being government handouts) and to have a chance at success, you have to put something into the game, minimal though it may be.

When his father was buying those orange groves in Florida his son remembers a particular parcel he bought cheaply on the outskirts of Orlando since he was traveling with him at the time. It was a small acreage plot with an old orange grove that was producing just enough to cover the taxes. His father knew the trees would have to be replaced in a year or so in order to make the grove productive, but his instinct still told him it was a good deal. Sure enough, before a year was up, he was approached by a company that wanted to mine the phosphate they found under the grove and offered to pay good money to do it. More importantly, they offered to replenish the mined area with topsoil and replant it with new orange trees. Not only did Roy collect a substantial sum of money for what was under the ground, but a brand new orange grove was put in place at no cost to him.

With the grove then producing a profit, the property substantially increased in value. That's when real estate offers spurred by the expanding Orlando market poured in and he eventually sold the property for many times what he paid.

But mostly Roy earned the hard way his public label, "communications mogul," and his interests and involvement roamed far and wide. You never knew where 'Pops' would pop up next. And pop up he did in my family's life," Johnnie said.

CHAPTER 20
A HELPING HAND?
by John B. Babcock

Park Broadcasting in the late 1970s was a thriving, highly profitable cash cow, more profitable than those listed broadcast groups that publicized financial results. Park credited much of our stellar performance to my drive as chief operating officer. Our relationship had never been closer. He had my full support and complete trust.

In June 1977, my youngest daughter Jeannie was graduated from Ithaca High school with a record fully as solid as was turned in by her sisters, Susan, who was finishing a tough curriculum at Smith College, and Nancy, who was headed for a fine arts degree at Cornell. Both degrees were being paid out of my own pocket. But Jeannie had lived through enough of our cold winters in the Northeast and passed up acceptance at an Ivy League school, preferring to head south, preferably to University of North Carolina at Chapel Hill. That choice had my enthusiastic support. My associate, Roy Park, Jr., was a recent graduate of UNC-Chapel Hill. He had high praise for the solid preparation at Chapel Hill that fortified him with the basic learning tools to go on and earn his MBA at Cornell's Johnson Graduate School of Management.

While his dad was a distinguished alumnus and key fund-raiser for NC State University in Raleigh, I presumed that Pops also had influence and would be given ready audience at The University of North Carolina at Chapel Hill. The senior Park had funded his own son's education at Chapel Hill and persuaded the university to accept him after he busted out of Cornell as an undergraduate.

Jeannie applied for entrance to UNC-Chapel Hill, and I asked Park to put in a good word for her. He warmly agreed. The summer wore on, and Jeannie grew anxious when no response was forthcoming. It became too late for her to apply to another institution. We relied on Roy Park to pave the way to easy acceptance. I knew about such arrangements because my dad had been chairman of the trustees at Cornell University. Jeannie, however, got the standard rejection letter from UNC-Chapel Hill.

I repeated my request for help and big Roy promised to make some calls. Time marched on, and September was at hand. Still no good news from Chapel Hill. Again, I urged Roy to give us a hand. Instead, he gave Jeannie and me the bad news.

He said he was so closely identified with NC State that his heavy support there made him less than welcome to seek a favor at Chapel Hill. He said UNC-Chapel Hill people told him they were full and unable to take more students. I expressed distinct disappointment, and Jeannie was crushed.

A few days later, while we were still trying to recover, he met with Jeannie and me and said the one thing he could do was see that she was taken as a freshman at NC State, where he was a heavy-hitter. He put in a call to Rudy Pate, his main contact for alumni fund-raising at NC State, and with Jeannie and me listening in, Rudy promised to secure immediate entrance approval, which he did. A very pleased Roy Park then elaborated at great length the virtue and quality of a degree from State, which, like Cornell, was a revered land-grant educational facility. I'm not sure that Roy really thought that girls required, or were capable of, the intensity of study that was requisite for their male peers. State had plenty of openings, and the college was eager for applicants who could pay full tuition.

Between a rock and a hard place, Jeannie gratefully packed up and reported to the Raleigh campus, where again, Rudy saw to her safe arrival and enrollment. She reported to a large freshman dormitory and got acquainted with her roommate. She signed up for the required freshman courses.

Because I supervised the Park Greenville TV and radio stations in eastern North Carolina, I had to visit Raleigh often. I would fly into Raleigh and rent a car for the two-hour drive to my stations in Greenville. I rarely stayed the night in Raleigh. Roy insisted that I spend as much time as possible on the ground, pushing the Greenville management group for sales profit.

I managed a new trip schedule such that I would have a night in Raleigh, preferably a Sunday on my way to Greenville, or a Friday after an exhaustive few days at the stations. That gave me some time to visit Jeannie on the Raleigh campus and share an evening together. It didn't deprive Park of my full week devotion to his agenda. Just my weekend was sacrificed, and, after all, Roy worked as long and hard both Saturday and Sunday as he did weekdays. He despised idle weekends as much as he did vacations.

As her freshman year progressed, Jeannie tentatively revealed to me that the coursework was far too easy. She wanted to major in economics and communications. But she found scant choices in either and shyly suggested that our family money might better be spent at an institution that offered the quality of business and communication courses she had wanted to take at Chapel Hill.

Jeannie moved the next academic year, enrolling in the Newhouse School of Communication at Syracuse University to pursue a degree in communications and business. After her sophomore year earning all As, her professors begged her to stay and earn a dual degree of business and communications. But, as at Raleigh, there was not enough depth and choice in economic courses. So, foregoing the communications component, Jeannie satisfied her appetite for demanding coursework in economics by taking her last two years at St. Lawrence University. Where? Way north at Canton, NY, up on the frozen St. Lawrence River, almost to Canada. Weather aside, she ended up well educated, a result she felt could have been achieved at The University of North Carolina at Chapel Hill, only a few minutes from Roy Park's alma mater. Jeannie went on to a career in banking and professional freelance writing for high-tech companies. She is happily married and lives in Atlanta.

CHAPTER 21
THROUGH OTHERS' EYES

With money in your pocket
you are wise and you are handsome
and you sing well, too.

—Yiddish Proverb

My father could never carry a tune, and I inherited this inability as well. But like many self-made men, he was susceptible to flattery. He got plenty of it. Nobody ever accused him of singing off-tune. As Johnnie Babcock points out, extravagant praise and accolades were heaped on Pops over the years with seldom a negative word. "But how many of these were the expressions rooted in the hope of someday garnering a piece of his pie? How many were from celebrants who would bristle at one harsh word directed at their reputations?" Johnnie asked, pointing out, "The fraternity of wealth and power remains faithful to itself.

"Consider for a moment all these rich accolades," Babcock said. "If all these quotes were glowing in a book from famous academic, publishing and political giants, true captains of industry, what weight would anybody give a couple of complaining serfs? They'd say those guys have problems. Look how the rest of the world worships this man."

Despite the accolades (Appendix E, A Few Accolades*)*, the scales have to be balanced with our personal experiences.

The *Ithaca Journal* did a feature on my father in May 1985. The headline was ITHACA'S MEDIA BARON KEEPS HIS EYES ON

THE FUTURE, and staff reporter Joseph V. Junod interviewed a number of people who had known or worked with him. Under a subhead reading VIEWS DIFFER ON PARK'S STYLE OF LEADERSHIP, he reported, "Like most people in the public eye, Roy H. Park, Sr. draws both positive and negative responses from people who have dealt with him."

There is no question that Pops treated different people in different ways and came across to individuals differently—no question about that. He was aggressive. Remember the way he courted and won my mother? To many, he was charming. But in dealing with me, he was frequently insensitive, vindictive and just plain mean-spirited. Some others were treated the same way, and he could be ruthless and grudge-bearing. He knew he had absolute control over all his employees and did not hesitate to exercise it.

Junod reported that Conrad Fink spent three years with the Park firm as executive vice president of the newspaper divisions, pointing out that he joined Park in 1977 after twenty-one years with the Associated Press, the last ten as a vice president. Junod wrote:

Fink left Park in 1980 and now divides his time between Athens, GA, where he teaches journalism at The University of Georgia, and his upstate New York farm. Asked to describe his years with the Park organization, Fink, 52, said, "I found it to be a very distasteful experience. It was educational in many, many ways, but I am glad it's over."

Asked if he was able to fully exploit his experience and imagination during his tenure on Terrace Hill, where Park maintains corporate offices, Fink flatly replied "No." Fink, hesitant to speak out on the record about Park, described his former boss's operating style as "highly individualistic." "He's built a fine company," Fink said. "With some adjustments, he could have built a company two or three times the size it is now." Asked about why he left Park, Fink responded, "We agreed to disagree."[16]

Another vice president of operations for Park Newspapers, Jim Harris, also parted company with my father after eighteen months. As reported by Dumbell in the *Charlotte Observer* in May 1982, Harris said my father was " ' brilliant and has unique management techniques. I resigned because I had differences with him over management philosophy. He'd surround himself with financial people,' Harris said, 'and I felt I was the only newspaper man on board. The emphasis is not on the editorial part.' "

One of the financial candidates interviewed by Pops was told in the interview there were no "yes men" in the management group. He said my father told him he wanted people to tell him what they thought, and that they had a "free enough environment" to agree or disagree. Not many management people who worked for my father felt that way after they worked for him. Before he was hired, one of them said my father told him he wanted him "to get all the information about a situation, to make an informed and rational decision based on the facts, and then move on to the next opportunity."

That part may be true. Decisions my father made were generally based on the facts, and usually well informed. But he made some decisions on less than rational grounds, and if you disagreed with him, God help you. The more you tried to express your thoughts, the harder he pushed back—his mind already made up. It wasn't wise to tell, let alone convince, Roy H. Park he was wrong, especially when his decisions were based on a skewed view of certain people, and the certainty of his power.

THE SUSCEPTIBILITY OF POWER

Power is the ultimate aphrodisiac.

—Henry Kissinger

Power feeds on itself. You lose sight of reality and believe only what you want to believe and what you think is the truth. If everything you do is right, how can anything you do be wrong? Therefore, power is susceptible to flattery.

If I had one piece of advice, it would be to make a list of the friends or people who flatter you who have not asked you for anything. More than likely it will be a short list. Those are the ones you can trust. Those are the ones who will be with you down the line when pandering and flattery are no longer meaningful, and when just being there counts.

I do not like flattery. It embarrasses me. Although I might make an exception if this book receives a few words of praise.

Power feeds on flattery. It insulates and divorces you from reality. It can lead to self-destruction. People with power become obsessed with it. But it backfires when you go that step too far. Dictators are overthrown, revolutions materialize, individuals crash. Allow power to consume you, and expect to go from a person revered to a person despised.

Still, the majority worship power, and if they don't have it for themselves, they worship those they think are powerful. Riding on the coattails of someone they regard as having power, they feel, gives power to them. It is never the case.

Babcock recalls that all the way through my father's North Carolina association, he was involved in fund-raising. There were individuals on campuses he raised funds for who served him like map-carrying messengers for a military officer. He refers to them as toadies making sure that potential givers were treated well.

But those in power don't reciprocate. They use power to entice, cajole and promise. In the end, they retain power for themselves. Power gives you *control* over other people. There is a country saying that sometimes you get and sometimes you get got. My father once told my wife something she never forgot after he fired someone who was supposedly a longtime family friend, "You get them before they get you." But despite his power base, he allowed himself to be trumped by flattery on occasion.

Anyone who has ever been taken advantage of by someone he trusted would, one assumes, become paranoid or at least skeptical. My father tended to be paranoid ever since he had been burned by his accountant in Ithaca back in their early days. His characteristic wariness should have countered his susceptibility to flattery. He said many times he never cared about the money. But money is power, and power succumbs to flattery from people who use you for their own agenda.

A striking instance of this is what happened when my father received a letter from someone claiming to be a distant relative from North Carolina, who was trying to set up an appointment to see him. The letter was flattering and referred glowingly to Pops's accomplishments. A meeting was set up, and a young man appeared in my father's office. I have no idea what he said, but he convinced my father he was distantly related and an avid admirer. He said he was looking for a job, and my father was so taken with his sincerity he hired him.

He had no experience in any area the company operated in, and there were no openings at headquarters. But he claimed to be a skilled photographer and suggested that he become my father's eyes in the field. He also convinced Pops to do a documentary. He visited every holding my father had, questioned the managers, saying he was my father's relative and emissary and photographed the buildings for the purported documentary. The managers were told he was my father's personal representative, and that they were to cooperate fully with him. My father funded his trips all over the country for seven months, accepting the young man's reports on each company as helpful.

As time went by, my father became somewhat obsessive about the relationship, relying on his reports and taking everything he reported as the truth. When this young "relative" returned several months later, richer by far by pocketing most of the excessive funding for his travels, he presented my father with his massive collection of photographs. He found a place to reside in Ithaca, and it was evident he intended to stay. He had gained my father's confidence but not my mother's. She hired a private detective to investigate. The reports that started coming back were suspicious. He was not who he said he was; he had no connection with the Park family.

When police executed a search warrant, they found in his apartment copies of letters he had written to the vast majority of the people listed in the *Forbes 400*. They were virtually identical, claiming he was a relative. Each letter was tailored to the individual history of the recipient, based on research he had done on that person. Apparently my father was the first, and possibly the only one, who fell for it. The man was finally escorted by police out of Ithaca and out of the State.

At any rate, if you ever wonder who you *can* trust, check out the movie *Screamers* as a good example of how difficult it can be to find out who you *can't*.

Johnnie Babcock remembers another example of Pops's susceptibility to flattery, involving someone my father thought could do no wrong.

GOOD OLE BOYS
by John Babcock

Native North Carolinians are an exclusive breed. Wherever they spend their life, whatever their career, they never abandon their roots to their home state. Roy Park spent more years in rural New York than he did in the South. But binding personal friendships, close business ties, political bonds—none of them had the warmth North Carolinians and Southerners in general have for one another.

Sitting across from his desk, as I did for thousands of hours over the years, I witnessed countless phone conversations between Roy and those who called him. Where most powerful businessmen take refuge behind screens of interceding assistants before picking up the phone, Roy listed his home phone and business numbers prominently and was as likely to answer the ring himself as to rely on a secretary. If the call originated from North Carolina, his demeanor softened. He would settle back in his stately leather chair and slip into a soft Southern welcome for his caller.

Be it the governor, an ex-governor, a college president, a business tycoon or maybe just old "Pea Vine" who wanted to talk about Roy's television station, the conversation oozed with first-name familiarity. They were all Good Ole Boys, and if they were flatterers they had an even greater edge. One southern boy really had Roy's number. This talented salesman flattered Roy to a degree that was disgusting to others on the station staff and to us in Ithaca. Roy loved it and boasted about the salesman's ability.

It wasn't long till he was promoted and became Roy's main contact at the station. He avoided the regular reporting channel through my office. I was never close to him and over the years had never been invited to his home, though I was a frequent visitor to the homes of other key employees. One jealous staffer let me in on the real scoop. He hinted that his boss acquired almost 100 percent of his furniture and personal items at the expense of the broadcasting station. Here's the way it worked:

Business clients buy commercial messages sold by broadcast station salesmen. The Federal Communications Commission requires that accurate and notarized records be kept for each and every commercial (spot) aired and logged by the station. As each spot is performed and verified, it is recorded and billed to the client at a contracted sales price. Some spots may be run at no charge, such exceptions brought about by technical failure in performing the spot, management granting a "bonus" spot to settle a viewer complaint, or in servicing a trade-out.

Trade-out was the culprit here. Almost every station acquires furniture, vehicles, equipment, even meals at a restaurant, with advertising schedules priced to compensate for the amount of goods or services received. It is a common broadcast practice to save cash expenses and at the same time get some value out of otherwise idle airtime, the station's sole product. An automobile dealer may trade out a car for a given dollar total of advertising spots. He gets "retail" or more for the car, and the station is spared a heavy cash outlay. Everybody's happy.

That is, until skullduggery enters the scene. Our internal auditor discovered a large number of ads for one auto dealer described as "bonus," "make-good" or simply "no-charge." A friendly bookkeeper at the car dealership was carrying these same spots on his books as payment for one of its luxury cars. Where was the car? It was registered to the employee's wife!

Further audits revealed that over time, this man had furnished his home, paid for personal entertainment, clothing, cars, etc., at the expense of Roy's station. False and illegal affidavits paved the way to my firing our fallen star. Without admitting any embarrassment or chagrin, Roy ordered that each and every trade for radio and TV advertising had to be preapproved by him personally, with written proof that the value received went to the station, not an individual. This was a detailed and messy chore, but recall that it was undertaken by an owner and CEO who already personally approved every salary increase for every employee, be it as small as $5 a week.

Controlling commercial advertising traffic on our stations achieved new prominence, though it had escaped Roy's eagle eyes these many years. Like cash boxes at a newspaper, it was just one more attraction for thievery that had to be tested and monitored. Roy actually enjoyed digging into such detail. He trusted no one 100 percent. He also learned in the course of improving controls that being a Good Ole Boy was no rock-solid guarantee of honor and honesty.

Flattery can dull the instincts of many powerful people. Perhaps Roy's instincts were more reliable when it came to acquisitions and balance sheets.

CHAPTER 22
RETURN TO THE FOURTH ESTATE

Every ceiling, when reached, becomes a floor, upon which one walks as a matter of course and prescriptive right.

—Aldous Huxley

A year after I joined the company to run the outdoor division, my father began to expand his fourth career in media into the Fourth Estate. He had reached the legal limit allowed at the time in ownership of broadcast properties (seven AMs, seven FMs, and seven TV stations), and his lifelong dream, as projected in his college yearbook forty-one years earlier, was to become "a lord of the fourth estate." He had to follow a long road to get there, but he finally did.

In addition, he needed new places to invest the burgeoning returns from his holdings. With $105 million cash in hand, he was ready for further acquisitions, and his love for newsprint persisted. "I'd always wanted to buy newspapers," he said. "Ever since I wrote features for the *Technician* or sold them to newspapers in Raleigh, Durham and Winston-Salem while I was in college, I wanted my own newspaper. I don't know anything that I could do that would give me more happiness than buying…newspapers."

On November 1, 1972, at the age of sixty-two when many people start thinking about retirement, my father bought his first newspaper, the *Daily Sun,* in Warner Robins, GA, for cash. The following year he went on to purchase the *Union-Sun & Journal* in Lockport, NY, and the *Journal Messenger* in Manassas, VA. These first acquisitions set the size standard that was the common bond for the rest of his acquisitions; they were small-town, mostly rural newspapers in the 10,000 to 25,000 circulation range. None of his papers had a circulation of more than 50,000. "We know how to operate in small towns," Pops said. "We wouldn't know how to operate in New York City, Buffalo or Oakland." Never forgetting his rural upbringing, he would say, "I'm a real country boy. I've still got a little hayseed in my hair."

In 1975 he acquired a daily in Brooksville, FL, and one in Nebraska City, NE. In northern New York State, he bought two in Ogdensburg and one each in Massena, Canton and Potsdam. In 1977, he bought papers in Plymouth, IN, and Norwich, NY, and in 1978, two in McAlester, OK, which he then merged.

With these newspapers added to his broadcast properties, my father, in 1978, headed the largest individually owned communications business in the country. As for the relationship between his electronic media and his venture into print, he did not foresee newspapers being replaced by television or news transmitted on cable channels.

He maintained that there are three characteristics of newspapers that would help assure that medium's survival: you can take it with you, you don't have to take notes on it, and you can clip stories from it.

In 1979, acquisitions really picked up, with the purchase of a daily in Macomb, IL, and two more in Broken Arrow and Sapulpa, OK. Then seven years after buying his first newspaper, he reached another milestone. He became a newspaper owner in his native state on May 2, 1979, when he bought the *Newton Observer-News-Enterprise*. This was followed in the same year with papers in Morganton and Statesville, NC. The Statesville paper, which he bought for a little over $10 million, became his biggest newspaper in North Carolina with a circulation of 18,000.

In 1980, Pops purchased a newspaper in Perry, GA, one each in Concord, Davidson, and Kannapolis, NC, and another in Coldwater, MI. In 1981, he bought two more in Phillips County, AR.

More North Carolina acquisitions followed in 1982, with papers in Clinton, Marion, Lumberton and two in Aberdeen all joining the Park Group.

Within four years, my father had picked up eleven additional newspapers in the Tar Heel State. As he told a senior in the School of Journalism in an interview for the *UNC Journalist*, "We like North Carolina because it is a rapidly growing, progressive state. It is also becoming a center of new industry. No matter how good a paper is, if you don't have a good and expanding market you aren't going to grow that much."

FURTHER INTO THE FOURTH

Along with the North Carolina newspapers already in hand, 1982 also saw papers in North Dakota, in Arkansas and another in Virginia joining the Park Group. In 1984, two more newspapers came aboard, one in New York and another in Indiana. Several more came aboard in 1985: two in New York, four in Kentucky and another one in North Carolina.

In 1986, the group picked up three newspapers in Pennsylvania, two in Iowa, one in Minnesota, and three in Oklahoma. In 1987, six more in Kentucky came in plus two in Idaho. In 1988, six more North Carolina newspapers came aboard, along with another in Kentucky and Indiana. The following year two more North Carolina newspapers were acquired, and finally in 1991, the group acquired its last newspaper, in Minnesota. This capped off his fourth career in communications, that of media baron fulfilling the prophecy of his 1931 college yearbook.

A chronology of his newspaper acquisitions and dates is also found in Appendix B, Building a Media Empire. By 1991, he owned 144 newspapers of which 41 were daily, 38 nondaily, and 58 controlled-distribution weeklies. Another seven were monthly tabloid magazines. Just as his broadcasting properties catered to medium-sized markets, the vast majority of my father's newspapers, as I said, had circulations under 20,000. But by 1991, his newspapers combined reached more than one million American homes. Adding his broadcast holdings, his media properties reached nearly a fourth of all American households in twenty-three states.

ACQUISITION METHODOLOGY

When he started purchasing newspapers, he said "I wouldn't be surprised if this didn't keep me busy for a while." Asked why people sell their newspapers to him, he said, "I believe it's because some people send someone else in. I come myself. I don't go with three offers in my pocket. I sit across the table and tell them what I can do." Pops would make an offer on the spot and "knock off a letter of agreement right there, and that's the end of it. I like to deal with the person who can make the decision and make it stick."

"In all acquisitions," he told students at Cornell Johnson Business of Management School in 1976, "offer to buy for cash. It sure gets you the best price and will knock out of the box the fellow who offers a small down payment and paper on the property he is buying."

Whether it was a broadcast station or a newspaper, my father was able to make personal assessments that pinpointed any weakness on the part of the seller that could be used to his advantage. Generally he was dead-on when it came to evaluating and persuading people when he was going after an acquisition.

As Babcock points out, "One owner was an old man with an unprepared son-in-law his obvious successor. Pops convinced the senior he would earn more from investing the cash purchase money and not have to worry about the future. Another was an owner whose family succession was to a twelve-year-old son. A third was a gentleman frequently at odds with his son's decisions. He took the cash, and his son was trained to be an exemplary manager. The seller was satisfied. He died happy, if not as rich as he could have been by shopping the property.

"In another case, a newspaper owner's wife had terminal cancer. Pops offered a pretty fair price—all cash and quickly—and wrapped up the deal overnight. After working with him closely over the years, Johnnie said, "There was almost always a highly personal weakness for selling to which Pops homed in on like a bird dog on scent." And he was persistent. Aside from studying his prospects, if the initial meeting did not result in a definitive possibility of a sale, my father stayed in touch with his targets through gifts and letters on a steady basis.

Other newspapers were sold to my father for tax reasons and included payments over several years to reduce the seller's tax liability. Rep. Morris K. Udall, D-AZ, pointed out, as reported in 1979 by Virgil Gaither in the *Tulsa Tribune*:

> Even if, in its wisdom and within its discretion, the IRS should find the value of this newspaper to be "only" $7.5 million, the tax rate would require payment of over $5 million. This would still be more than one owner could borrow, since interest charges would be better than double the earnings of the newspaper. Is it any wonder that the heirs must sell, or that an owner sells prior to death to put his estate in order? There are no other options.[17]

But most of the time the newspapers did not come to him, so Pops went after them with an offer that was too good to pass up. "Some people want cash, and we'll pay cash," he said. His method of operation was the same: he courted the owners using his Southern charm and reputation as a sharp businessman. He promised to keep the papers just as they had always been, and his offer usually included a deal in which the owner kept control of the paper for a few years.

As an example of how aggressive his approach to prospecting and recruiting was, I came across this letter to my father from the publisher from the *Sampson Independent* dated July 21, 1981:

> I wanted to write you to explain my actions at the

banquet for the NC Press Association. I am not sure what I said to you when you asked me about joining your organization—frankly I was so shocked I did not know what to say. After reflecting back, I think I told you that I was happy where I am, which is the case.

I am 57 years old and have lived in Clinton for 16 years. I have a good job here, I have a pleasant relationship with Jim Boone and others in this organization and the portion of the newspaper, plus some other publications have found the job of continuing this paper in what we would like it to be is a job that greatly interests me. Neither my wife nor I have any great desire in moving, unless of course, we become bored with our situation here.

I hope I was not rude to you, and I am still not quite sure what I said to you. In any case, I am flattered that you would consider me for a job in your organization.

But more often than not his persistence and ability to close the deal paid off. As Gaither reported in the *Tulsa Tribune:*

Such was the case with C.A. McWilliams, who sold the *Broken Arrow Ledger*, a daily, and three weeklies, the *Jenks Journal*, *Bixby Bulletin* and *Tulsa Southside Times*, to Park Newspapers, a New York–based chain which now owns a total of nine Oklahoma newspapers, including the dailies *Sapulpa Herald* and *McAlester News-Capital & Democrat.*

Although he did not disclose the selling price, McWilliams said he and his wife "always had a policy that if anyone wanted it [the newspapers] badly enough, we would sell it. They [Park] wanted it, so they bought it."

McWilliams indicated he had been approached about selling by publishing firms within Oklahoma, but said their offers were much lower than Park's. "The key is that they [the chains] are aggressive. They have people out all the time looking for papers to buy," McWilliams said.

"At one time I had the ambition of owning several papers, but I was so busy running what I had that I didn't have time to go out chasing down leads," he added. "A lot of people, for instance, would like to have bought the Sapulpa paper, but they [the Park chain] were in there after it. The same with the McAlester paper."[18]

As Jim Dumbell reported in his interview with my father in the *Charlotte Observer:*

> Some newspaper experts say Park has a reputation for being more interested in the financial than the journalistic side of newspapers....
>
> John Morton, a Washington, D.C., newspaper analyst, says of Park, "He has a reputation for being a very tight-fisted operator. I'm not aware of any of his papers being notably improved. But not otherwise, either. And I gather he's paid fairly good prices. I understand he's been willing to pay somewhat more dearly than others." When it comes to a purchase price, Park says, "If you get a good property and a good market, it doesn't really matter if you pay a little too much for it. It's what you can do with it that's important."[19]

Pops' strategy after acquiring a newspaper with cash, if not on hand then readily borrowed from a bank, was to let the local management run it. He was mainly interested in seeing that the properties turned a profit. Only twenty-five or so people were employed at Park headquarters in Ithaca, and my father was cautious about the speed at which his acquisitions grew. "We may add one [paper to the chain] per quarter. If we added more than that, we would have to increase our staff," he explained. God forbid his payroll would have to go up.

LOCAL AUTONOMY (WITH A LEASH ON THE BOTTOM LINE)

A.J. Liebling said, "Freedom of the press is guaranteed only to those who own one." My father gave his newspapers plenty of freedom but only if they came through on the bottom line.

J. Montgomery Curtis, retired vice-president of Knight-Ridder Newspapers, says, "Park had a reputation in New York State of being a very, very clean and highly ethical man about money. There was nothing unethical ever, but he's shrewd. I recall he did not oppose his newspapers doing anything good, but neither did he encourage it, unless it helped him make money....There's nothing wrong with that as long as you put some of the money back in the paper."

"A lot of people are greedy," my father said, "They want to make money at somebody else's expense. I think what you have to do is put up as many safeguards as you can that you don't make money at other people's expense. Or by making your product less desirable by raising advertising or circulation price, for instance, or by cheapening the product."

As Gaither reported in the *Tulsa Tribune*:

Park also makes no apologies for his newspapers, and claims that one of the chief criticisms of chain operations—namely that they are just out to make a buck—is just so much nonsense, at least in his case. "Last year, 1982, we won upwards of 50 awards for editorial work and community service. From my farm background, I remember the statement that 'You can't starve a profit out of a cow.' In many cases we lose money on these properties for two or three years.

Sure you can go for the short buck, but it is better in the long run to strengthen the paper. We try to build the community, because that is the best way for the newspaper to grow. Show me a dormant community and I'll show you a dormant newspaper. We encourage and motivate growth in every way we can.[20]

As my father told Clifton Metcalf, Jr., writing for the *UNC Journalist*, when he "buys a paper, he tries at first to keep the staff as it was before the sale. 'We don't go in, and lop off heads,' he said. 'Instead, we just let attrition take its effect. At first, we don't know who the good people are.' Park said, 'This initial stability was a responsible business practice. It is also something responsible owners were often concerned about.'"[21]

When Pops asked a former owner to stay as general manager during a transitional period, however, he was expected to live strictly by budgets approved in Ithaca. The Ithaca office also expected detailed records and reports, down to the disposition of every copy the presses ran off. He retained decision-making power over capital purchases. His management style was not to send many corporate directives to his newspaper executives except when the profit picture seemed to be getting dim. "Veto power over major business decisions is held in Ithaca, but day-to-day operations are under individual control. These are subject only to precise reporting and business decisions which measure accountability and ensure good performance," he said.

My father was well-known as an entrepreneur who knew how to read a financial statement. He was a patient and relentless builder, not a reformer, and he didn't use his papers or stations to advance any political or ideological cause.

Known for his hands-on management style in running his newspapers, he showed no apparent interest in using the power and influence that might come from newspaper ownership. He supported editorial autonomy and encouraged his editors to maintain each paper's local identity and image, from typeface to editorial content.

As reported in *Business Week* in 1977:

Unlike other owners of multiple broadcasting or newspaper properties, Park has not attempted to give the components of his empire a single look. Headquarters supplies market research, pointers on salesmanship, and capital for improvements in facilities, but says little about editorial viewpoints, program choices, or how news should be covered.

"Park insists on local autonomy," the article reported, quoting Babcock as saying, "That's more than just a slogan with us."[22]

It was the same policy he established from the beginning with his broadcast properties. His belief in local autonomy was confirmed by setting up a separate corporation for each newspaper and broadcast station. His headquarters staff provided leadership, motivation and financial guidance and capital but rarely, if ever, interfered with editorial viewpoints and content.

As he told Gaither during his interview for the *Tulsa Tribune*:

> The fear among some people that chain newspapers will "control" the news or dictate editorial positions is completely unjustified. We have Republican newspapers, Democrat newspapers, and Independent newspapers. Wherever possible we retain the original owners of the paper to operate it. Our only instruction to them is to serve the community as best they can. We do not send out editorials to our newspapers. We never send out an article saying "use this," he said.

As Jim Dumbell of the *Charlotte Observer* noted in his 1982 interview with Pops over lunch on the enclosed porch of his home:

> We were high above Cayuga's [lake] waters, as the words of nearby Cornell University's alma mater [song] go, [the melody would be familiar to North Carolinians, but in Chapel Hill the verse is "Hark the sound of Tar Heel voices"], when Park [again] said, "I never said to my newspapers anything that was to be printed. I never urge them to write editorials that agree with me.

We've got Democratic, Republican and Independent newspapers, but we've got no Communist papers—at least I hope not."

For lunch there was barbeque Park had brought back from Parker's Barbeque in Wilson during a recent trip to North Carolina.

Park discussed his view of the mission of a community newspaper. "We do try to build our communities," Park said, "and tell our people to support things that are good for the community, such as jobs, and less crime. We want decent living, good government and all the things that make an area a nicer place to live." He asked that each of his newspapers devote more than 50 percent of their front-page space to local news, and make their editorials local.[23]

My father felt strongly about emphasizing local news coverage, with more than 50 percent of the front page covering feature stories about people and events in the community, and plenty of local sports coverage. Where larger newspapers had circulation in Park markets, he wanted "nobody to beat us with local news." He said, "We write on subjects people can do something about, rather than put in two columns of canned stuff from some [wire] service."

My father told *UNC Journalist* reporter Metcalf his emphasis was on the time-tested and home-grown staples of small-town journalism—lots of news about churches, Boy Scouts, high school football games—saying, "If your kid is playing, you're going to watch it." And he expected his reporters to get into that. He told Metcalf, "One of the most important characteristics a reporter could have was a broad background and an interest in a wide variety of subjects. You can't be dull and be a good reporter," he said.[24]

As reported by Byrd in the *Winston-Salem Journal*:

His chain of papers is often overlooked in the industry because of its niche: "community newspapers," the world of small-town publications where who came to dinner can sometimes make the front page. In the aggregate, Park's chain is large. But individually, the papers are small, all under 20,000 circulation. And the subjects he insists they cover don't necessarily excite.

"Group [picture] shots are supposed to be taboo," he says of most newspapers' practice. "But how are you going to get all those people in? It's not uncommon for us to have the faces of 100 people distinguishable in one issue. Some journalism schools say that's pretty bad, but it sure helps you at home where the people are reading the paper."

He knows big-city newspapers scoff at so-called "chicken-dinner journalism," but it doesn't bother him. "They do a good job of covering the big stories, but they don't cover the stories we cover in our newspapers," he says. "We think a small businessman remodeling his store or taking in a partner, we think people ought to know about that."[25]

My father did not go after rundown newspapers or papers in communities lacking growth potential. He wanted his newspapers to be good community newspapers. Al Neuharth said the Park properties' reputation is topnotch: "It's considered generally that he took a small handful of communications properties and parlayed them to what's now a substantial and growing institution—quite highly regarded everywhere."

Pops did hire professionals to critique his newspapers but did not have an overall editorial director because he felt that would tend to stereotype them. He also did not see the critiques until after they were shared with the managers. As reported by Dumbell in the *Charlotte Observer*, one of the consultants my father hired to critique the papers to his managers was:

> Ken Byerly, a former professor at the UNC School of
> Journalism, and then publisher of his own newspaper in
> Lewiston, Montana. "After Roy buys a paper it becomes
> a better paper," Byerly said. "There's no question about
> that. When he's needed an editor I've had him ask me,
> 'Can you help me find one who's good, and good for
> the community?' He's always after quality and services
> to the community, but he watches the bottom line like a
> tiger."[26]

Apart from fanatical attention to financial details, Pops was
about as laissez-faire as he could get. (Of course, the papers were
in distant parts, so the managers did not have to endure the ordeal
of the 8 AM meetings.)

Ten years after Pops purchased his first newspaper, the *Daily
Sun,* in Warner Robins, Jim Dumbell of the *Charlotte Observer*
interviewed Foy S. Evans, who started and operated the newspaper
for twenty-three years. At the time, Evans had become the mayor
of Warner Robins, and he said,

> I stayed on for 18 months during the transition. The
> paper was five days, now it is Sunday too, and advertising-
> wise it has grown a lot. The subscription price is up too.
> There was some staff turnover, but I won't say it was
> Park's fault. I had held together a staff that was better
> than the newspaper deserved. There was no wholesale
> firing or housecleaning.

> Park gives you," Evans said, "as a general manager,
> guidelines where money is concerned, but as for editorial
> directions he leaves that to the local people. He gave me
> no editorial direction whatsoever.

Asked if the guidelines were aimed at making more money, Evans laughed. "I'd say yes. He has his own ideas with the budgets and reports. But he lived up to the contract, and as a lawyer I have come to know what is in the contract that counts." Evans did not elaborate.

As Dumbell reported,

If Evans has unspoken reservations having sold to Park, there are none where the former owners of the Statesville Record and Landmark, purchased in 1979, four years before the interview took place. The owners were Chester Middlesworth and his mother, Pauline Middlesworth, who together owned 50%, along with former editor and general manager, J.P. Huskins, who had 12%.

Middlesworth was later named Pops's regional coordinator for his North Carolina newspapers.

Park had courted him for five years before completing the deal, which is not his longest courtship. It took him twelve years to persuade the owners of the Robesonian before they would let him buy it. Middlesworth said he was "comfortable with my father," and "For the first year to two we didn't even talk business during our negotiations. We had offers from six buyers, including the New York Times, Harte Hanks, and Freedom Newspapers. A couple of them offered more than Roy did, but we checked him out and he appealed to us.

"One reason," Huskins added, "was that Park was a native of this State. I am as pleased as can be with the new ownership, and I can't see any change in the paper. Really, the employees are better off in that as a group you are less affected by adverse things in the economy,"

Dumbell reported.[27]

Huskins also told Byrd of the *Winston-Salem Journal*:

"Park doesn't fit the image of a newspaper mogul who uses his properties to mold public opinion." J.P. Huskins, the former majority owner of the Statesville Record & Landmark, decided to sell his paper to Park in 1979 partly for that reason. "I don't think he is trying to build a communications empire where he can wield great influence like a lot of them think they can," Huskins said. "I don't think that's on his mind at all.

"I worked on the paper as publisher for two years after we sold it. And I never had a letter advising me to do one thing one way or another thing another way or a telephone call [from Park] the whole two years I was there."[28]

In McAlester, OK, Pops actually bought two competing news-papers, the McAlester *News-Capital* and the McAlester *Democrat* and consolidated them into one, the McAlester *News-Capital and Democrat*. As Gaither reported in the *Tulsa Tribune:*

The two newspapers had been bitter enemies up until the time of the sale about a year ago and, according to residents, created quite a bit of dissension within the community. Now, according to Delmer McNatt, manager of the McAlester Chamber of Commerce, there is peace in the valley.

"We came out on top of the deal," McNatt said. "They [Park] have improved the quality of the newspaper, and have done a real service for McAlester." The people of McAlester are very well satisfied. They have very high-caliber people and are doing a super job of editorializing.

It also has assisted our advertisers. The rates are a little higher, but the coverage is better and the merchants don't have to advertise in two newspapers so their ads have much better impact.[29]

In another case, as reported by Ken Allen of the *Charlotte Observer* on February 11, 1980,

Cyril "Shorty" Mebane of Newton, NC, about 45 miles northwest of Charlotte, is a typical seller. The Newton Observer-News-Enterprise had been in his family since 1904. He was the third generation publisher and feels his family would have wanted him to sell. Under conditions today, they would have figured it was the smart thing to do. "I'll tell you about my ancestors: They were all interested in putting out the best paper in the county. I feel like Roy Park can do a better job than I can do."

In this case, Pops had some difficulty proving it. "Unlike other papers, where the publisher has kept control," Allen reported, "he put in a consultant until he could name a general manager. The general manager didn't work out, the consultant came back, and last month Bob Coppage was brought down from New York to run the paper. In the shuffle, the paper dropped its daily stock listings and the weekly roundup of district and superior court news. It also dropped about 400 of its 4,500 subscribers. Coppage has replaced the stocks and court news and is after the drifted-away subscribers."[30]

This was an exception. A spot-check of other people where Park bought North Carolina newspapers showed that few detected changes after the sale. Belie Banks, a former editor of the *Mecklenberg Gazette,* published in Davidson, said, "I can't see any change," and Tom Williams, who sold the *Gazette* to Park in 1980 and remained general manager until 1982, said, "If their payroll check wasn't from a different office, nobody here would know the difference."

And former Senator Sam Ervin, one of the three trustees of the *News Herald* in Morganton, said he thought the decision to sell it to Park in 1978 was the secret of Roy Park's success—that he allowed the local newspaper to determine how it presents the news and editorial opinions. "I really haven't noticed any changes," he said.

STEADY AS HE GOES

As his newspaper group grew, my father was aware of, and took full advantage of, the economics of scale of group ownership. Besides the obvious advantage of central or mass purchasing, a chain can afford to do things a small independent paper could not do. Hire a man to do nothing but travel from newspaper to newspaper developing advertising sales, for instance, or developing circulation. "This consolidation applies to many businesses," he said. "There are not as many mom and pop food stores today, or as many family farms."

But changes were kept to a minimum. "He does not want to change just for change alone," Middlesworth said. "If change is necessary to improve the product, we make that change gradually. You can't or don't want to change the paper's image to the reader. He's a very patient man."

As Ken Byerly said, my father may be best understood as a collector or a builder. "He likes to see things grow. He takes in accomplishment. He's very proud of the fact that his group of newspapers is now up to whatever it is up to. He feels this is accomplishment."

One new technology in the newspaper field, the video-display terminals that allowed copy to be set directly into type from a reporter's VDT, did cause Pops some concern. VDT's placed more responsibility on the reporter to keep his copy free from spelling or grammar errors. "When we hire somebody now, we have to give them a spelling and grammar test," Pops said. "I can't say this is a great advance. It doesn't make interesting writers. Some of the best writers I know can't spell worth anything."

And so my father was active in managing his companies even into his later years. A 1990 graduate of Ithaca College, Rodd Perry remembers being a "little awestruck" working for Pops his senior year: "He's probably one of the only people I've called 'Sir' in my life....He really had a presence....He was very much involved in the running of his newspapers and radio stations down to minute details." Ed Adams, general manager of WNCT in Greenville, said, "Mr. Park knew you on a first-name basis, and he knew what an operation was doing."

He had no plans to retire. When he was seventy-one, he said, "I've seen a lot of my friends retire and get out of the stream of things. They're not only unhappy, they get dull. They get very sensitive and feel people don't treat them right. In business, I meet some of the most interesting and stimulating people. Besides, I enjoy it." As banker John Watlington put it, "There are people who just don't recognize time or age restrictions, who just go on doing what they want to do."

CHAPTER 23
DEFINING HIS OWN LEGACY

Going through the notes and memos my father wrote to me, I came across one to which he attached an editorial from the *North Carolina Leader*. The article was dated September 28, 1978, which was during my third year as vice president of Park Broadcasting.

His note said: "This is my friend Margaret Knox of the North Carolina Leader, and I must say I am in agreement with this." The editorial was headed A SPECIAL BREED and it read:

Evidently most persons associate the definition of workaholic with something intrinsically bad and downright un-American.

This has come to the Leader's attention in recent months; the fact that other employees and many others regard anybody they pinpoint as a so-called workaholic as someone not to be trusted, even a threat.

This editorial is in defense of those called workaholics.

What is commonly misunderstood is the very fact that work is fun. Yes, fun. Workaholics—those this newspaper knows—don't work for a larger paycheck, or even anything material.

It takes someone with spirit and knowledge to so apply himself. Work must be so absorbing that the body and mind don't tire.

Elation, the drive for excellence, and the ability to lose oneself—only to find oneself—are some of the rewards.

It is the Leader's contention that most people do not understand this or relate to it at all.

The workaholics the Leader knows are extraordinary well-rounded men and women.

Because their own work is so absorbing to them [leads to]... an appreciation of excellence in other fields—sports, music, books, drama, a fine wine—and yes, even a perfect pizza.

Something has crept into the English language called "super-achiever." This is classified by most in the same twilight category as the workaholic.

What is wrong with trying to be the best?

Let's bring workaholics and super-achievers out of the closet. One does what one has to do. This is still a free society, and if one is a workaholic, think of the names he is not called—lazy, slothful, selfish, greedy, etc., etc.

Come on now, is there something evil about being a workaholic?

The Leader salutes them, and regards them as a very special breed. They generally help make the world better, relieve it of drabness.

Workaholics we know are the most caring people around. They are actually LIVING their dream.

The Lord must have a gleaming corner for them all.

As for that gleaming corner, in my father's case, and being a closet workaholic, myself, I hoped so. But as the Bible says of the virtues of faith, hope and charity, "The greatest of these is charity." With Pops, charity did not begin at home. Bringing home the bacon, did.

I got a kick out of the comment from my contact in tracking down permission to reprint the editorial. Jim Heavener, president of Vilcom in Chapel Hill, owned the newspaper at the time. He wrote, "Mr. Park was a distinguished broadcaster and it was a pleasure to be in touch with you this way. If he had owned the *Leader*, he would have figured out something that the previous owner...and I couldn't. He would have made it make money."

CHARACTERISTICS OF MEN AT THE TOP

I wasn't aware of it back then, but studies have shown that executives who make it to the top do not have the usual human characteristics. Men who build their own empires are not so good at inspiring individuals one-on-one as they are at motivating masses or large numbers of people.

When Dr. Mortimer Feinberg, president of BFS Psychological Associates, polled thirty corporate presidents and board chairmen, he found interesting facts about motivations, habits and actions of the American corporate hierarchy. His findings showed that such executives "have an instinct for the jugular, and can tell immediately what is wrong with *you*. They know that in building their corporate empire, any one of their underlings can cause their demise by just one blunder," and they have a lack of trust. "These executives are killers, without the killer instinct. They only kill those who try to encroach on their territories. You can enter with their permission, but only if you are not threatening to them. They invent, create and improvise, and have a capacity to see what the run-of-the-mill executive cannot see."

Although such entrepreneurs generally play within the rules (my mother always referred to my father as a Boy Scout) and have a certain amount of humility, in their case humility is *power*, Feinberg reported:

> They're humble because they feel that if they fail, they will do so because failure is a condition or fate which can happen to anyone. But they have a tremendous— although sometimes hidden—need for power. And while they may not call attention to their personal or corporate power, if you intend to deal with these men you had better be aware that they indeed have this power.

Feinberg warned:

> It doesn't pay to cross these power figures. They always keep score, always collect their IOUs. They never permit a favor to go unrepaid; neither do they ever forget an insult. And those who wish to play their game had better play it by their rules....They are also ruthless, but not wantonly ruthless. They don't set out to hurt for the sake of hurting. But they know their enemies, whether these enemies are competitors or business or personal rivals. They know how to use their power for their particular purposes.

> But whatever else the chief corporate executive may or may not be, one thing is certain, he is organized... highly organized.... They organize time brilliantly... know approximately how much time each step or each operation should take, and allow for it perfectly in their planning, without fuss or ado. And only enough time is spent on each individual problem to provide a solution to that problem.

They also never forget their basic purpose. Neither

women, nor family, nor obstacles, nor challenges can divert them from their goals. They run a race that few of us are capable of running, or would want to run even if we could....

While these top executives are not necessarily happy people, they are fulfilled in the sense they know what they want; they've found themselves. They know what is expected of them. They know themselves well enough to realize just how far they can stretch their capabilities. And they constantly and consistently stretch them to their absolute functional limits.[31]

These attributes applied to my father and to his treatment of me and the outdoor division.

THE DECLINE OF THE OUTDOOR DIVISION

During the five years I was assigned to Park Broadcasting, the outdoor division had been run by two managers hired as professionals in the industry, one from the mid-to-late seventies and the other in the early eighties. As I said, my father installed these managers thinking our inventory would be easier to sell and far more profitable, since the billboards had been fixed up. Under new management, my father expected to see the bottom line improve dramatically. It went up and down under the management styles of my replacements, but posting a loss of $275,000 at the end of the six years, left him no choice but to bring me back to try to turn it around a second time.

As the two who most closely supervised and worked with these managers, Babcock and Feldman recall the first general manager had a practice of parking his briefcase outside his front door when he arrived home at 5:15 PM. He was also a believer in not having dinner or socializing with the managers when overnighting at one of the field offices. I am not saying his method of management was wrong. It might have been suitable in many companies. But it wasn't suitable for Park Outdoor. He was also a firm chain-of-command manager, never taking time to meet or talk to any of the employees reporting to the managers in the field. Once, a field office manager invited a female employee to meet with him behind closed doors to show her pornographic material. When she complained about this to the general manager in Ithaca, he accepted the field manager's denial, never talking to the employee, who quit.

Crucial was his refusal to react when competition moved into our markets. He was apparently not worried when brand-new competitive boards started springing up in Scranton, making our boards look shamefully outdated, and when cigarette businesses started to appear on those boards, he sloughed it off. He also made little effort to bring in national business, since his New York City agency sales trips consisted of flying out of Ithaca early and arriving back at 5:30 the same evening. Questioned on how he could possibly make the many necessary contacts needed at the many agencies in New York, his reply was, "You can't expect to influence their buying decision, anyway, so why waste the time and money?"

During his tenure, tobacco advertisers voluntarily removed themselves from TV, creating a huge influx of tobacco advertising into outdoor. But as large national cigarette and liquor advertisers pulled their accounts from Park in Scranton, he resigned to take a position with another outdoor company in 1979.

When I came back to outdoor, I also learned the manager passed over an incredible opportunity for a productive addition to our business. My father was given the chance to buy from three different plant operators their separate ownership of billboards in a major metropolitan area in New York State and to put the combined operation under our outdoor advertising roof. I can't imagine it was because it would have meant more work for him without a corresponding salary increase, but he convinced my father and Johnnie not to do it. An Indiana outdoor company bought the three companies at a bargain price and eventually sold the entire major market for what was probably a handsome profit to another outdoor company.

A second manager Pops brought in from another outdoor company also had a reputation of being an industry professional. He overturned each division's autonomy, believing management should be centralized in Ithaca with specialists under his management experienced in sales, leasing, and operations. General and sales managers at the branch level were unnecessary, since the home office would do the planning and decision-making for the field operations. He opted to have people in Ithaca traveling to the various markets, which at that time were spread out over half of New York State and a good part of northern Pennsylvania. As a result, by the time I returned, he had either dismissed or put so much pressure on our former general managers, they all left.

This manager also made a deal with a large tobacco company to get its business on our billboards posted on key locations in all of the Park markets by switching Lorillard, our biggest single advertiser ($600,000 per year), to less desirable locations far removed from metro areas. When the market rep from Lorillard came in to inspect his company's showings, he was incredulous. He requested a meeting with the general manager, who refused to meet with him, saying he had "worked out all the changes" with the rep's boss in New York City. When the Lorillard rep told him he was canceling the rest of his inspections and would recommend that all Lorillard contracts be cancelled in our markets, the manager told him to "Do whatever you want, but I have no time to meet with you."

The following weekend, certified letters came in canceling all of the contracts with a 60-day notice. Dave Feldman said my father opened the letters over the weekend and at the staff meeting on Monday passed them on to the manager. He glanced at them and flipped them aside, saying, "This man is just a checker and I have it all worked out with his boss." Pops then asked Dave Feldman, "What do you think, Dave?" Feldman replied, "I think that in sixty days we will no longer have six hundred thousand dollars of annual billing with Lorillard." Feldman said that was the beginning of the end for this manager.

This was followed shortly by a visit from an R.J. Reynolds rep, who after asking for the general manager and being told he was traveling, then asked for Dave Feldman. After remarking that he could tell from our basement location what my father thought of his outdoor division, he promptly informed Feldman that all R.J. Reynolds business in Binghamton, Utica, Elmira, Ithaca, Auburn, Scranton-WilkesBarre, and western New York was cancelled. He told Dave it was necessary because of the condition of the boards and their remote locations. With this, we lost another $300,000–$400,000 in annual billings.

The end for this manager followed a new New York State Department of Transportation law requiring that metal plates with license numbers be affixed to all billboards on federal and interstate highways. For Park Outdoor, that meant roughly 75 percent of our signs. The manager reported periodically on his progress in installing the licenses, saying he had personally checked out a number of the markets. He reported in late summer 1981 in a weekly manager's meeting that the project was complete, and all license plates were on display.

Feldman said my father and his CFO looked at him quizzically. After the meeting, the CFO called Feldman up to his office and asked him what he thought. His answer was, "I would be surprised if not more than a handful of plates, if any, had been installed." Feldman then volunteered to go out and physically spot-check each market and report back. When he got to the western New York market of Dunkirk, Jamestown and Olean, he noticed that not a single plate had been installed. In fact, they were all lying neatly in boxes in the garage in our Jamestown office, still unopened.

Coincidentally, a registered letter arrived at the Jamestown office that morning from the Buffalo regional office of the DOT, pointing out that a spot inspection by one of their real estate people noted that none of Park's plates were on display. The letter asked for an explanation to keep the billboards from being declared illegal and subject to removal.

Feldman drove to the Buffalo office, met with the DOT regional director and explained that due to extensive turnover in Jamestown, we were behind in getting the plates installed. He asked for time to get them up. They granted us an additional sixty days. After spot-checking Utica, Rome, Auburn, Ithaca, Elmira and Binghamton, Feldman reported back to Babcock and Park that some were still not up, and the manager was fired.

To make matters worse, Feldman was asked to make sure the manager removed only personal articles from his office. Feldman was to drive the manager home in a company car, remove his personal belongings from the car, and return the car to headquarters. The manager's parting comment to Feldman, who had some trepidation driving him home, was, "I have no hard feeling toward you because you were just doing your job, but Park Outdoor is still in the dark ages and will always be that way."

He still insisted that he had an "understanding" with the Lorillard media director regarding changing locations, but he did not elaborate why or what sort of deal he had made. The upshot, Feldman recalled, was that "after going through two professional outdoor managers the outdoor division had little if any cigarette business, strong competition with new inventory in Scranton, no managers, and ineffective local sales executives."

Given the forward movement everywhere else in the Park empire, problems with outdoor were the last things my father wanted to be concerned about. But it wasn't going to be too long before the problem was to be dumped back into my lap.

PREPARING TO GO PUBLIC

Forgive me for jumping ahead just a bit to 1982, because 1981, the year I returned to outdoor, was a sad year for me. It was the year without my friend and mentor, John B. Babcock. That said, in late 1982, with his broadcasting acquisitions slowing and his newspaper group growing, Pops began thinking about a new name to encompass all of his holdings, since both Park Broadcasting and Park Newspapers were too limiting to encompass his growing media empire. As you might guess (and explained in Chapter 25), I was back running the outdoor division by this time, and Pops asked me as the *former* vice president of advertising and promotion for Park Broadcasting, Inc., to come up with a new name for his media companies.

It took less than thirty seconds. I suggested the name I had given to our tabloid newspaper, *Park Communications*, and he immediately bought it. The name was changed in early 1983, and he became chairman, director and chief executive officer of the newly named Park Communications, Inc., which went public in October of that year.

At the time the name was changed, the 1,400 outstanding common shares split 6,000 to 1. The split increased outstanding shares to 8.4 million. After the offering, 9.2 million shares were outstanding, with a total stock authorization of 18 million shares.

But we went public without Johnnie Babcock. After nineteen years of managing the enterprise, and being promised the presidency of the company, he had finally confronted my father and demanded that Pops make good on his promise. Giving up that title was too much for my father, even though he would always remain chairman of the board. The meeting did not go well. Johnnie recounts the way it went down with four final words next.

CHAPTER 24
FOUR FINAL WORDS

In Johnnie Babcock's own words:

"My personal relationship with Roy H. Park had a few ripples but seldom a storm. I functioned as operations coordinator of his companies through 1981 for nineteen years. Abandoning a well-earned corporate post to return to Ithaca at age forty-two, I elected to invest my business experience and productive energy in a new career full of promise. I hit the ground running, and Roy saw to it that I ran full speed for all those years. I learned to deflect his habitual and predictive bossism and served as a buffer between him and regular targets such as Bob Burns, Dave Feldman and his son, Roy, Jr. He deluged these unfortunates with critical memos and impossible-to-achieve demands. He particularly relished skewering and demeaning young Roy at our weekly management meetings. I was the instrument of destruction if Roy Sr. wanted, for whatever reason, to get rid of a station manager or key supervisor. He relied on me as the torpedo to do the deed. He never personally fired anyone. For some, he made life so difficult that they resigned.

"In a company environment that emphasized slow career and pay growth for all employees, I was, as they say in upstate New York, 'brought along' with regular but modest salary increases, and edged up in title from operations manager to operations VP, and ultimately to executive VP for operations. I was too visible on the management scene to be named president, as he had promised. One theory was that he thought too lofty a title might dim the spotlight on his unique management image as chairman, president and chief executive officer.

"In the 1980s, the broadcasting industry entered the digital age and acquired the information and management tools made possible by computers. Radio and television groups were becoming sophisticated, and they were growing fast through acquisitions to threaten Park's proprietary claim to owning more U.S. broadcast stations than anyone else. Many already served larger markets with more people than Park Broadcasting did.

"I represented our firm at industry gatherings that bored Roy, such as the National Association of Broadcasters convention, which annually introduced the newest engineering products and production techniques. He allowed me to make capital commitments for major items of broadcasting gear. I could bargain effectively for multiple purchases to update several of our stations at one time. State-of -the-art equipment was necessary to be competitive, Park acknowledged, but personally he couldn't distinguish a transmitter from a microchip and didn't much care.

"I learned that top management people in other firms made much higher salaries than I did. Some owners had approached me with a better deal than I had with Roy, but I fended them off because of the carrot Roy had held out of eventual equity and a handsome retirement program. And I had no desire to live in and commute from a major city such as Los Angeles, Chicago, New York or Boston. My young brood of three girls was growing up in my birthplace, Ithaca, NY. They loved the fresh air and the lively college campuses in their hometown. The lure of greater things for me paled in light of these attractions, but I did think I deserved more money, and I wanted Roy Sr. to live up to the commitments he made when he hired me.

"Although I was paid more than anyone on my management team, I grew increasingly disenchanted. Knowing that Roy often picked up the mail at the post office on Saturdays, and that he would expect me to be at the office catching up after a week on the road, I made sure to be there one weekend. When he showed up, and after an hour of ripping open envelopes to ferret out viewer complaints or information that would embarrass a staff member on Monday morning, he rang my number and summoned me to

328 _____Sons In The Shadow

his huge office.

"I was loaded for bear. Before he could engage in the usual business exchanges, I spoke up and said I wanted to have some direct talk with him. Sensing that I was on the muscle, he shrugged back into the depths of his plush chair, and good listener that he was, warily heard me out. I told him that I did not think that I was paid as well as some other group managers whose pay had been reported in our most prestigious trade magazine. His hand inched forward toward that formidable center top drawer, home of the memos and hand-written notes he squirreled away for future reference after each hiring interview with top management candidates. He quickly sorted through his notes and clutched the memo dealing with my first day as his key assistant.

"Feeling that I was about to be jerked around, I asked him to read the notes in his hand. I asked that he pass by the words granting medical coverage, etc., and get to the critical part that clearly said that I would be rewarded with stock in his company, and the promise of a substantial retirement. Where were options or awards of equity? Where was my retirement agreement? On the rare occasions when Park was on the defensive, his dark eyes under the bushy eyebrows shown with threatening intensity. His speaking voice, normally so muted that it could hardly be heard, rose sharply.

"He responded with his almost-patented observation that he never paid a dividend, even to himself, and that he had no plans to change. Going public was way in the future. I pressed my request for an answer as to when and how much I could expect in stock or options, and what retirement plan I might expect. I noted that he had in hand the letter confirming his original promise that I would be named president and be granted equity and retirement. With a dark cloud in his eyes, he tilted his head defiantly and said loud and clear: *I changed my mind!*

"I stood up, took my key chain out of my pocket, separated the building and office key, and tossed them on his desk. Two decades of loyal service and contribution had been wiped out by four vindictive words.

"I immediately started to build my own retirement portfolio through management consultancies, affiliation with a well-regarded broadcast brokerage firm, and a commitment to work with a major investment firm in New York City interested in communications industry ownership. All three ventures took off positively and kept me busy cashing in on almost four decades of management experience. Meanwhile, Roy Sr. resorted to communicating with me through his very expensive Washington, DC, attorney, and soon we just fell out of touch. My wife and I would see him at social occasions. While she would not speak to him, I engaged in sufficient small talk to indicate that I did not hold a grudge. Indeed, I did not.

"If there was any satisfaction in my departure from Park, it was to observe him at various luncheon spots, huddling with his financial people. Park lunches were traditionally work sessions but accommodated and encouraged lively give-and-take conversation. Now I imagined they radiated the warmth of a 1930 vintage adding machine. Those lunches prompted one to recall something from my earlier career, when I reported to a top executive who was to die an alcoholic. Wife Nancy wryly suggested that for Christmas I present my undeserving boss with a fifth of whiskey. It was poetic justice that my former employer, the most sophisticated and gifted numbers man ever, should have for lunch a continuing compendium of indigestible statistics.

"A few weeks after I turned in my keys, my daughter, Jeannie, was married in the First Presbyterian Church in Ithaca. Roy and Dottie declined the invitation, but Roy, Jr. and Tetlow came to the wedding to support our family at this important time in our lives.

"Over time, Roy retreated to the plush office in his home, increasingly withdrew from day-to-day involvement, and missed savoring the crowning glory of a full life of accomplishment and financial enrichment. He would not like this said, but I was truly sorry for him. And I had good reason to feel compassion for his son, who also received precious little praise for his years of effort and achievement at Park Communications."

AN ARRANGEMENT CUT SHORT

My father had to explain Johnnie Babcock's departure, so shortly after Johnnie resigned on December 8, 1981, he scheduled a number of conference calls with his various managers. He started the telephone conference by saying that he had, or was calling, all members of our three management groups to make an important announcement and that he wanted them to hear it at the same time, and directly from Johnnie Babcock. He said "Johnnie, you are on first."

Babcock's statement said:

"I am going into my nineteenth year with Roy Park on a different basis than that full-time position I have filled as the operating head for Broadcasting. It may be a different basis, but I want you all to know that I shall still be on the scene. Roy and I have talked about this for a good long time, and we arrived at a balance that will allow me to pursue some personal projects that have been gathering dust, and at the same time continue to be helpful to Roy—and to all of you.

"My plan is to make myself available for up to one-third of my time, and on a different basis, I'll be working with Roy, Jr. on outdoor and with Bill Fowler on radio. Of course, I'll remain available as needs arise for other problems that Roy might call me in on, and we have agreed on a retainer arrangement so that will be possible.

"One thing for sure, I am shifting to a part-time basis when the company is probably as strong at the top as it ever has been. We've got Bill Fowler and George Lilly in Broadcasting operations, and Roy, Jr. in outdoor. Tom Thomas, Randy Stair and Dave Feldman and the combined financial control staff are now providing us with the support needed in the financial area.

"Those of you who run back with me a few years know that I have a lot of farm and scenic land in the Ithaca area. I want to work on managing and developing some of that. I may also accept some consultancy work in Broadcasting, as long as it is with folks who are not competing with Park stations in our markets. I'll be working at Park a day or two a week as Roy and I plan our time and needs, and soon after the first of the year, I'll set up my permanent office right in my home here in town."

Following Babcock's statement, my father said: "As a person who has had more than one career in his lifetime, I could not honestly disagree with Johnnie's decision. I want to reiterate that this was not a sudden development, and as Johnnie has indicated, it has been carefully thought out and planned for by the two of us. Over the years, Johnnie and I have worked as a team, with my job being to find good stations, provide the money or credit to buy them—and for Johnnie to run them once they became part of our group. We are fortunate that Johnnie will be working with us on a continuing basis with online responsibility for radio and outdoor and to consult with George and me on television.

"Johnnie, we enter into this new relationship at your suggestion—and it should be a fulfilling arrangement for you, for me, and for all of us."

But Johnnie wanted to give his side of the story, so a little over a year later, in January 1983, he issued to key Park personnel a letter that read:

My participation in Park management during 1982 did not work out the way it was described to the managers December 8, 1981. I was not called for any consulting for television, and the authority that is a necessary part of line responsibility for radio and outdoor was removed.

When it was made clear that I would not be asked to be part of the January meetings in Raleigh this month, I opted not to perform consulting work for Park in 1983.

My 19th year with the Park Companies was rewarding in two respects:

I enjoyed helping Roy, Jr. restore respectability to the

outdoor division. He won back many key customers.

During a year that was grim for radio generally, it was pure fun to work with Bill Fowler as he restored profit growth to radio, including a spectacular fourth quarter.

Roy Park is building a newspaper business that may one day rival broadcasting in volume, if not in profitability. You are part of a communications group that continues to grow at an impressive rate. Probably no individual can match Mr. Park's record of achievement. I shall continue to cheer him on from the sidelines just as I did directly as a member of his line management team.

I intend to stay extremely active in broadcasting, and hopefully my future endeavors may make it possible for our paths to cross. I surely hope so, for my association with you is one treasure no one can take away. I could not leave the active ranks of the Park Companies without thanking you for your personal contribution to whatever track record I leave behind.

Good luck to you and all the Park Companies for 1983.

He signed it, "Warm Regards, John Babcock."

CHAPTER 25
DARKENING OUR SHADOWS

Years after Johnnie Babcock resigned, my mother told me that things didn't work out because he wanted to take over the whole broadcasting operation. I asked her what she meant, and she said Johnnie wanted to be the head of it. Of course, she was right, since he was already the man running Park Broadcasting for my father and had been promised the eventual title of presidency, *in writing,* over the years. That commitment was not honored and Johnnie left the company. I don't know if my father ever realized the magnitude of that loss of talent and loyalty.

My father explained to my mother that the reason Babcock did not get the presidency of broadcasting was because all of his managers said they would quit if he were given that position. The very position he had been in, effectively, from Day One as he undertook the duties and responsibilities required to oversee operations during the building of Park Broadcasting. Johnnie hired the managers, fired people on demand for my father, set the salaries and budgets and managed the entire operation.

That's when I realized that the story my mother heard from my father was the one he wanted her to hear. I'm sure he was shocked when Babcock resigned, but in his version of events he painted Johnnie with the same black brush he had used to keep me in the shadow with my mother. Now I fully realized that through all of the seventeen years I worked for my father, my mother's picture of me had been shaded by what my father told her.

Looking back through all the letters she wrote to me during that period, I suddenly made sense of the whole situation. Time and time again she would quote what my father told her about the "problems" he had with me, and most of it was simply not true.

In effect, here were two sons, me and Johnnie Babcock, who was the son of the man who gave her husband his first real break. What my mother knew about our performance in the business came only from what my father told her. So he was able to rationalize his treatment of both of us to her. Johnnie survived quite well. As he told me:

"When I resigned from Park's firm grip on my daily life, I also ended day-in-day-out contact with the management team I had built in broadcasting. I gamely deflected involvement in the affairs of the company despite pleas from many of my old team for ongoing advice.

"I could not simply terminate friendships, many held for over a decade. Even twenty years later I have retained firm and warm friendships with Roger Turner, who ably headed the radio group, and with George Lilly, who headed the television group."

He pointed out, "There are station managers and former owners with whom I worked closely, and whose stations I visited several times a year. Hanes Lancaster in Johnson City, TN, has remained a close personal friend and confidant. Ron Philips from Richmond is another. I have spent many happy days with Hanes, whose family took me in as a member when we worked together. I have enjoyed continuous contact with other group members too numerous to list.

"Often our existence flourished under Park's iron and sometimes unreasonable demands. They only made our bonding stronger. I miss working with them, and always will."

WORKING FOR A SELF-MADE MAN

I kept hoping my father would mellow. I had been working in a number of capacities for him and hoped that some rapport could be established. There were plenty of successes, but there was always plenty of criticism.

By not joining him right out of college and establishing a career with other companies, I was able to earn a measure of respect and escaped the absolute control that would have been characteristic of an entrepreneurial workaholic who successfully built his own company had I gone right to work for him. Even while working for other companies, I was subjected to his negative judgment.

When I was in creative at JWT, I should have pursued account management. When I became an account manager, I should not have gone to a smaller firm and when I was with a smaller firm, I should have chosen one with larger, nationally known accounts. But it mostly rolled off my back.

On the other hand, employees who work for a self-made man can be treated fairly as long as they work the long hours that are expected, and turn in a strong bottom line. They can survive as long as they do what they are told, don't disagree publicly with their leader, and devote a certain amount of their time to assuring him he is right in all the decisions he makes, even if they feel some are wrong. This allows just enough self-respect to survive, and helps to assure financial reward.

But as I found out, the relationship changes when the son who has been independent goes to work for a father who achieved what my father had. I was just one of the latest to discover what perhaps millions of sons working in family-owned businesses had already experienced—what it was like to be the son of a boss.

A friend sent me, in mid-1980, an article on the father-son working relationship where the son was working for the father. It appeared in the People section of the Raleigh *News & Observer* and was written by staffer Angelia Herrin. The point is made that founders of their own businesses are independent people with a drive to control their own environments. And their experiences and drive make founding fathers a different breed, according to Dr. Leon Tanco, head of the Center for Family Business in Cleveland, OH.

There are more than 10 million family-owned businesses in the United States. The spokesmen for Sons of Bosses, Stephen Klein, said, "Many sons of bosses have trouble proving themselves to their dads and taking their place in the business." He said that statistics show that only 30 percent of family businesses survive into the second generation. Some of the sons quoted in the article said that the dissension frequently spills into social occasions, which the father cannot divorce from the place of work, and that the mothers are upset, wives are ready for a divorce, and children are neglected.

I was still part of the Park Broadcasting division when I came across this article, but I knew that the outdoor operation, under its new managers, was not performing well. Herrin, who wrote the article, pointed out that two refrains that most of the SOBs were hearing from their fathers were, "I made it all on my own," and "Son, I did this all for you." There was also the promise that "Someday, this will all be yours."[32]

I never heard those quotes and knew that my father had absolutely no intention that someday he would turn the management of the company over to me, or that someday any part of it would be mine. I was just grinding my teeth and doing my job and trying my best to enjoy the work.

Little did I know that in less than a year, I was going to be asked to go back into the outdoor division to clean up the mess that had been made. And my problems would be compounded by the fact I would no longer be working with Johnnie Babcock, who had been so closely involved in the needs and problems of the outdoor division. I would be reporting directly to my father without the welcome management buffer he provided that had earlier been in place.

AN OFFER I COULDN'T REFUSE

When my father asked me to take back the job of heading the outdoor operation in 1981, I said I wanted no part of it. I felt it would be like trying to bring his outdoor division back from the dead, making it more than just a tax write-off before he took me out of it. I had no desire to take on for a second time the massive amount of work needed to turn around something which had been run into the ground.

But two things changed my mind. The first was Dave Feldman, who had stayed with the outdoor division through the two managers. He pointed out that I had nothing to lose. The outdoor division couldn't be in any worse shape, and there was no way it could go but up. I had my doubts about that until I found out the other reason why I would have to take on the job. My father told me that if I didn't go back to the outdoor division, I would need to look for *another job.*

 Park Communications

| Vol. 8 No. 5 | Terrace Hill, Ithaca, New York 14850 | October 1981 |

Park Heads Up Outdoor

ITHACA, N.Y. — Roy H. Park, Jr., has been promoted from vice president and director of promotion for the Park Companies, to vice president and general manager of Park Outdoor Advertising.

Commenting on the appointment, group supervisor John B. Babcock noted that Park has greatly broadened his base of experience through his recent assignment publishing the company newsletter, "Park Communications," and handling advertising, promotion and publicity for the Ithaca-based group of 21 broadcast stations, 45 newspapers, outdoor advertising companies and real estate in 19 states.

"Roy Park also has management experience in outdoor advertising at a time when we need it. He brings back to the operation fresh perspective rising from a depth of media experience. He has held major advertising agency posts that ave contributed good, basic understanding of how the oldest advertising medium — outdoor · can most effectively be utilized in advertising plans. here is no substitute for the maturity, experience and integrity which Roy brings to our

outdoor operation," Babcock concluded.

2 State Operation

The Park Outdoor Advertising group maintains over 2,500 poster and paint units in central New York from the St. Lawrence River to Lake Erie, and across Northern Pennsylvania. The companies serve the key markets of Utica, Rome, Binghamton, Elmira, Jamestown and Dunkirk in New York, and Scranton, Wilkes-Barre, Towanda, Sayre,

Bradford, Warren and Oil City in Pennsylvania.

A 1956 graduate of the Lawrenceville Preparatory School in New Jersey, Park holds a BA in journalism from the University of North Carolina at Chapel Hill and an MBA in marketing from Cornell University.

Agency Background

In 1963 he joined the world's largest advertising agency, J. Walter Thompson Co. in New York City, and was assigned to the Ford account as a copywriter.

He later served at JWT as review board executive, advertising planning director, awards chairman and account executive on Pan American, Institute of Life Insurance, U.S. Department of Defense and RCA Sales Corporation, where he was promoted to senior account executive.

After seven years at JWT, he was named the vice president of marketing and account Continued on Page 2

I asked him what was going to happen to the company newspaper, and he said it might be dissolved. He said if he could get somebody who was up to continuing it, he would, but I could tell he had no plans to do that. In the same issue of the *Park Communications* tabloid that contained the news of my return to outdoor, Babcock reported (in a box I did not write) that my new responsibilities were a demanding, full-time job that would leave no time for me to continue editing and publishing *Park Communications*, which I had done for the past four-and-a-half years. "For the time being, we will suspend publication," he said.

That was the end of that.

Saving the outdoor division was much more important to my father, and I certainly could understand that, even though I wasn't looking forward to being the one to do it. When I agreed to take it on, I laid down some conditions for my return, among which was his commitment to invest more capital in the plant.

A key reason I was brought back was evident. Operating profit, as I noted earlier, posted a *loss* of $275,000 in 1981. I will give the two managers credit because they accomplished something I couldn't. They convinced my father to undertake some capital improvement in the plant. It was better than performing cosmetic repairs on deteriorating inventory to keep costs down, which could only lead to flat or declining sales.

BACK TO OUTDOOR

At the time I returned, the Park Outdoor Advertising companies maintained more than 3,000 poster and paint units in upstate New York from the St. Lawrence River to Lake Erie, and across northern Pennsylvania. The companies served key markets of Utica, Rome, Binghamton, Elmira, Jamestown, Olean and Dunkirk in New York; and Scranton, Wilkes-Barre, Towanda, Sayre, Bradford, Warren and Oil City in Pennsylvania.

This time my father agreed with Babcock and me to commit *substantial* amounts of money to modernize the Park Outdoor poster and paint locations, "as Park moves dynamically into the '80s with new experienced and professional management across the board." He had already allowed, in the Scranton division, the installation of new trim on the poster panels, and in other branches, the installation of new unitized panels, white baked-enamel trim kits and new fluorescent lighting.

We had gone to prepasted posting in our divisions by this time and we created a new rotary paint program in Scranton. My father had allowed me to double our construction crews to expedite the work and provide continuous upgrading of the appearance of our outdoor units. I also had convinced him to join in the Traffic Audit Bureau (TAB) program, and he agreed to pay the cost of having all of our branches being audited by TAB to provide accurate circulation figures for our locations. We also were able to join the New York and Pennsylvania Outdoor Associations as well as the Institute of Outdoor Advertising and the Outdoor Advertising Association of America (OAAA).

My father promised: "After total modernization is completed, we will continue into the decade with unipole poster and paint structures, new rotary paint programs in every branch and halophane lighting on our paint units." With this upgrading in progress, we began an active new leasing program and worked closely at the local levels with planning and zoning officials to protect our place in the market to provide the best possible coverage.

In putting me back in charge, my father also knew that although I had been out of the New York City circuit for six years, I still had my contacts with the large national accounts, some of whom went back to my J. Walter Thompson days.

Metamorphosis. An example on the left of one of the outdoor boards initially inherited, and on the right, one of the replacement structures built by Park Outdoor.

One of the major reasons for stagnant growth while I was

out of the outdoor picture was the decline in our share of the national cigarette business. Competition had moved into Scranton, financed by one of the cigarette companies because our boards looked so bad. Another major tobacco company had pulled its business.

Slowly but surely the national tobacco companies who had come back to Park Outdoor in Scranton after the massive upgrading we had done in the plant began to expand with us in our central New York markets. R.J. Reynolds, Phillip Morris, Brown & Williamson, Liggett & Meyers, Lorillard, and American Tobacco came back as key advertisers. Lorillard had been the most difficult to bring back because it had been treated so badly during my absence. It took five years before Lorillard gave Park Outdoor another chance. The field inspector who was snubbed by my predecessor became the media director of the company, and he had a long memory. It was only after others he had brought up through the ranks recognized that they could trust our people that Lorillard began to expand into a major factor with our company.

During this time, we also expanded our inventory. In 1986 we built some boards in the Syracuse market and then extended the coverage with the purchase of ten bulletin faces. We also negotiated for some bulletin locations on I-81 leading into Syracuse on the Onondaga Indian Reservation. Our lease manager met with the thirteen chiefs in a real longhouse, smoked the appropriate pipes and came to an agreement for several locations on the reservation. The deal was signed, it would bring good money to the reservation, and all was in order.

That's when Dennis Banks, a fugitive from justice, came to the reservation to hide out from the authorities.

About the time the construction for the first unit started, the construction team from Scranton found themselves, along with our lease manager, surrounded by Indian braves with chains, chainsaws and shotguns. The Indians had damaged the construction machinery and put sugar in the gas tanks. Then the hostility accelerated. I remember receiving a call from a phone booth on the reservation from our lease manager describing the situation and asking what he should do. My reply was "Get the hell out of there."

I found out later that Banks had stirred up the tribe. The braves overruled the agreement made by the chiefs, and white men were driven off the reservation.

I was amazed when, later, the chiefs returned the thousands of dollars of lease payments we had given them in advance, right down to the penny, but I still feel anguish as I ride up I-81 knowing a belowground pad for the structure still exists at the location where our first eighty-foot structure was to go up under the agreement. Later, the tribe took over the other boards owned by our competition that already existed on the reservation, and the units still carry graffiti to I-81 travelers today.

It should be noted that Banks later was sentenced to life imprisonment for the 1999 murder of a nineteen-year-old.

While I was with Park Broadcasting, it is interesting that I remained in the same corner office on the fourth floor of Terrace Hill that I had when I first ran outdoor, but the outdoor division had been moved from the second floor to the basement. So I moved into the dungeon quarters which, aside from being damp and moldy, had no drop ceilings to cover the overhead piping, and natural light only from window wells. I quickly renovated the space the best I could, but many pipes hung too low to be covered. I installed cheap carpeting over the cement floors and built out offices to give individual privacy in what used to be a bullpen. The only separate office space before I moved down had belonged to the former general manager, and was set up by him to keep an eye on the workforce in the bullpen through a window.

We put up with live animals, including chickens, in the window wells, and either freezing from being below ground or burning up from our location next to the building's main furnace. And I recall with some embarrassment national clients stumbling down the musty steps to the basement side entrance. They could see what my father thought about the outdoor division. And I remember the day when my six-year old niece came to the basement to visit. After open-mouthed silence, she looked at the exposed pipes in the ceiling and asked, "Doesn't Grandpops like you?"

At any rate, 1982–83 were turnaround years, going from a loss of over half a million because of the problems and huge maintenance expenses I re-inherited in 1982 to a small $40,000 operating profit in 1983. Which was a good thing since the improvement on the outdoor bottom line helped to contribute to the overall fiscal health of Pops's empire, which at this time included over 30 newspapers along with television and radio stations.

It was time for a great leap forward.

The Park Radio Group during their summer sales meeting in front of the Terrace Hill entrance of Park Broadcasting in 1979, four years before Park went public.

CHAPTER 26
GOING PUBLIC

Six years before he took his company public, my father told *Business Week* in an interview that he "cherishes his ability to spend his money as he pleases and turned down brokers who suggested going public in the bull market of 1968 for that reason." He explained:

> I like the freedom of not being responsible to other people. I want to be able to make a deal on a handshake. People will think I'm a real square, but I didn't think my stock was worth as much as the brokers thought it was. They wanted to sell it at something like thirty times the earnings. I didn't want to have a lot of people hurt if it went down.

His twenty-one-year old media company, one of the largest privately owned conglomerates in the nation, was known as a "quiet organization." Aside from Park Communications, Inc., and his real estate holdings, *Forbes* estimated in 1983 that my father also controlled some $10 million in P&G stock and almost the same amount of ConAgra, the parent company of the Nebraska flour mill that made the Duncan Hines cake mix.

In October 1983, Park Communications, Inc., became a public company, and the stock (symbol PARC) was listed on the Nasdaq National Market System. Goldman Sachs & Co., which managed the underwriting group, had planned to price the shares between $17 and $20. The company earned $4.8 million on revenues of $44.7 million in the first half of 1983. It employed over 2500 people and operated in twenty-three states, with a major concentration in North Carolina.

On October 26, 1983, my father sold 11 percent of Park Communications in a public offering. The opening offer was $19 per share, and the stock bid on May 17, 1985, was $34.50. There were 9.2 million shares of stock outstanding on May 13, 1985, and 750 stockholders. Park remained the sole owner of 8.2 million shares, or 89 percent of the remaining stock. It was a decision, he said, that was prompted by the need to place a value on his holding for estate purposes and to offer some protection from estate taxes.

In an article in the *Ithaca Journal* on May 17, 1985, Joseph Junod reported that through it all, my father had built a personal fortune that he refused to discuss. He wrote,

> Park says he won't talk about money, how much he is worth, how much he gives away and who will benefit from his estate, for three reasons. "It's nobody's business, it's stupid and it's a good way to make enemies."

Park Communications in 1984 increased its gross revenue over 1983 by 13 percent and its net income by 26 percent, which set a new high in revenues and profits. Gross revenues were $93.8 million and net income was $11.1 million. Earnings per share climbed 22 percent to $1.31. By this time, the circulation figures ranked Park newspapers at thirty-eighth, with 73 publications, in the country among 153 group publishers. With twenty-one broadcasting stations also under his belt, my father was positioned to expand the company even more.

This growth, in one way at least, bothered the man who built a media empire by focusing on midsized television markets (Richmond, VA) and smaller daily newspaper markets (Statesville, NC). "We're sorta getting away from being a person," Pops said. He also admitted to having some qualms about going public. He told Junod it would mean: "[H]aving to stand naked 'bout every quarter." Junod goes on to report "[Park] said, with a touch of chagrin, 'that it cost him 72 cents to mail each 1984 annual report,' a document that contains hints about the man and his company. In an era of sophistication, colorful, expensive annual reports, Park's is simplicity itself. Clear, focused, easy-to-understand and containing but one photograph of an individual, that of the founder."[33]

In 1990, the country entered a recession, and Park Communications' stock dropped from a high of $22.25 during first quarter 1990 to a low of $10.25 during fourth quarter. It closed at $15.25 a share. The nationwide recession that began in July had taken its toll on media companies, which saw huge drops in operating revenues and slashed staffs and closed news bureaus in response.

In contrast, Pops got through 1990 with a 2 percent decline in operating revenues. By controlling costs, the company's net income was up 1 percent and earnings per share equaled those for 1989, according to the company's annual report.

Though he was feeling the pinch, my father was still upbeat, saying that, in many ways, he was enjoying the recession. In 1991, advertising linage was down at Park Communications for the year, as were profits. For its 1991 fiscal year, the company reported net income of $11.9 million, compared with $18.9 million in 1990. Yet in a January 1992 interview with C.E. Yandle, a staff writer for the *News & Observer*, Park said he was optimistic about his company's operations, expecting a slight upturn in sales that year. His company's strong cash position insulated it from problems that plagued other media corporations, he explained.

Yandle wrote:

> The 81-year old chairman of media giant Park Communications, Inc., is taking advantage of sagging profits at the nation's newspapers and radio and television stations. Using a cash arsenal of more than $100 million, the Ithaca, NY, firm has bought three newspapers, a television station and a radio station over the past four months.

> And Park, who was in Raleigh for the corporation's

annual shareholders' meeting, says he and his company are hungry for more. "We squirreled away some money," he said in an interview at the McKimmon Center, the site of the meeting. "I don't like to use the word depressed in relation to prices, but there are more newspapers available at a fair price right now. Let's put it that way."[34]

COMING UP FOR AIR

There are only two lasting bequests we can give to our children. One of them is roots, the other, wings.

—Hodding Carter

At this point in my life and the life of Park Communications, I had to wonder what was to be my role in this era of change and growth. In other words, why was I in Ithaca? I had my roots. The leaves of my family tree had called me back home. Back to the family. But wings were another matter. My wings had been clipped, and I lost my father the day I came back to work for him.

I know the answer to Sam Johnson's question: "Does my father love his business more than he loves me?" I had thought I could live with that. But even with accepting that, the relationship with my father continued to go downhill. I finally began to understand why.

Based on my years at J. Walter Thompson, it was natural to become close to agency people who handled our national outdoor business. We had a natural affinity for one another. A lot of them understood the struggle that was taking place in my attempts to bring Park Outdoor out of the dark ages and into the modern world. They knew it was not easy going, and one of them sent me pages 128 to 131 on father-and-son relationships from a book by Harry Levinson, entitled *The Great Jackass Fallacy.*[35] My friend passed it along knowing the words definitely applied to me.

I tried to understand. The pages pointed out that for an entrepreneur founder, the business is an extension of himself, so he had great difficulty giving up his instrument of power. The pages made many of the same points that the articles mentioned earlier in this book had made. They pointed out that a founder's business is his baby, almost his "mistress," and noted the great difficulty a founder had in delegating authority to a son. While he might consciously want his son to attain his place in the sun, he unconsciously feels that yielding any portion of the business to him is like losing his masculinity, and he did not want his son to win in every area in which he was assigned.

Typically, the desire not to be replaced by a son in his summit position deals with a situation where a son eventually is expected to take over the entire business. That was hardly my case, since I only ran a small portion of what he owned. It was at the bottom of the pile in terms of importance to the company. But even my attempts to succeed with this tiny portion of his company bothered him. It seemed like he had one set of rules for me, another for everyone else.

Levinson went on to point out that these conflicting emotions cause a father to behave in an unpredictable and contradictory manner, leading those close to him to think that while on the one hand he wants the business to succeed, on the other, he is determined to make it fail. I realized (it was slow in coming, I admit) that he really never intended for outdoor to become much more than a vehicle for depreciation and a source of fees and rent payments to his company. All this put me in the tenuous position of swimming upstream. He wanted the business to be run honestly in order to maximize the bottom line but not necessarily grow into a respectable and meaningful part of the company.

A son naturally seeks increasing responsibility, Levinson wrote, given his growing maturity. The son strives for the freedom to act responsibly on his own. He is totally frustrated by his father's intrusions and resents being kept in an infantile role, always the little boy in his father's eyes, with the accompanying contempt, condescension and lack of confidence that characterize the father's attitude. Characteristically, the son is terribly torn by these conflicts, and the father sees the son as ungrateful and unappreciative. The son feels both hostile to his father and guilty for feeling that hostility. While the father believes that the son will never be man enough to run the business, at the same time he tries to hide his feelings from his son.

Then Levinson made a devastating point. He said that sometimes the competition can lead to a manipulative alignment with the mother against the son and result in the mother siding with her husband whenever the battle peaks. This was also happening, and I began to realize that my father worked hard to poison my mother's mind against me. He constantly characterized me as "creative," argumentative, and lacking financial awareness.

Creating something that can be touched, seen or heard, and which others appreciate, can bring peace to the mind and soul. People who do physical work, paint, sculpture, write, or compose can experience the value of their work. Without positive feedback from the boss in a management job, where you are dealing with people, strategies and ideas, it is impossible to gain a feeling of self-worth. The worst stress a human can face is not having guidelines by which they can gauge their own value.

I was "creative" (not a term of praise in my father's vocabulary), but I also knew what needed to be done to bring in the bottom line. I knew, faced with the physical wreck most of the outdoor division was in, you "had to spend money to make money." I had come in with the goal of improving the outdoor division. I was trying to repair the billboard structures, along with the organizational weaknesses that existed, neither of which my father really wanted repaired. Things were made even more difficult when other executives in the organization running the glamorous side of my father's businesses expressed dismissive or contemptuous opinions about my job and functions. In truth, the last thing anyone should have been was envious of my position. Under my father's iron hand, there was nowhere to turn. Not to my mother, not my colleagues.

That left my immediate boss, Johnnie Babcock. Entrepreneurial fathers are unable to resolve their dilemma themselves, tending

to be rigid and righteous and finding it difficult to understand any
other point of view. Well-meaning associates, such as Johnnie,
who try to help the father see the effects of his behavior, have
a difficult time bringing up this thorny subject and usually find
themselves ignored.

This is what could have happened to Johnnie, despite the fact
that he was fully aware of the situation. He was sympathetic and
frequently defended my point of view. He risked putting himself
in the position of losing whatever beneficial influence he might
have to help the situation. He faced this struggle the entire time I
reported to him. I remembered what Rose Kennedy told me back
in 1958. When I asked why Jack's father stayed in the background
during his run for president, she said, "It's easier for a son if a
famous father gives him the complete stage." Johnnie or I could
not begin to imagine my father yielding the stage.

I would abhor the *complete* stage, wanting only a small place
on it. I needed free reign to run what I had been responsible for
since 1971, but even after being hired back to clean up the mess
left by the two managers who replaced me in 1976, this did not
come. My feelings of disappointment, frustration and tension
were mounting. When this is the case, the son thinks of leaving.
Levinson's book helped me to understand the relationship, but it
did not provide any answers.

So I reread an article sent by Shelly Smith, a longtime friend
and one of the sons in the Smith family that ran the Ithaca Gun
Company. He had sent it to me some ten years earlier in 1974,
knowing even back then what I was going through. I had thought
at the time that it provided some hope.

The article was entitled, WORKING FOR THE OLD MAN. It was
written by Richard S. Morrison for *MBA* magazine. Morrison, who
was a graduate of the Stanford School of Business, had joined
his father's company, Molded Fiber Glass, some three years after
he left college.[36]

I remembered I had seen some grounds for hope in that article,
which asked, "Should I go to work for my father?" Morrison
shared the problems he encountered in doing so to be helpful to

other MBAs facing this decision. Morrison said you could do your own thing working for your father, and that if your father was smart and really wanted you to prove yourself, he would put you to work in the worst, most troublesome segment of the company. The job I took in outdoor was not only the most troublesome, it was the worst, and only a tiny part of the company. Morrison went on, however, to point out that when he took on the most troublesome part of his father's business, his father kept his nose out of the day-to-day operation. My father didn't.

Morrison said that most MBAs don't get excited about walking in someone else's footsteps. The key is whether you believe that your employer will treat you fairly and provide opportunities and promotions based on your ability and desire. Even after years of horror, this had given me some hope, but I hadn't begun to see any light at the end of the tunnel.

It was as if I had told my father to be sure to wait until my annual review and then tell me what my goals *should* have been. Dwell on everything you feel I did wrong and avoid acknowledging anything I did right. Give me a mediocre performance rating with a cost-of-living increase. I'm not here for the money, anyway. And while you're at it, make sure you give me enough work to keep me out of town on business during the week and in the office late and on weekends and holidays. I adore the office, have no family responsibilities, and really have nowhere to go or anything else to do. I have no life beyond work.

Morrison also pointed to the common element present with everyone, that you were foremost "the Old Man's kid." This identity, he warned, can serve you both well and badly. If your father is respected, you might carry part of his halo, but at the same time you can be resented because you are that "lucky kid who had it made." This certainly didn't apply to me. I didn't have it made and worked in a division that was looked down upon by the rest of his employees.

The tongue-in-cheek definition of a boss's son—a young man who is willing to start at the bottom for a few days—didn't apply to me. Try seventeen years.

Another problem with working for a father, Morrison wrote, is that you might be thought of as wealthy. That never applied to me, nor did the other employees think so. It was clear that I was living on limited means, making far less than his other management people. In my father's case, the business's earnings were plowed back into the business, as actually was the case with Morrison's father. "Your salary will be lower than you would receive on the open market," Morrison said. Then he pointed out the worst premonition I had when I finally accepted the job: If you fail in the family firm, you are likely to be looked upon as a complete incompetent. The risk of failing is to virtually eliminate your chances to be taken seriously as a candidate for positions in other companies in the future.

As time went by, and as things got meaner, I knew that it would be tougher and tougher for me to leave for another job. And the longer I waited, the worse it would be.

A SUPPORTIVE FAMILY

If poetry comes not as naturally as the leaves to a tree, it had better not come at all.

—John Keats

Here I am talking about my lot and my suffering, but my family suffered as well. It's unfair to think back on how rough it was on me without remembering it was even rougher on my wife and kids. It's not much fun to have a father who would drag himself home beat up every day but still be determined to work late into the night and on weekends to keep up with what needed to be done to satisfy the needs of the company and his own father.

In New York, my commuting ate up the hours. I left early and came home late. In Ithaca, the job pressure was much worse, and I was spending two or three nights a week out in the field. If I wasn't traveling to my divisions, with Scranton and Utica both being two hours in opposite directions from Ithaca, and Potsdam, NY, and Erie, PA, being five hours apart, I was traveling to New York, Chicago and other cities. Then for five years it was network promotions, sales and annual meetings, four-hour drives to and from Ogdensburg and overnight stays there each month for the newsletter, and trips to the individual broadcasting properties for promotional events. In contrast to the substantial amount of travel I had done on the RCA account at J. Walter Thompson, my schedule now doubled the time I spent away from home.

As legendary CEO Jack Welch pointed out in his 2005 book *Winning*, his children were raised, largely alone, by their mother. In the April 14, 2005 *Newsweek* in a sidebar on WORK AND FAMILY, Welch said from his earliest days at GE, he would show up at the office on Saturday mornings. "For 41 years, my operating principle was to work hard, play hard and spend some time as a father," he stated, and if there was ever a case of "Do as I say, not as I did, this is it."

Sometimes my children were involved in sporting events I couldn't attend. My wife filled in, alone. It was tough for her to see mothers and fathers of other children cheering on the crew, soccer, lacrosse or football team. Those weeks of not having time for my kids rolled into years. I had been there before, but on the other side. But my children turned out fine without a more full-time father, and my wife didn't really complain. Her disappointment was evident. She didn't like it, but she understood what I was going through.

My children were not sent away to private school as I had been. Both went to Ithaca High School, where their grades were good enough to get into a first-class college. They had their sights set on my alma mater, UNC-Chapel Hill, which accepted only a small percentage of its student body from out of state. Getting in meant getting out of Ithaca, which did not hold the happiest of memories for them. With my father being a big fish in the smallish Ithaca pond, his reputation ran from good to bad, and my children carried whatever fame, or stigma, was associated with the Park name.

My family in Ithaca. Who somehow managed to hold up well under stress.

It may only take a village to raise a child if that child is an orphan or if both parents just don't care. It's good to have two parents to raise a child, but just one caring parent can still turn out a shining young product. In our case my wife raised our children mostly on her own.

Lee Iacocca said, "No matter what you've done for yourself or for humanity, if you can't look back on having given love and attention to your own family, what have you really accomplished?"

How could I pay back my wife for all those silent years of suffering? Nothing with a price tag. I could only fall back on words. Only one way to try to express my understanding of what she had been through and how I felt. "Poetry, an outward expression of instinctive insight, must be summoned from the vast deeps of our mysterious selves," said Hughes Mearns. "Therefore, it cannot be taught; indeed it cannot be summoned; it may only be permitted." I permitted my thoughts to flow in these untitled words for my wife:

A wife, my darling, is something a man may seem to take for
granted.
Like the sun, the stars, the currents of the wind.
Love may not be expressed obviously or often,
For something so much a part of a man's life.
But cold is the day without the sun.
How bleak the night sky without its diamonds of light.
How suffocating the world without wind.
And empty a man without his wife.
Love is a growing thing.
At first like a child it is suddenly born.
Nourished with warmth and bursting with energy,
It takes toddling steps on chubby legs with the conviction of
Worlds to conquer in its brand-new heart.
It fathoms the first brightness with sparkling eyes,
The darkness with irretractable persistency,
The swift transition to adolescent adjustment with hope and
bailing wire.
And emerges, for the very lucky, as the finest,
Most precious and mature love of all.
The kind that is strong enough to exist unexpressed—
As endurable and lasting as the light and diamonds of the
universe,
And the winds through the willows of earth.
A wife, my darling, is one of those fine truths a man does take
for granted,
And this, simply love which can be taken for granted,
Forever and ever,
Is what I share with you.

Being taken for granted is asking a lot, and except for weekends during this time, I wasn't much of a husband or a father. The
one exception was that every year we packed up for one week of
vacation, driving straight through for sixteen hours from Ithaca
to Bogue Banks, an island off Morehead City, NC. (Remember,

I had only two weeks of vacation working for my father, and one of those weeks was used, if used at all, to try to spend some time around Christmas and Thanksgiving with other family members.) The beach trip wasn't much of a vacation for the kids when they were young, either, because with my penchant for aquariums, I had them dragging nets in the ocean and in Bogue Sound before they got too old to protest.

FINDING I STILL HAD VALUE

The ability to deal with people is as purchasable a commodity as sugar or coffee. And I pay more for that ability than for any other under the sun.

—*John D. Rockefeller*

As the feeling of claustrophobia became too much to bear, I finally decided to take a chance and look for another job. My wife and I both wanted to go back south, so I used a couple of vacation days and flew to Atlanta, GA, for an interview with Rollins Outdoor. As part of the interview, I had to take some stringent psychological tests in the office of a prominent PhD who Rollins used to assess all of their management people plus top management recruits. The tests took a full day. At 4 PM in the afternoon I was told to take a break while the results were determined. At 5 PM, Dr. Wayne Helms called me into his office to give me the results. He was reluctant to spell out the details at first, but I prodded him to do it.

He finally agreed to share some post-test highlights with me, while I took notes. I saved the notes I took, and he finally, to start with, told me that I made a very good first impression. "Good eye contact, firm handshake, confident." he said. He went on to say:

IQ 127-132. Higher than 96% of the general population. Shows excellent learning ability. Missed only two on test for logic, rational thinking. (Four on vocabulary). Excellent problem solver. Excellent vocabulary. Clear choice of words.

On people, tests indicate like to spend 80% of time with them; only 20% as a hermit. Do require periods of solitude. But like people, controllable with these, warm-hearted, outgoing, and can deal easily with all types.

Show complete confidence in self. Believe in self. Independent. Resourceful. Perfectionist. Not a procrastinator. Innovative. Decisive. Show initiative. Good aggressiveness. A realist.

Tactful. Diplomatic. Good emotional stability. Not volatile. Work well under pressure. Mentally tough. Goal-directed. Evaluate your performance on the bottom line, so no trouble establishing priorities.

Management style: training-orientated. Can work with all types of people, and not bothered by those you dislike. Treat people as individuals. Manage by objectives. Communicate well with everybody. Good crisis manager, turnaround manager.

So there it was. Everything my father said he needed but didn't realize he had. And, probably, he didn't really want, or least want to recognize in his son.

I'd learned a great deal from my father over the years, entrepreneurial wizard that he was, but it was good to confirm that in my case, as the 1974 song by *America* went, "Oz never did give nothin' to the Tin Man, that he didn't, didn't already have."[36a]

Needless to say, the next morning I was called for a final interview at lunch by Rollins' senior management, and a number of alternatives were discussed for assignments in Atlanta. I flew home feeling pretty good about the whole thing and felt that I might be offered a job.

Two days later, the job I was offered was not what I expected. They wanted me to head their Philadelphia division. Although the assignment was far higher than I expected, the location was not what I wanted. As flattering as it was, it also did not fly with Tetlow, who after having put up with a dozen brutal years of Ithaca winters, had no intention of moving only slightly south to Philadelphia. I reluctantly turned it down and continued working for my father without missing a beat. I was buoyed up by the experience. At least I was marketable and after years of being beat down working for my father had not been rendered unfit.

As I said, the words of Feinberg, Levinson and Morrison on father-son relationships helped me to understand what was going on but did not provide any answers. The same relationship continued without relief, and it became more and more evident that the only answer was to leave another company as the constricting nature of my job continued to grow.

I'm sure Maya Angelou didn't mean it the way I interpreted it then, but she said, "I've learned that people will forget what you said, people will forget what you did, but people will never forget how you made them feel." And the feeling I had was not good.

The answer finally came when an interview with my father in 1984 appeared in *Forbes* magazine, with implications that were too much to bear. As soon as it hit the newsstand, I received sympathetic phone calls from all over the nation from friends and business associates, and I finally realized that working with my father was forced to come to a close.

Tuesday, Sept. 4, 1984 • ITHACA JOURNAL **3**

Local

More local news
Page 4

Park quits father's firm after magazine appears

By HELEN MUNDELL
Journal Staff

Roy H. Park Jr., of 55 Highgate Circle, resigned Friday as vice president of Park Outdoor Advertising, in response to an "apparent vote of no confidence" of his father in Forbes magazine.

"I had no choice," Park said today. "This was a public vote of no confidence, and it was even more distressing in the light of the success we've had in turning around Park Outdoor."

Park's father, Roy H. Park Sr. was featured in a profile in the Sept. 10 issue of Forbes magazine. He was quoted as saying that his son would not inherit control of Park Communications, a publicly traded corporation headed by Park Sr. The magazine said, "The implication is clear: Park's son has yet to prove himself. 'You can't treat somebody special just because he's your son,' says Park. 'When NBC was at the bottom, young

Sarnoff was running it, and they lost a lot of good employees.'"

Young Park said his quitting has nothing to do with his father's statement that he wouldn't inherit the corporation, "since I've always known this was a possibility." He said he has no connection with Park Communications, since Park Outdoor has never been a part of the public company.

He said his resignation was "directly in response to his implication that I had to prove myself," the younger Park said.

He said he was asked to take over Park Outdoor three years ago, when the company was losing money. "It had been badly mismanaged, and it really had a bleak future — almost an impossible future. Right now, it's successful, and profitable. And while I'm not solely responsible, because I've had the best people in the outdoor advertising business — I brought them in — I think my management over the past three years

deserves some credit. But when this happened, and success is called failure, in a public, nationwide media, it's kind of hard to work in an environment where hard work and loyalty go unrecognized."

He said he's had about 60 people working in two states for Park Outdoor, "and I think this is a kind of an indictment of all of them, and I don't like it."

Park said he's worked for his father for the last 13 years.

After graduating from Cornell University with an M.B.A. degree in marketing, he went to work for J. Walter Thompson advertising agency in New York City, where he was a senior account executive for RCA, among other things. He also was a vice president and account manager for Kincaid Advertising Agency in Charlotte, N.C., before returning to Ithaca to work for his father.

Concerning the "special treatment" his father mentioned, Park responded, "You can't give special treat-

ment to a son. I'm just talking about fair treatment. I think everybody deserves respect — from the clerk to the owner's son." He said he didn't think that "to call the success of our division a failure" was showing respect.

He said his father's "values and priorities are different from mine."

Park said there has been virtually no turnover at Park Outdoor, since he took the division over at his father's request. When he took it over, he said, "The turnover was a big problem. We didn't even have a manager in six different divisions in two states, when I came back. And I think that's important."

Park said he was also upset that his father "didn't feel the need to tell me the way he felt, man to man. It had to come out in a nationwide business media."

He said that in the past year, his father "hasn't had anything to say except everything is going well."

Roy H. Park Sr. could not be reached for comment.

CHAPTER 27
FORBES AND FALLOUT

*When a man's knowledge is sufficient to attain, and his
virtue is not sufficient to enable him to hold, whatever he
may have attained he will lose again.*

—Confucius

And so my father lost a son.

The profile by Jeffrey Trachtenberg in the September 10, 1984,
issue of *Forbes* magazine was headlined EVERY DECADE, A NEW
CAREER, and it said, "Don't be deceived by his flashy jewelry and
his fancy cars. Roy Park is a serious man, a onetime newspaper
reporter who became a centimillionaire."

The interview covered my father's workaholic path from Duncan Hines to Park Communications and closed with Trachtenberg
reporting:

Park sold 11% of his company to the public last
October. He didn't really need the $3.5 million cash he
personally collected, rather he wanted to avoid estate
problems. By going public, he established a fixed value
for the company. That avoids a messy dispute with the
IRS like the one that plagues the estate of publisher S.I.
Newhouse. Being public also lets Park's firm use stock
for acquisitions.

Roy Park has a son and a daughter, but neither is
likely to succeed him. Roy Park, Jr. runs Park Outdoor, a
family-owned billboard business, but he will not inherit

control of Park Communications. The implication is clear: Park's son has yet to prove himself. "You can't treat somebody special just because he's your son," says Park. "When NBC was at the bottom, young Sarnoff was running it, and they lost a lot of good employees."

Park says he will name a successor someday, but even then he won't retire. "Twelve years ago I got a new lease on life when I started buying newspapers," he explains. "If we get another president, I might start something again. We've already applied for 45 low-power television licenses. I do better on new projects, where you can be creative. Every decade or so, I need a different career."[37]

I knew then I needed a new career, too. The denigration I suffered within the company I could live with, even being kept in the position of a second-class citizen. But as the calls began coming in about my father's statement to the world, from my friends, colleagues and many of the people I had met and worked with in my life, it was the final blow.

OUT OF A JOB

What lies behind us and what lies before us are tiny matters, compared to what lies within us.

—Oliver Wendell Holmes

As Sylvia Robinson said, "Some think it's holding on that makes one strong; sometimes it's letting go." My son, Trip, and I went down to my basement office over the weekend and cleaned out my personal belongings. On Monday morning, I walked into my father's office, handed him my letter of resignation and returned my credit cards and the keys to my car.

My letter of resignation, on which my mother was copied, simply said:

> This is to inform you that I am resigning from Park Outdoor Advertising effective today, August 31, 1984. The *Forbes* article expressing your true sentiments leaves me no choice.
>
> I regret having left a productive eight-year career to join your company only to have you feel that my efforts over the past thirteen years have not been worthwhile.

I'm sure he was shocked as I left his office, and Dave Feldman gave me a ride home. I left the nondescript company car in the parking lot, figuring my replacement would have as tough a time finding it as I had.

I was still in shock myself. Why the public vote of no confidence when after seven years with J. Walter Thompson and Kincaid Advertising I was asked by my father to come home to straighten out the outdoor division he owned and restore it to profitability? And why after a couple of years, when that was done, did my father hire professional managers to run the company and move me into his broadcasting company?

And after the outdoor division had slipped back into a loss situation, five years later, why was I asked to either take back its management or find another job? Was it because my father and I differed on which direction it should go? It was not easy to come to blows in the office and try to act like nothing had happened sitting around the dinner table at night.

I want to make it clear that his statement that I wouldn't inherit the company had nothing to do with my resignation. I had always known taking over the company was not possible. Further, I had no formal operating experience with Park Communications. The outdoor company was never part of this public company. My resignation was in response to my father's statement that I had "not proven myself," and I could not continue to work in an environment where success is deemed failure and where commitment, hard work and loyalty are put down.

My issue was not "special treatment" but "fair treatment." Every employee deserves to be treated with respect, from a clerk to the owner's son. To refer to the success of our division as unproven was unfair.

This all happened quickly. I had to let my former employees know. Temporarily having no access to typing help, Johnnie Babcock, on his first computer, helped me draft the following memo that went out the next day:

TO: All Park Outdoor Employees
FROM: Roy H. Park, Jr.
DATE: September 1, 1984

With deepest regret I inform you that on Friday, August 31, 1984, I resigned as vice president and general manager of Park Outdoor Advertising.

Exactly three years ago, my father asked me to take back an operation which had been badly mismanaged, was losing money, and was faced with a bleak future. Hard work and teamwork from people like you in the field restored the company to profitability, and indeed, this year we are headed for all record profits for Park Outdoor.

In the September issue of Forbes magazine, a prominent business publication just out on newsstands across the nation, my father conveyed the impression that I had failed to prove myself, and, at the least, was unworthy of succeeding him.

I have no connection with Park Communications, and our outdoor divisions were never a part of the public company. The issue certainly is not "special treatment," but fair treatment. Every employee deserves to be treated with respect. To infer that our success with the outdoor divisions is a failure indicates a lack of confidence in all of us. It is hard work in an environment when commitment, hard work and loyalty go unappreciated.

To further compare our long tenure together with the terrible turnover experienced by another company, when we know that turnover among our key people has been virtually nonexistent in the last three years, is also unfair. We all know about the rampant turnover in the outdoor divisions before I returned.

My father's nationally published vote of no confidence left me no choice but to resign. Based on our successful outdoor turnaround, he did not feel the need to tell me this personally. It is sad that he saw fit to do this, but I must admit my values and priorities are different from his, and they will remain unchanged.

I regret that this all occurred on such short notice. I was not made aware of the article until a flood of phone calls from friends nationwide came to me at the end of last week. These callers were all shocked and expressed both sympathy and support, proving once again that there is nothing more valuable in this world than trusted friends.

I count each of you among those good friends, and on my departure, thank you from the bottom of my heart for your tremendous efforts to help rebuild Park Outdoor to its present healthy position.

Good luck to each and every one of you.

I'd had little time to prepare for a new job search and realized that finding one was going to be a long process. It certainly wasn't going to be in Ithaca.

I had some savings by then but realized they would soon run out until I remembered I still had some P&G stock that could be used as collateral on a loan. Frankly, I had forgotten that, and after scrambling through papers in the basement I located the shares.

I remember Dave Feldman telling me that my father asked Wright Thomas, his president and chief operating officer, on a couple of occasions to ask Feldman to talk to me, saying, "He will listen to you." Dave assured him that I would not listen to him, regardless of our long-term relationship, and that the only person who might be able to change my mind was the person who caused the departure. My father also summoned Dave and another key employee, Fran Clines, for a meeting in his office to discuss the situation. He knew Fran since she had been the corporate receptionist before becoming human resources director for Park Outdoor, and he appealed to both of them to hold the fort and not jump ship, telling them he was working on negotiating my return.

Of course, I kept in touch with a few other employees, the most critical being my secretary, Angel. I remember meeting with her at her house while she was on maternity leave, since I needed her help in getting out resumes and job letters. While she worked, I was relegated to winding up the mechanical swing to keep her four-week-old infant occupied and quiet while she typed.

News from the office was shared with me by employees, so I had general knowledge of what was going on. Dave told me my father also asked him to tell me he was worried that people would quit and our national business would cancel if I waited too long to return. I did, in fact, have a number of my former employees call and ask if I could find a way to write reference letters for them. I told everyone who called to sit tight and hold on for the time being.

Calls also began coming in from media people with national agencies such as Leo Burnett, SSC&B, and Asch Advertising, and from buying services for R.J. Reynolds, Philip Morris, Lorillard, Seagram, and American Tobacco.

From someone who signed off as a native, caring Ithacan, a letter arrived saying, "Someday your dad is going to be sorry." A letter written to my father from one of our local outdoor advertisers calling himself a concerned longtime customer said, "As a user of billboard advertising and frequent traveler to the Binghamton and Syracuse areas, I have been able to watch the dramatic improve- ments in the quality of the boards…[and] impressed and amazed that your company could obtain such outstanding locations to build such beautiful boards."

Forbes. A beautiful, gentle Rottweiler that joined the family when a dog's love was needed the most.

One of the letters from my employees said, "You've attained something 350 million can't buy—your sanity and peace of mind. Everything happens for the best, and we have a feeling of calm that you will be happier and more relaxed than you've ever been in your life."

One bright spot was a new puppy my son had been wanting a long time that joined our family. During this period an eight- week-old female Rottweiler my mother purchased from a friend and breeder, Ted Fox, came through, and check Appendix I for more on why we named her Forbes.

WORKING THE MEDIA

It didn't take long in this small town for the *Ithaca Journal* to get wind of my resignation, and the same person, Helen Mundell, who frequently wrote articles on my father, contacted me. I thought about it, made some notes, and as we had learned to handle things at Park Outdoor, had asked her to put her questions in writing so I could give some thought and accurately answer each one. Just four days after I resigned, on September 4, 1984, her article at the top of the local section of the newspaper appeared under the heading PARK QUITS FATHER'S FIRM AFTER MAGAZINE APPEARS:

Roy H. Park, Jr., of 53 Highgate Circle, resigned Friday as vice president of Park Outdoor Advertising, in response to an "apparent vote of no confidence" of his father in Forbes magazine.

"I had no choice," Park said today. "This was a public vote of no confidence, and it was even more distressing in the light of the success we've had in turning around Park Outdoor."

Park's father, Roy H. Park, Sr., was featured in a profile in the September 10 issue of Forbes magazine. He was quoted as saying that his son would not inherit control of Park Communications, a publicly traded corporation headed by Park Sr. The magazine said, "The implication is clear: Park's son has yet to prove himself. 'You can't treat somebody special just because he's your son,' says Park. 'When NBC was at the bottom, young Sarnoff was running it, and they lost a lot of good employees.'"

Young Park said his quitting has nothing to do with his father's statement that he wouldn't inherit the corporation, "since I've always known this wasn't a possibility." He said he has no connection with Park

Communications, since Park Outdoor has never been a part of the public company.

He said his resignation was "directly in response to his implication that I had to prove myself," the younger Park said.

He said he was asked to take over Park Outdoor three years ago, when the company was losing money. "It had been badly mismanaged, and it really had a bleak future—almost an impossible future. Right now, it's successful, and profitable. And while I'm not solely responsible, because I've had the best people in the outdoor advertising business—I brought them in—I think my management over the past three years deserves some credit. But when this happened, and success is called failure, in a public, nationwide media, it's kind of hard to work in an environment where hard work and loyalty go unrecognized."

He said he's had about 60 people working in two states for Park Outdoor, "and I think this is kind of an indictment of all of them, and I don't like it."

Park said he's worked for his father for the last 13 years.

After graduating from Cornell University with an MBA degree in marketing, he went to work for J. Walter Thompson advertising agency in New York City, where he was a senior account executive for RCA, among other things. He also was a vice president and account manager for Kincaid Advertising Agency in Charlotte, NC, before returning to Ithaca to work for his father.

Concerning the "special treatment" his father

mentioned, Park responded, "You can't give special treatment to a son. I'm just talking about fair treatment. I think everybody deserves respect—from the clerk to the owner's son." He said he didn't think that "to call the success of our division a failure" was showing respect.

He said his father's "values and priorities are different from mine."

Park said there has been virtually no turnover at Park Outdoor, since he took the division over at his father's request. When he took it over, he said, "The turnover is a big problem. We didn't even have a manager in six different divisions in two states, when I came back. And I think that's important."

Park said he was also upset that his father "didn't feel the need to tell me the way he felt, man to man. It had to come out in a nationwide business media."

He said that in the past year, his father "hasn't had anything to say except everything is going well."

Roy H. Park Sr. could not be reached for comment.[38]

Despite the fact that my father couldn't be reached for comment, it didn't take long for him to respond. The very next day, on September 5, a boxed commentary from him, reported by Mundell, appeared on the Local page of the *Ithaca Journal* under the heading PARK SAYS HE REGRETS SON'S DECISION:

Roy H. Park Sr. said today he regrets the decision of his son, Roy H. Park, Jr., to resign as vice president of Park Outdoor Advertising.

The younger Park resigned Friday after what he called an "apparent vote of no confidence" of his father printed in the September 10 issue of Forbes magazine.

The article indicated that Park Sr. had said his son would have to prove himself if he were to inherit control of Park Communications, a publicly traded corporation headed by Park Sr.

The younger Park, 46, indicated he thought he had proved himself by returning Park Outdoor to profitability in the three years he has run the company, which is owned by the Park family.

Park Sr. said today that Park Outdoor "has shown marked improvement under his direction in the past three years." He declined further comment.[39]

I later was told that my mother had hung a sign over my father's office toilet at home, TIME WOUNDS ALL HEELS. She appeared to have been unaware of the quote my father made in the *Forbes* article after my (what proved to be unlucky) thirteen years of hard work for him, that I had "yet to prove myself." Or his implication that turnover during my years was rampant, when in fact, it had been rampant all through his reign and that of his other managers, and had stabilized considerably under mine. Needless to say, my mother was shocked when I resigned, and she let him know it. We spoke a few times on the phone, and she indicated that she was urging my father in every way possible to work things out.

NEGOTIATIONS

During this time, my father tried to contact me directly. I took my time calling him back, but when I did he told me he had a written proposal and would like me to listen to it. A day or so later, I sat down with him on the terrace one afternoon. He gave me the proposal in writing. He went through the provisions in detail, and I told him I would get back to him. As Will Rogers said, "Lettin' the cat outta the bag is a whole lot easier than puttin' it back in."

The two keys that began to turn the lock in my mind included the title of president and a CEO status, which I had not had before, and an agreement to sell me the outdoor companies in ten years. The biggest sticking point was the time lapse before the sale. Why he picked ten years I'll never know, but it was certainly too long for his heavy hand to continue to rest on the company. That's probably why he picked it, and since he would remain the owner, there was a lot he could do. There was always a chance he could make my life miserable enough to force me to resign, rendering the agreement null and void.

There was another catch in the agreement, but it seemed so far-fetched I eventually let it pass. The agreement to sell the company to me in September 1994 had a provision that my father could sell Scranton but only if he did so by December 31, 1984. With only a few months to go, I remember that he *never* had sold anything unless he was forced into it, such as the FCC regulations requiring a sale in Roanoke, VA. Further, I felt there was no way the local competition could get their hands on that kind of cash; they had already borrowed heavily to build the boards to compete against me, and I had begun to overtake them.

I shared the entire agreement with one of my attorneys, a personal friend, whose advice was quite practical. There was nothing wrong with returning as long as I did it on my terms, he advised. I wanted five years, but compromised on splitting the difference and settling on seven.

As my father had done when he negotiated the antique automobile, this time I got the benefit of the split. But in the end, my father, as the seller, still tried to keep 100 percent control. Despite my CEO status, I knew he couldn't resist keeping a heavy hand in the outdoor division. I was right.

THE RETURN

The *Ithaca Journal*'s headline on October 22, 1984 read: YOUNGER PARK BACK IN FAMILY BUSINESS. The article, by staff writer Helen Mundell, read:

> Roy H. Park, Sr. and his son, Roy H. Park, Jr., have patched up their quarrel, which was revealed publicly in late August in an article in Forbes magazine.

> The younger Park, 46, has been named president and chief executive officer of Park Outdoor Advertising of New York, Inc., a newly formed corporation. He will also serve on the board of directors, along with his father, who will be chairman. Park Jr. said an agreement has been reached to allow him to purchase control of the newly formed company during the next several years.

> Dave Feldman, who has been with Park companies for 15 years, will be treasurer of the new company and will also have an option to buy stock. Park Jr. resigned August 31 as vice president of Park Outdoor Advertising, in response to what he called "an apparent vote of no confidence" of his father, as stated in a profile in the September 10 issue of Forbes.

> "The management authority afforded by this new position, as well as the opportunity for controlling ownership of the company, have provided the basis for my return," the younger Park said. Park Sr., 73, said, "We're happy to have Roy at the helm of the outdoor operation."

Park Outdoor is a privately owned company, separate from Park Communications, Inc., which has stock that is publicly traded.[40]

Following my agreement to return were written comments from my employees such as: "Thank God you're back!" "Wow, what a fighter!" "You certainly won one hell of a battle! We all must carry on now and give you the support you will need to make this company more successful."

I also received a warm letter from my sister saying:

Congratulations: I heard the news. I'm totally confident that you're going to give them hell. You're going to do a wonderful job. One real positive thing that came out of this whole mess is I know you have the loyalty of the people who work for you. Well, Mr. CEO, it ain't going to be easy, but I know you have it in you to at least quadruple your earnings (especially without all the negative feedback): I'm 100 percent with you.

Roy, I'm really proud of you. Roy Senior ain't an easy person to stand up to...but we've both done it in our own ways.

She signed it, "I love you," and she attached a letter she had just received from a good friend, Bryant Mangum, suggesting I share it with Tetlow and my son. She said, "It's a pretty perceptive, feeling and beautiful letter." It read, in part:

Today on the way home...I [bought] the September 10 issue of Forbes magazine...."My feelings about the article on your dad are not so simple...[along with] the tears that came into my eyes. The first tears obviously were for myself....

The second tears were for your father. They were like

tears that I have shed for my own father, who has come in some ways—though by monetary standards, no—to the same place that your father has come.

Both have succeeded in dramatic ways; both have come to the top in the things that they have chosen to do....And yet neither of them, or so it seems to me, has come to the point that Jung describes as the development of a philosophy of life independent of society, which equates power over people with success. Perhaps both of them are cultural casualties, victims of the Depression, or of growing up on farms in the 1930s. But I do know that both of them are special people who somehow never learned that their children are separate from them and have a legitimate right to the pursuit of their own visions, and that those visions are real and honest.

People like you, and like me, and like Roy, have to deal with the irony of loving someone whose requirements are impossible and yet whom we love, precisely because they are our fathers and because we respect their eccentricities.

I've strayed from the *Forbes* article. Most people who read it will applaud what your father says about not treating a person differently because he is your son. But to me sons must be treated differently, precisely because they are sons; and daughters must be treated differently, precisely because they are daughters....And hopefully we will give them something that has less to do with dollar marks than with the human spirit that comes to them through us.

I've completely lost the *Forbes* article....But I've not lost the main thought that it has led me to: that we can not disinherit our fathers whether or not they disinherit us.

I don't feel my father intended to "disinherit" me, but as Johnnie points out in the next chapter, he intended to diminish the company he had agreed to sell me in seven years by some 33 percent. Buried in our 1984 sales agreement was a provision I could not imagine would become a reality. It gave it him less than two months to execute, which he did and put me through hell.

But I should have anticipated it. After all, I was dealing with my father. But at least it was long before a purchase price was established, and together with my Park Outdoor team, we were able to weather the storm, handle the transition and redirect our efforts to continue to thrive today.

Eight years after I purchased the New York outdoor companies, in 1996 our sales and management team gathers outside former corporate headquarters in downtown Ithaca, NY.

Six years later, our sales and management group in 2002, after we purchased our own building on a wooded lot in the Village of Lansing, an Ithaca suburb.

CHAPTER 28
NEVER SELL—NEVER?

As Johnnie Babcock points out, "Park watchers who liked to say they knew Roy H. Park inside and out insisted that he was an aggressive business buyer who never sold anything. They were right when it came to his main leverage capital: stock in Procter & Gamble, its spin-off company Clorox, and the food giant, ConAgra. There were also some local securities that he steadily accumulated as limited offerings became available, among them: First National Bank of Ithaca (ultimately Bank of America) and locally owned Tompkins Trust Company, where at his death he was the largest stockholder.

"Pledging parts of those solid assets to secure loans for desirable communications purchases, he paid cash for the many TV and radio stations that became Park Broadcasting. He also built significant real estate holdings and became an active player in outdoor advertising. Park made some brilliant purchases, but along the line he did sell off a few things. He rarely mentioned his sales, and with good reason. Most were not good deals.

"When he bought AM and FM radio stations in Minneapolis, Park also picked up radio properties in Duluth, MN. This far-north site was a management problem for me, who secured a manager for the Duluth stations who was so talented as to rise through the ranks to supervise all the Park radio stations. The advertising market for the stations was small, however, with dim prospects for growth. The stations lost money. After a winter sojourn to stir up business and quell a union organizing drive up north, I told my boss that the only hot place in the Duluth-Superior, WI, metropolis was an indoor rink devoted to curling, that occult sport where contestants push a heavy stone toward a far-off goal and team members sweep the ice ahead of the slowly sliding object to ease its course to bump other stones out of a score.

"I told Roy no alarm clock was needed at the Duluth motel. Cars starting up outside the room door woke you up all during the night. Nights are so cold up that way that automatic engine-starters fire up periodically during the night to prevent the oil from being so frozen that a battery can't turn the engine in the morning. The more frequent the starting noise, the colder the night. And come morning, you had to kick the motel room door open from the frost.

"Park sold the Duluth stations to a native who made a success of operating small stations in limited markets. The price was minimal. The rationale expressed by Park was that the weather was just too cold up International Falls way. Of course, he'd never been within hundreds of miles of the market. The real reason was an ice-bound operating statement.

"The Federal Communications Commission forced the sale of two Park radio stations when rules prohibited purchasing radio and TV stations in the same market. The prize was NBCTV affiliate WSLSTV in Roanoke, VA. Park readily agreed to sell off the sister radio stations. A broadcast broker came up with a client who impressed Roy. The billionaire Bass brothers of Fort Worth, TX, would buy the radio stations! Roy gloried in chatting with Perry Bass, a glib and attractive oil and cattleman and sophisticated business executive. He and Roy settled on a price of $1,500,000. Roy was openly tickled. Finally, the time came to submit the proposal to the FCC, and the official written offer from Bass hit Roy's desk. And Roy hit the phone. The purchase price was a stark $1,350,000. After chatting up Perry Bass for a few minutes, Roy pointed out that the written offer was $150,000 short of their agreed price.

"Perry Bass's laconic response was that down his way in Texas, his folks always got a 10 percent discount for cash. Park swallowed his complaint, but it was obvious that he had met his match in rough and tumble negotiating. He was faced with accepting the cash offer or being labeled a northern cheapskate by a well-known financial heavyweight. Roy folded like a lead balloon.

"These were two deals where the sale was not as satisfactory to him as a masterful purchase. He was to suffer one more costly business sale. Having agreed to sell all his outdoor plants to son Roy, Jr., Pops had buried an 'out' in their agreement allowing him to sell for himself the Scranton–Wilkes-Barre poster and paint plants, the largest and potentially most profitable. Despite a senior secretary's statement to Mundell in the *Ithaca Journal* article published July 8, 1991, that one of Roy's mottos was "We never sell anything," he undertook personal negotiations in secret and dumped the Scranton plant at a discount price to thwart and hopefully discourage his son from acquiring and operating the balance of his outdoor empire. The expensive and unsuccessful transaction was never discussed before or after with his son or his staff. It was a preemptive strike not easily justified, and in any event vindictive."

THE SALE OF SCRANTON

An old Florida farmer decided to visit a pond in the back of his property that he had not visited in a long time. As he neared the pond, he heard voices shouting and laughing with glee. As he came closer, he discovered a bunch of young women were skinny dipping in his pond. He politely made the women aware of his presence, and they all went to the deep end of the pond. One of the women shouted to him, "We're not coming out until you leave!" The farmer replied, "I didn't come down here to see you skinny dipping. I'm just here to feed the alligator."

Moral: Old age, cunning and treachery will triumph over youth and enthusiasm every time.

About the time I got to writing this part of the book, I had another lunch in a Chinese restaurant, and yet another fortune cookie read: "Love truths, but pardon error." I certainly love the truth. That's what this book is about. I also pardon error, to use an old Procter & Gamble advertising slogan 99⁴⁴⁄₁₀₀ percent correct, but there is one error that my father made that took me years to forgive. I was sure naïve to agree to that little provision about Scranton in my agreement to buy the company in 1998. He might as well have said, "Thanks a million," when I signed off.

That's what he got: $3.75 million to be exact. And little did I know the whole time my competitor in Scranton had GE Capital behind him.

The sale of Scranton came in just under the wire of my father's deadline of December 31, 1984. The last thing that you want are phone calls from your employees thrown out of their jobs on Christmas Eve. It's not the best time to hear that one of your companies had been sold and your employees sent home to celebrate their jobless status on Christmas with their families. I found it impossible to believe that my father would construct an agreement to sell me the company, *after* he was in negotiation to sell a third of it to my competitor. It was beyond comprehension that a father would do that to his son, but I should have realized that if the possibility was even mentioned by him, it was already fact. I had trusted him but should have known better. There were no opportunities my father missed.

It's one thing to sell a company and another to sell it to the competitor your father had pitted you against. The terrible thought crossed my mind that the entire reason the money had been spent to upgrade Scranton and Wilkes-Barre, eliminate the union, and make massive capital improvements to bring national business back in was to make the company more valuable for a sale.

But I mentioned that this was *his* error. It was mine to be duped, but the irony of the entire deal was that the proceeds of $3.75 million were reinvested in buying and expanding a building housing a bank in Ithaca. The building was a white elephant. When I was assigned to sell it after my father died, the most we could get was $1,250,000, and it had to be put in the hands of a real estate holding company to get even that. On the other hand, the Scranton operation is now probably worth some $75 million, based on some industry valuations. Funny how things work out, and I would have to consider it one of my father's worst management decisions. Of course, the entire burden of that bad decision was carried by his son.

I would not like to believe that Christmas Eve was the date chosen by my father for the cruel exodus wreaked on my employees. But the timing was perfect for my former competitor to crush my employees and demoralize me. It sent the meanest message possible and totally ruined one of the few Christmases that our family was to spend together.

During the brutal sweep when the employees were fired and escorted out the door with no time to gather their personal belongings, most of them were told they would be invited back to interview and apply for a job. Over the next several weeks, those who had exhibited the most disdain for my competitor and his methods were not asked back or not rehired after an interview. My former competitor's game plan was geared to make them hurt. Former employees of my company who had held positions not requiring competitive contact with him in their day-to-day jobs were hired back.

I quickly offered jobs in our Binghamton division to any former employees who were not hired back in Scranton. Our general manager, William Piatt, was immediately put on our payroll there and he commuted faithfully from Scranton into our Central New York territory for years. One of our former salespersons felt the commute would be too much and found employment in Scranton. Our other Scranton salesperson, a young man I hired directly out of college 45 years ago and who served with us in leasing before sales, remained with the surviving company in Scranton. But he ended up joining us a number of years later as our vice president and general manager in Binghamton after the Scranton operation was resold.

THE ENSUING YEARS

The young often live
In the future
The old, too often,
In the past
Those who have age,
But never grow up
Live the Present
As if it were last.
Now Past and Present
And Future
Each one an important Key.
But the Gate to Success
As Life meant it
Has not just one lock
But three.

—Roy H. Park, Jr. unpublished (1980)

As the 1970 song by *America* goes, "I've been through the desert on a horse with no name," but, in my case, I still didn't get out of the rain. The past had been turned upside down, emptied; the future, for growth, anyway, pretty much cut off. So I was left with the present.

The timing on the sale of Scranton at the end of 1984 was particularly sad for me since the operating profit that year came in at $587,000, the largest in the history of our outdoor companies. During the next four years, I was thankful that while we had been pumping capital improvement money into Scranton, the division now gone, we also had initiated a capital-improvement program in New York State.

Being concentrated there, I moved quickly to get involved with our state outdoor advertising association, which at the time was called the Roadside Business Association of New York. In

1985, I was elected president and in 1986 we strengthened the association to represent all of the outdoor companies doing business in New York outside of New York City. We changed our name to the Outdoor Advertising Council of New York, Inc., and I served as president until 1991, and then chairman, until 1995. Dave Feldman, from 1996, has served as chairman to this day.

Despite the loss of the vast majority of our national business (when buys were made in Scranton, they used to overflow into our New York markets), operating profit in 1985 increased from $587,000, as I said, (when we had the billing from Scranton) to $603,000. In 1986, operating profit went up 58 percent to $943,000, and the following year 43 percent more to $1,328,000.

But even though our sales and profit ratios were growing and doing well, the weekly management meetings continued, and I learned that my CEO status didn't mean much. With everything going well for the company I ran, my father could still not avoid involving himself in the day-to-day operation of Park Outdoor. He still owned the company, and the proceeds of my efforts were his. Every move I made was closely monitored, and many good opportunities were restricted or thwarted.

I had endured seventeen long years of rough road working for my father, and the road ahead didn't look any better. I learned a lot, but that knowledge taught me that to survive I had to look to the future. Despite the fact that I had returned as president and CEO of Park Outdoor Advertising, my father had no intention of taking his finger out of the pie.

When I had an opportunity to expand into Erie, PA, where our corporate sales manager lived, in order to give our company another large city to help attract business, I faced strong resistance from my father. Even though the company had enough money to make the acquisition, he told my mother that Erie was a bad place to do business, was infiltrated by organized crime and that expanding into that area would be dangerous. As usual, she believed him, at first, but I am reminded that at our next board meeting, when my case was laid out, she supported me in making a bid to buy a small paint bulletin plant in the market.

My father reluctantly agreed, but it was increasingly evident to me that he had little interest in seeing my operation grow or expand, other than making sure there was growth on the bottom line. The meeting with the two partners took place in a hotel in Erie over a late dinner; they had requested that neither of us have lawyers present. I had prepared a letter of intent that required their signatures, in which my offer was stated in writing. The owners tried every tactic to try to keep a copy of the unsigned agreement overnight, which would have given them the ability to shop it with other buyers. The meeting dragged on into the late hours without their signing. I laid a check for $50,000 on the table as our good-faith down payment and told them they could cash the check as soon as the agreement was signed.

Their eyes kept focusing on the check, but they still held off signing and finally insisted on calling their lawyer. He came to the meeting in the restaurant with pajamas on under his coat, and I exercised an equal right to call my own lawyer 250 miles away in Ithaca. I made sure I gathered up the check and the unsigned agreement when I left the table to make the phone call to him at home at 11:30 PM. We stuck to our guns, and shortly after midnight the agreement was signed, the check collected by them. The deal was done.

But my father's tight reign on making the moves that we needed to make, as well as constant nitpicking each week in the management meetings, made me realize that if I waited out the next four years we had agreed upon before exercising my right to purchase the company, there would not be much of a company to purchase.

Our company was also being drained with rental payments. Along with the outdoor companies, my father originally bought several parcels of land occupied by billboards belonging to the sellers. Some fifty parcels of land were purchased along with the billboards, and in some cases as many as six billboard structures were located on a single parcel of land my father then owned.

These lands were transferred from the outdoor division and put into his real estate operation, RHP Incorporated. Park Outdoor was paying lease rental to the real estate company under this arrangement, and some of these lease rentals were exceedingly high.

After he concluded the agreement with me, I noticed some of these parcels were being sold. Our outdoor division would have matched any offer, both to preserve the boards as well as eliminate the leases, but we were not given a chance to do so. Each time a piece of land on which we owned billboards was sold, we were faced with negotiating a higher lease rental, or removing the boards. Hardly the act of a father who wanted to see the operation run by his son succeed.

As I have said, the outdoor division also paid rent to RHP Incorporated for the ten of us housed at headquarters, and I use "headquarters" loosely. Remember my description of our dismal, belowground quarters. We had been put in the basement because Pops couldn't find other tenants desperate enough to rent the space.

When I got word through the office grapevine that plans for a new lease with a substantial increase in our rent were in the works, I exercised my right as president and CEO. I began looking for new office space and learned 3,000 square feet was available in a building recently vacated by the telephone company in downtown Ithaca that was owned by a friend. At the time, the space was an open shell and had to be built-out into individual offices. I designed the build-out, my friend started construction and I went out looking for new office furniture.

I knew the move, when it took place, had to be swift. If my father had known ahead of time, he would have tried to prevent it and certainly wouldn't have sold us the decrepit, second-hand furniture and equipment we were using but didn't own, even at its depreciated value.

I negotiated trade-outs with current and new advertising clients for furnishings and state-of-the-art office equipment, and just before the new lease was drawn, the space was finished and fully furnished. In one weekend our entire staff, using our own vehicles, made the move. On Monday morning we were fully operational in our new quarters. We even transferred our telephone number.

When Bob Burns, my father's real estate representative, came to the basement on Monday for a signature on a new lease, he returned to tell my father no one was there. The first thing my father asked was if the furniture was still there, and Burns replied yes, but no humans were evident. There was no way my father could imagine we had all taken the day off at the same time, and I let him sweat it for a while before I told headquarters we had moved and that there was no need to bring down a new lease.

After we vacated the basement office space, my father's real estate division was never able to rent it again. It was used mainly as storage.

PURCHASING PARK OUTDOOR

Park Outdoor now had an independent office but our Monday meetings were still held at Terrace Hill. The bottom line was still in my father's control. I knew the only way that the company could survive, and I could survive, was to buy it. Soon. I had to buy it while it was still viable or preside over its slow death.

The most difficult job I ever faced was to convince my father to sell Park Outdoor to me. Despite the fact that I had come back as CEO, and was immediately blindsided by the sale of Scranton, I had continued to build a base of operations with what remained and upgrade the integrity of the entire company. I had retained a loyal set of managers, sales people and production workers, and I managed to salvage a good deal of national business despite the loss of our Scranton operation. It was time to expand, but the restrictions placed on my goals continued, with my father keeping his fingers in every move I made, despite the autonomy that should have been granted to my CEO status.

As I said, while we had poured $600,000 in capital improvements into Scranton, I had the foresight to invest some of the additional money in refurbishing and upgrading the inventory in New York, so it was in much better shape than the year before I had returned. Our overall sales were going up, along with modest increases in operating profit, but certainly not to the extent my father would have wanted. I knew the only way to bring peace back to the family was to, again, become independent and eliminate the working relationship. So after legal counsel, I developed a plan to approach my father to purchase the company early.

He was adamantly opposed and immediately flew in his tax attorney to explain all of the reasons, aside from our agreement, that he couldn't sell it early. I point out here that this, and ensuing disagreements with my parents over the years cost me hundreds of thousands of dollars in legal fees, a far cry from the first twenty-one years of my life, and in fact all of the years before I came back to work for my father. Except for the last two years of his life, I lost a father when I came back to work for him in 1971. And later, and I'll come to this, I lost for a while my mother when a decision was made to divide our family foundation, a decision endorsed by our outside trustees.

Life is simple, and we only have to look at nature to understand ourselves. When a plant is under stress, it blooms freely, the object being to spread its seed. The older animals head the flock, pack or herd because they are the survivors. It's no wonder that old men chase their nurses around the bed before finally packing it in. The ones that survive, be it plant, animal or man, are those nature has properly designated to continue the species. But it is unfortunate that as men get older, understanding, generosity and wisdom often go by the boards. If not chasing women, they are chasing power and control, the sad fact of human nature. It is a depressing truth that fathers and grandfathers do not always mellow when they enter old age. I have always thought that as you grow older, you tend to seek serenity. I had pictured my father dispensing wisdom like Uncle Remus in *Br'er Rabbit,* or even the guy behind the curtain in *The Wizard of Oz.*

But, as Sherwood Anderson wrote in "Discovery of a Father," a son's wish for what he imagines to be a perfect father does not always come true: "One of the strangest relationships in the world is that between father and son. I know it now from having [a son] of my own. A boy wants something very special from his father.

You hear it said that fathers want their sons what they feel they cannot themselves be, but I can tell you it also works the other way. I know that....I wanted my father to be a certain thing he was not."[41]

I had hoped for a sharing of wisdom from him, not hardened aggressiveness, and always thought that as I got older, I would spread wisdom, love and compassion to the younger members of my family. But maybe that won't happen. It didn't happen with my father. Despite all the books and movies where "on Golden Pond" people mellow, I am not sure that it happens much in real life.

For no real reason I could see, he was determined to hold on to Park Outdoor. But this time also, my mother was on my side, and she also could see no reason why my father could not sell the company to me. His tax attorney, on the other hand, was asked to come up with every reason in the book to make the case that my father could not sell ahead of the agreed-upon date. And he was good at it. In the early stages, I relied on my attorney, a personal friend, but this time he urged me to add first-class counsel. As the saying goes, if you want peace, you better be prepared for war. So I hired the managing partner of one of the largest law firms in New York. The tax counsel working with his firm was the best I could find, after all, he was up against the tax attorney who had represented my father and his dealings over the years.

My approach, despite an unyielding legal opinion of my father's tax attorney that the company could not be sold, was simple. I repeated the mantra that went to the heart of their position each time we met over a two-month period, "You can, but you won't." The stalemate was finally resolved when my lawyer came up with a formula that factored in the value of what an immediate outside buyer might pay with the understanding that under my agreement they would have to sell it back to me in three years. In other words, the formula took into account the value of the company to an outside buyer by positioning me as an outside buyer at the time, and the logic was irrefutable.

Only after my mother threw her support behind the idea of selling it to me without fully understanding why my father wouldn't, or comprehending the formula that made it impossible for him to deny the sale, were we able to move ahead.

Better times. Trip opening graduation presents from his grandparents while "Grandottie" looks through a family photo album in 1989, a year after she supported my purchase of Park Outdoor.

Working as I had been for an extremely low salary over the seventeen years, I had been unable to put aside much, and to accomplish the sale I obviously had to pledge the company, as well as everything I owned, as collateral. But at age fifty, I was able to convince Chase Bank to lend me the money. As far as the inventory, I would have felt a lot more secure about my personal pledge if the majority of the boards were not unsightly, rickety old structures built some forty years ago.

After the sale my father tried to convince my mother he had given me a "sweetheart deal." But after I pledged the inventory I bought, along with my family's house, car, furniture and whatever else we had of value, and owing a mortgage, car payments and student loans, and with the purchase price being over thirty times my annual income before taxes, the deal wasn't all that "sweet" to me.

It was a gamble, but with all my employees still in place, I knew I had a fighting chance. With the huge debt load of principal and interest the company had to meet, and with Chase breathing down my neck at every turn, we started back to work. The pressure was intense for the next couple of years with the bank hovering over my shoulder more than any board of directors ever could. The debt load left little to spare for capital improvements or the construction of new locations even though we had the leases. My father did not have to struggle with that sort of tough situation with the proceeds he had after he sold his Hines-Park Foods company to Procter & Gamble.

But slowly and surely we climbed out, and even our suppliers helped us by allowing us to pay them back over longer periods of time.

REBUILDING PARK OUTDOOR

Now I've learned you only get to keep what you have earned.

From the song "Weekend Lover"
by Rupert Holmes [41a]

In a sales meeting with my managers in 2001, I recapped some of the things we had to do to get the company I bought in 1988 moving again. I highlighted our history, which, most of them already knew, pointing out that starting in mid-1985, our acquisitions included 24 eight-sheets in Utica we bought from Sweet Outdoor and 12 faces from Howard Signs in Erie, PA. The following year we purchased 10 bulletin faces in Syracuse from Roberts Outdoor, which followed our entry into that market the previous year without objection from Norm Simpson, the dominant Syracuse plant operator, building five structures on I-81 and I-690, some costing as much as $80,000.

In 1986 we also bought 64 eight-sheet faces from Maypat Outdoor in Watertown. Then in 1989 we strengthened our position in Binghamton by acquiring Midstate Outdoor with 400 faces in the Triple Cities market. That same year we bought 600 faces from Matthew Outdoor in Northern New York and the Mohawk Valley.

We made one small and sometimes not-so-small acquisition after another, and one September morning in 1990, while I was shaving, I realized I personally owed $8.8 million dollars. Chase Manhattan was still my bank at the time, and although it was small change for them, it was big bucks for me. Not to be deterred, in 1993 we bought three bulletins and 7 thirty-sheets from Mincom in Syracuse. That same year we also bought four bulletins in our Southern Tier from the Meigs-Street Corporation. The following year we traded inventory with Penn Outdoor in two counties in Pennsylvania for 55 thirty-sheet faces in Elmira, Watkins Glen, Bath and Utica, mostly as a defensive measure to prevent further expansion by competitors in our markets.

By this time, we were stretched from along the Canadian border to the north into Erie, PA, to the west and all along the Southern Tier of New York (and into a number of northern counties in Pennsylvania) from Jamestown to Oneonta. It's a lot easier to control cost when you are concentrated in a single large market, and we were very labor-intensive, covering an area that encompassed about half the state of New York. We were able to make payments on the loan but had very little left over to maintain and upgrade our inventory. There were always other outdoor operators out there wanting to buy, and we finally decided to look at some of the offers.

In October 1994, we carved off our western division. It took at least four hours to drive from Ithaca to Jamestown and down into Erie. Because of the requirements in the Western New York and Pennsylvania divisions and building in the territory from national outdoor competitors and local individuals, selling the division was prudent to reduce overhead and debt.

Then we took a hard look at what we called our northern division, which covered north from Oswego and Watertown up to Ogdensburg, Canton, Potsdam, Massena and Malone and even Chateaugay along the St. Lawrence River. This included new boards we had built in Watertown, but most of them were old. The weather was so cold in this part of our territory for five months of the year that we had to mix calcium chloride in the paste to freeze the poster paper on the boards. When spring came, the ice and paste dissolved and the paper slid off, leaving us with massive cleanups and reposting jobs. And every time a storm blew in several structures suffered damage. In November 1995, northern became our second divestiture. We did retain some boards from this sale for our Utica plant, but overall the proceeds from both sales were enough to reduce the principal on our loan dramatically. We were then able to concentrate on improving the remaining inventory, which covered some 15,000 square miles, an irregular circle averaging 240 miles wide around our headquarters in Ithaca.

In 1999, we bought 12 bulletin faces on the fairgrounds in Syracuse from Empire Outdoor, and in 2001, 49 faces in Utica-Rome and the Mohawk Valley from Seifert and Stannard Signs. In 2003, we bought 43 faces in Fulton and Montgomery Counties from Lang Media and added them to our Utica operation, and our company continued to explore opportunities for further expansion.

We also continued to obtain new leases in legal areas and follow up by building on these sites. Through the energetic efforts of our Outdoor Advertising Council of New York, we were able to pass a vegetation bill in New York State, and the ability to trim trees in front of existing boards was like finding or building new inventory.

In our 2001 meeting, I also told my employees about a speech I heard in October of that year. It was one of the Cornell Business School Durland Lecture Series, which had been created with help from my father. The CEO of American Express, Kenneth I. Chenault, spoke just after the World Trade Center attack. This was a company that had to evacuate its New York headquarters housing 4,000 employees after the September 11 attack. The company lost ten people in the World Trade Center collapse and had to relocate its remaining employees all over Westchester County and elsewhere in New York City to continue operations.

He spoke of his company's rules for success, and I shared them with our people.

Chenault said all employees, top to bottom, must be held accountable for their actions, and to be an effective sales person, aside from humility and honesty, you also need a sense of humor.

He said for every problem there is a solution. There's never a problem without one. He also said you must be innovative and able to develop value-added ideas in order to make fundamental breakthroughs and be a consistent winner. Take the complex and make it simple, he said. And although cooperation and collaboration between employees is critical, he said confrontation with leadership is allowed as long as it is constructive. As a team player, he expects you to raise the performance bar for everyone so that in coming together, you can move your company forward and equally share the results. Finally, *anticipate.* Be adaptable to possible setbacks, not just react to them. Prepare in advance to confront change, not just cope with it after it takes place. This, Chenault said, is the single most critical ingredient for survival and success.

Although not part of his talk, Chenault also knows the value of showing *appreciation.* At the end of last year I received a pair of Tiffany wine glasses with a signed letter from him thanking me for five decades of loyalty as an American Express Card Member.

During our sales meeting I also stressed the importance of being *organized.* It is critical to the survival of any small business in New York State. History repeats itself so keep organized files and throw nothing out, the absence of which can come back to bite you later. Those files allow you to confront any challenges or problems that come up again and provide a history behind your arguments. The points you need in your counterattacks. It allows you to stay on course without having to 'reinvent the wheel.' Staying on course means survival. In short, I said, *organization* applies to any business you run, the people you manage, your personal life and any commitments you may make to your spouse, children, supplier, bankers, lawyers or brokers.

There was one other business asset that is often overlooked, but central to success. In *The Art of the Deal* Donald Trump touts the importance of *showmanship*. He says let people know how successful you are. My father's achievements spoke for themselves, but there was no question that among things he had in common with Trump was *showmanship*.

And speaking of The Donald, remember my mention of returning to New York with JWT and inappropriately dining at the Four Seasons Restaurant at the company's expense? During a trip to New York on foundation business in the early 1990's, I returned there with family and friends for a late dinner. We were headed up the stairway when I thought I recognized someone coming down.

I intercepted the gentleman and his stunning companion on the landing and asked how everything was going. After a brief and friendly exchange, I told him how good it was to see him again. We parted, and when I came up to join my group, they commented they didn't realize we knew each other. Then one of them said, "But you called him Jim." I said yes, that's James Rosenfield, my father's colleague when he was president of the CBS TV Network. My friend said, "That was Donald Trump and Marla Maples. You didn't see his double-take when you called him Jim. He's probably going to need to see his psychiatrist in the morning."

In more recent years I came across our President in New York restaurants several times. Without knowing who I was, he courteously acknowledged my eye contact by nodding his head as I walked by his table at Jean-Georges where I was dining with then Cornell Chairman of the Board Stephen Weiss, who told me Trump was "sitting with the good guys." And again, at a later time he stood up and shook my hand when I approached the table he shared with Melania at Le Cirque.

Shortly after our sales meeting, our then national sales representative, John Roberts of Power Sales Advertising, who was in attendance, wrote me the following note. He represented our client, R. J. Reynolds Tobacco for many years before that company was forced to drop billboard advertising. John sadly passed away at a young age in August 2016, but at the time because he admired the integrity with which we ran our company, he asked if he could represent us when he started his own business in 2005. We were the first outdoor company to sign him up.

> *I wanted to drop you a note of thanks for including me in the annual Park Outdoor meeting a few weeks back. The development of the attached photos from the 'awards' ceremony affords me this opportunity to send regards.*
>
> *What I take away from that session is the quality and continuity of the people of Park Outdoor. Dave mentioned this as a 'strength' of the company in his remarks and it truly is.*
>
> *I recently cleaned out my Rolodex and discarded more than one-half of my Lamar business cards for departed managers and changed addresses. I have Park Outdoor cards from the 80's that could've been printed yesterday. In my mind, this is the mark of a remarkably stable company.*
>
> *And while most outdoor vendors continue to wring their hands over a downturn in national business, Park Outdoor has positioned itself for any "uncontrollable" economic dislocations. It's a great regional economic story."*

Teresa and John Roberts with Tetlow. As our national sales representative who spent most of his time in the City, John was affectionately known by us as "Mr. New York."

In 1989, the first full year I owned the company, our sales increased by a million dollars, exceeding $5 million and within the next two years, we reached $6,000,000. The sale and loss of billing from both our northern and western divisions in 1994 and 1995 dropped us back into the $5.5 million range and it took us a couple of years to recover from the loss of this inventory. In 1998 we were back above $6 million, and growing at an average rate of 5 percent, fiscal sales are well over $10 million today.

Small potatoes to the communications empire my father built, but for something he bought primarily for depreciation, not bad. We pay plenty of taxes and Park Outdoor means a lot to our over a hundred employees with their extended families that depend on the company for their livelihoods.

Our company's success is due to our employees and we share it with them. Through incentives, bonuses and profit sharing, over the past four years we have turned back up to 27 percent of our net income to our employees.

Members of our Syracuse and Utica divisions gather in Utica, NY after a staff luncheon.

Our Elmira and Binghamton teams take a photo op after a joint staff meeting in Binghamton, NY.

CHAPTER 29
IN RETROSPECT

There are times when a man needs to rise above his society, his culture, even his teachings and surroundings. He must exercise God-given self-determination to question claims of the world around him. He must discard the parenthesis of his life and step into the endless vistas beyond. Often an individual is not right, a society is not right, a continent is not right, perhaps, a world is not right. We must bend to society, but not snap under it. Individual freedom is not easily given by others, so it must be taken. A man must believe in himself, live his own life, carve his own destiny. He can learn from others, but the better lesson is self-taught. Human nature ensures that there will never be a perfect world, but there can be a perfect dream. Our Creator has seen to it we are given the capacity to think for ourselves. Our minds are private, but if breached, our souls certainly are. God gave us a soul. Our duty is to give it meaning, and He wants it back. If returned without meaning, His preference may be to send it back from the hereafter to earth through you, to give you a second chance, but it may be reassigned to another. I think one way or other, until it has meaning, His intent is to re-use it.

—Roy H. Park, Jr.

I wrote that in 1958 when I got back into The University of North Carolina. I had a lot of thinking to do, being isolated my first year there, living alone in a room at the Carolina Inn. In going through my father's papers after his death, I also went through my own and came across this passage that reminded me of him, and his philosophy on life. The way my words defined his independent drive during his life was pretty scary.

My father was a God-fearing man. Not a Bible-thumper, but he certainly paid his dues at the Presbyterian Church. He was raised at an early age by the Bible, by his mother, and he believed in the hereafter. The apple doesn't fall far from the tree, and as I delved into his life, I began to believe more and more in, "Like father, like son." Although I have actively tried to avoid the things he did I didn't like, I'm coming to believe that I'm more like him than I ever thought.

After all those years of trying to understand and know him, Ethan Canin comes close to describing my own realization of this through the words the father expresses to the son in his story "The Year of Getting to Know Us": "[Y]ou don't *have* to get to know me. You know why?...You don't have to get to know me... because one of these days you are going to grow up and then you are going to *be* me."[42]

Eight years after I resigned from my father's business, and then returned under the agreement giving me the right to buy the company, which I did in 1988, I was approached by *Town & Country* for an interview for a special section the magazine was doing on sons and daughters of famous parents. I was among five people written up: Wallis Annenberg, the daughter of billionaire publisher Walter Annenberg; Phillip Fisher, the son of oil investor Max Fisher; Bernard Petrie, the son of Milton Petrie, the clothing store czar; and John Lennon, whose father manufactured specialized instruments for everything from power plants to NASA rockets.

They wanted to know how I felt being passed over to head my father's company. Not aware that I had purchased the company, they had seen a second article in *Forbes* about fathers and sons and wanted to know what had happened. I was hesitant to speak out and put off the interview as long as possible. When I finally decided to give the interview, I told my parents I had been interviewed for an article by Evan McGlinn called "5 of the Fortunate," and they waited with trepidation for its publication, as did I. I tried to be discreet, but also honest, and my father was relieved and somewhat pleased at the way it came out. The article appeared in October 1992. Here is the pertinent part:

"Fifty-four-year-old Roy Park Jr. decided he would follow in his father's footsteps and join the world of advertising and media. After seven years of working at J. Walter Thompson on such accounts as Ford and Pan Am, Park was asked in 1971 to run one of his father's companies. But son and father found that they couldn't work together.

"His father wanted to see if Park could turn a profit for Park Outdoor Advertising. He did, but was soon replaced by experienced outdoor-advertising managers and shuffled off to the Park Communications broadcasting division. Within a few years, the billboard division was again losing money, and, according to Park, his father basically said, 'Look, either you take the billboard division back over, or look for another job.'

Six Years After returning to Park Outdoor after fallout from Forbes, *Town & Country* published an article on the sons and daughters of famous parents.

"The pair's problems were not confined to working hours, either. 'There would be some blowout at the office,' said Park, 'and then we would be sitting at the dinner table, and I would be chewing my tongue ragged because I was still furious at the end of the day, trying to act like nothing happened.'

"The real blowout came while Roy, Jr. was again making the billboard division profitable. His father second-guessed him until, as Park says, 'I had to make a decision, either leave the company, again, or buy it for my own sanity.'

"So in 1988 he borrowed the money and bought the billboard business. It now controls some 3,000 billboards in New York and Pennsylvania and has revenues of nearly $7 million, a 60 percent increase over what it was when his father owned it.

"Even though his father is estimated to sit on a fortune worth some $515 million, Park says he received only a nominal gift from his dad. 'He paid for my college education, except for $3,000, and that was it. I see fathers who spoil their kids, and then the kids really aren't worth a hell of a lot. I certainly wasn't spoiled, I'm glad I wasn't. Our relationship is excellent now.' [43]

WINDING DOWN

In July of 1991, my father was interviewed and given a large spread headlined "At 80, the lion of Park still runs this show" in *The Ithaca Journal*. His health had been failing a bit, but he had no intention of thinking about retiring. On the front page of the business section, Helen Mundell reported:

"Retirement does not figure in 80-year-old Roy Park's future. At an age when most of the Ithaca-based media mogul's contemporaries have been retired for 15 years or more, the chairman and chief executive officer of Park Communications, Inc. works 70-hour weeks. And that's after Park cut back on his workload—on doctor's orders. This spring, a bout with illness briefly hospitalized the workaholic multimillionaire, who counts among his close

friends the cream of Ithaca's business community as well as national media luminaries such as Katherine Graham and Al Neuharth, both now retired from their respective journalism empires, The Washington Post and Gannett Co., Inc.

"The octogenarian's illness, from which he now says he's fully recovered, focused media industry attention both near and far on Park Communications. "

It went on to say:

Some industry watchers suggest that top Park managers have been running the fiscally sound company for perhaps several years, leaving Roy Park free to pursue other interests. 'Somehow, I've got the info that...the president has been effectively running the show for the last two years or so,' said J. Kendrick Noble, Jr., a former analyst at Payne Webber who left that firm in January to found Noble Consultants Inc. of Bronxville, NY. Park President Wright M. (Tommy) Thomas flatly denied that scenario, saying his boss is still firmly in command.

"If I was going to retire, I'd like to retire like Al Neuharth,' Park said, with a smile. Neuharth, retired chief executive officer of media giant Gannett, now is part-time head of the Freedom Foundation—formerly the Gannett Foundation. 'I don't think (Park's) the retiring kind,' Neuharth said last week in a telephone interview from Washington, D.C. 'There's no reason why he should retire. He gets better and stronger as the years go on. '[44]

In a front-page insert headed "Park Sets Fast Pace," Mundell reported that Pops' friend, former U.S. Senator Harry F. Byrd Jr., of Virginia, said he never heard Park mention retirement. "'If you have, let me know,' Byrd said with a hearty laugh."

During the interview, my father said he was feeling fine again.

"'There was no cancer, or anything like cancer,' he said, responding to rumors in the community at the time of his illness. Park, who had recently spent three days at a CBS network affiliates' meeting in New York City, wouldn't say how many hours a week he put in before his illness. He said his company, which has grown steadily since he bought his first paper in 1972, is 'in the market for more' newspapers,

*particularly in states where the company already has papers.
'I'm still interested in our newspapers and scan them,' said
Park, a newspaperman since he was 12. In fact, if he sees
a dull headline in a Park paper, the editor who wrote it is
likely to get it back in the mail, more colorfully rewritten by
Park or his top managers."*

In the article, she also asked, "Is there life after Roy Park
for the tightly-run newspaper and television chain?" My father
indicated he had several good people who could take over the
helm, but made it plain that "he is not budging." It was clear
that Pops didn't intend to turn his company over to any family
member, and Mundell reported that "Park's future doesn't include
turning the company over to anyone else to run, at least in the
foreseeable future."[45]

Knowing my father as well as I did, I just knew it wasn't in
him to turn over what he had taken a lifetime to build for someone
else to continue to run. He had already made up his mind on how
it was going to end, but during the interview he continued to play
the game. He said that if something were to take him out of the
picture, the company has several good people available to take
over, and in Mundell's article, started by naming Wright Thomas,
who my father said was:

*Not only president, but also chief operating officer,
treasurer, assistant secretary and director. 'Tommy is not
only a good manager, but a CPA and a good organizer,' Park
said, smiling affectionately at Thomas, who was ensconced
in Park's office with other top company managers during a
recent interview.*

Toward the end of the interview, my father said what he really
intended to have happen when he was gone. Mundell reported:

*"Park said he plans to leave a large block of stock to
the Park Foundation, which he set up to make charitable
contributions in communities where the company has
properties. Employees will then be able to buy the stock from
the foundation at a low interest rate. 'It's the idea of giving
the employees a stake,' he said. 'They helped me build (the*

company) and I don't want to see it sold out to some fellow
who's going to let it be run down.'"[46]

That was in 1991, and the following year my father began to slow down. After we moved out of the building in 1990 and I was no longer working at the Park Communications headquarters, I would occasionally see my father with his business associates during lunch at the same restaurants, but was unaware of whether or not he continued to report to his office every day.

I do know the things men fear the most as we grow older began to take a toll: cataracts, high blood pressure and prostate problems that would eventually require surgery. I think his physical decline was partly the result of all of his years from Duncan Hines on, enjoying good food and drink, the lack of exercise that came with all work and no play, and the stress he appeared to be shedding like rain water which all the while may probably have been building up inside.

As I said, I'm not sure at which point he began to spend more time at home and less and less time going to the office, and I know that during this period his office personal met with him in his study at home. And as a consequence, I was also able to see more of him, and during this time, my father and I got along well. There were no points of conflict. I was no longer working for him and finally had the time to re-establish a father-son relationship.

Then, following cataract surgery, my father suffered a series of pin strokes which slowed him down physically and to some degree affected his mental acumen. I remember my father would ask, "How's our Outdoor company doing, son?" I would reply that it was doing just fine, never giving him any indication that he no longer owned the company. I began to drop by on weekends, to see how he was doing, and Tetlow and I would go out to dinner with my mother and father more frequently to keep him occupied and happy.

It was during this time I began to feel what Sherwood Anderson describes as having felt in "Discovery of a Father": "It was a feeling of closeness. It was something strange. It was as though there are only two in the world. It was though I had been jerked suddenly out of myself...he had become blood of my blood."

I thank God for that last year and for the time we were able to spend together in a non-working relationship. As writer Harriet Beecher Stowe said, "The bitterest tears shed over graves are for words left unsaid and deeds left undone."[47]

Free to continue rebuilding the company I now owned, and at ease in leaving behind whatever fate might be in store for Park Communications.

THE PASSING OF THE FIRST

No sidewalk playground now to meet my friends,
They've put a roadblock at the rainbow's end.
We're driving faster now than Orville flew,
We leave our mark on every single thing we do.
Ashes to ashes, dust to dust
It's the way the West was won.
Amos and Andy and nickel candy
Have fallen to the gun.
Ashes to ashes, dust to dust
It'll never be the same.
But, we're all forgiving,
We're only living,
To leave the way we came.

—From the song "Ashes to Ashes"
by Dennis Lambert and Brian Potter[48]

These lyrics sung by *The 5ᵗʰ Dimension* in 1973 made their way into my life again after my father passed away. The playground at the Cayuga Heights School in Ithaca is still there. A few of my friends have passed away, but most of the ones I grew up with are still around. Spread out all over the country. Of those who have died, Pops left the biggest hole in my life. He put me through some of the worst times in my life, but he taught me a great deal. I wish he were still around to see what I learned from him being applied. He left his mark on everything he did. And he left his mark on me.

In October 1993 doctors determined Pops needed prostate surgery. The pin strokes he had suffered combined with a weak mitral valve as a result of his bout with rheumatic fever as a child, placed him at high risk for the surgery in Ithaca. Our family chartered a private plane staffed by a nurse to fly him from Ithaca to the Columbia Presbyterian Hospital in New York City, while we followed in another plane.

After he had been carefully situated in a room overlooking the Hudson River, he seemed to be at peace and commented on how beautiful the river was. Leaving him with a private nurse and thinking everything was OK, the family went out to dinner. Before we left his room, I wish I had said words similar to the ones the son says to his father in Ethan Canin's "The Year of Getting to Know Us": "I told my father not to worry, that love is what matters and that in the end…he can look back and say without blinking that he did all right by me, his son, and that I loved him."[49]

But I hadn't, and when we arrived back at our hotel rooms, we got the bad news. After all of my father's work-filled days that ran late into the night, as Dean Koontz wrote in his book *By the Light of the Moon*, "in the story of his life, death put its comma, and he was gone."

Pops died on a Monday night, October 25, 1993. He was eighty-three years old, and the cause was reported to be cardiac arrest.

When he died, Park Communications owned seven TV stations, 21 radio stations and 144 newspaper publications in 24 states. He had 2,650 employees, including 35 at his Ithaca headquarters.

A SON'S LETTER

Once you've loved someone, the love is always there, even after they're gone. Love is the only thing that endures. Mountains are torn down, built up, torn down again over millions and millions of years. Seas dry up. Deserts give way to new seas. Time crumbles every building man erects. Great ideas are proven wrong and collapse as surely as castles and temples. But love is a force, an energy, a power. At the risk of sounding like a Hallmark card, I think love is like a ray of sunlight, traveling for all eternity through space, deeper and deeper into infinity;

like that ray of light, it never ceases to exist. Love endures.
It's a binding force in the universe, like the energy within
a molecule is a binding force, as surely as gravity is a
binding force. Without the cohesive energy in a molecule,
without gravity, without love—chaos. We exist to love and
be loved, because love seems to me to be the only thing
that brings order and meaning and light to existence. It
must be true. Because if it isn't true, what purpose do we
serve? Because if it isn't true—God help us.

—Dean Koontz, From the book Darkfall, 1984[50]

At the time of his death, my father was survived by his wife
of fifty-seven years, her mother, his daughter, a sister in Winston-
Salem, three grandchildren, one great-grandson, and me.

One of those grandchildren was my son Trip, twenty-six at
the time, who left this message on my answering machine the day
after he learned his grandfather died:

After hearing eleven beeps, I guess that must mean you
already have plenty of messages. I just wanted to check
in and add one more to it and see if you guys are OK, and
to let you know what our flight plans are. Anyway, give
me a call tonight. I know you are probably tired of the
phone ringing, so I will wait for you to call back.

I love you, Dad, and I hope you are OK and take care.
I will either see you tomorrow or the next day, and am
trying to get there as soon as I can. I love you very much,
and I hope you guys are doing all right. I mean it, Dad, I
love you. Talk to you later. Bye.

Two days later, on October 27, Trip delivered the following
letter, one I treasure because this is what families should be all
about. It started:

Dear Dad:

Now it's just Roy Park, Jr. and III.

Funny how generations meld together. Specifically, look at what Grandpops perfected, then at the areas in which you excelled...then there's me.

See what I mean? He had a tremendous business mind with a particular sense of timing and making swift, corporate decisions. You had a struggle between a skill for art and a desire for corporate accomplishment, while at the same time, your timing was still good. The two of you differ mainly in the "Friends" category. I don't think anybody who has met Roy Park, Jr. can say they weren't treated with compassion, respect, and honesty.

This I noticed from the early days of visiting you in the dungeon of a workplace called Park Outdoor. With pipes running over your head and dehumidifiers running to keep the papers from sticking together, an environment like that would have driven anybody mad (and I know you came close), but you always treated everyone around you like a United States Senator. You still do. This accounts for secretaries, contractors, colleagues, and college-buddies, to name a few.

Even Ted, your yardman, from Pine Knoll Shores. Laura thought you two were old friends by the time we came down. I merely told her, "That's Dad, he can make anybody feel wanted, needed, and respected, all within minutes of meeting him. He does not even need connections, he's just incredible with people."

So, what I gathered is that there was more of a personable side that you acquired from God knows where. That I liked. That I learned.

Then there's me. My timing often sucks. My business philosophy... well, when I develop one I'll write you later. But, I guess it all got overloaded in the creative side. Sometimes I feel helpless in this family since about all I contribute is an annual Christmas card.

But you've asked me what I've learned from you two.

You've already found out I do like my independence. With total disregard to your clear-cut advice, I stormed down to an advertising agency in North Carolina, for a change of pace. That decision almost drove me to requiring a pacemaker. But a gamble on my career once in a while never seemed to bother me.

Because I believe my "autopilot" has been good all along, nothing seems to have scared me. I never was afraid of fitting in. Ithaca High School taught me that. I never feared making new friends. Dumping everything and getting my education in Chapel Hill, then a job in Chicago, not to mention back and forth again, only made me stronger.

Still, I had learned that people will trust you after you trust them first. They will only respect you after you give them respect. Finally, they will love you, only after you show love. You were never afraid of any of this; neither was Grandpops, and neither was I.

Perhaps it is here, in this esoteric limbo, that I have learned the most. I had to find parts from both of you since we are all uniquely different.

From Grandpops, it is to never, and that is never, give up on your goals. When you feel they are getting closer, build confidence from your efforts, and throw new goals way out ahead again. For me, I never want to feel like I've accomplished everything. My best work is still ahead of me, whether it be the creation of my own animation house or simply a house full of kids (had to see if you were still awake). Unfortunately, this was never advice that came from him directly, but something I observed over twenty-six years of time. I'm sure he had a list of things he still wanted to get done in his last thoughts, and I don't want my list to end, either.

From you, compassion. I know I won't get anywhere in this world without treating others around me with as much respect as I feel I deserve back. This undoubtedly pays off on a daily basis. The neat thing I've noticed here, is that whether it's college, work, or just an outside collective friend, compassion is the true litmus test. It's how you can find others that are "mutually respectful and understanding" (to quote from "Pops").

These come to mind for me as invaluable lessons…not the only two, but probably the most inspiring. If you haven't noticed, I sometimes feel I don't, and never will, have the level head with which the two of you have been gifted. It all kind of sways to the right side. Perhaps if it weren't for you two, things would be a lot worse for me. I believe I needed to see both of your lifelong philosophies carried out, and witness what you have accomplished first.

I am terribly saddened that it has come down to just you and me. But the fact that I am the Third should offer you some comfort. I know I'll be making plenty more mistakes in the future, but that can't be helped. The funny thing is that I wanted to write this letter on my Bayer Bess stationary since there's no telling what it will be one, two, or twenty-six years from now.

But at least we both had the chance to learn from
Grandpops, for now that's what we can be thankful for.
From now on, we have each other. I think that's a hell of
a lot.

Love,
Trip

After my father died, one of his television stations put together a videotape biography on him, which did a good job of tracking his life. It is a short tape, maybe fifteen minutes long, but it gave a good overview of how he developed his many careers during his life. We have shown this on occasion to incoming or graduating Johnson School Park Leadership Fellows, after which I point out that my father was an entrepreneur, a pioneer who constantly sought and took advantage of opportunities, as well as a civic leader in his community who continuously strove to do the same for others, and that these are also the ideals on which the Park Leadership Fellows Program at the Johnson School are modeled.

I tell them, "You carry the responsibility to continue to emulate these ideals. A responsibility to lead a productive and successful life in whatever endeavor you choose, as well as a responsibility to serve your communities, your families, and those who will follow you as future business leaders. This is a high standard to bear, but it is also a model of leadership our country desperately needs in the new millennium."

As I said, the Johnson School at Cornell is named after Sam Johnson, and I never had to ask the question he asked in his memorable and moving movie tribute to his father: "Did he love his business more than he loved me?"

My father might have loved me the last couple of years of his life, but I loved him all his life, and still do. The *Forbes 400* list of richest Americans that came out one week before his death ranked my father 139th. Knowing what I know now, I wish I could bring him back. I'm sure he would remind all of our family members where the money for the foundation he founded came from, how it was earned, and having run his smaller Park Foundation for thirty years, what he had in mind for its use.

THE MEMORIAL SERVICE

A memorial service was held at the First Presbyterian Church at 1 PM, Friday, October 29, 1993, in Ithaca. The burial was private with the immediate family only. The family requested contributions to the charity of one's choice in lieu of flowers. But there were plenty of flowers anyway, as is usually the case. Jim Whalen, president of Ithaca College, gave the eulogy at my father's service. He was one of my father's closest friends; his remarks are in Appendix F, Eulogy from a Friend.

The obituary in *USA Today* stated the annual income from his Park Communications empire was $160,000,000 and went on to say that "Park, who collected antique cars, rare watches, and French provincial office furniture, made his first media purchase in 1962—WNCT TV and radio stations in Greenville, NC. In keeping with his philosophy of 'We don't sell, we only buy,' Park still owned them at his death."

In the final paragraph, the newspaper reported, "There has been no decision about a successor. President and Chief Operating Officer, Wright Thomas, said in a statement on behalf of the board that 'Park built a sound organization that will carry on.'" (Unfortunately, it didn't, and was sold within a year.)

As reported in the Raleigh *News & Observer* on Wednesday, October 27, 1993, "Raleigh friends of 50 and 60 years standing who mourned his loss Tuesday characterized him as a steadfast friend and a workaholic who took far more pleasure in working and doing business than in money."

Tributes to memories of my father from friends, associates, educators, and people from all walks of life flowed in from around the country. Many are reported in Appendix G, Memorial Tributes.

Several years after my father died, my mother passed along to me the following piece. I don't know if she had it before Pops died, or after, but different versions of it are attributed to both Mother Teresa and Dr. Kent M. Keith. But I thought this version, which borrowed from both as seen in Footnote 51 seemed to pretty much capture the best in my father, and I guess she thought so, too. It's entitled, "Anyway."

> *People are unreasonable, illogical and self-centered. Love them anyway.*
> *If you do good, people will accuse you of selfish ulterior motives. Do good anyway.*
> *If you are successful you win false friends and true enemies. Succeed anyway.*
> *The good you do today will be forgotten tomorrow. Do good anyway.*
> *Honesty and frankness make you vulnerable. Be honest and frank anyway.*
> *People favor underdogs but follow only top dogs. Fight for some underdogs anyway.*
> *What you spend years building may be destroyed overnight. Build anyway.*
> *People really need help but may attack you if you help them. Help them anyway.*
> *Give the world the best you have and you'll get kicked in the teeth.*
> *Give the world the best you've got, anyway.*[51]

Much later, in 2014, I was asked by a Junior in the Dyson School of Applied Economics and Management what was the most challenging aspect of management and why. My answer is in Appendix L.

CHAPTER 30
AFTERMATH

As to his legacy, after a succession of ownerships, the Duncan Hines Cake Mix line my father started is still going strong. It was sold by P&G to Aurora Foods in 1998, then acquired five years late by the Pinnacle Food group which in February 2007 agreed to be acquired by affiliates of the Blackstone Group for $1.3 billion.

The media empire my father created was massive, but what's left to carry our Park name today is pretty small. Park Outdoor is one of the few remaining family-owned outdoor companies operating in New York state. Each year, the *Central New York Business Journal*, published in Syracuse, NY, selects 52 companies out of the hundreds of thousands operating in central New York to be featured as "The Business of the Week." In the August 24, 2001, issue, our company was featured under the heading, BILLBOARD FIRM PROFITS BY STAYING LOCAL. The article by Annemarie Kropt pointed out that the "sign business has been in the Park family for more than 35 years," and said, "By focusing its efforts on local businesses, Park Outdoor Advertising of New York, Inc. remains a booming company despite the economic times." It went on to say:

Though the Ithaca-based company sells advertising space to regional and national companies, over the last 20 years, revenue from local businesses increased from 20 percent to over 97 percent....

The company currently owns approximately 1,700 billboards covering 15,000 square miles in 21 counties throughout New York State and Pennsylvania.

Park's father began the company in 1964 by acquiring billboards from General Outdoor and the estate of Max Andrews. Park Outdoor Advertising initially covered an area from the St. Lawrence River to the north, Jamestown to the west, and Scranton, PA to the south.

The article pointed out that "in 1984, the senior Park sold the Scranton–Wilkes-Barre market." When that happened I acquired other territories in Watertown and Erie, PA, to make up the loss, and also expanded the company's holdings in Binghamton, Syracuse and Utica. The article reported,

Park, Jr. went on to purchase the company from his father in 1988, and in the 1990s began consolidating the operation, selling its western and northern divisions.... Concentrating on Utica, Rome, Syracuse, Binghamton, Elmira, Auburn and the Finger Lakes Region has proved successful.

Though the company faces competition from other media, including radio, cable television, and newspapers, Park says that many of these other venues also use Park Outdoor to put out their message. Advertising with Outdoor based on cost and immediate impact is the most economical way for a local business to operate, he says. Park attributes his company's success to the company's employees, whom he says are long-term and dedicated. 'The company is a family business, with our employees treated like family.'[52]

One of the best things about Park Outdoor, that makes me proud, is the loyalty of our employees. 2017 saw the retirement of the first of our long-term managers I hired some 35 years ago. In his final letter to me Paul Panara wrote: "Over the years we've had many good times and some difficult ones, but through it all we've grown tremendously not only in revenue, but also in industry innovation. It has been a rewarding career for me, both professionally and because of the many friendships I have made. I wish you and your family the very best in the years to come."

But Dave Feldman, the first person I met when I joined my father's company in 1971, is still with the company as Executive VP and Chief Operating Officer. In a meeting in 2001, I told our managers, "Having worked under my father for 17 years, and having been subject to his almost fanatical hands-on management, I have tried to go in the opposite direction and allow each of you to run your own division exactly as if it were your own company, for which you and your people share in the rewards. I respect your dedicated efforts, and can say the outdoor medium needs more examples such as you to keep the industry honest and raise its level of responsibility.

"Even in tough times, you have all come through for the company, and I respect your dedicated efforts tremendously. I thought it was interesting that in looking into our history, we have actually brought back or recruited over the last 10 years a dozen individuals that have worked for Park Outdoor or Park Communications in the past. Six of you are in this room."

I also urged them to continue to deal fair and honestly with our suppliers and customers, to maintain humility in their dealings, and above all, to keep a sense of humor at all times. After all, as Mark Van Doren said, "Wit is the only wall between us and the dark."

I think my father would have been proud at the way the company he started, and the one I ran for him for many years, turned out. And I think my mother may be pleasantly surprised, too.

I've often heard my mother use the expression when somebody starts complaining, "try walking in my shoes sometime." I told our managers it's good practice to put yourself in the other person's place. This brief transference into the mind of another will help you gauge and understand how what you are saying or doing is impacting the other person. It's helpful whether you're selling something, giving advice or dealing with your employees, friends

Front: Kevin Fischthal, Sam Salamida, Rocky Conte, Paul Savka. Back: Christopher Culver, Michael Dickinson, Edward Hirthler, Andrew Croft, Christine Tevyaw, Elizabeth Kaminski, Matthew Gray, Jason Paff, Timothy Wells.

Our Park Outdoor Advertising team Binghamton, NY headed by Sam Salamida where members of our staff and creative team Conte, Savka and Kaminski have all been with Park for over 21 years and our operations manager Culver, for 17, and administrative assistant Gray, 16.

Front: Jamie Whitson, Olin Wood, Michael Crawford, Anthony Clark.
Back: Kerry Leipold, Mike Sigler, Steven McCormick, Raymond Vough, Peter Fahs.

The Park Outdoor division in Elmira, NY is headed by Kerry Leipold who has been with the company 37 years and includes other long-termers Wood, 40 years, office manager Whitson 36 years, operations manager Fahs, 31, and regional sales manager Sigler for 16.

Front: Edward Ditata, John Reid, Susan Topa, Vicky Jones, Matthew Stubley, Heidi Davis, Jackson Maurer, Joseph Entelisano. Back: Christopher Brillante, Leon Davenport, Richard Misiaszek, Gennadiy Karpovish, James Lutz, Yuriy Potapchuk, Jonathan Rice, Chad Biamonte, Shawn Biamonte.

Park Outdoor's division in Utica, NY headed by Matt Stubley, also services our inventory in Syracuse under operations manager Ditata with Park for 29 years and foreman Davenport for 17. Other long-termers include office manager Jones, 34 years, creative director Topa and regional sales manager Maurer, both 30, and production team members Lutz, 30, Karpovich and Misiaszek, both 19, Potapchuk, 18, Davenport, 17, and Rice, 16.

Stephen Frank, Debbie Peck, Bill Dugan, Sarah Janson, Mark Daniello.

Park Outdoor in Syracuse, NY headed by Bill Dugan where creative director Daniello has been with the company 28 years and office manager Peck, having worked for the company for a stint in the 1970s, came back on board almost 20 years ago.

or family.

MOVING A LIFETIME'S WORK

But I'm getting ahead of myself again. Before my father passed away, Jim Dumbell wrote in the *Charlotte Observer:* "Probably no one amasses that kind of wealth and reaches the age of 71 without considering what will become of it when he's gone." The newspaper quoted my father saying, "Park Newspapers will remain, we hope, but you can't run anything from the grave." It reported, "He has provided an opportunity for some of his key employees to buy sizeable shares of his holdings at low interest rates, and for the remainder of his empire to go public when he's no longer there to run it."[53]

As reported by Byrd in the *Winston-Salem Journal* in February 1983, my father "left instructions for after his death that he says were modeled on those of Frank E. Gannett, the founder of the Gannett Co., the country's biggest newspaper chain." The newspaper reported the family will get part of his company stock and that: "The Park Foundation, which already gets part of his companies' profits, will get enough stock to 'have considerable influence.' The remainder will be offered to the Park companies' management, at low interest rates." Quoting my father, the newspaper said: "'Hopefully we'll have enough good key people [to buy] that they'll be able to carry on.'"[54]

Park Communications did not need to be sold. It had competent management and could have continued to run like a well-oiled machine, at least for a while. My father owned 89 percent of the shares at Park Communications, valued at $429 million, when he died, and he willed 57 percent of his shares to the Park Foundation. This was an outright bequest of 51 percent of the Park Communications stock to the Park Foundation, and his Residuary Bequest also willed the remaining residue of his estate to the Foundation.

Pops's will, dated November 19, 1992, stated "[I]t is my belief that it would be in the best interests of Park Communications, Inc. and its stockholders to have selected employees of the company acquire some of its stock. Accordingly, it is my wish that the Park Foundation, Inc....from time to time, permit those employees who have three or more years of consecutive service to the Company, to purchase from the Foundation appropriate amounts of such stock on terms and conditions as favorable to such employees as are consistent with maintaining the Foundation's status as a charitable organization." In the will my father said, "I believe that this would tend to encourage such employees to devote their best efforts to the improvement of the company and the enhancement of the value of its stock."

This did not happen, since my mother made the decision to sell Park Communications as quickly as possible. In 1993, I was named to the Park Communications, Inc., board of directors, joining my mother, Wright Thomas, Senator Harry Byrd, Mark Green and John McNair in having the responsibility of selling the company. My mother and I briefly entertained the idea of my purchasing the radio, television and newspaper properties that were in the territory that my outdoor company served, but this was precluded by the estate attorney who, because I was on the board, pointed out I was a disqualified person. With the job I had running Park Outdoor at the time along with a number of other outside responsibilities, I had no objections to a sale which would immediately maximize cash funding for the Foundation.

After interviews with numerous investment bankers, Goldman Sachs, which originally took Park Communications public, was selected. Various bids were received and reviewed by the board, with the surprise high bidder being two investors who were financed by loans from the Retirement Systems of Alabama. These investors came in at $711 million, between $10 and $15 million more than the highest bidder from media conglomerates, and its bid was qualified and accepted.

The sale closed May 1995. During 1996, the new owner of Park Communications sold off the twenty-two radio stations to pay down the debt to the Alabama retirement fund and then refinanced the whole transaction by issuing company bonds through Merrill Lynch and Goldman Sachs enabling them to pay off the entire remaining Alabama Retirement System debt. Park Communications was then sold to Media General, a leading communications company located in Richmond, VA, who owned and operated television stations and newspapers in the southeastern region of the United States. Media General, following its corporate policy, immediately sold the TV stations and newspapers not located in the southeast to other communication companies. The majority of the Park properties, the television stations and newspapers in the Southeast my father bought over the years based on his belief that this region would continue to have above average economic growth, remained intact operating under the Media General banner.

After the sale of Park Communications, the estate still owned my father's two real estate companies: RHP Incorporated and RHP Properties, Inc. This included Ag Research, the ad agency where my father started out and which Johnnie Babcock and I both formerly ran which had survived through it all. My father still owned the first building he bought in Ithaca, and most every other piece of real estate he had bought. The real estate holding and operating companies included orange groves, timberland, and dozens of parcels of land in Pennsylvania and central and western New York, apartment buildings, houses, parking lots, and commercial establishments.

While negotiations for Park Communications were taking place in 1994, I was named director and senior vice president of these companies with the responsibility for selling my father's real estate holdings in New York and Pennsylvania. Most of these properties had to be sold one at a time, and the proceeds from these sales amounted to approximately $9 million, of which a substantial part went to fund the Park Foundation.

...INTO A FOUNDATION

As the proceeds from the sale of the Park Communications began to flow into the estate in 1995, the decision to designate the trustees for the Park Foundation had to be made. In his will, my father specified that my mother and the president of Park Communications at that time, Wright M. Thomas, made sure that promptly after the founder's death the existing Park Foundation qualified as a not-for-profit corporation for charitable purposes, and when 501(c)3 status was assured, to elect *up to* three additional persons to serve on such.

Since Wright Thomas was committed to help the new owners of Park Communications during the transition period, my mother asked five additional people to serve as trustees. Three were family members: my sister and me as vice presidents, with my sister also named secretary, and my daughter as treasurer.

My mother asked the attorney who handled my father's estate and continued as her legal advisor and estate planner to join the board as a salaried trustee with a trustee-initiated grant fund equal to that of the four family members. He was also assigned to serve as attorney for the Park Foundation. This was the attorney who represented my father when I was trying to buy Park Outdoor.

A second nonfamily trustee—the consultant I had hired, despite initial resistance from my mother and daughter, to help with the sale of Park Communications—was asked to join on the same terms. My mother also retained his services as her personal financial advisor. Shortly thereafter, my son and niece were named junior advisors to the Park Foundation.

When all was said and done, only my mother remained out of the four original trustees of the private foundation my father had founded on September 1, 1966. Members of the board at that time were my father and mother, the then treasurer of Park Broadcasting and ironically, Johnnie Babcock.

With the five-person board complete, my mother was reaffirmed as president. At the recommendation of the attorney, I was later elected first vice president at our June 1998 meeting, and my sister who was already secretary, elected second vice president. As first vice president, I was assigned as the contact person between the trustees and the executive director and other foundation staff employees. The bylaws stated that the first vice president "shall, in the absence of the president…perform the duties and exercise the powers of the president and shall generally assist the president and perform such other duties and have such other powers as may from time to time be prescribed by the board. Upon the death, resignation or removal of the president, the first vice president shall automatically become the president."

I wrote to the board members in 1997 on the need for a mission statement, suggesting that "the primary objective of the Park Foundation is to aid and support higher education in the fields of communications, business and scientific research, with emphasis on colleges and universities with which the founder was active during his distinguished career." I also suggested the mission statement should specify that:

In higher education, preference is given to academic institutions with which Roy H. Park was affiliated during his career. Scholarship and fellowship programs have been established at these institutions in furtherance of his desire to encourage young Americans to take advantage of the opportunities offered by their country.

In line with this, five core grantees were selected: North Carolina State, Ithaca College, The University of North Carolina at Chapel Hill, Cornell University and Boyce Thompson Institute, on whose board my father served until his death.

In dividing up the responsibility for the core grants, I suggested that the outside trustee who lived in North Carolina take responsibility for NC State and asked the then chairman of the board of trustees of Ithaca College to work with my sister. I took Cornell and UNC, the two colleges I attended, as well as Boyce Thompson, since I was already on its board of directors.

All the other suggestions I made in my memo were approved and incorporated in our guidelines for making grants, and read as follows:

The Park Foundation was established by the late Roy

Hampton Park. He was founder, chairman and chief executive officer of Park Communications, Inc. The Park Foundation makes grants primarily in the areas of education, public broadcasting and the environment.

In higher education, preference is given to academic institutions with which Roy H. Park was affiliated during his career. Scholarship and fellowship programs have been established at these institutions in furtherance of his desire to encourage young Americans to take advantage of the opportunities offered by their country.

Support for other educational and charitable programs is generally restricted to the Eastern seaboard where Roy H. Park had lifetime interests, or to communities where Foundation trustees currently reside. In evaluating requests, the Foundation seeks to support and encourage established and worthy nonprofit organizations.

The Foundation will consider small lead gifts for new or enhanced programs, matching gifts to encourage the participation of other donors, "last dollars" to achieve a campaign goal, and one-time, short-term gifts to sustain a program until its long-term funding is established.

The Foundation will provide neither sole nor primary funding to an organization, and will not replace governmental support. Generally, the Foundation does not encourage requests for endowment, capital campaigns, construction, equipment purchases, debt reduction, or ongoing general operating support.

As was clear throughout his life, my father's primary interest at all times was on education, and university scholarships in particular. As confirmed to me in a letter dated April 27, 1999 from our Park Foundation trustee and attorney, "The real emphasis on scholarships came from your father in the late 1990s."

The letter continued: "I think your father would be very pleased with the scholarship programs we have set up at the four core schools and the other core programs we have put in place." Along with NC State, UNC-Chapel Hill, Ithaca College and Cornell University, in 1999, the Boyce Thompson Institute for Plant Research was one of the Park Foundation's five core programs.

KEEPING ON THE PATH

Shortly after my father's death in 1993, and during the next six years serving with the Park Foundation, I picked up where my father left off. As I mentioned, my father said "give of your time or your money, but *never* both." Unfortunately I did not heed his advice, and have a full plate on both counts.

Pops was a member of the Board of Advisers of The University of North Carolina School of Media and Journalism.. In 1994 I was named a member of that Board. In 2005 I received a Distinguished Alumnus Award from the University, and in 2011 was inducted into its North Carolina Advertising Hall of Fame. In 2015 I received the prestigious William Richardson

UNC Chancellor Carol Folt (left) and MJ-School Dean Susan King at the presentation of *The Order of the Long Leaf Pine* from Governor Roy Cooper.

Davie Award, the highest honor given by the University of North Carolina Board of Trustees. In 2017, I was inducted into the North Carolina Media and Journalism Hall of Fame, and was awarded *The Order of the Long Leaf Pine* from the Governor of North Carolina for exemplary service to the community and the state.

My father was a director of the Boyce Thompson Institute for Plant Research, Inc. on the Cornell campus for nine years until his death. In 1995 I became a director, serving on the selection committee for the new president in 2004. I was elected vice-chairman in 2008, and a member of the executive, investment, finance, audit and compensation committees. In 2016 I returned to director status, remaining on the executive committee.

My father's ties to Cornell began back in the 1950s when he engaged the University to research American eating habits in conjunction with the establishment of his Duncan Hines food line. He also became a member of the Advisory Council of the Samuel C. Johnson Graduate School of Management at Cornell University in 1977.

In 1996 I was named to its Advisory Council. In November 2004, Dean Bob Swieringa wrote, "Like your father before you, your voice of reason and clarity of thought continues to drive the opinions of others while galvanizing our efforts to move the school to new heights and accomplishments. Johnson would not resemble the top-10 school it is without your years of lasting commitment and contribution. When I think of the handful of great leaders who have left a lifetime imprint upon this institution's very being, you are in the forefront of that group."

That year I was the thirteenth alumnus to be inducted into the School's Hall of Honor, the highest form of recognition that can be rendered by the dean on behalf of the Johnson School community. During the induction Dean Swieringa said:

> *If you want 1 year of prosperity, grow grain. If you want 10 years of prosperity, grow trees. If you want 100 years of prosperity, grow people. Roy Park grows people. He invests in individuals with leadership qualities, professional and personal life accomplishments, academic achievements, and commitments to community service. The Park Leadership Fellows Program is among the richest leadership development experiences in any top business school both in scope and impact. Roy grows people! His investments change lives. And he is looking forward to 100 years of prosperity.*

In 1999, I was named a trustee of Cornell University, serving on the governmental, alumni affairs and development and trustee-community communications committees. In 2007 I was named a trustee emeritus and Cornell Presidential Councillor, the highest honor the Board of Trustees can bestow. In 2017 I was asked to serve as one of 13 founding members of the Cornell

SC Johnson College of Business, which was at the time, the third largest business school in the world.

As for my father's years of involvement with Ithaca College, not least of which was his position as Chairman of the Board, when asked to serve as a trustee by the College's Chairman I suggested it be offered to my sister, instead. As for his extensive history and long-term relationship with North Carolina State University, his alma mater in Raleigh, NC, I was pleased that another Park Foundation trustee offered to represent us there at one of these four core educational grants established as part of our Park Foundation mission statement.

REMEMBERING HIS LEGACY

Silent Sounds

There are sounds in this world
Other than the beating of
Tin hearts to the time of
Gold pieces dropping in
Silver cashboxes.
Sounds other than the fanatical ravings of
Self-inflated,
Antlike, little men
Waving feeble antenna
And trying to explain away
The World.
And these – the Sounds of Life –
Are the ones that bear listening:
Cicada wailing in rustling sun,
And trout breaking crystal water

In its dying light.
Cut off by insulated office,
Crowded laboratories,
Classrooms and white collars,
These sounds –
Independent of civilization –
Are the true foundations
Of our future.
Despite us and all we uncover,
They and this world will go on
Voices from the beginning of
Time may pass over our
Machine-deafened ears,
But when these sounds stop,
We will stop, too.
When lowly insect ceases
Its song.
The Great Chain of Being ceases
Its cycle.
And when earth dies…
We die with it.

I wrote that poem in January 1959, about midway through my journalism studies in Chapel Hill. It appeared as TODAY's NC POEM in *The News & Observer,* and of all the poems, articles and letters I wrote, this was my parents' favorite. My father liked it because of what it said. My mother, because she felt it made my father think of other things besides work.

I liked it because it contrasted the self-importance of man to the hidden machinery of nature that keeps this old world going, and puts a little depth into the admonition: "Take time to smell the roses."

My mother felt it put me squarely in the environmental category. Where it actually put me is a comfortable understanding of the environment, from fungus and bacteria that break down matter to earthquakes and tornados, the storms, hurricanes and tsunamis that devastate our shorelines, and all the roles that nature plays in between. It is the nature of nature, and a rational understanding of the environment. I'm not an advocate of scaring the hell out of people to raise money by trying to convince them the balance of nature and the natural order of things (including human nature) can be meaningfully changed.

I have nothing but contempt for the radical activism of the "Angry Young Man" in Billy Joel's song, "with his fist in the air and his head in the sand."

I believe in evolution and adaptation because the wisdom behind creation has made provision for it. And I have always been an optimist, as my father was before me. As his friend Paul Harvey said, "I have never seen a monument erected to a pessimist." While writing this book I came across a provocative thought from the *New Yorker* that "there are many species for the same reason there are many sentences. You might know only a few thousand words, but you have no trouble or prospects of running out of sentences." The environmental directive for life is simple: to reproduce its species, through spores, bulbs, seeds, rhizomes, binary fission, mitosis, division, fragmentation, budding, eggs, or live birth. For humans, birth creates families.

Blood is thicker than water. Isn't it? Families can have their wars and fights and squabbles but still recover over time if there is balance. But balance can be tipped by nonfamily enablers who alter the normal ebb and flow of family relationships and lead to its dissolution.

I know. My father caused me some anguish and pain for many years, but he kept us together and my family still loved him in the end. When all was said and done, there was healing and enduring respect for his legacy.

My father's legacy is not one to be forgotten, and what he worked for all his life should not to be ignored or refuted. I was sensitive to erosion of his hardworking lifetime ideals, and despite the absence of his intentions for the foundation's mission in his will, the philanthropic objectives that best reflected the interests of my side of the family were evident in the previous thirty-year history of its grant making, when my father, mother, and Johnnie sat on the board. As far as my family was concerned, no one was going to trample on his grave.

For three decades the Park Foundation made grants in support of education, religion and human services. Having researched the entirety of my father's relationships and interests during his lifetime, I felt I knew where his interests were and where they weren't.

I have no objections to environmental grants as long as they are defined and directed to realistic and obtainable goals. While I was a trustee of the Park Foundation, my trustee-initiated grants to environmental causes were the largest of any trustee and the percentage of my environmental funding was larger than that of the Park Foundation as a whole. But they were not directed to some of the environmental groups Michael Crichton makes reference to in his 2004 book *State of Fear*.

What I objected to was an increasing use of general board-initiated funds directed to environmental activism crowding out other grant categories. Nor did I have problems with public broadcasting programming such as *Nature* and *Nova*, if it did not expand to the point that it wiped out the foundation's ability to issue grants to other educational, charitable, faith-based and community human service programs. But our foundation's grants were beginning to be based on barely concealed political activism, pessimism, criticism, radical environmentalism and other anti-isms. When grants for programming to which the Park Foundation's logo would be linked were controversial, including criticism of specific organizations or corporations, or politically partisan, I had real concerns.

A conflict had already arisen with another family member when my mother named me first vice president. Shortly after this I became aware of discussions behind my back objecting to what was believed to be my "heir apparent" status. My mother resisted complaints at that time, saying it was "Roy's turn," and refused to believe another family member was complaining, even though it was common knowledge to the rest of the trustees. My children and I felt the Park Foundation was beginning to move in directions I felt were very different from those my father would have approved of or taken, and I knew our attempts to hold to his legacy were putting a strain on my mother.

I remember in one of our board meetings, I was sitting next to my mother, and while other family members were proposing some unusual environmental grants, my mother shook her head and whispered to me, "If your father were here, he wouldn't believe this." The attorney trustee, who worked for years for my father, overheard the comment and said, "If Roy had attended any one of these meetings, the Board of Trustees would have been a committee of one."

To try to gain some balance, my mother requested the addition of two more trustees to the foundation: Senator Harry Byrd and John McNair III, a former CEO of Wachovia Bank, both of them having been lifelong directors of my father's companies. These appointments did not have a noticeable effect, since they were not full trustees.

The meetings were run by the book, but differences continued to exist beneath the surface. It was heartbreaking for me and my family to watch how the majority of what my father worked so hard to make was directed to grants funding directions I felt were not in accordance with what he believed. In a joint attempt to calm the situation an outside advisor who professionally consulted family foundations (he was also in charge of one of his own) was engaged in early 2000 for a two-day session in New York. By the time it was all over, a family member summarized the progress of the meeting by declaring it "a waste of time." By then it was too late to hope for a family reconciliation, although both Senator Byrd and John McNair tried to talk my mother out of the family split.

Without input from me or my children, it was decided that the solution to pursuing the philanthropic objectives best reflecting the diverse interests of the trustees, was to separate the trustees who followed the conservative philosophy my father held during his lifetime and who were trying to keep the foundation within the bounds of what we felt had been his "donor intent."

I had invited all of the trustees over to my home for dinner the night before the meeting where the decision was to take place, and while they enjoyed my hospitality, one of them told me that my mother would not change her mind.

THE SECOND SHOE IS DROPPED

Professionalism is knowing how to do it, when to do it, and doing it.

First, my father made it difficult to run the business he had assigned to me, then he balked at allowing me buy it so it could be run properly. He was a tough taskmaster on his workers and his family, but as I said, he kept the family together. My mother took a different course.

All families have rifts and in time they can heal. But not easily, or not when alliances are formed with people in a position outside the family to influence family relationships. Non-family enabling on one side or another can result in disruption and irreparable damage to a family unit. Somehow, my mother had been persuaded that siding with two people on one side of the family and sending the other three on their way would bring the whole family back together again. It didn't, and I worried about Dottie's ability to detect deception.

People who met her liked her. She had a sharp wit and a keen sense of humor. But she had so many people pulling at her. She was generous to a fault, and a generous person with a big heart needs to take a chapter from her husband's book. He never gave anything away, and nothing was ever handed to him. You *earned* what you got, like he did.

Pops said in an interview with Marilyn Green of *The Ithaca Journal* published January 25, 1980, "You have to give to get. So many people want to talk about 'what am I going to get.' In my business life, in the 10 years I worked for other people, I never asked for a raise. If they asked me to take on additional duties, I did it and did it well. I didn't ask 'Will you pay me?' I just did it. And in every case they treated me fairly. I figured if I did a good job I would be rewarded, and if I wasn't rewarded I would learn something from that, too."

As I've said before, everyone should make a list of the people who spend time with you who haven't asked you for anything. Those on the short list are those you can trust. They will be with you down the line, and when the giving is done, remain by your side.

At any rate, with my mother's decision made, during the Board meeting the next day when it became clear that the division of assets proffered by her attorney was grossly unfair, our family walked out of the meeting. Shortly after it was agreed that a joint press release would be issued announcing the split in our family foundation. On February 3, 2003, datelined Ithaca, it was issued:

> *The trustees of Park Foundation, Inc. announced today the formation of a second Park family foundation, Triad Foundation, Inc. The new structure will permit the two foundations to pursue the philanthropic objectives that best reflect the diverse interests of their respective boards.*
>
> *In the area of higher education, the Park Foundation will continue to support the undergraduate Park Scholar programs at Ithaca College and North Carolina State University in Raleigh. The Triad Foundation will assume responsibility for the Park Fellowship programs at Cornell University's Johnson Graduate School of Management and the School of Journalism and Mass Communication of the University of North Carolina at Chapel Hill. Other Triad grant-making will concentrate on early childhood education, marine ecology, plant research and human services in the home communities of its directors.*
>
> *Dorothy D. Park will continue to serve as President and Chairman of the Board of Trustees of*

the Park Foundation, which includes her daughter and granddaughter and two non-family trustees. Roy H. Park, Jr. is the President and Chairman of the Triad Foundation, with his son and daughter serving as directors.

Dottie visiting with a guest in her home in Ithaca in 2003. It was not until after this picture was taken of their cordial meeting that both noticed and got a laugh out of the wording on the pillow.

On February 6, 2003, Dan Higgins wrote in *The Ithaca Journal*, "The Park Foundation, Ithaca's philanthropic powerhouse with assets of about $600 million, announced Wednesday the creation of a new spinoff organization", going on to report:

> *"Called the Triad Foundation, it will manage Park Fellowship programs at Cornell's Johnson Graduate School of Management and North Carolina's School of Journalism and Mass Communication. Roy H. Park, Jr. will be president and chairman of the board of the new organization."*

Higgins' article went on to say that:
> *"Other journalism schools would do virtually*

anything to have (a Park Fellowship program),"
said Richard Cole, dean of the Journalism and Mass
Communication at the UNC Chapel Hill.

Cole said the Park Foundation provides nearly
$2 million per year and benefits 60 students. A Park
Fellowship pays tuition and fees, and gives cash stipends
of $10,000 annually for masters' students, and $18,500
per year for Ph.D. students

At the Johnson Graduate School of Management at
Cornell, Park Fellowships also support 60 students,' said
Clint Sidle, the director of the Park program.

The Park Foundation gave out about $30 million to
433 organizations in 1999, according to its 2000 IRS
tax return. Some gifts were relatively modest, others
are considerably larger and ongoing, including a $3
million donation to the Boyce Thompson Institute for
Plant Research's Biodiversity Program. "[55]

The following day, Higgins headlined in *The Ithaca Journal,*
"Triad focuses Park mission." He wrote:

"The Triad Foundation, the new organization
recently split off from the Park Foundation, won't make
any changes to the way it manages fellowship programs
it will take over in Ithaca and Chapel Hill, NC, according
to its director.

Roy H. Park, Jr., the president and chairman of
the Triad Foundation, said the new foundation, 'was
established to allow it to pursue the philanthropic
objectives that reflect the interests of its board of
directors. "

Higgins continued to write,

"The Triad Foundation was formed with a grant
from the Park Foundation. Florino (Park's Executive
Director) said that the final grant amount hasn't been yet
confirmed by the group's auditors. But according to Park,
Jr., it was enough for Triad to continue administering the

grant programs at the two Universities."[56]

On July 10, 2003, the *Cornell Chronicle* reported, in part:
"A program at Cornell's Johnson Graduate School of Management that builds commitment to community service among MBA students has a new name and the support of a new foundation.... The Park Leadership Fellows Program...supports 60 exemplary MBA students yearly at the Johnson School, in return for their involvement in significant service projects that are of lasting value to the community and their participation in leading training. It is the only MBA program in the world offering such full support for service and leadership training.

(In December 2017, 500 Park Leadership Fellow graduates celebrated their 20th Anniversary as covered in Appendix N.)

The report continues, *Triad also will continue the Park Foundation's support for the Cornell-based Boyce Thompson Institute for Plant Research, specifically for plant research with strong promise for improvements in human health and medicine. Park, Sr., served on the board of directors of the private research laboratory from 1984 until his death, and Park, Jr. currently serves on the Boyce Thompson Institute board as a vice chairman."*[57]

And so we went our separate ways, and some of the conflicting family pressure on my mother was relieved. I made sure I stayed close to her as the next 13 years rolled by to make sure she was able to remain independent and be well cared for in her own home where she died peacefully on June 18, 2016 at the age of 103.Her obituary appeared in a dozen newspapers including the *Raleigh News and Observer* and the *New York Times* in its entirety and my remarks at her memorial service which capture the character of this wonderful woman appear in Appendix M on page 523.

CHAPTER 31
A NEW BEGINNING

TRIAD—a group of three persons; three related things that form a group; three people considered as a unit; a union of three.

There are also a couple of other definitions of Triad, one having to do with music, "a chord of notes," and the other, a secret Chinese organization involved in illegal activities such as selling drugs. But I can assure you that our new family foundation is not heavily into music and definitely not into drugs, except for the kind that cure human ailments and illnesses as a result of scientific research on plants and the resulting discoveries.

We settled on "Triad" because it means a union of three. The three of us wanted to protect and honor my father's heritage by calling ourselves the "Roy H. Park Foundation," but in the last face-to-face meeting we had with the other five Park trustees, my mother was opposed to this. She said I could name it the "Roy H. Park, *Jr.* Foundation," but it wasn't my hard-earned money that funded it, so the Park Foundation will eventually be run by family and outside trustees who do not carry his name or never knew the founder.

As reported in the *Cornell Chronicle*, the foundation's new name "'reflects the desire of the Triad directors to honor the legacy of my father,' explained Roy H. Park, Jr., president and chairman of Triad. Serving as directors and officers of the Triad Foundation are Park, Jr. and his children, Roy H. Park, III, and Elizabeth Park Fowler. The unit of three inspired the name Triad as well as the foundation's logo, a pyramid transected into three parts by the letter *T.*"

"We chose 'Carolina Blue' for our logo, since six members of the family attended The University of North Carolina at Chapel Hill. This blue is the color of the sky and the oceans covering over 70 percent of our planet. The logo also represents the three of us living in three key states equally spaced along the East Coast, where my father conducted most of his business.

The *Cornell Chronicle* continued:

"As part of the change, the fellowships themselves have been renamed the Roy H. Park Leadership Fellowships, for the founder of the Park Foundation, the late Roy Hampton Park. An entrepreneur, Park launched the Duncan Hines food group in the 1950s and also was the founder and chair of Park Communications, a media company that included newspapers, TV and radio stations and outdoor advertising.

"Park Sr., who died in 1993, used Cornell expertise and laboratories to research Americans eating habits and perfect his company's food products. He served on the advisory councils of the College of Agriculture and Life Sciences and the Johnson School and helped create the Lewis H. Durland Memorial Lecture series at the school.

"Park Jr. is a 1963 graduate of the Johnson School and is a member of its advisory council and a Cornell trustee. He is president and CEO of Park Outdoor Advertising of New York, Inc., headquartered in Ithaca."[59]

There are very few conservative foundations left in America. James Piereson, executive director of the John M. Olin Foundation, pointed out in a *Wall Street Journal* opinion article in July 2004 that organized philanthropy, like the academic world, remains firmly in the grip of orthodox liberalism. Liberal ideas have effective control over key institutions, thanks to support from large liberal philanthropies. "Death, retirements, along with changing circumstances, have brought changes in leadership and focus to many of these institutions," he wrote. He said, as a consequence, the Olin Foundation will be closing its doors at the wishes of its late founder, who feared that what happens to many large foundations could happen to his—that it might eventually be captured by people hostile to views he held when he was alive and in control. As Steve Forbes, editor-in-chief of *Forbes* said in its July 24, 2006 issue, most foundations "are dominated by proactivist-governmental types vibrating with barely concealed hostility to entrepreneurial capitalism."

Adam Meyerson, president of the Philanthropy Roundtable, stated in a June 13, 2000 memo, "Our members are deeply disturbed that so many of America's large philanthropic foundations violate the most cherished values of the business leaders who endowed them." And as reported in the July 1, 2006 issue of the *Economist*, philanthropists…"like the notions that their foundations will live on after them, carrying their name down from generation unto generation. But, after the founder has died, foundations tend to become sclerotic and directionless—the fiefs of administrators who have lost sight of the original aims."

Our Triad Foundation Mission Statement was more specific but not much changed from that of the Park Foundation, and we intend to honor it. It simply reads:

> *The Triad Foundation, Inc. is a Roy Hampton Park Family Legacy. The Foundation honors the legacy and donor intent of its founder, the late Roy H. Park, founder, through graduate education fellowships at academic institutions with which he was affiliated during his lifetime and through grants for scientific research.*
>
> *The graduate fellowship programs reflect his desire to encourage American citizens to take advantage of the opportunities offered to them by their country. Triad Foundation, Inc. continues his commitment to democracy and free enterprise, religious liberty and freedom of thought and broad access to education and employment.*
>
> *Charitable and educational grant-making is generally restricted to the East Coast where Roy H. Park had lifetime interests, and to areas where Foundation Directors reside.*

As said earlier, these areas, which coincide with my own stomping grounds, are along the Atlantic Coast. Although other members of my family have traveled to the west and overseas, I'm basically a home boy and territorial in nature. My life and travels mostly kept me near water, surrounded by the sea or along shorelines from Cape Cod to Key West. Memorable and current ports of call range from Coral Gables on one side of Florida to Tampa and Gasparilla Island on the other, from Bermuda to Sea Island, GA, Charleston, SC, and Charlotte to Pine Knoll Shores, NC, and from Manhattan Island's Carlyle Hotel to our home far above Cayuga's waters.

Four members of the family live in Ithaca, and Triad, through the astute professional management of its assets, has created enough growth beyond that needed to cover our three initial commitments to be of help to the Ithaca community and to much broader goals.

The history of the Park Foundation before the Park Communications funding, and before the division, included substantial donations to religious organizations. Recently, my mother sent me a note saying she discovered "more than we thought we knew about him." Her note said, "One of his goals was that his offspring would live lives to help others—to make this world a better place because they had lived," and attached were several quotes he had pasted to the back of a framed picture on his desk.

They included a quote by Emerson reading, "All that I have seen teaches me to trust the Creator for all that I have not seen," and by Pasteur saying, "The more I study nature, the more I stand amazed at the work of the Creator." These confirm my father was a religious man, aside from the years he spent as an elder and president of the trustees of the First Presbyterian Church.

He always held to his conservative principles and, as I said, my family will not be the ones who trample on his grave. Our foundation is doing fine, and a sample of the grants we have made that continue his legacy are listed in Appendix J, Triad Grants: Continuing the Roy H. Park Legacy.

With our emphasis on higher education our Roy H. Park Fellows through 2017 now number 1,000, higher than indicated in my August 2015 welcoming speech to Cornell Park MBAs (Appendix K). We need to remember that only in a free enterprise society where hard work allows the accumulation of wealth would Fellowships like these which send graduates back into the world debt free, be able to exist. We are reminded as Winston Churchill said, "we make a living by what we get...we make life by what we give."

Since 2003, Triad has approved over 4,450 grants totaling over $160 million through grants ranging from $1,000 to $2.5 million a year. Making money is hard but philanthropists know smart giving is much harder.

As a penguin in the movie *Happy Feet* said, "Let me tell something to you." Managing a family foundation is no easy matter, even with our small and highly dedicated staff.

Without program directors, Triad family members serve in that capacity, putting in hours that range from 30 to 60 percent of a normal nine-to-five work week to keep up with a hundred or more grants that are active at any given time. It's intensive, exhaustive, time-consuming and difficult to make grants that are meaningful and are effective and measurable against their intended goal.

Photo by Jon Reis/www.jonreis.com

The Park Family. Four generations in August 2005 with the electric carriage WTRV-TV in Richmond had used in parades.

Though it is sad to leave behind a foundation carrying his name and going in a number of directions in which he had no interest and probably would not have supported during his life-time, Triad has moved on to honor and support the traditions his life represented. His life was worth it, and the legacy of his story is not yet finished.

It's interesting how people try to redefine the legacy of a person who's gone. A deliberate remaking to fit their own images and justify their own pursuits, which may be quite the opposite of what the deceased believed in. My father's legacy included education, to which he made commitments all his life. It took him off the farm and sparked the entrepreneurship that led to his success.

He was not into environmentalism, though he may have enjoyed those fleeting moments he took from work to acknowledge the natural world. When he bought land, he bought it to make a profit, to build on, sell or rent. He bought orange groves to harvest oranges and timberland to cut and sell the timber. He did not buy land to take it off the tax roles. He paid taxes on the land he bought and taxes, again, on the income he made from that land.

Nor did my father look kindly on public broadcasting stations that competed with his commercial properties. He bought stations and newspapers to sell advertising and *never* used his ownership for political purposes. He allowed his managers to take whatever positions, political or otherwise, that the advertisers, subscribers and viewers in each area believed in. He *never* forced his beliefs on others.

Throughout his life, Roy Hampton Park was committed to democracy and free enterprise, religious liberty and freedom of thought, community responsibility and broad access to education and employment. The true legacy of my father was that of a God-fearing, persevering business entrepreneur who pulled himself by his own bootstraps, took reasonable risks and worked hard all his life.

If the soul of a person who has given it meaning is granted the chance to hang around and watch over this world for a while, I hope one option may be the one offered by this beautiful Hopi prayer:

When you awaken in the morning hush,
I am the swift uplifting rush of quiet birds in circled flight.
I am the soft stars that shine at night.
Do not stand at my grave and cry. I am not there.
I did not die.

As Sean Connery said in the movie *The League of Extraordinary Gentlemen*, "Old tigers, sensing the end, are at their most fierce. And they go down fighting." That goes for my father and the son who once upon a time was able to survive in his shadow long enough to find the light.

My interview with Marquis Who's Who about carrying on my father's tradition is found in Appendix O.

EPILOGUE

It is said one never really finishes a book. They abandon it. Thomas Wolfe wrote, "The reason a writer writes a book is to forget a book and the reason a reader reads a book is to remember it." I wrote this book to remember it.

My father will not be forgotten by me. His chapter is finished, but events in my life are ongoing and there is more to tell.

But I have now told about the role my father played in my life and in the life of others, and the role I played in his. In the words of O'Keeffe, I hope *"what* he did with *where* he has been has been of some interest." I know this. Our Triad Foundation will honor his past as A Roy Hampton Park Family Legacy.

As the years roll by and memories return, time grows short. You know this when old friends start leaving you behind. I didn't write the eulogy for my father, but I did for the first person I met when I transferred to UNC-Chapel Hill. *Eulogy for a Friend* is Appendix H if you want to read it.

I know if my father were running his business today, he would not be a happy camper. The newspaper and broadcasting stations that were the basis of his media empire are hurting, while the smallest part of his former empire is holding up well. A 200-plus year old medium, outdoor advertising provides a powerful ad format with low cost, demographic reach and instant impact with a quiet, pervasive, continuous presence. Compare this to the up to 10 loud ad messages crammed into four or five TV commercial breaks each hour with often irritating narration and music, and to the intrusive ad pop ups on the internet.

A prediction for the future I don't think a lot of us will take kindly to is our replacement by robots and this includes self-driving cars. Outside of cities, there are those of us who will still want to drive our own cars, since they reflect who we are. Carrying people from point to point, there will always be eyes in those cars, and our signs will cover the routes they take. In the event they are able to go off road then how do you keep their computers from being hacked, turning them into killing machines?

And how will insurance work when the cars are involved in accidents?

At any rate, software disruption to our traditional industries is the result of free-market capitalism. Things change, and as a pioneer business entrepreneur who took responsible risks and worked hard all his life, my father believed, as do I, in capitalism. As Nicholas Longworth, Speaker of House at the onset of the Great Depression wrote:

> *The capitalistic system is the oldest system in the world, and any system that has weathered the gales and chances of thousands of years must have something in it that is sound and true. We believe in the right of a man to himself, to his own property, to his own destiny, and we believe the government exists as the umpire in the game, not to come down and take the bat, but to see that other fellows play the game according to the principles of fairness and justice.*

I also think my father, born on a farm as the grandson of a Baptist preacher, might also agree with Dr. Adrian Rogers, former three-term president of the Southern Baptist Convention who said:

> *You cannot legislate the poor into freedom by legislating the wealthy out of freedom. What one person receives without working for, another person must work for without receiving. The government cannot give to anybody anything that the government does not first take away from someone else. When half of the people get the idea that they do not have to work because the other half is going to take care of them, and when the other half gets the idea that it does no good to work because someone else is going to get what they work for, that, my dear friend, is about the end of any nation. You cannot multiply wealth by dividing it.*

The 2009 recession which took the Dow down to 6,500 was deeper than the one that followed 9/11, shortly after I began this book. The Dow recovery during the past year has been historical.

Warren Buffet wrote in Berkshire Hathaway's Annual Letter

to shareholders back on February 26, 2011 that *"Human potential is far from exhausted, and the American system for unleashing that potential — a system that has worked wonders for over two centuries despite frequent interruptions for recessions and even a Civil War — remains alive and effective."*

But during the last decade that potential was exhausted. The system died and became ineffective. Government policies worked to undermine free enterprise in America, especially for small businesses such as ours who employ the majority of our nation's middle class. They were the new downtrodden. With a new administration in place the red states are now seeing the truth in the song by Simply Red that "the growth of a nation cannot be achieved by keeping the downtrodden down."[59a & b]

Our hope for our American middle class is if those they believed in enough to vote for are able to accomplish what they voted for. The American system must reestablish the rungs hardworking Americans can climb to reach a better life. This is well on its way.

In the meantime if you've read this far, Johnnie and I use one of my father's favorite expressions to say, and we mean this without irony, "Thanks a Million."

Front: Park, Cottrell, Nesbitt, Feldman. Back: Simonet, Clines, Spencer, Richards, Stickane, Magacs, Tiffany, Steele.

The headquarters staff of Park Outdoor Advertising of New York, Inc. An American small business that has survived in Central New York for over 50 years.

APPENDIX A
WHY I BUSTED COLLEGE[60]
(Reprinted with permission from *Seventeen*)

I am a bustee from an Ivy League college. I'm not alone. One out of every six students who enter a major eastern college or university leaves without a diploma. Here is my story, representative of many, told with some degree of shame and with the hope that it might keep someone else from doing the same thing.

I'm not dumb. I have an IQ upward of 140. I graduated in the upper half of my class at a top eastern preparatory school, and I applied to only one university—Cornell in Ithaca, New York. Like many of my classmates, I wasn't sure what career I wanted and felt that college was probably the best way to find out. There was also a definite angle of glamour and intrigue that went with the thought of college. Then, too, I considered college the next step toward maturity—a step that parents and others expected of me. Put simply, I had been working, eating and breathing college, until college—in my case Cornell—had become a goal in itself. I came through satisfactorily on my entrance examination and in the fall of 1956 was proud to become one of the 1,611 men freshmen "on the hill."

Since I was not sure what I wanted to do, I entered the liberal arts college with some thought of law. I felt I would enjoy working with people, researching and compiling cases, preparing them with the common sense, presenting them with logic and winning them over with the zeal of a crusader. I'm the kind of guy who likes to argue.

Also, I reasoned, law would give me an excellent background for business.

Since Ithaca was my home town, Cornell was familiar to me. I faced no problem of adjusting myself to a new environment. I moved into the men's dorm to continue life on my own—away from home—and to meet more people.

Classes began September 19, two days after formal registration. I brought my books and thumbed through them, but put off reading the first assignments. Everyone was trying to meet everyone else. Orientation rallies, dances and coed parties followed one another in rapid succession. I wasn't worried about grades. I was confident that my prep school background would carry me through.

Within two weeks, I became fast friends with seven other freshmen, most of whom had also attended prep schools. When a person enters a large college, he can't help feeling lost. But it is a sort of contest as to who can appear the most casual and unconcerned. I doubt that I came close to winning, but I know this—I tried hard. And among my friends I had some tough competition. Ours was a varied and closely-knit crew.

John was from Ithaca, and we had been close friends long before college. Rip had attended prep school with me. We had both wrestled on the school team, and we managed to get into the same dorm at Cornell. His roommate, Sabu, was a foreign student from Iran who welcomed the American routine.

Just down the hall from me, on the same corridor, was Binge. He and his roommate, Brew, had both gone to a military academy. Later, we fell in with Skoal, a graduate of a different prep school, and a high school graduate named Jud. Each of us was different; that's what made the group dynamic.

Wherever we went, we went together, and many were the nights we'd go out looking for excitement. Since I had access to a car, there were always the safaris to nearby colleges. All this time my books collected dust.

I went into my first quizzes cold and unprepared. And I busted them flat.

Well, it bothered me, but I really wasn't worried, and I wasn't alone. We all felt that we could do better on the next test, get a high mark and bring our averages back up.

But the difference between the prep school I had attended and Cornell was becoming more apparent. It pervaded the atmosphere—both academic and social.

At prep school, twelve students would sit about a huge elliptical table with the master at one end. The masters were instructors, advisors, debate leaders and friends, all in one. Classes would often start with a joke and continue in a chatty style. Students entered into discussions, and if you didn't understand a particular point, just raise your hand to get an explanation.

At Cornell, for the most part, the classes were larger—some of the lecture classes had more than two hundred students. Often I found myself sitting mutely in huge lecture rooms, rapidly, almost frantically, jotting page after page of notes, which usually were merely so many meaningless and unrelated words.

There was no respected companion *drawing out* each student

and inspiring him to participate. The exalted professor was *telling*. And when a professor would rapidly join the rest on the page; only later, after reviewing, was I able to discover extraneous material and weed it from the important.

At prep school also I had a strong goal. The goal was to get accepted into college. Toward this goal, it seemed, every master, advisor and headmaster was intent on helping us travel.

Once prep school was behind, I lost this goal. I was in college and figured I would have no trouble staying there.

Beyond high school had lain college, with its promises, intrigues and freedoms. Beyond college lay life—which is a lot tougher than college, and most of us inwardly realize this. We each had four or five years before leaving our warm, secure, little world, and we wanted to enjoy every moment of it.

With the sudden release from personal guidance, interest and pressure came a slack in my studious intentions. At Cornell, my time was my own, and an endless variety of functions were beckoning. It was easy to become a glutton.

But the assignments kept pouring in—a report here, a short quiz there, a paper today, and an hour exam tomorrow. I failed to stay on top of them, let alone catch up on my back work. Why? I've asked myself that question a hundred times.

Most of the time I spent "studying" was really an exercise in self-deception. I would sit in front of a book for hours on end. When I had finished, I would find that I had merely substituted the putting of words on paper for learning. The brainwork still lay before me.

I was taking courses in English, French, psychology, English history, basic military science (ROTC), and physical education. The minimum number of required course hours in most colleges today is fifteen per term. With six for French, I was carrying eighteen.

My English course was primarily theme writing. I had always enjoyed that, and I liked my professor. He spoke our language. I enjoyed English immensely.

Not so with French. It was a grind. I had terrific instructors, but I had already taken three years of French and was tired of it. A language was required at Cornell, so I had to take it.

Psychology, I found extremely interesting, although the professor sometimes lost me in the shuffle of terms and philosophies.

I liked my professor for English history, but not the course. History came hard for me, and that was my first inkling that I could never be a lawyer. The inkling grew later.

Military science was a valuable experience. It was required, as was physical education.

I found this combination of courses a good brainful, but we were all in it together. And my friends and I were having our fill of college fun, too.

One night about eight, the six of them (Jud was already in bed) came into my room and asked me to go stir up a little excitement with them. Since I had put off a five-thousand-word theme until the last minute, I said no. That was one of the few times I can remember saying it. They went on, anyway. At two that morning I had finished and was deep in sleep.

An hour later, they were banging at my door.

Spreading myself thin. I made the wrestling team at Cornell, front row fourth from left, but dropped out when I was headed for scholastic probation during the first semester of my freshman year.

When I saw Binge grinning there, a bale of way hay strapped to his back, a huge "Bridge Out" sign under one arm, I couldn't help laughing. Then Rip came thumping down the hall behind a "No Parking" sign. A squeaking noise signaled the arrival of Brew, pushing a wheelbarrow full of wet cement. The rest of the fellows each held a red blinker-lantern.

While the rest of the dorm slept, we scattered hay in every crack and corner of the building. We rolled the wheelbarrow into another dorm, hid the signs in a nearby graveyard.

This was the most extravagant of many escapades, none of which was allowed to end when it was over. We kept each adventure going for nights on end, rehashing it in bull sessions. Hardly a day passed when at least one of us didn't feel he had something important to relate, and we would gather in a room and talk late into the night.

All these ill-conceived doings bit huge chunks out of my study time. Extracurricular activities stole even more. All through the year, we freshmen were warned by counselors and advisors against "spreading yourself thin." But I had dreamed of wrestling for Cornell when I was in prep school, and I had to make the team. I was also the art editor of Sounds of Sixty, our class newspaper.

At the end of the term, the little blue probation slip ended my extracurricular career.

I had passed all my courses; 60 is passing and I had an average of 69.4. But in Cornell liberal arts school you must have three courses over 70 to stay off pro. I had only two—English (80) and History (75). If I wanted to stay in Cornell, I had to get off pro.

And make no mistake, I wanted very much to stay in Cornell.

Fraternity rushing went on for the first two weeks of the second term. I should not have rushed on pro, but I did. So did my friends. And we all made good fraternities.

There was the usual orientation to fraternity life, pledge raids, meetings, and parties. And then things calmed down a bit. My fraternity brothers were concerned over my grades and tried to help. I began in earnest to raise my marks.

The courses were a little more to my liking this term. English,

French, psychology, English history, ROTC, physical education again, and biology, a subject in which I had done well at prep school. We even used the same text.

A Cornell tradition is "freedom with responsibility," and class attendance is, within limits, up to the individual students. In biology, each cut over three took a point off the final grade. I knew this but figured incorrectly that if I did well, the rule wouldn't apply. Overconfident, I cut some lectures.

Then I had two bad breaks.

I knocked my right thumb out of joint falling off a motorbike when I tried to carry a girl sidesaddle. I had to wear my arm in a cast and couldn't write for a full month. Lectures were completely forsaken, but *without* getting special permission from the lecturers. Later, I contracted a virus that put me in the infirmary for a week.

My English dropped to a 75, partly due to the extra time I spent pulling my grade in psychology. I got a 70 in French. The other two courses I busted from cuts. Twenty-one points for cuts were subtracted from my final average of 80 in biology. Cuts influenced my history professor to give me a disciplinary mark of 55.

The biology incident, in particular, set my teeth on edge. I spoke to my biology teacher, but he turned a deaf ear. So I received my suspension notice. One hundred thirty-two boys in my class didn't make the grade. It was pretty sad to see some of my closest friends walking out the back door with suitcases in their hands. It was sadder still to be among them.

I got two jobs and began working a twelve-hour day, driving myself to relieve my depression. I walked two miles to get to my second, and another half-mile in the evening to get back home.

Finally, I got my courage back and, urged by one of my professors, I sent a letter of appeal to the reviewing board at Cornell. I cited my broken thumb and illness and vowed never to cut again. Then I could only wait.

Each day I took my stand beside that mailbox expecting the board's decision. When it finally arrived, I remember holding the envelope for a while, turning it over and over in my hand until I could work up courage to open it. I tore it open. A glance. I was back in! I was to be readmitted that fall. There was one condition: I had to take two courses at Cornell summer school and get at least 75 in both.

When summer school began, I quit my morning job to attend classes. I made it through with a 75 and an 80, and I was back at Cornell that fall!

This time I lived at home instead of the fraternity house. I didn't waste time with friends. I didn't cut lectures. I didn't date. I went up to my room and closed the door and studied. I spent hours each day bent over my books. And I think I had the neatest collection of notes, typed on bond paper and bound, of any student since the University opened in 1868. I really worked.

And college today is work. You can't stay in a good college any more just because you can pay. You have much less time than years ago for coeds and drinks at Zinck's. The toughest thing about education today, in my opinion, is learning how to go about getting it.

A Sigma Phi Fraternity party which explains why the fun I had with some 39 brothers may have helped me take a less serious path at Cornell. I'm at the far left, and this particular party was chaperoned by my mother and father who are dead center in the picture. Because I was still in the pledge class of 1957 when I busted out, in a surprise event on May 27, 2013 I was initiated as a life member of the Epsilon Chapter of Sigma Phi.

My hard work did pay off. Up to the finals, I had an 83, 78 and 77 respectively in sociology, biology and far eastern studies, with a lower average of 68 in Great English Writers and of approximately 60 in British government. These averages would easily get me off pro, and I was beginning to feel like a human being again.

I moved into the fraternity. I was finally going to be initiated;

I had a 1952 Nash-Healey sports car of my own; a group of us were going to start a combo in which I was to play the drums, and I knew the courses I would be taking next term would be primarily of my choosing. Everything was finally going right.

Then came the finals. I laid out my study plans, I sweated and crammed. I forgot about sleep and taxed myself to the limit. And the results began to come in.

My final mark in English, 65, was consistent with my work for the term, and I was content with it. I had passed and I hadn't particularly enjoyed the "jug-jug, pu-we, to-witta-woos," and "hey nonny nonnies" of the old English writers anyway. I passed ROTC again. Biology was easy. I made an 88 on the final, got an 80 as a final mark. Government, which had been giving me trouble all term, I busted. But I was still in the running.

I was sure I had done well on the Far Eastern exam, but I

Not an Animal House, even though this fraternity picture bears a strong resemblance. Sigma Phi at Cornell in 1957 was definitely a cut above and not a boring place to be.

was worried about the sociology final. Much to my surprise, my sociology grade came in at 85. I had still to get my Far Eastern studies mark.

Then it came. My final in Far Eastern had been low, so low that the final mark was 63. That was a blow I had not expected.

I couldn't understand what had happened. I saw my professor and asked to see the exam. He told me it was "inaccessible," that it and another quiz had counted more than I expected. He was as immovable as a concrete wall and offered about as much sympathy.

All I could do was wait for the drop notice.

The board didn't meet for a while so I continued to go to classes. I wrote another appeal letter, but I had no real basis for an appeal this time. When the board met, I was dropped from Cornell. This time for good.

Well, the end had come and I left Cornell. Again, I wasn't alone. Of the eight in our group, only three are now in Cornell. Five of us failed to meet the pace.

This time I lost all hope, and friends and acquaintances didn't help much. For each person who genuinely cared, there were two who cared more about extracting a sadistic pleasure from it. Many

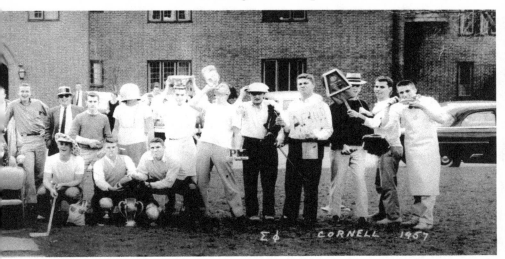

his was the year I broke my thumb in Bermuda which provided me with a ready-made ostume for this Sigma Phi moment by sporting a cast on my right arm as shown above.

who asked me about it would, under the guise of sympathy, stick in the knife and give it a little twist.

Of those few who genuinely cared, I remember two. One was a wonderful girl I had known and felt close to most of my life. We went for a long drive soon after I learned that I had busted and she proceeded to outline my weaknesses and lay bare the reasons for my failure. She strongly suggested I go into the army to get back on my feet. She meant well, but what she said really challenged me to prove I could continue my education somehow.

I got the confidence to back up the challenge a few nights later. I had a long talk with one of my fraternity brothers, who told me to hold up my head and keep working until I could get back into a college that would give me what I wanted. He said he knew I could do it.

That really helped. The next week, I took a series of aptitude and interest tests to help me plan my future. All the results pointed to writing and journalism. I signed up immediately for two journalism courses in the Cornell Extension School.

I enjoyed them immensely, and then I was sure. I was going into the writing field, and somehow I was going to get into another college so that I could develop my ability. I knew the shadow of my bad record loomed over me. One possibility presented itself: The University of North Carolina in Chapel Hill. It has an excellent school of journalism, and since I was born in that state, I seemed to have at least a chance.

Dad and I flew down one weekend to see what my chances were. We talked to everyone, my records were studied and the admissions director decided to give it a try. I was to take two more courses by correspondence and make at least B's in both. Then I was to go to a double session of Carolina summer school, take four more courses and come out with a B average in all.

It was a lot of concentrated work—study, eat and sleep, with a little black coffee on the side. But I was working to get into a college again, and all the determination I'd had at prep school came back.

By June 9, 1958, I had finished the correspondence courses,

taken the exams and was attending my first classes at Carolina summer school. The correspondence marks had come through a day before—an A in English, a B in math. The Cornell marks came soon after—86 in advertising, 83 in writing.

So far so good.

The summer started off fine. I was pretty lonely, but since I was there to do a job, it didn't matter.

To fill in all the loneliness, I began writing on the side. I'll never forget my first published editorial. I had written it to a local paper, the Chapel Hill *News Leader*. Over a cup of coffee on the morning of July 3, I saw my name in print for the first time.

Later, missing a girl back at Cornell, I began pouring my feelings into poems. My first poem appeared in the Raleigh *News and Observer* in August. I bought every paper in Chapel Hill, and then I drove to Raleigh to buy more.

Life was great.

When I registered for the fall term at Chapel Hill, I lost exactly half of my Cornell credits. But fall term was fine. I stuck pretty close to my B average and made a lot of new friends. I got to know my instructors. I went to my advisor if any trouble developed.

Spring term went well too. I'm on my way now. I'm in a good university—the oldest state university in the nation. I'm enjoying my studies. I know where I'm going

There have been some basic changes in my study habits. I spend less time organizing, typing notes and outlining material, and more time just plain learning. I read the assignments and keep up with the professor, day by day. I enter into discussions as I did at prep school.

If I dislike some of the professor's ideas or philosophy, I listen anyway. I'm in college to learn, not rebel, for I have begun to realize that the truly educated man has very few prejudices.

Carolina is no easier than Cornell. But it's easier for me. Why? I'm working harder, I'm back in college—to stay.

To stay until I walk out the front door, a diploma in my hands.

YOUR LETTERS –

COLLEGE INS AND OUTS[61]
(reprinted with permission from *Seventeen)*

"After I finished reading 'Why I Busted College' by Roy Park, Jr. in the October issue, I turned off my radio and got down to some serious studying." M.S., Detroit, Mich.

"Every time I start daydreaming while I study, or wonder how I'll get everything done, I shall take out Roy Park's article and read some of it!" C.G., Lafayette, La.

"I can doubly appreciate Roy Park's story, since I, too, lived for the mailman and the college board's verdict. I'm back in school now, with great hopes of receiving my diploma in education someday. Thanks for the most sincere story."
M.H., Park Forest, Ill.

"Few of your many excellent articles have impressed me as much as 'Why I Busted College.' As a high-school senior with my hopes set on Cornell, I am grateful to Mr. Park for his frank account of his experience. Am I discouraged? Not at all. I feel that I can now face college, be it Cornell or not, with a more realistic idea of what obtaining further education requires. Everyone who attends or plans to attend college should read this article." Z.W., Havertown, Pa.

"Upon reading this article, I received a severe blow; for as a college freshman I am following in the exact footsteps of Mr. Park. But I think his article has helped me a great deal to realize my mistakes." V.I., Salisbury, N.C.

* * *

"Roy Park's article is a timely reminder that college is no place to goof-off. So now, back to my homework." K.McK., Oakland, Calif.

"I have just finished reading your superb article 'Why I Busted College.' When I met you a few years back, just about the time you were dismissed, I had not the slightest idea I was talking to the person who was going to write my biography of college. This article fits me so perfectly in every factor of my college days – it is difficult to believe...It has been said that if just one person understands what another person is trying to say the author's means of communication has been successful — it has." J. B., Notre Dame

"Congratulations to you, not only for good article but for your courage in putting on paper what is certainly going to help thousands of young men (and girls) across our USA." G.D., Philadelphia, PA

APPENDIX B
BUILDING A MEDIA EMPIRE

1952	RHP Incorporated	Ithaca, NY
1961	WNCT AM/FM	Greenville, NC
1962	WNCT TV	Greenville, NC
1963	WDEF TV AM/FM	Chattanooga, TN
1964	WJHL TV	Johnson City, TN
1964	Park Outdoor Advertising, Inc.	New York & PA
	Park Displays	
1965	WTRV TV AM/FM	Richmond, VA
1966	Park Foundation, Inc.	Ithaca, NY
1968	KRSI AM/KFMX FM	St. Louis Park, MN
1968	WNAX AM	Yankton, SD
1969	WSLS TV	Roanoke, VA
1969	WUTR TV	Utica, NY
1969	Park Outdoor Advertising of	Scranton, PA
	Scranton-Wilkes Barre	
1972	*The Daily Sun*	Warner Robins, GA
1973	KWJJ AM KJIB FM	Portland, OR
1973	WBMG TV	Birmingham, AL
1973	*The Union-Sun & Journal*	Lockport, NY
1973	*The Journal Messenger*	Manassas, VA
1974	KJJO AM/FM	Eden Prairie, MN
1975	KEZX AM/FM	Seattle, WA
1975	*The Daily Sun & Journal*	Brooksville, FL
1975	*The Nebraska City News & Press*	Nebraska City, NB
1975	*St. Lawrence Plain Dealer*	Canton, NY
1975	*The Journal*	Ogdensburg, NY
1975	*The Massena Observer*	Massena, NY
1975	*Potsdam Courier-Freeman*	Potsdam, NY
1976	WHEN AM	Syracuse, NY

1977	WONO FM	Syracuse, NY
1977	*The Pilot-News*	Plymouth, IN
1977	*The Evening Sun*	Norwich, NY
1978	*News-Capital & Democrat*	McAlester, OK
1979	*Macomb Daily Journal*	Macomb, IL
1979	*Daily Ledger*	Broken Arrow, OK
1979	*Newton Observer-News-Enterprise*	Newton, NC
1979	*The News Herald*	Morganton, NC
1979	*Statesville Record & Landmark*	Statesville, NC
1979	*Sapulpa Daily Herald*	Sapulpa, OK
1980	*The Concord Tribune*	Concord, NC
1980	*Mecklenberg Gazette*	Davidson, NC
1980	*The Daily Independent*	Kannapolis, NC
1980	*Coldwater Daily Reporter*	Coldwater, MI
1980	*Houston Home Journal*	Perry, GA
1981	*Helena West-Helena Word*	Phillips County, AR
1981	*Twin City Tribune*	Phillips County, AR
1982	*The Sampson Independent*	Clinton, NC
1982	*McDowell News*	Marion, NC
1982	*Sandhill Citizen & Robbins Record*	Aberdeen, NC
1982	*The Robesonian*	Lumberton, NC
1982	*Devils Lake Daily Journal*	Devils Lake, ND
1982	*Courier News*	Blytheville, AR
1982	*The News-Virginia*	Waynesboro, VA
1984	*The Journal Register*	Medina, NY
1984	*The Evening News*	Jeffersonville, IN
1985	*The Register-Star*	Hudson, NY
1985	*The Chatham Courier*	Hudson, NY
1985	*Sentinel-Echo*	London, KY
1985	*Grayson County News Gazette*	London, KY
1985	*Logan Leader*	London, KY
1985	*News Democrat*	London, KY
1985	*Mooresville Tribune*	Mooresville, NC
1986	KWLO AM/KFMW FM	Waterloo, IA
1986	WPAT AM/FM	Clifton, NJ
1986	*The Wayne Independent*	Honesdale, PA

1986	*The Evening Centennial*	Shenandoah, IA
1986	*The Essex Independent*	Shenandoah, IA
1986	*The Pioneer*	Bemidji, MN
1986	*The Milton Standard*	Milton, PA
1986	*Lewisburg Daily Journal*	Milton, PA
1986	*Sand Springs Leader*	Sand Springs, OK
1986	*Maniford Eagle*	Sand Springs, OK
1986	*Sand Springs Extra*	Sand Springs, OK
1987	*The Morehead News*	Morehead, KY
1987	*The Shopping News*	Morehead, KY
1987	*Grayson Journal-Inquirer*	Morehead, KY
1987	*Olive Hill Times*	Morehead, KY
1987	*Menifee County News*	Morehead, KY
1987	*The Greenup News*	Morehead, KY
1987	*The World River Journal*	Burley & Hailey, ID
1987	*South Idaho Press*	Burley & Hailey, ID
1988	*The News Herald*	Ahoskie, NC
1988	*North Hampton News*	Ahoskie, NC
1988	*Index*	Ahoskie, NC
1988	*Common Wealth Enfield Progress*	Ahoskie, NC
1988	*Murfreesboro Advantage*	Ahoskie, NC
1988	*Southwest Halifax Advantage*	Ahoskie, NC
1988	*Eden Daily News*	Eden, NC
1988	*Commonwealth-Journal*	Somerset, KY
1988	*The News-Gazette*	Winchester, IN
1989	*Richmond County Daily Journal*	Rockingham, NC
1989	*The Hamlet News Messenger*	Rockingham, NC
1991	*Blackduck American*	Blackduck, MN

APPENDIX C
MEMBERSHIPS AND HONORS

Out of the best and most productive years of each man's life, he should carve a segment in which he puts his private career aside to serve his community and his country, and thereby serve his children, his neighbors, his fellow men, and the cause for freedom.

—*David Lilienthal*

My father served as a director of the Tompkins County Hospital Corporation, a trustee of the Ithaca Festival of the Arts, a president of the Tompkins County Chamber of Commerce, president of the Tompkins County United Fund, associate chairman of the Laymen's National Bible Committee in New York City, president of the Board of Trustees of the First Presbyterian Church of Ithaca, a member of the New York State Council on Crime and Delinquency, and a member of the Governor's Committee on Hospital Costs by appointment of New York Governor Nelson Rockefeller, and a trustee of the Hospital Review and Planning Council of Central New York from 1966 to 1969.

He was chairman of the New York State Newspaper Foundation, in Albany, New York, from 1977 to 1982, and a director of the New York State Publishers Association beginning in 1975, becoming vice president in 1980 and president in 1981. While there, he founded and became a trustee of the New York State Publishers Foundation.

He also served on the Committee on Regulatory Review of the National Association of Broadcasters from 1984 to 1987, was a member of the Board of Trustees of The Museum of Broadcasting in New York City, and a trustee of the Chowan Graphic Arts Foundation. In 1984, he was also named to the Corporate Advisory Board of the National Association of Securities Dealers, Inc. in Washington, DC.

He was a member of the Rotary Club, the Public Relations Society of America, the American Association of Agricultural College Editors, the Agricultural Relations Council, Phi Kappa Phi (Blue Key Honor Society), the National Press Club of Washington, the North Carolina Association of Broadcasters, the Southern Newspapers Publishers Association, American Newspaper Publishers Association, Inland Daily Press Association, Press Associations of Florida, Oregon, Georgia, North Carolina, Illinois, Virginia, Nebraska, Oklahoma and Hoosier State, the Sales Executives Club of New York, and the Broadcasters Associations in New York, Minnesota, Alabama, South Dakota, Tennessee, Virginia and Washington State.

He became director of the Sales Executive Club of Greater New York in 1979, becoming its vice president in 1981, its secretary in 1982 and its treasurer from 1985 to 1987. But back in the '60s he attended as an ordinary member, and an incident disclosed in the *North Carolina State University Alumni News* in 1971 showed his devotion to his native state and to his career.

Rudolph (Rudy) Pate, a close friend of my father at NC State, reported, "It was just before Christmas of 1962. The Sales Executive Club of New York was conducting its Christmas party at the Roosevelt Hotel. The program chairman had retained the services of a number of highly attractive dancing girls who were performing some intriguing steps on the stage.

"Roy Park had a platform-side table where he and a member of the staff of the Governor of North Carolina were discussing economy, the politics, and education and the life of North Carolina. The discussion was earnest, and it continued with scant interruption throughout the luncheon and the door-prizes and the dancing.

"After the party, a club member asked Roy what he thought of the beautiful dancing girls. 'Oh,' answered Roy with apology,

'I'm afraid I didn't see much of them. We were talking North Carolina business.'"[62]

On October 27, 1989, North Carolina Governor James G. Martin conferred on Park its highest civilian honor, the North Carolina Award, created in 1961 by the General Assembly and given only to men and women who made significant contributions in science, literature, fine arts and public service. "Park was recognized as a pioneer in food packaging and communications as well as one of the state's leading philanthropists," Pate said. He was recognized for making significant contributions to the welfare and quality of life of his native state and the nation.

In 1977 he was named an honorary member of Cornell's Beta Chapter of the marketing fraternity, Pi Sigma Epsilon; in 1987 an honorary member of the Delta Upsilon Chapter of Alpha Kappa Psi, a business fraternity at NC State; and in 1990, an honorary member of Alpha Epsilon Rho, the National Broadcasting Society at Ithaca College.

On the lighter side, Park held memberships in the Commonwealth Club of Virginia, Lucullus Circle, the Marco Polo Club, the Classic Car Club of America, the Packard Club, the Shenandoah Club, the New York Athletic Club, Cornell Club of New York, Raleigh Capital City Club, the Sphinx Club of Raleigh, Ithaca Country Club, Antique Automobile Club of America, the Union League Club of New York City, the Auburn-Duesenberg Club, and, yes, the Ithaca Yacht Club, which took him despite him ruining their regatta when he first got his boat in the '40s.

In addition to his work with the Presbyterian Church in Ithaca, he also received the Ethel Nestell Forner Writer and Community Award from St. Andrews (Presbyterian) College in Laurinburg, North Carolina, in 1991. As one of ten winners of the 1971 Abe Lincoln Awards, presented annually by the Southern Baptist's Radio and Television Commission, he was specifically cited for his outstanding utilization of his radio stations to advance the quality of life in the communities they serve, as well as his broad participation in the religious programming of interest to the audience served.

Among the other honors he received was a special citation for Distinguished Service to Agriculture in 1947 from the American Institute of Cooperatives; a Distinguished Service Award from the Tompkins County United Fund, 1961; a Life Membership Award from the Tompkins County Chamber of Commerce, 1983; a Giants of Achievement Golden Plate Award from the American Academy of Achievement in 1984. In 1990, he was awarded the Broadcast Pioneers prestigious Golden Mike Award for his flagship radio stations, WPAT FM/AM, serving the greater New York City area. In 1982, he was also inducted into the North Carolina Broadcasters Hall of Fame.

Pops was awarded "THE GOLDEN PLATE" at American Academy of Achievement's Annual Golden Plate Banquet in Minneapolis, MN on July 7, 1984. The caption reads: AWARDED TO AMERICA'S CAPTAINS OF ACHIEVEMENT "REPRESENTING THE MANY WHO EXCEL" IN THE GREAT FIELDS OF ENDEAVOR.

Again, on the lighter side, he was appointed a County Squire by Governor W. Kerr Scott in1953; an Honorary Citizen of New Orleans by its mayor, de Lesseps Morrison in 1958; an Admiral in the Great Navy of the State of Nebraska by Governor Frank B. Morrison and an Honorary Citizen of the State of Tennessee by Governor Buford Ellington in 1961. In 1963, he was commissioned as a Kentucky Colonel by Governor Bert Combs, and another governor of North Carolina, Terry Sanford, appointed him to the Society of the Prodigal Son the following year.

APPENDIX D
DEEPER CONNECTIONS TO
EDUCATION

North Carolina State University

Soon after graduation, Roy H. Park became involved in re-activating the NC State Alumni Association. "It was slow going, and for the year 1932 the grand sum of all contributions totaled $901.50. Of course, this was during the Depression and dollars were hard to come by," he said.

His first official post with North Carolina State after graduation came in 1937, when he was appointed to the Public Relations Committee of NCSU Alumni Association. He later became president of the association, and in this capacity, was a key figure in the creation and promotion of the "Nickels for Know-How" program. Through this program, North Carolina farmers could contribute $.05 on each ton of feed and fertilizer purchased to support agricultural research and education at the NC State College of Agriculture and Life Sciences. The program brought in a total income of over $17 million since 1951 and yielded as much as $500,000 annually.

When he was president of the NCSU Alumni Association in 1961, he also initiated the university's most prestigious annual giving club, according to Al Lanier, the Alumni Association's executive director. It was called the Chancellor's Circle.

His principal address to the NCSU Development Council Meeting in 1970 was said to have set the tone for the University's Development Program in the decade to come. During that address, my father demonstrated his faith in education. He warned that both "the radical fringes of youthful society and their counterparts" on the extreme right are endangering America's free universities.

He noted: "The extreme left is operating through sit-ins, riots, and burnings. They rant for the irresponsible, illogical and ignorant goal of pulling down the towers of learning." On the other extreme, he added: "Some of our older generation are almost as bad. These range from the type who always have cast a suspicious eye on free education and free expression to mossbacks who cling to the idea that anything new or different is an abomination in the eye of God and man. The radical right," he observed, "presses for repressive legislation, while the young radicals clamor for no laws at all."

Pops stressed that most of the current generation of students are constructive citizens who will make solid contributions to the state and nation. He urged business and educational leaders to retain their perspective "and to project to others our faith in the long-range progress we know will be made."

My father became a trustee of NC State in 1977, and during his tenure until 1985 worked closely with the governor's Commission on Literacy. He was awarded an honorary Doctorate of Humanities Degree by NC State in 1978, and that same year, on May 13, he gave State's Eighty-ninth Annual Commencement address.

In his "Call for a New Coalition," he spoke of the need for land-grant and state universities to enlarge their national program of support for public universities. "The time has come," he said, "for business and industry and the land-grant colleges and state universities throughout the country to form a new coalition that can develop into a permanent alliance to protect themselves against big government, both national and state.

"The only way freedom of thought and learning can be carried on at the land-grant colleges and state universities in this great country of ours is through dollars given without strings or stipulations. Our college administration needs the flexibility that goes with unrestricted private funding. Unlike tax dollars that come with rules and ultimatums, the private dollars instead can provide the freedom necessary to nurture quality on the campus, and build faith on the part of the public. From this alliance, immense direct benefits will come to the nation and the economy of our state," he said.

"Throughout the years this university has helped the economy and our people in many ways. For example, university research on plant disease has saved North Carolina's tobacco industry on at least two occasions. It's now a billion dollar industry for the State.

"Today we are waking up to the fact that the dollars from Washington come with strings attached. The mission has degenerated from general and applied research to the control of the academic standards for great and proud institutions, such as ours and our sister university at Chapel Hill. This may take a radical change in thinking of my fellow entrepreneurs and in the executive suites of North Carolina and the nation.

"I suggest the new alliance would be a natural alliance—one that flows naturally from the existing and growing links between the American business world and these great land-grant and state universities. Business and industry have received significant help from land-grant and state universities. Now business and industry must help finance them. Every business, large or small, benefits— so every business and industry should contribute," he said.

In talking to the students, my father gave a lot of insight into himself. "I've had four careers—writer and editor—advertising and public relations—food marketing—and now, communications. When my work gets routine and becomes dull, I move on to another challenge," he said. "If I have prospered, it has been a combination of luck and hard work...with luck the ingredient once in a while, and hard work, *the rule every day.* At sixty-five, I should be newly retired, but my work is too exciting. In communications I'm in the thick of what is going on in a fast-moving world...and I *love it.*"

He told students to "go out in the world and do the things that give you fulfillment. Above all, don't get stuck in a job that is a bore or a drudgery. Involve yourself in a career that you enjoy so much that you never count the hours, and in a job that is so much fun that you look forward to going to work every morning.

"We must not be a tired, complacent nation, but a nation of eager explorers determined not to be outdone by the past but rather to emulate our forefathers by seeing that each generation continues to outdo the other in providing a better life, a better living, a better mind and a bigger heart," he said.

In concluding his address, he said he could think of no greater honor for an old grad than "being asked back to make a commencement speech. This glorious university gave me a good start in my professional life. I am indebted to it and to the men and women who have made it the great institution that it is today."

In calling attention to my father's remarkable career and seemingly limitless energy and drive, the *North Carolina State University Alumni News* featured him on the cover of its August 1955 issue. It called him "a harnessed hurricane—not like Hazel, of course, but with enough force, appeal, and insight to team up with famous foodman, Duncan Hines, in a business venture now topping $50 million a year." In 1971, he was described in this publication as "an executive with a restless mind and steel-trap memory."

Cornell University

In 1971, Pops cosponsored seminars for the Cornell University Department of Communication Arts through his company, and this continued throughout the 1971–1972 academic year. In this capacity, he spoke to the students on December 11, 1971, in an address entitled, COMMUNICATIONS MEDIA: MORE THAN A BUSINESS.

In 1976, when he spoke to the Cornell University Graduate School of Management about his time with Carolina Cotton and Duncan Hines, he said his experience in broadcast and newspaper taught him "the basics in print and communications that have never left me, and I learned work habits borne of a deliberate self-discipline that are unchanged today."

He summed up his advice to the students on getting ahead in the business world, saying, "You might realize that in your new highly competitive business world, you will be lonely. Basically, you'll have to be logical and unbiased in arriving at the right decisions. Your associates must realize that you are dedicated to the business.

Then there are the Durland Lectures, which my father helped create and fund, and which continue to be the Johnson School's most prestigious business speaking event. Each year, the dean of the school invites a distinguished business leader to the campus to meet with students and faculty members and to deliver a major address. Income from the fund is used to conduct the lecture and support speaker programs.

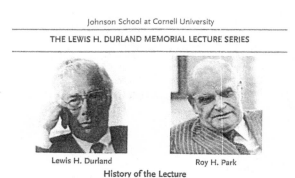

Johnson School at Cornell University

THE LEWIS H. DURLAND MEMORIAL LECTURE SERIES

Lewis H. Durland   Roy H. Park

History of the Lecture

Roy H. Park, the late chairman of Park Communications, Inc., and a past member of the Johnson School Advisory Council, was instrumental in creating the Lewis H. Durland Memorial Lecture Series. Park and a group of supporters endowed the Durland Memorial Fund in 1983 in honor of Lew Durland.

When my father passed away, Cornell University Professor Emeritus William B. Ward said, "Park had a vision on the business world that is extremely unusual. He pulled himself up by his own bootstraps....It seems that he had the Midas Touch. Everything he touched turned to gold."

And Gray Thoron, emeritus law professor and former dean of the Cornell University Law School, and his good friend, said, "We've lost a wonderful friend....He not only built a tremendous media empire, but he did it on his own. He had tremendous drive, he had tremendous energy and ability. He never boasted about it like [Donald] Trump or some of those other people like that. He was very low-key in talking about his accomplishments."

Ithaca College

At the dedication, Ithaca College president, James J. Whalen, said, "The Roy H. Park School of Communications is not only our first named school, but it is named in honor of a man whose service and commitment to this institution are exemplary in American higher education. Roy Park's universally recognized leadership in the world of communications will henceforth and in perpetuity be associated with Ithaca College and its School of Communications."

After twenty years of service on the board, eleven as its chairman, Pops became the board's first chairman emeritus. But he continued to serve as a special adviser to the newly elected board under Chairman Herman E. "Skip" Muller, and to President James J. Whalen. In stepping down, Pops said, "It has been both a pleasure and a privilege to be a part of the Ithaca College community for so many years. Even as I concentrate more fully on my corporate activities, I look forward to continuing my service to the College in a new role. I am confident that under the continued leadership of my good friend and colleague James Whalen, and the able guidance of my esteemed vice chairman, Herman Muller, the course has been set for what will remain a strong, vibrant institution of higher education."

President Whalen praised Park's interest and involvement in the life of Ithaca College, noting that the role of board chairman is paramount to the success of any institution. "A president can only lead if those who hold the college in trust, and especially the chairman, are people of talent and strength and integrity," said Whalen. "My chairman, Mr. Roy H. Park, is that and more. He is my friend. He is a man of substance and prominence, who has assisted Ithaca over the years with his kindness and generous attention, his strength, leadership, and his deep caring for our students. I want to express my appreciation for all that he has done and will continue to do for Ithaca in the years to come."

In July 1991, Gray Thoron told Helen Mundell of the *Ithaca Journal*, "Ithaca College has been very lucky to have had him give them as much of his time and interest as he has. A lot of people think his only interest is business—and it's not."

In the same article, President Whalen said, "Roy had done so many wonderful things for Ithaca College I just can't say enough about him. His trusteeship has been exemplary, especially his work as chairman of our board....He has been readily available to me. He's brought wonderful people to our boardroom, to our classrooms, and lecture halls.

"In sum, he had consistently demonstrated the kind of genuine interest and support for the institute that few college presidents have an opportunity to enjoy."

When my father passed away two years later, in 1993, Ithaca College history professor Paul McBride said, "We've lost a real friend. He's been an extraordinary benefactor of the college...both in his business and his many contacts....If we needed something, background or expertise, Roy had some connection and he could call on those connections to benefit the college."

He even surprised the superintendent for custodial services at Ithaca College, Richard Coulture, who said, "He was a much more funny and fun-loving person than I had anticipated."

APPENDIX E
A FEW ACCOLADES

On his seventy-fifth birthday, one of my father's television stations taped a tribute to him from three rather distinguished associates. The first was Paul Harvey, who said, "Roy, I kind of invited myself to your birthday party because you for so long have been such a credit to our sometimes incredible industry. Others may do what you've done over the years yet to be, but you always have been first and they, only because they were encouraged by a pioneer who has moved on the mountain alone, then to beckon us more timid ones to follow. Roy, as the politicians say, I want to wish you many happy returns and on behalf of our industry, may I plead with you, sir, to lead on. Good Day."

Next came a salute from William S. Paley, founder and former chairman, CBS, Inc., saying, "As a broadcaster, as a businessman, as a family man and friend, you continue to show a boundless enthusiasm that the years cannot give. In a career filled with re-markable achievements, you have earned a place in the history books as the first broadcaster to acquire the full limit of seven television stations, seven AM radio stations, and seven FM radio stations. To these broadcast properties and your other business and perpetual interest you have brought an enlightened leader-ship and dedication. I congratulate you on your successes, past, present and future, and wish you all the best. Happy seventy-fifth Birthday, Roy, from all of us at CBS."

Finally, Allen H. Neuharth, former CEO of Gannett Co., Inc., said, "Nothing could be more worthy of a celebration than seventy-five years of Roy Park. And as we think about that up here in Washington, and envy you leading in Carolina, I want you to know, Roy, that even after seventy-five years, those of us who have been watching you are well aware of what the next seventy-five are likely to be with your company. I know you and Dick Gilbert and others are down there plotting about how you are going to take over the Gannett Company and move the whole thing to Ithaca, and we are ready to talk with you about that anytime you are because we admire you and envy you for all you have done, and for everything I know you are going to do in the future."

Neuharth also said, "Park has several other outstanding characteristics. He's a real entrepreneur in the very best spirit. He's also a great patriot. He has combined that patriotism and entrepreneurship in a way that has benefited not only his own business but the communities, the institutions he's served, his state and the nation. Not only the high and mighty have nice things to say about Roy Park."

Another Park associate was the vice chancellor for development and university relations at North Carolina State University. Like any aggressive college, NC State pays attention to its wealthiest graduates, both for their influence and for what might be earmarked for the college in their wills.

Rudy Pate was enthusiastic in his praise of Park's role in helping the university. He was quoted as saying, "He's been an enormous influence," Pate said, adding that Park played a leading role in developing more corporate support for the university. "Mr. Park is also the hardest working man I know," Pate said. "He's got an enormous capacity for work. He has already been recognized as one of the most successful corporate executives in the twentieth century."

Past NC State Chancellor Larry Monteith had said, "Roy has added to the great strengths and excellence of all functions of the University...he was an advisor to four chancellors, a leader and was prominent in advancing his alma mater."

It was Park's philanthropic endeavors and dedication to North Carolina citizens that prompted the late NC Senator Sam J. Ervin to say, "He is one of the finest human beings the good Lord ever created...and he has one of the most important characteristics of all—an understanding heart."

"I've never seen anyone who works like Roy Park works," said James J. Whalen, president of Ithaca College. "When you're leaving, Roy Park is working. When you come back, Roy Park is working. He has tremendous energy, tremendous drive."

In 1985, when Whalen awarded him an honorary degree, he said, "Yours is the greatness of the self-made man who has made of himself more than most men dare to attempt."

Former NC State Chancellor, Joab L. Thomas, said, "Roy Park's life has been characterized by a high degree of integrity, motivation, and discipline, a trait finely honed by a demanding regimen in the busy realms of advertising, newspaper, radio, television, and corporate leadership. Nothing escapes his attention or his interest. A voracious reader, world traveler and philanthropist, his thoughts and actions encompass the world."

And Bill Friday, president of The University of North Carolina System, who had known Park for twenty years, summed up the Ithacan and his success this way: "He remembers the small things. He knows the little things make the big things come."

To Sam Ervin, there was nothing offensive about Park's interest in profitability. "I don't know that it's any cardinal sin to try and make money," Ervin said, "I don't think everybody's afflicted with that desire."

Pops had many articles written about him in the *Ithaca Journal*. In 1991, Helen Mundell wrote an article headlined, How Park Enraptured a Small City.[63]

"He's a very acquisitive man," said Betty Boniface, when she was secretary to Park Communication's president, Wright Thomas. "One of his mottos is, 'We never sell anything.' Someone once asked him what he did for fun. He said he worked, because he just loved running his company."

His own secretary, Barbara Iorio, when she was working for him said, "I really enjoy working with him because it's been like getting a master's degree without paying the tuition."

"He's a marvelous person," commented Sandy Kuntz, owner of Hal's Deli in downtown Ithaca. She was a longtime renter in a building owned by Pops, where he and his top aides frequently ate lunch. "He's done so much for the community." Kuntz was thrilled when Park constructed a new building near her Ithaca Aurora Street eatery, to replace the burned-out Leonardo Hotel. Kuntz loves that Park patronized her deli, "when there are so many fancier places he could eat." And what did Roy order? "Chopped liver or a pastrami or corned beef sandwich," Kuntz said. She added that "He liked our kosher dill pickles—and coleslaw."

Park had a great influence on the career of another great eatery owner, former Ithacan Forrest Smith, who grew up playing with Park's children and calling Park "Uncle Roy." "Roy Park," Smith said, "taught me to enjoy the other person's success, as opposed to begrudging them their successes." Park also told Smith to pay attention to detail, told him that he loves the Bible, and that the most important thing in his business life is to teach people to learn to love what they do. The last thing Park taught Smith is that everybody needs a role model, Smith said. "He's mine, and I've got the best."

Friends for many years—My father with Doris and Chuck Smith of the Ithaca Gun Company.

In other comments reported by Mundell, Fred Weeman, vice president, First Albany Corporation, said: "He's one of the true long-term investors. The only time I've ever seen him part with a stock is when he's made a gift." Randel Stair, his financial vice president, said, "I learned very early on that while he was willing to listen to anything you wanted to comment on or propose, you'd better have your homework done."

Once Anthony DiGiacomo, retired president of the First National Bank said, "I've known Mr. Park well over thirty years. He's a stickler for detail. If he makes a promise to you, he keeps it—a rare quality and a good quality," and Harry F. Byrd, Jr., former U.S. Senator from Virginia, who served 36 straight years in elected public office, said, "I regard him as...a great businessman, a splendid newspaperman, and overall, just a very superior person."

My father and mother's best long-term friends, Charles and Doris Smith, were also quoted. Chuck, who was a family member and an official with Ithaca Gun when my father helped him negotiate his sale, said, "I first met Roy right after I came back from World War II, in about 1946. Then...[along] came Duncan Hines. He got hold of Duncan Hines and made him famous." And Doris Smith said, "He's been a sincere friend. He was helpful in arranging the financial aspects of the sale of Ithaca Gun. He's sort of a genius at that."[64]

APPENDIX F
EULOGY FROM A FRIEND

Jim Whalen's eulogy for my father began:

"I want to take a moment to thank Larry and the Choir, Jean Radice, and Angus Godwin for providing so much beautiful music today. I am very proud of all of you, and I know Roy would have been too. As so many of you know, Roy appreciated very much the efforts involved in special presentations. Gray Thoron, he would love knowing that you were here to share one of his favorite poems. And, of course, I want to thank Reverend Lewis and Reverend Hill for their special kindness and help.

"And to my vice president, Bonnie Gordon, a very special thanks for your superb efforts during these last few days in bringing it all together. You were special to Roy and I know he appreciates it as well.

"I also want to acknowledge Cornell President Frank Rhodes, and our colleagues from The University of North Carolina and North Carolina State.

"It was very hard to even imagine us all being here today… Roy's family, his business associates, staff, friends and neighbors, students and faculty from the educational community he served so well—from this whole community that he served so well. But here we are, in part to grieve, in part to remember…and perhaps most of all, to share our stories about Roy and the ways in which he touched our lives so that we could each see a little more of him through each other and take comfort in that sharing.

"I did take comfort, Dottie, in being able to share part of Tuesday with you, as you and the family returned from New York. I must tell you that I watched that plane touch down on the runway with such sadness. I remembered the many times when you and Roy would offer me and Gill a ride, and we would come into that airport together after having had such good times. When the door of the plane opened on Tuesday, I couldn't help but expect what I had seen so often before…a great tumbleweed of crumpled newspapers from Roy's daily reading, armfuls of wonderful Christmas treats from Sulka ties and Tiffany scarves to those fantastic singing bears with the red noses, and that visible sense of tired but happy satisfaction from having had a good trip.

"Instead, I saw in all your faces that certain knowledge that somebody was missing. There was a tremendous sense of emptiness around us, and I recalled the words of a good mutual friend who said that no one would know until Roy was gone how much space he occupied in our lives—how large a presence he really was.

"As we sat together afterwards, Dottie, with Adelaide, Roy, Jr., and Tetlow, you said something to me that I will never forget. Amidst your own deeply personal loss, you turned to me and said, 'Jim, you are part of the family.' That meant so much to me—more than you will ever know, because 'family' means love, and caring, and having someone to share the good times with, and the difficult ones as well. We have had all of that in the eighteen years since you and Roy first welcomed, so warmly, Gillian, Marjorie, and myself to Ithaca, and it has been a truly generous wonderful gift. Your constant friendship and kindness have been a source of strength this week in particular, and I thank you so much.

"I have often described Roy Park as my friend and mentor, and I have always meant it. I learned so much from him—some of which was terrific fun, and some of which was just not easy. I learned for example, how to be wrong and still feel that something good has happened. Roy had a special way of teaching that, but it was hard to be a willing pupil sometimes. And there were lessons about never settling for second best, but always, always striving for perfection. In fact Roy could be absolutely maddening in his insistence on doing things 'right'—which really meant doing them the way Roy wanted them done. But the fact of the matter is that so very much of the time he was right—and you would learn to see things a little differently.

"You would learn, from watching and participating with Roy, about seeing the bigger picture. Now for most people, that means seeing the forest instead of the trees. Well, that wasn't enough for Roy. When Roy talked 'big picture,' it wasn't just the forest and the trees, it was a question of who owned the land, and what was on either side of it, and what the plans for it were. Roy's view wasn't oriented so much to what would happen next, as much as to what would happen eventually, in the future. And I learned that as far as Roy was concerned, every step was to be taken in consideration not only of today's gain, but tomorrow's plan.

"I think about Roy Park and I think about the words we typically use to describe successful business people—hardworking, driven, determined, creative, dynamic—they all applied to Roy, but there was nothing typical about him. He had singular instincts, an uncanny sense of opportunity, and the intelligence and willpower it took to transform his dreams into reality. Roy was a genius. His accomplishments made an indelible mark on his industry and brought him stature, prestige, and tremendous power. But Roy was even more special in another way. Those of us who have known individuals of stature, prestige, and tremendous power so often also find coldness and something not quite complete in them. Roy Park had the warmth and the humor, and in many, many ways, the sensitivity that made his presence whole and even more substantial.

"And one of Roy's very finest qualities was his humility. He was an important man, but he did not think he was *too* important. He never forgot his own modest beginning, and he had a special place in his heart for people who worked hard and perhaps had to struggle, but who were determined to improve in life. Roy related to that; he respected those efforts and supported them, with everything from a phone call to help out with a job, or a kind note of encouragement, to something as simple as a smile.

"Roy genuinely and deeply appreciated the kindness and devotion that were extended to him, whether it was from Matty, or Oscar or Bernie as they shared all those trips in the car, or from Barbara or Maria at the office, or from Emilita or Cipriani at the house, or from the dozens of others in Ithaca or more distant places who discovered that with this particular captain of industry, graciousness extended meant graciousness returned.

"We had fun together, Roy and I. There are hundreds of stories I could share with you, but let me tell just a couple about my friend Roy.

"I mentioned earlier a comment by a friend who said something about Roy being such an enormous presence in our lives. There was one place in which Roy and I often met where that was amply demonstrated to me over and over again. When I first came to Ithaca in 1975, I had a call during the first week or so of my presidency asking if I would come downtown to a luncheon meeting of the bank board. I asked people in my office what that was about, as I was a little surprised to be invited so early to such an august gathering. They dutifully explained that it was a long-standing tradition for the president of Ithaca College to serve on the bank board and that they were quite sure that I was going to be asked to do so. I was, of course, delighted, and gladly agreed to attend this lunch with Mr. Roy Park and his good friend and colleague, Mr. Lew Durland. We had a wonderful lunch with lots of good discussion, and an opportunity for me to meet other people who were involved in this community. They did ask me to join the bank board, and again, I gladly accepted.

"I returned to my office and happily announced that I had joined the board of the First National Bank of Ithaca and was completely taken aback by the look of surprise on the faces of my staff members. 'What?' they said. 'Wrong bank, wrong bank!!!' And they proceeded to tell me that I had made a terrible, terrible mistake because in fact, the tradition, long established in Ithaca, New York, was for the Ithaca College president to serve on the Trust Company Board. Now perhaps we won't visit today what Roy knew about that particular tradition, but it sure was a slick move, and Charlie Treman didn't talk to me for quite a while.

"I actually came to appreciate so much the many, many opportunities that were borne of that one luncheon. Over the years since, I have participated in many different ways with what became the 'First National Bank of Ithaca / Security New York State / Norstar / Fleet' whatever....Along with many other things, it provided me a chance to spend even a little more time with Roy regularly as we would gather in that boardroom downtown. And I even learned something from that.

"When I first arrived, I noticed fairly quickly that there was a definite pattern related to who sat where in that room. Lew Durland, as chairman of the board, would sit at the head of the table, and Roy Park always sat immediately to his left. Not only did Roy sit there when he *was* there, it seemed clear to all of us that Roy sat there even when he *wasn't* there. Nobody used that chair except for Roy Park. All kidding aside, it went on that way for years and years. Even when I became chairman of the board, the only time that seat was occupied was when Roy Park himself was sitting in it. I think it is safe to say that no one else will ever fill that space.

"People often think of Roy in material terms, and that's a mistake. He certainly appreciated fine things—and collected some of them—but he did not lead the ostentatious life he could have led. He did have some things, some prized possessions that were prized as symbols of deeper, more meaningful parts of his life. One of these was a pen, a beautiful Tiffany pen that he cherished, carrying it in the pocket closest to his heart.

"One day, I was in his office to sign some papers and asked to borrow a pen. He handed me his, and I signed the papers and left a little while later. The next day, Roy called, and as only Roy could, in the most gracious manner, he inquired about the possibility that I might have inadvertently walked off with his prized, beautiful, cherished Tiffany pen. I searched everywhere and could not find it.

"During the next few days, I spent a lot of time talking to St. Anthony, who my mother had always told me could help find lost things. I begged St. Anthony to find that pen, because I knew it was important to Roy, and consequently, that it was important to me. It wasn't so much that he could not replace that pen. Lord knows he could have dozens of them if he wanted them. The point was that he loved this one because it was given to him by someone he loved more dearly than anyone, his wife, Dottie. He carried that pen like a talisman, and he could not and would not rest until he found it.

"Well, it took a couple of days, and I am not sure who rescued me, whether it was St. Anthony or the cleaning lady, but Roy found it, and he was very happy. And I was, too.

"Over the years, I have been asked so many times why Roy and I were such good friends, and what it was that made it work so well for us. I don't really know the answer entirely. I just know that over those years we were both very glad that we were close friends. I suppose I like to think that maybe it had something to do with Roy's ability to see people as they really are. I like to think that there was something in that poor boy from Dobson, North Carolina, that recognized something in this poor boy from Pottsville, Pennsylvania, and thought, as Roy often said to me, that we made 'a pretty good team.' 'Isn't that right, Jim,' he would say. And believe me, I'd say, 'Yes, Roy, we make a pretty good team.' And we did.

"I owe a great debt of thanks to Roy Park. Apart and aside from his friendship, he gave me the best kind of working partner a president of a college could ever have. With his sound counsel and strong support, with his drive for excellence, and relentless determination to make things better, he enabled us to realize some dreams for Ithaca College that will have a lasting impact not only on this community, but on the lives of generations of students who have had the opportunity to participate here. And when you multiply that by his assistance to Cornell, to The University of North Carolina, and to his beloved alma mater, NC State, it is almost hard to imagine that there is anyone left out there whose life hasn't been touched in some way by Roy Park.

"One day in the spring of 1988, Roy allowed us to pay tribute to him with an honorary degree at graduation and we tried that day to capture some of the essential Roy Park. I would like to share just one passage from that citation:

There is no greater accomplishment than the fulfillment of a dream and none greater to fulfill than the American dream. You, Roy H. Park, have realized that dream and so achieved greatness.

Yours is the greatness of the self-made man who has made of himself more than most men dare attempt. Yours is the greatness of having the insight to recognize opportunity and the skill to seize it. Yours is greatness borne with quiet dignity, rather than public fanfare; the greatness of being considered wise among the knowledgeable, expert among the able, and tireless among the diligent. Yours is the greatness of serving as an example to succeeding generations of men and women who would realize their own dreams—an example that proves that vision, ability, hard work and creativity lead to success. Yours is greatness that speaks eloquently of man's capacity for achievement and his dedication to progress.

"In closing, let me again say to you, Dottie, that I am honored and deeply touched to be part of your family. And to my friend Roy, I just want to say that I will miss coming home from various journeys—whether it was just for a day or several weeks—and knowing that within moments of my arrival the phone would ring and I would hear your voice say, 'Welcome home, Jim.' I'll just have to take comfort in knowing that earlier this week, the good Lord said to you, 'Welcome home, Roy, welcome home.'"

APPENDIX G
MEMORIAL TRIBUTES

"We were very close," said Rudolph Pate, who retired from NCSU in 1985 as vice chancellor for development and university relations. He and Mr. Park became friends in the 1940s when Mr. Pate was the university's public relations representative and Mr. Park was working with the Cotton Growers Cooperative Association. The families have visited in each other's homes over the years.

"He seemed to thrive on work. It made him tick," Mr. Pate said in the *News & Observer*. "He shied away from any mention of wealth."

Frank Daniels, publisher of the Raleigh *News & Observer*, called my father "a remarkable builder who built quite an empire in radio and television, then devoted himself to acquiring newspapers throughout North Carolina and around the country and knit them into a viable, strong organization."

Other comments from friends and associates in his native state included:

William C. Friday, former president of The University of North Carolina, who said, "Among North Carolina's illustrious achievers during this half century, none stands taller than Roy Park. Native born, his attention to his homeland never varied and his great talents were constantly in the service of Commonwealth. Always of good humor and with a generous heart, he moved among his peers sharing of himself gladly in the service of others. We shall greatly miss this warm and kindly man who was admired by so many of his fellow Carolinians."

Larry K. Monteith, Chancellor of North Carolina State University, who said, "Roy had added to the great strengths and excellence of all functions of the University, including his distinguished service as a trustee, as president of the Alumni Association, longtime chairman of the Development Council and generous supporter. While he was chairman of the Development Council, he generated literally millions of dollars of support from virtually every county in North Carolina and outside the state. He is one of the greatest graduates the university has ever produced, and is one of America's greatest entrepreneurs. He loved his alma mater and serviced it nobly. Among the university facilities that has benefited from Roy's generosity is the D.H. Hill Library. He was an advisor to four chancellors, a leader, and was prominent in advancing his alma mater. He was a friend and benefactor who will be missed deeply."

From Governor James B. Hunt, State of North Carolina, who stated, "Roy was a special friend to me, a small-town boy who achieved great things, but never forgot his roots. We shared a deep love of our native state, and a lifelong devotion to our alma mater, North Carolina State University. He supported the University with his time, his talent, and his treasure, whether serving on the Board of Trustees, heading up fund-raising campaigns, or just making suggestions about what the University needed to be doing. Roy's newspapers, radio, and television stations enriched and informed our state. Most importantly, Roy's energy and enterprise inspired everyone who came into contact with him. He was a deserving recipient of our highest honor for service to the state, North Carolina Award. I will truly miss him."

John McNair, III, former chairman, Wachovia Bank, said, "Roy Park's career is not unlike a novel, from a crossroads-reared young man in rural North Carolina to one of our country's most successful and recognized entrepreneurs. The amazing trait he always honored is the fact he never forgot his roots. He was always a gentleman and most importantly a true and loyal friend to a host of men and women all across our nations. He will be missed by each one of them."

James K. Dorsett, Jr., attorney, Raleigh, said, "He was an exceptional person in almost every way, with great talent and wisdom, but complete integrity. He was trusted and liked by all of the people with whom he did business and from whom he made acquisitions. His capacity to do and his intuitions were so good. Additionally, he was just an enjoyable, interesting person to be with. It was a remarkable experience to know Roy."

The comments from some of his managers included:

From the *Richmond Times-Dispatch*, Wednesday, October 27, 1993, Executive Vice President / General Manager Rich Pegram, WTVRTV: "Mr. Park was intimately involved in knowing what was going on with the company.... He had an incredible mind for detail and knew the specifics of each operation....He was a true pioneer. He started this broadcast company when he was fifty-two, at a time when most people are thinking of retiring.... [His death] is a shock. He was one of those larger-than-life people you assume will go on forever."

From the *Post Standard*, Syracuse, New York, Wednesday, October 27, 1993, Vice President of Newspaper Operations Robert J. Rossi, Park Communications, Inc.: "You find very few people with his drive and dynamic approach. There aren't very many of him left in the country."

From the *Press & Sun Bulletin*, Binghamton, New York, Wednesday, October 27, 1993, Regional Coordinator Chester P. Middlesworth, Park Communications North Carolina Newspaper: "He was a workaholic who never worked a day in his life because he enjoyed everything he did in the business world....I've known him to wear as many as six watches at one time. I've seen him with two watches on one arm, another watch on the other arm, a pocket watch and cufflinks that were watches....He was always a stickler on time....As we would be driving down the road, he would be handing me pieces of paper and asking my comments on them even though I was driving seventy mph."

From Binghamton's *Evening Press* on August 3, 1983, "Work is his recreation, not just his job," said former senator Sam Ervin, who was a director of one of Park's papers in Morganton, NC.

From educators:

Professor Rick Wright, Jr., S.I. Newhouse School of Communications at Syracuse University, said, "I think we've just seen the last breed in Mr. Park...where we had one person who controlled it all. He was definitely one of a kind."

Others said:

Chairman and CEO Erland Kailbourne, Fleet Bank, wrote, "I just wanted to drop you a note to extend my deepest condolences on the passing of your father.

"As you know, I had the privilege of knowing him for the past twenty years, and he truly was an individual that set his own pace and direction. During the past twenty years I, of course, have seen the significant changes that occurred at the First National Bank of Ithaca, Security New York State Corporation, as well as the Norstar organization as it evolved to the current Fleet configuration. Roy, too, witnessed and was a significant part of the chain of events.

"I also had many enjoyable breakfasts and lunches with him in Ithaca as we discussed a number of business subjects over the years. He was an individual that I will never forget."

And Senator Alfonse M. D'Amato from Washington wrote, "I would like to offer my heartfelt condolences for your loss and indeed the New York community's loss.

"Mr. Park's life is the epitome of the American success story. Rising form humble beginnings in a rural farm community, his hard work mixed with savvy business skills allowed him to build an extensive communications company. But Mr. Park not only contributed greatly to the strength and vitality of America through his business endeavors, he followed the altruistic spirit that is the hallmark of so many of our entrepreneurial leaders. He remained an active and committed force in education, serving in various capacities with Ithaca College, The University of North Carolina at Chapel Hill, and Cornell University. I salute Roy H. Park for the tremendous contributions he made throughout his life. I know he will be sorely missed."

President James J. Whalen, Ithaca College, said, "Roy had that rare combination of business genius and personal insight that enabled superb service to his industry and to education....He was always there for me and for Ithaca College, and we will miss him very much....Roy had an appreciation of undergraduate education. He really liked students. Most of all he enjoyed challenges. He saw education as a challenge...[we often discussed] what it takes to educate young people. We used to talk all the time about being able to read and write well and articulate. He provided a lot of direction for the institution....Roy was one of those people who liked to cut to the chase. He was a very efficient guy and used his time well. When you were working with Roy, it was high intensity (and) it was stimulating. One time he said something I won't forget. He started to say, 'Time is...' I thought he was going to say, 'Time is money,' but instead he said, 'Time is time.' That was sort of a measure of the guy. That always impressed me a lot."

James J. Whalen – "Part of the Family"

APPENDIX H
EULOGY FOR A FRIEND
By Roy H. Park, Jr.

Jim Frazier was my best friend, and I think he would agree that I was a good friend to him.

We knew each other for almost half a century, over forty-five years, and always kept in touch. We were both beginning our sophomore year in college when we met. He was working his way through The University of North Carolina waiting tables at the Carolina Inn, and I was housed there my first year in a tiny room with a dormer window under a stairwell. My father wanted to make sure I was isolated from any distractions that would take my mind away from my studies. Living by myself, in a small room at the Carolina Inn was sure one way to do it.

As my wife and I flew back from seeing Jim at the nursing home here in Rocky Mount just a month ago, for what was to be the last time, I was flooded by memories of all the happy times Jim and I spent together, starting in those early days at Chapel Hill.

Our friendship grew as we studied together, crammed for exams together, enjoyed sports and campus events, double-dated, and traveled together to various North Carolina campuses.

In those early years, although I called him "Jim" from the start, in his strong and somewhat abrupt manner, he usually referred to me as "Park."

We did just about everything together, and I never saw Jim out of control. He was always even-tempered and steady. Although I had raised a lot of Cain at Cornell before I transferred to Carolina, I knew when I first met him, I had met a mature person, and by that time I had matured enough to welcome a stable friend like him.

Although through our three years at UNC, we always moved together from one rooming house to another, Jim was smart

enough not to be my roommate. He would have had to put up
with possums in the bathtub, a Russian wolfhound sleeping in
his bed, fish tanks, and all-night games of poker, chess, double
solitaire, and Risk.

Although he was at the very least, somewhat opinionated, Jim
never expressed his feelings through emotional outbursts. The
most he might say was "damn" in a quiet way, or "shoot." There
were a lot of worse words I used frequently, and it's a good thing
Jim never picked up on them.

I can assure you that Jim did not suffer fools gladly. Despite
that in Ralph Waldo Emerson's words, "It is one of the blessings
of old friends that you can afford to be stupid with them," one
thing I can say about Jim is that during the entire time I knew him,
I never saw him do anything stupid. He had a low tolerance for
anyone who was a phony or acted foolishly, but once you proved
yourself to Jim, he would always be there for you.

At the Beach, with good friends in September 2000. Behind me in the left
foreground, are Rosalie and Jim Frazier, and circling the table to Jim's right,
Tetlow, Irene and Dave Feldman, Chief Operating Officer of Park Outdoor, and
Trip leaning around his wife, Laura Park

We attended each other's weddings, and through the years
Tetlow and I would look forward to our vacations in Atlantic

Beach where we could spend time with friends, family and Rosalie and Jim. Jim and I shared a love for fishing, and fishing came second only to his devotion to his wife, Rosalie, the great pride he had for his sons, Randy and Lyle, and the delight he felt at the birth of his first grandchild, Thomas.

Every year we would charter a boat and head for the Gulf Stream, and we always made sure we had the essentials. These included tasteless sandwiches sealed in plastic from the Scotsman, plenty of ice, and at least a fifth of bourbon.

I'll never forget one time when the fishing got pretty slow. About half a day had gone by and we had hooked only two fish, and we decided it was time to break out the bourbon. About that time something big hit my line, and turned out to be the most significant catch I ever made during all the years Jim and I fished together. Of course we turned the sailfish loose after the captain measured it for a mounted replica, but we were both proud of the little flag our boat flew of a sailfish upside-down when we pulled back up to the dock. The flag signified we had caught and released a treasured billfish, but the picture of us holding only two fish and a tiny flag did look a little foolish.

Over the years, Jim and Rosalie, Tetlow and I also enjoyed our Sunday drives when we vacationed together, and after enjoying a late brunch would head for the Core Sound Waterfowl Museum on Harker's Island. When he wasn't working, one thing Jim loved to do was to get in his car and explore.

As I said, Jim never let his emotions get the best of him, and he was always "steady as (s)he goes." But I remember his last words to me just a month ago when I left his room. As I was parting, I said "Love you, Jim." He replied, "I love you, too, Roy Park."

Neither Jim nor I are particularly fond of the French, but I have to agree with the French essayist Michel Eyquem de Montaigne, who wrote, "If you press me to say why I loved him, I can say no more than it was because he was he, and I was I."

God rest your soul, Jim Frazier, and good fishing with the Big Guy, forever.

August 17, 2004

The kindness that was Jim during one of our fishing
trips where no dog was left behind.

APPENDIX I
DOG STORY

Following the death of my Russian wolfhound, our family had a number of dogs including a Belgian shepherd, Alaskan malamute, and inherited from a member of our family, a mixed breed that died of old age. After that, we went dogless for a while until 1984 when my mother gave my son an eight-week old female Rottweiler puppy we named Forbes.

Forbes and family at the beach.

We named her after the magazine that ran the interview with my father that resulted in my leaving his company, since she arrived during that time. With her name later being a reminder of an altercation that actually became a turning point for better days, Forbes grew up as a devoted, playful and treasured member of the family.

Sadly, Forbes died of advanced bone cancer at age eleven in my wife's arms on our kitchen floor. When you lose a dog, it rips your heart right out. The wrenching sadness that eats into your soul can only begin to be relieved by the happiness a new puppy can bring.

Forbes showing that a "beached" dog can metamorphose into a "sand shark" dog when she found a way to rise from the depths through hammock netting.

As Dean Koontz recognized in his book *The Darkest Evening of the Year,* "...you can't support the illusion that a dog can be your lifelong companion: There's such beauty in the hard honesty of that, in accepting and giving love while always aware it comes with an unbearable price."[65]

It took me a year to convince Tetlow to get another Rottweiler, but we did. We named the puppy Brook after Tet's father. As Brook grew up and the years went by, we began to remember the sadness at the loss of Forbes and the reality of a dog's short life span. I knew my wife could not again survive the gap between the loss of a beloved dog and the decision to even entertain the idea of going through it again with another.

Brook before we adopted Spencer.

So while Brook was still young, we decided to get a second dog, this time an Australian shepherd, a smaller breed which was said to have the same intelligence (but a much more active temperament) as a Rottweiler. And like a Rottweiler, they also have no tails. Spencer came to us through the Aussie Rescue Society when he was four months old, and Brook immediately adopted him.

So our male Aussie was raised by a female Rottweiler and this upbringing not only had a calming influence on the Aussie, but showed great tolerance on Brook's part, which was a good thing. Because Brook also died with cancer, this time at the early age of seven, leaving the Aussie she mentored grieving and alone.

Raised by a Rottweiler. Spencer the male Australian Shepherd we adopted when he was four months old was raised by Brook, and he mourned her when she passed away after only seven years.

It was then Tetlow and I decided that although dogs, being pack animals, bond well with humans, they do better when they have a second dog to bond with. And we needed that second dog to carry on the tradition of the first dog, and to help us bridge the gap when, God forbid, the oldest went to the place where Will Rogers said he wanted to go to be with all the dogs that have died.

Not easy at first for Spencer to accept an annoying little puppy not much bigger than a rat.

That said, we bought a totally hyperactive eight-week old puppy we named Sadie for Spencer to raise. It was painful for Spencer to put up with at first.

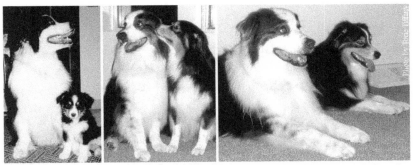

Spencer eventually accepted Sadie and took her under his paw to raise, for which she showed her appreciation.

But then the relationship improved and as Brook had done with him, he raised her as his companion and a responsible part of our family.

But then the inevitable as Spencer grew old and developed cancer at the age of 11 years. After he lost an eye we knew the end was near, so a puppy we named Charlie was added to the family.

The family of three thrived until the invasive nature of cancer no longer allowed Spencer to swallow and Charlie hung out with him until the end.

So again, we have two, but as I write this Sadie is deaf and wobbly at the age of 15 and Charlie at 7, is some 50 in dog years. So soon we may face the hard work and happiness a new puppy can bring.

We realize the need to carry on the tradition of a two-dog bond to avoid the heart-wrenching confusion the surviving dog feels when its partner disappears and the sorrow you feel inside when this happens from which it's almost impossible to recover.

APPENDIX J
TRIAD GRANTS
CONTINUING THE ROY H. PARK
LEGACY

Roy H. Park's commitment to democracy, free enterprise, and freedom of religion and thought are the values which drive the philanthropic mission of Triad Foundation, Inc. in its grant-making.

In our efforts, we are guided by his entrepreneurial values, hard work, perseverance and leadership, his humility, integrity, creativity and willingness to take responsible risks, and by his sense of charitable and community responsibility.

Triad Foundation, Inc. makes grants primarily in higher education for graduate fellowships carrying his name, for scientific research and public policy institutions that represent his legacy, as well as for educational programs serving children and youth development, health and human services, animal welfare, and marine and tropical ecology.

—Triad Foundation, Inc. Values Statement

Animal and Marine Welfare
Amber Lake Wildlife Refuge and Rehabilitation Center, Inc.
Andrew Harris Foundation, Inc.
Aussie Rescue and Placement Helpline, Inc.
Billfish Foundation, Inc., The
Broome County Humane Society and Relief Association
Cayuga Dog Rescue
Coral Restoration Foundation, Inc.
Cornell University / College of Veterinary Medicine
Cornell University / Laboratory of Ornithology
Cornell University / Shoals Marine Laboratory
Corolla Wild Horse Fund, Inc.
Desert Cry Wildlife, Inc.
Dreamchaser PMU Rescue and Rehabilitation
Florida Aquarium, Inc.
Friends of the Rosamond Gifford Zoo at Burnet Park, Inc.
Friends of Bermuda Underwater Exploration Institute
Friends of Orange County Animal Shelter
Friends of Stokes Shelter, Inc.
Humane Society
Lowry Park Zoological Society, Inc.
Marine Aquarium Council
Marine Stewardship Council, Ltd.
Messinger Woods Wildlife Care and Education Center, Inc.
Misfits Animal Rescue, 2nd Sanctuary, Inc.
Mote Marine Laboratory, Inc.
National Aquarium in Baltimore, Inc.
New England Aquarium Corporation
North Carolina Aquarium Society / Pine Knoll Shores
North Carolina Zoological Society
Ocean Conservancy, Inc.
Peaceful Valley Donkey Rescue, Inc.
Reef Relief, Inc.
Reef Environmental Education Foundation
Rottweiler Recovery Foundation, Inc.
Sea to Shore Alliance
Shark Savers, Inc.
Solutions to Avoid Red Tide, Inc.
South Carolina Society for Prevention and Cruelty to Animals
Suncoast Humane Society
Thoroughbred Retirement Foundation
Tiger Creek Wildlife Preserve
Tiger Haven
Tompkins County SPCA

Town of Pine Knoll Shores Municipal Dog Park
Utica Zoological Society
Veterinary Care Foundation

Triad Foundation Inc. headquarters in Ithaca. Front row: Executive Director **Melinda Oakes**; Administrative Assistant **Isabella Corina**; Assistant to President **Jennifer Cottrell**; Associate Director **Stephanie Parente**; Grants Assistant **Linda Swan**. Top row: Triad Consultant **Ezra Cornell**; Communications and Program Director **Jeff True**; aquarist and horticulturist **Mary Alyce Kobler** and Controller **John Dentes**.

Children and Youth
A Child's Place of Charlotte, Inc.
Alexander Youth Network
All Sports Community Service, Inc.
Baden-Powell Council, Boy Scouts of America
Big Brothers Big Sisters
Boys and Girls Club
Camelot Community Care, Inc.
Caroline After School Program, Inc.
Cascadilla Boat Club, Ltd.
Center for Transformative Action/Vitamin L
Challenge, N/A/Pure Fashion
Champions for Children, Inc.

Charlotte Mecklenburg Police Athletic League, Inc.
Child Care Services Association
Child Development Council of Central New York
Children for Children
Children's Dream Fund
Children's Flight of Hope, Inc.
Children's Home, Inc.
Children's Theatre of Charlotte, Inc.
City Federation of Women's Organizations
City of Ithaca—Ithaca Youth Bureau
College of the Holy Cross/Holy Cross Club Hockey
Computer Mentors Group, Inc.
Congressional Sports for Charity
Cornell Cooperative Extension
Cornell University/Team and Leadership Center
Corporation to Develop Communities of Tampa, Inc.
Creative Kids Count, Inc.
Drop-In Children's Center
Elon Homes for Children
Enfield Community Council
Family Center, The
Family Enrichment Network
Family First
Florida Elite Basketball, Inc.
Frameworks of Tampa Bay, Inc. (formerly OPBI, Inc.)
Freedom Playground Foundation, Inc.
Friends of the CanTeen, Inc.
Friends of Ithaca Youth Bureau
Gary Koch Invitational Pro-Am, Inc.
Girls Incorporated of Central New York
Girls on the Run International
Girl Scouts of NYPENN Pathways, Inc.
Girls Talk, NC, Inc.
Global Giving Foundation
Ithaca High School Booster Club, Inc.
Lansing Community Council
Madison County Children's Camp
Mary Lee's House
Metropolitan Ministries, Inc.
Momentous Institute
Myers Park United Methodist Church
Newfield Project Graduation
New York State Department of Agriculture and Markets
New York State Sheriff's Association Institute, Inc.

North Carolina Partnership for Children
OASIS Network of New Tampa
Ophelia Project
Orphan Society of America
Pace Center for Girls, Inc.
Palma Ceia Little League
Pat's Place Child Advocacy Center
Positive Coaching Alliance
Relatives, Inc., The
Search Institute, The
Seigle Avenue Partners, Inc.
Seven Lakes Girl Scout Council, Inc.
Special Olympics of New York, Inc.
Tandem Productions, Inc./Beauty and the Beast Storytellers
Tampa Bay Little League, Inc.
Tampa Fastbreak Youth Basketball Club, Inc.
Tampa Knights Futbol Club
Tampa Metropolitan Area YMCA, Inc.
Thompson Children's Home
Tompkins Community Action
Town of Lansing
Town of Newfield
Twin Rivers Council, Boy Scouts of America
United Family Services, Inc.
University of Alaska at Fairbanks/The Boys Project
Uptown Day Shelter, Inc.
Victory Junction Gang Camp
Village of Dryden
Voices for Children of Hillsborough County, Inc.
YMCA
Young Life / Tampa Urban Young Life

Education and Culture
74 Media, Inc., The
Academy Prep Center of Tampa, Inc.
Achieve Tampa Bay (United Cerebral Palsy of Tampa Bay)
Alliance for Public Schools Foundation, Inc.
Alliance for School Choice, Inc.
American Council of Trustees and Alumni
American Islamic Congress
American Woman's Economic Development Corporation
Andreas H. Bechtler Foundation
Arnot Art Museum
Arts & Science Council Charlotte Mecklenberg, Inc.

Arts Council for Chautaugua County
Arts of the Southern Finger Lakes
Ashland University
Aurora Free Library Association
Auburn Public Theater, Inc.
Bill of Rights Institute
Bob Moog Memorial Foundation
Boca Grande Area Chamber of Commerce Scholarship Fund
Canterbury School
Carolina Artist Studio Gallery, Inc.
Cazenovia Collge
Center for the Arts at Ithaca
Central Piedmont Community College
Central New York Community Arts Council
Central New York Jazz Arts Foundation, Inc.
ChairScholars Foundation, Inc.
Charlotte Country Day School
Charlotte Symphony Ochestra Society, Inc.
Chemung County Performing Arts, Inc. / Clemens Center
Children's Scholarship Fund-Charlotte
Cicero Historical Society
Clare Boothe Luce Policy Institute
Classroom Central, Inc.
College Mentors for Kids, Inc.
Communities in Schools/Charlotte-Mecklenburg
Community Arts Partnership/Tompkins County
Community School of Music and Arts
Community School of the Arts
Cornell University
Cornell University Campaign
Cornell University/Bailey Hall Plaza
Cornell University/Big Red Leadership Institute
Cornell University /Campaign for Big Red Hockey
Cornell/Department of Athletics & Physical Education
Cornell/Department of Mechanical & Aerospace Engineering
Cornell University / Entrepreneurship@Cornell
Cornell University / Entrepreneurship and Personal Enterprise
Cornell University / Herbert F. Johnson Museum of Art
Cornell University / Johnson Graduate School of Management
Cornell University / Cornell Law School
Cornell University / Office of Donor Relations
Cornell University / Presidential Research Scholars Program
Cornell University / Prison Education Program
Cornell University / Program on Freedom and Free Societies

Cornell University / SC Johnson College of Business
Cornell University/School of Hotel Administration
Cornell University / Student Activities Office
Cornell University / Student Aid Development and Stewardship
Corning Painted Post Historical Society
Corporate Development Committee of Lansing Central Schools
Cortland Repertory Theatre
Council of Urban Professionals/Rise to College
Cristo Rey Tampa High School at Mary Help of Christians, Inc.
Crossroads Corporation for Affordable Housing and Community
Development
David A. Straz Center for Performing Arts, Inc.
David Horowitz Freedom Center
Discovery Place, Inc.
Discovery Trail
Displaced Homemakers Center in Tompkins County, Inc.
Dress for Success
Dryden Central School District
Duke University Libraries
Edith B. Ford Memorial Library
Education Equals Hope, Inc.
Educational Foundation, Inc.
Elizabeth Ann Clune Montessori School of Ithaca
Elon University
Empire State Special Needs Experience, Inc.
Eric Carle Museum of Picture Book Art, Inc.
Family Reading Partnership
Finger Lakes Musical Theatre Festival
Finger Lakes Re-Use
Finger Lakes Wine Center
First Tee of Charlotte
Foundation for Excellence in Education
Foundation for Individual Rights in Education, Inc.
Foundation for Outdoor Advertising Research and Education
Franklin County Public Library
Fred & Harriett Taylor Memorial Library
Freedom Alliance
Freedom School Partners, Inc.
Friends of Lansing Community Library Center
Friends of the Daniel Parrish Witter Agricultural Museum
Friends of the Groton Public Library
Furman University
Gary Sinise Charitable Foundation
Gasparilla Island Maritime Museum

Golden Opportunity GO, Inc.
H. B. Plant High School
Hillsborough County Public Schools
Hillsborough Education Foundation, Inc.
Historic Ithaca, Inc.
History Center in Tompkins County
Homer-Cortland Community Agency
Hopkins Street Community Center, Inc.
Hunter R. Rawlings III Cornell Presidential Research Scholars
Immaculate Conception School
Independent College Fund of New York, Inc.
Institute for Energy Research
Institute for Humane Studies
Intercollegiate Studies Institute
Interlochen Center for the Arts
Iraq and Afghanistan Veterans of America
Island School, Inc.
Ithaca Aviation Heritage Foundation, Inc.
Ithaca City School District
Ithaca City School District/Belle Sherman Elementary School
Ithaca College
Ithaca College/Community Fireworks
Ithaca Montessori School
Ithaca Public Education Initiative
Jack Miller Center
James B. Hunt, Jr. Institute for Educational Leadership
    and Policy Foundation, Inc.
Jazztorian, Inc.
Johann Fust Community Library of Boca Grande
John Crosland School, The
Johnson and Wales University
Kansas State University Foundation
KIPP Charlotte
Lansing Central School District
Lansing Community Council
Lansing Theater and Performing Arts, Inc.
Leadership Institute, The
Learning Collaborative, The
Learning Disabilities Association of Central New York, Inc.
Levine Museum of the New South, Inc.
Light in Winter
Lincoln Institute for Research and Education
Louisburg College
Lynnwood Foundation, The

Management Assistance Program, Inc.
Manhattan Christian Academy
McColl Center for Visual Art
McDonogh School
Mint Museum Auxiliary
Mint Museum of Art
Montpelier Foundation
Muse America
Museum of Modern Art
Myers Park Presbyterian Church Pre-School
National Park Foundation / Flight 93 National Monument
National Press Foundation
Network of Enlightened Women
Newfield Central School District
Newfield Public Library
New York Historical Society
North Carolina Community Sailing and Rowing
North Carolina Dance Theatre
North Carolina Partnership for Children
North Carolina Performing Arts Center at Charlotte Foundation
North Carolina State University
North Syracuse Central School District
Onondaga Community College Foundation, Inc.
Opera Carolina
Peachtown Elementary School
Peter M. Goodrich Memorial Foundation
Plant High School Academic Foundation, Inc.
Plant High School Athletics Foundation, Inc.
Plant High School PTSA
Powers Library Association
Powerstories Theatre of Tampa Bay, Inc.
Public Library of Charlotte and Mecklenburg County
Purple Heart Homes
Queens University of Charlotte
R. Bruce Irons Camp Fund
Regents of the University of California, The
Roberson Memorial, Inc.
Roberson Museum and Science Center
Robert C. Parker School
Robert W. Woodruff Arts Center
Running to Places Theater Company, Ltd
Salesian Sisters of Tampa, Inc.
Science Discovery Center of Tompkins County (Sciencenter)
Shared Journey's

Sigma Phi Educational Foundation, Inc.
Society of Illustrators
Southern Cayuga Central School Parent Teacher Organization
Special Operations Warrior Foundation
Spencer Van Etten Central School District
St. John Presbyterian Learning Center
St. Mary's Episcopal Day School
St. Peter Claver School
State Theatre of Ithaca
Step Up for Students, Inc.
Students for Liberty
Syracuse University/Institute for Veterans and Military Families
Tampa Bay History Center, Inc.
Tampa Museum of Art
TCSD Foundation
Teach for America
Teens, Inc.
Theatre Charlotte
Thomas Moore College of Liberal Arts, Inc.
The Hill Center, Inc.
The Tampa Theatre, Inc.
The University of North Carolina at Chapel Hill
The University of North Carolina at Chapel Hill/Department of
    Computer Science
The University of North Carolina at Chapel Hill/School of
    Journalism and Mass Communication
The University of North Carolina at Chapel Hill/The Triad
    Foundation First Generation Fund
The University of North Carolina at Chapel Hill/The Triad
    Foundation Interns in Admissions Communications
The University of North Carolina at Greensboro
The University of North Carolina School of the Arts Foundation, Inc.
Tompkins Cortland Community College Foundation
Tompkins County Public Library Foundation
Tompkins Learning Partners
Tompkins-Seneca-Tioga BOCES
Tri-Cities Opera Company, Inc.
Trumansburg Central School District Foundation
Trustees of the Lawrenceville School
United States Holocaust Memorial Council
University Cooperative Nursery School, Inc.
University of Florida Foundation, Inc.
University of South Florida Foundation, Inc. / Tampa Bay Area
Virginia Foundation for the Humanities and Public Policy

Writing Project
Village at Ithaca
William A. Farnsworth Library and Art Museum, Inc.

Wings for Kids, Inc.
Wings of Eagles Discovery Center
Wounded Warrior Project, Inc.
Young America's Foundation
Young Entrepreneurs Academy

Faith Communities
American Jewish Committee
Cornell Catholic Community
Crossroads Life Center, Inc.
Danby Federated Church
Emerald Isle Baptist Church
First Congregational Church of Ithaca / United Church of Christ
First Presbyterian Church of Ithaca
Good Shepherd Catholic Community
Greenville Presbyterian Theological Seminary
Hillel: The Foundation for Jewish Campus Life
Immaculate Conception Church
Jesuit Retreat House
Museum of Jewish Heritage
Myers Park Presbyterian Church
Our Lady of Mercy Parish / Boca Grande Child Care Center
Palma Ceia Presbyterian Church, Inc.
Roman Catholic Diocese of Rochester
St. Andrew's Church
St. Anthony of Padua Shrine Church
St. Catherine of Siena Church
St. Francis Foundation, Inc. / Everyday Blessings
St. John's Church
St. Mary's Episcopal Church of Tampa, Florida, Inc.
St. Paul Center for Biblical Theology
Temple Beth-El
Trinity Lutheran Church of Ithaca
University United Methodist Church
West Huntsville Church of Christ

Government and Citizenship
Alliance Defense Fund
American Business Defense Foundation
American Center for Law and Justice
American Civil Rights Union

American Conservative Union Foundation
American Enterprise Institute
American Land Foundation
American Legislative Exchange Council
American Spectator Foundation
American Transparency
Americans for Prosperity Foundation
America's Future Foundation
Capital Research Center
Center for American Greatness
Center for Class Action Fairness
Center for Competitive Politics
Center for Consumer Freedom, The
Center for Governmental Research
Center for Immigration Studies
Center for Urban Renewal and Education
Citizens Against Government Waste
Citizens United Foundation
Civitas Institute, Inc.
Committee for a Constructive Tomorrow
Competitive Enterprise Institute
Daily Caller News Foundation
Energy and Environment Legal Institute
Empire Center for Public Policy
Foundation for Government Accountability
Foundation for Economic Education, Inc.
Franklin Center for Government and Public Integrity
Free Congress Research and Education Foundation, Inc.
Freedom Works Foundation
Genesis Institute
Government and Justice Center, Inc.
Frontier Lab, The
Heartland Institute
Heritage Foundation
Independent Women's Forum
Institute for Justice
Institute for Responsible Citizenship
John Locke Foundation
Judicial Watch, Inc.
Liberty Day Institute
Manhattan Institute for Policy Research
Mountain States Legal Foundation
National Center for Police Defense, Inc.
National Center for Public Policy Research

National Legal & Policy Center
National Right to Work Legal Defense and Education Foundation, Inc.
National Taxpayer Union Foundation
National Women's Hall of Fame, Inc.
Patrick Henry Center for Individual Liberty
Prager University Foundation
Project Veritas
Property and Environmental Research Center
Reason Foundation
Reclaim New York, Inc.
Southeastern Legal Foundation, Inc.
State Policy Network
Tax Foundation, Inc.
Think Freely Media, Inc.
Washington Legal Foundation

Health and Medicine
Achieve Tampa Bay (United Cerebral Palsy of Tampa Bay)
Alcohol and Drug Council of Tompkins County
Alzheimer's Association and Related Disorders Association
American Cancer Society-Southern New York Region
American Council on Science and Health
American Heart Association
Angel Flight New England
Asthma and Allergy Foundation of America
Beachtree Care Center
Boca Grande Health Clinic
Boca Grande Health Clinic Foundation, Inc.
Bright Focus Foundation
Cancer 101, Inc.
Cancer Resource Center of the Finger Lakes
Carolina Breast Friends
Carolina's Healthcare Foundation, Inc.
Carteret County General Hospital Foundation Corporation
Cayuga Addiction Recovery Services
Cayuga Medical Center Foundation
Central New York Area Health Education Center
Chicago Medical Innovations
Children's Hospital Corporation
Christopher and Dana Reeves Foundation
Compos Mentis
Cornell University/Department of Neuro Biology and Behavior
Cornell University/Student & Academic Services
Cornell University/Weill Cornell Medical College

Cortland Prevention Resources
Cystic Fibrosis Foundation
Enable / United Cerebral Palsy and Handicapped Children's
Association of Syracuse, Inc.
Epilepsy Foundation of Northeastern New York, Inc.
Finger Lakes Independence Center
Fistula Foundation
Foundation of St. Mary's Hospital at Amsterdam, Inc.
Food Allergy and Anaphylaxis Network, Inc.
Greek Peak Adaptive Snowsports/Disabled Sports USA
H. Lee Moffitt Cancer Center & Research Institute Found.
Hospicare and Palliative Care Services of Tompkins County
Hospitality House of Charlotte
ICSD/South Hill School
Independent Institute
Ithaca Breast Cancer Alliance
Ithaca Health Alliance
Ithaca Triathlon Club
International Food Information Council
Juvenile Diabetes Research Foundation
Juvenile Diabetes Research Foundation International
KEYS Corp.
Leukemia & Lymphoma Society
March of Dimes Birth Defects National Foundation
Medical Foundation of North Carolina, Inc.
Memorial Sloan-Kettering Cancer Center
Mercy Flight Central, Inc.
Mira's Movement
More Health, Inc.
Morehead Memorial Hospital/Rockingham County Student
    Health Centers
National Breast Cancer Foundation, Inc.
National Foundation of Dentistry/Dental Lifeline Network
National Kidney Foundation, Inc.
National Multiple Sclerosis Society
Newton-Wellesley Hospital Charitable Foundation
New York Chiropractic College
Novant Health Foundation Presbyterian Medical Center
Population Services International
Receptions for Research - the Greg Olsen Foundation, Inc.
Reconstruction Home, Inc.
Retina Associates, Inc. / SRA Foundation
RHA Howell Care Centers, Inc.
Rural Health Network of South Central New York

Shelter Health Services
Smile Train, Inc.
Southern Cayuga Instant Aid
Special Olympics New York, Inc.
St. Elizabeth Medical Center Foundation, Inc.
St. Joseph's Hospital Health Center Foundation, Inc.
St. Joseph's Hospital of Tampa Foundation, Inc.
St. Jude Children's Research Hospital
St. Baldrick's Foundation
Starlight Children's Foundation
Susan G. Komen for the Cure
Sydney's Angels for Autism, Inc.
Thompson Child and Family Focus
Trustees of Columbia University in the City of New York
University of Texas Foundation / MD Anderson Cancer Center
Upstate Foundation, Inc.
Visiting Nurse Service of Ithaca and Tompkins County

Human Services
Access to Independence of Cortland County, Inc.
AHA Foundation
Alcohol and Drug Council of Tompkins County
Alpha House of Tampa, Inc.
Alternatives Venture Fund, Inc.
American Red Cross
American Red Cross International Response Fund
Angels of Mercy, Inc.
Area Congregations Together, Inc.
Autism Foundation of the Carolinas
Bed for Kids, Inc.
Better Housing for Tompkins County, Inc.
Birthright of Ithaca
Boca Grande Woman's Club, Inc.
Brooktondale Community Center, Inc.
Canine Companions for Independence
Camp Good Days and Special Times, Inc.
CARE
CaringBridge Corporation
Caring House, Inc.
CASA of Johnson & Wyandotte Counties, Inc.
Catherine's House, Inc.
Catholic Charities of Tompkins-Tioga
Catholic Relief Services
Central New York Ronald McDonald House Charities, Inc.

Centre for Women, The
Challenge Industries
Challenge, N.A., Inc.
Charlotte Center for Urban Ministry, Inc.
Charlotte Family Housing
Children's Dream Fund
City Federation of Women's Organizations
Clear Path for Veterans, Inc.
Clothes to Kids, Inc.
Common Grounds of Charlotte
Community Dispute Resolution Center
Cortland Prevention Resources
Created Women, Inc.
Crisis Assistance Ministry
Crisis Pregnancy Center of Finger Lakes, Inc.
Crossroads Corporation/Community Development
Crystal Coast Hospice House
DC Central Kitchen
Danielle House, Inc.
Day Care and Child Care Development Council of Tompkins
County, Inc.
Down Syndrome Association of Greater Charlotte
Drop-In Children's Center
Elizabeth Brewster House Foundation, Inc.
Elmcrest Children's Center
Faith in the Family International
Families and Children Under Stress, Inc.
Family and Children's Service of Ithaca
Family Services of Chemung County
Feeding America Tampa Bay
Finger Lakes Musical Theatre Festival
Food Bank of the Southern Tier
Foodnet, Nutrition for the Elderly in Tompkins County, Inc.
Foster Care to Success
Franziska Racker Centers
Freedom Guide Dogs for the Blind
Friends of Boca Grande Community Center
Gadabout Transportation Services
Genesis Group, Vision to Reality, Inc.
Gift of Adoption Fund, Inc.
Give an Hour Nonprofit Corporation
GlamourGals Foundation, Inc.
Good Fellows Club, Inc.
Goodwill Industries of the Southern Piedmont

Habitat for Humanity of Charlotte
Harvest Center, The
Hebron Colony Ministries, Inc.
Heifer International
Hope for the Warriors
Hope Way Foundation
Hospice and Palliative Care, Inc.
Human Services Coalition of Tompkins County, Inc.
Human Rights Foundation
Immaculate Conception Food Pantry
Inter-Faith Council for Social Service
Intrepid Fallen Heroes Fund
Ithacare Center Service Company/Longview
Junior League of Tampa
K9s for Warriors
KinderMourn, Inc.
King Ferry Food Pantry
Knights of Columbus Charities, Inc.
Ladies Union Benevolent Society
Lamplighters, Inc.
Lansing United Methodist Church
Learning Web Inc., The
Light on the Hill, Inc.
Loaves and Fishes of Tompkins County, Inc.
Louise du Pont Crowninshield Community House, Inc.
Love Knows No Bounds
Love Living at Home
Meals on Wheels of Tampa, Inc.
Men's Shelter of Charlotte, Inc.
National Alliance on Mental Health - Finger Lakes Chapter
Nest Foundation, Inc.
New Creation Outreach, Inc.
New Life Ministries of New England, Inc.
One Mission Society
One Student
On-Site Volunteer Services, Inc.
Operation Homefront
Orphan Foundation of America
Pat's Place
Planned Parenthood of the Southern Finger Lakes
Redeeming Joy, Inc
Ronald McDonald House of Charlotte
Safe Alliance
Salvation Army

Samaritan Counseling Center of Tampa, Inc.
Samaritan's Purse
SECU Family House at UNC Hospitals
Senior Services, Inc.
Service Year, Inc.
Shelter Box USA
Social Ventures, Inc./Friendship Donations Network
Southeastern Guide Dogs, Inc.
Spring of Tampa Bay, Inc., The
Start Right Now
Suicide Prevention of Tompkins County, Inc.
Sydney's School for Autism, Inc.
Tampa General Hospital Foundation
Tompkins County Department of Social Services
Tompkins County Senior Citizens Council
Trinity Café, Inc.
Twin Tiers Honor Flight
Union County Community Shelter
United Way
Unity House of Cayuga County
Varna Community Association, Inc.
Venison Donation Coalition
Wheels of Success, Inc.
Women's Opportunity Center

Media
American Studies Center / Radio America
Carolina Liberty Foundation
Charlotte Regional Partnership
Eternal World Television Network
Film / Video Arts, Inc.
Foundation for Cultural Review/The New Criterion
Free to Choose Network
Fund for American Studies
Just Facts, Inc.
La Mancha Media
Media Research Center
Mission Film Works
Moving Picture Institute
National Review Institute
Society of Illustrators, Inc.
Watch What Counts

Natural Resources/Environmental Education
Barrier Island Parks Society, Inc.
Bogue Banks Beach Preservation Association, Inc.
Cayuga Nature Center, Inc.
Cayuga Lake Watershed Networks, Inc.
Centers for Nature Education, Inc.
Central New York Resource Conservation and Development
Project, Inc.
Cornell University / Center for the Environment
Cornell University / Cornell Botanic Gardens
Crooked Trails
Danby Community Park Association
Discovery Trail, Inc.
Dump and Run
Fred L. Waterman Conservation Education Center, Inc.
Friends of Stewart Park
Gasparilla Island Conservation and Improvement Association
Gasparilla Island Maritime Museum
Hobart and William Smith Colleges
Ithaca Children's Garden, Inc.
Lime Hollow Nature Center
Marie Selby Botanical Gardens, Inc.
National Audubon Society—New York
North Carolina Beach, Inlet and Waterways Association
North Carolina Shore and Beach Preservation Association
Property and Environmental Research Center (PERC)
Tampa BayWatch, Inc.
Tanglewood Nature Center and Museum
Tompkins County Chamber of Commerce Foundation/Cayuga
Waterfront Trail
Tompkins County Chamber of Commerce Foundation /Sustainable
Tompkins
Town of Caroline
Tree Foundation, Inc.
Wing Haven Foundation, Inc.

Philanthropy
Association of Fundraising Professionals / Finger Lakes Chapter
Association of Small Foundations
Central New York Community Foundation, Inc.
Committee to Encourage Corporate Philanthropy
Community Foundation of Tompkins County
Community Foundation of Tampa Bay, Inc.
Cornell University/Public Service Center

Council on Foundations
Donors Choose, Inc.
Florida Philanthropic Network
Foundation for the Carolinas
Foundation Financial Officers Group
Foundation of the State University of New York
NY Funders Alliance
Ithaca Rotary Charitable Trust
National Center for Family Philanthropy
Nonprofit Leadership Center of Tampa Bay, Inc.
Observer Charities, Inc.
Philanthropic Collaborative, The
Philanthropy Roundtable
Rochester Grantmakers Forum
Rotary Foundation, The
Southeastern Council of Foundations, Inc.
The Giving Back Fund, Inc.
Tompkins County Chamber of Commerce Foundation
Women's Impact Fund

Public Safety
Cayuga Heights Police Department
Cayuga's Watchers, Inc.
Charlotte Fire Department
Charlotte Mecklenburg Police Department
City of Ithaca Fire Department
City of Ithaca Police Department
Cornell University Campus Police
Danby Fire District
Enfield Volunteer Fire Co., Inc.
Gulf Coast Community Foundation of Venice, Inc.
Jon Francis Foundation
Lansing Fire Department
Neptune Hose Company No. 1, Inc.
North Area Volunteer Ambulance Corps, Inc.
North Arlington Volunteer Emergency Squad
Raleigh Police Memorial Foundation, Inc.
Salter Path Fire and Rescue Department
Tompkins County Sheriff's Office
Town of Chapel Hill Police Department
Town of Indian Beach Fire Department
Town of Pine Knoll Shores Police Department
Town of Pine Knoll Shores Public Safety Department

Varna Volunteer Fire Department
Vestal Fire Department
Village of Cayuga Heights Fire Department
Village of Cayuga Heights Police Department
Village of Lansing

Science and Research
American Chestnut Foundation
American Society of Plant Biologists
Boyce Thompson Institute for Plant Research, Inc.
Cornell University / College of Agriculture and Life Sciences
Cornell University / Cornell Alliance for Science
Cornell University / Department of Biological and
Elm Research Institute
Environmental Engineering
Paleontological Research Institution

APPENDIX K
CORNELL PARK FELLOWS
WELCOMING TALK
August 24, 2015

The Dean and I bid welcome to our new Roy H. Park Leadership Fellows. So begins the start of your new life.

You've had a chance to meet your colleagues and the preceding class of Park Fellows and I am sure the bond between the 48 of you will grow. The last 17 years has resulted in 489 Johnson School Roy H. Park Fellows and another 402 from the School of Media and Journalism at the University of North Carolina. Your time here will fly by a lot quicker than you may think. I predict that you feel regret, and not relief, when it is over and you head out on your new careers.

Speaking of which, you should know that the last two years has seen 100% employment for graduating Park Fellows and it's a good time to be one when a student loan for an Ivy League MBA can run over $120,000. Be comforted that you will leave the Johnson School of Graduate Management basically free of this burden and with sound job opportunities.

There are entrepreneurs in this room and there will be many more among when you graduate. My father was one and his success is why our Foundation is able to award these fellowships. He came down from a farm in the hills of North Carolina at the age of 16 to put himself through college just in time to graduate at the height of the Great Depression. He used his education to survive at tough times and to succeed with one entrepreneurial idea after another. This along with perseverance and just plain hard work.

You may have seen in my book one of his favorite quotes written by the late Peter Kiewit, entrepreneur and former owner of the Omaha World-Herald, the largest employee-employer-owned newspaper in the United States:

I do not choose to be a common man. It is my right to be uncommon if I can. I seek opportunity, not security. I want to that the calculated risk; to dream and build; to fail and succeed. I prefer the challenges of life to the calm state of Utopia. I will never cower before any master nor bend to any threat. It is my heritage to stand erect, proud, unafraid, to think and act for myself, to enjoy the benefit of my creation and to face the world boldly and say "This I have done."

You have earned a place as a Park Leadership Fellow since you already represent a clear success in American society. But each of you has also developed an even clearer idea on the contributions you would like to make in our society. And so you come to Johnson with proven track records, to provide a meaningful service while preparing for your new role. And then you will go back into the world to fulfill your dreams and to inspire the dreams of others.

And when you reach for the ceiling above the floor you stand on, that ceiling will become your new floor, and the next ceiling another floor you will reach. I know you will conquer each ceiling you encounter in building your own towers of success, and tread proudly on those floors by prescriptive right.

And when that happens, don't forget the Johnson School, and the bonding, respect and lover you will have had for your time here, and be proud of the Park Fellow title you carry into your new life.

APPENDIX L
RUNNING A FAMILY BUSINESS
AN INTERVIEW

*In September 2014, I received a request for an interview from a student in his Junior year at the Dyson School of Applied Economics and Management located in the College of Agriculture and Life Sciences at Cornell University. His assignment for the Business Management and Organization course in the school, which is the No. 2 ranked undergraduate business school[66] in the United States, was to **ask someone in a managerial position in a business what is the most challenging aspect of management and why.** The interview as reported by David A. Relihan follows.*

"Be kind, for every one you meet is fighting a hard battle." Not what I was expecting to hear from the CEO of an advertising business and graduate of Cornell's Johnson Graduate School of Management. As a highly successful businessman in his own right, Roy Park Jr. was one of the last people I would expect to advocate such a seemingly "soft" approach to business and business management. However, as I was soon to learn, the "softness" in his approach is really just empathy. Furthermore, empathy and the willingness and ability to apply it to professional life is absolutely essential in dealing with the biggest challenge in management from Mr. Park's perspective.

The most challenging aspect of management according to Park is not represented by algorithmic financial models. It is not the third variable in the latest formula and it can't be tabulated on an excel spreadsheet. The most challenging aspect of management is something much more fickle, ephemeral, and ultimately, much more rewarding. Simply put, it's people.

The first few seconds of my phone-call with Mr. Park immediately put me at ease, and set the tone for the rest of the interview. His warm tone and easygoing manner were readily apparent, and his anecdotal style of narration foreshadowed his emerging philosophy on business, and on life.

Going into the interview I was all set on "getting down to brass tacks" and using plenty of buzzwords such as "leverage" and "innovate," in an attempt to connect on a professional level with Mr. Park. Instead, he insisted on first providing me with his backstory, assuring me that context is as important to understanding as discussing the actual issue at hand.

As a student at Cornell, Park flunked out due to the youthful propensity to chase girls and good times instead of good grades. He ended up instead finishing his undergraduate education at UNC, Chapel Hill, majoring in journalism. Accepted by the Johnson School at Cornell, after receiving his MBA he went on to work for some of the premier advertising agencies in NY, Miami, and North Carolina for the next seven years. He was then asked to take over the outdoor advertising division of his father's media-empire. He returned to Ithaca to find a business in shambles, ministered to by a demoralized work force and poised to be consumed by the unions in both upstate NY and Pennsylvania.

This is when Park's nascent philosophy on empathy's place in business really came into focus. In order to turn his company around and wrest control away from the unionizing forces daily beleaguering it, Park found that he had to win the trust of his employees back. In order to do this, he instituted a policy of "treating your company as your family." This included assigning achievable goals and consistently rewarding their completion, as well as appointing managers who shared his vision. Slowly, trust was re-established between the employees and management, having been so carelessly squandered in the past by the previous administration's unofficial policy of neglect and indifference.

Mr. Park concluded the interview by pointing out that under his administration, employee turnover had reached an all-time low, while profits have steadily increased from the dark days with an enervated work force.

David Feldman, Mr. Park's Chief Operating Officer, enthusiastically shared both his and Mr. Park's vision for the future direction of the company, including plans for a greater presence in digital online billboards that maximize revenue by cycling through different advertisers in the same advertising space.

The optimism and genuine concern for their employees welfare from both Park and Feldman was palpable, and, from a purely visceral standpoint, I would concur in that their current successes are almost wholly derived from Roy Park Jr's philosophy, by way of Plato, that "everyone is fighting a hard battle" and that therefore an attempt to understand and empathize should be the first step to gaining trust, and with it, loyalty and commitment to cooperate and work towards a common objective, be it in business or in life.

By. David A. Relihan

APPENDIX M
EULOGY FOR A MOTHER
By Roy H. Park, Jr.
June 30, 2016

Dorothy Dent Park.
October 8, 1912-June 18, 2016.

Our mother, as most of you know, was never called "mother" or mom" because my grandmother, teaching me to talk and trying to say "Dorothy," it came out "Dottie," and it stuck. Dottie felt it kept her the way she always felt. Forever young.

She met my father while she was still a Junior at Meredith College on a double blind date set up by her cousin. My father was not intended to be her date. But somehow she told me people got switched around and they both ended up in the back seat together. She suspected he planned it all along. On their first date, she told me, she didn't like him from the start. She loved to dance and learned he couldn't, and he also had the effrontery to tell her he intended to marry her.

"Boy was he persistent" Dottie told me. Among the strategies he used to eliminate his competition was to pull up in front of the fraternities whose members he knew she had been dating. This left her in full view in his convertible when he told her he had to run in to see somebody. He showered her with baby chicks and rabbits at Easter, and after he prevailed upon his secretary to keep it in her bathtub for a week, gave her a Pomeranian on her birthday. But it all worked and they were married in 1936.

I came along two years later, and from the age of four when we arrived in Ithaca, I was dragged along on her downtown shopping trips. Dottie was always dressed to the nines and she maintained the Southern tradition of wearing hats, from pill boxes with artificial cherries dangling down the sides to a Robin Hood hat with pheasant feathers sticking up in the air. These were during the days when there were department stores and grocery stores, five and dimes, bakeries, butcher shops and women's clothing stores on State Street. But she never worried I could be lost or separated since I could always spot her hat from anywhere.

Flash forward to my pre-teen years. Every Christmas my father would take me and head to Holly's, the fanciest women's store in town. There to pick out negligees for my mother of the Victoria's Secret sort, which after Christmas Dottie would promptly return. Their taste in sleepwear ran in different directions, and the routine was always the same.

Flash forward, again, to my early teens. To establish the Duncan Hines food products line, Dottie and Pops took the road with a vengeance along with Hines and his wife to promote "Duncan Hines Days," and for three months I was taken out of school to go along. Covering the country, my mother was driving down a back road in our convertible one day with my father reading newspapers spread up and open on the passenger side. With her view blinded, Dottie pulled into the intersection of a major highway and a car crashed into the rear of our vehicle. She was thrown through the open door of our spinning car but held on while the tip of one foot was crushed under a tire. Needing a cast, even this did not slow her down. In a few days when she could hobble on crutches, my crippled mother was packed into the repaired car along with the baggage and the safari continued.

(As an aside, nothing ever slowed Dottie down. In her late nineties, she fainted in the foyer of her home and broke her pelvis. When x-rayed in the emergency room, the doctor saw evidence of a previous pelvis break that had healed. No one even knew about it since she just ignored it and kept right on going.)

During childhood years when Dottie was a friend and

a companion we would often travel together and meet my busy father at the other end. She never complained about taking us to the movies and parties and retrieving us afterwards. I remember when I told her a birthday party had been overlooked for one of my friends since his parents had marital issues. She had a party for him at our house the very next day.

Dottie was terribly honest, and sometimes her honesty did not have great results. I remember our Foundation members having dinner

Dorothy Park

at a small resort that catered to weddings when she disappeared from our dining and came back holding the hand of a beautiful young bride. After sharing her admiration of the young lady in her bridal dress with all of us, in exiting the lobby, Dottie spotted her with the groom. He was far below her opinion of the stunning bride, balding with a droopy mustache. In a stunned manner she said: "You are the groom?" Later that evening we spotted the bride, seemingly after her new husband had gone to their room, sitting on the steps of the resort entrance holding her head in her hands.

At the tender age of 88, Dottie scheduled another summer party in the tradition she and my father always had. For a humorous twist, she planned to mount a life-sized stuffed monkey in the trees surrounding the area, along with fake rope vines. Then 9/11 hit, and Jack Simrell, her arborist, was surprised when she called him the very next day to ask him to follow through on the project.

At first he said it felt strange to him to continue plans for a party at that time, but then he felt it was the right thing to do. It showed the perseverance of the woman she was, and that we all needed to carry on. Then, while he was in the trees she yelled up to him in her southern accent "Mr. Simrell, do you like Tequila?"

In response to his puzzled "yes" she disappeared into the house, shortly reappearing with a silver tray and two silver goblets. He said he has never forgotten her "Mr. Simrell, would you care to come down and join me for a Margarita?"

A couple of weeks later, he remembers, when she asked him to do some additional work he said he couldn't schedule immediately, she replied "Mr. Simrell, you know I don't wait well."

Being the extremely generous and gracious soul that she was prompted frequent visits by people asking for support. She found it humorous that placed between them at one of her favorite places to sit was a pillow that we gave her. No one seemed to notice, during these lengthy sessions, that it read "Do not mistake endurance for hospitality."

However, she endured, forever strong, forever young. A great and wonderful woman, our mother. Dottie.

In the words of Edna St. Vincent Millay, "I only know that summer sang in me a little while, that in me sings no more."

With my mother when she reached the regal age of 97.

APPENDIX N

Roy H. Park Leadership Fellows
20th Anniversary Celebration

In 2007, 10 years after the Roy H. Park Leadership Fellowship Program was launched at the Johnson Graduate School of Management, an anniversary celebration was held for the roughly 250 graduates of the program in the Rainbow Room at the top of Rockefeller Center in New York City.

Last year, in 2017, the number of Park Fellow graduates had doubled to 500 and their 20th Anniversary Celebration was held at the same location. It's interesting to note that between these two Celebrations the Rainbow Room was closed for a while to undergo a major renovation. It was fortunate that the timing of the celebrations for the Park Fellows took place when they did.

Roy H. Park Leadership Fellows during the 20th celebration dinner in the Rainbow Room at Rockefeller Plaza on December 2, 2017.

The next two pages illustrate the opening of the "Celebrate 20" 62-page color brochure incorporating the role our Triad

ROY H. PARK, JR. AND THE
TRIAD FOUNDATION

In the history of the Samuel Curtis Johnson Graduate School of Management and Cornell University, there have been few benefactors as influential as Roy H. Park, Jr., MBA '63.

Park is a trustee emeritus of Cornell University and serves as a presidential councillor, the highest honor its Board of Trustees can bestow. A member of the Advisory Council of the Samuel Curtis Johnson Graduate School of Management since 1996, he was inducted into its Hall of Honor in 2004. In 2017, the Cornell Board of Trustees asked Park to be a founding member of the Dean's Leadership Council for the Cornell SC Johnson College of Business. Since 1995, Park has also served as a vice chairman and member of the Board of Directors of the Boyce Thompson Institute for Plant Research, located on the Cornell campus, and is a lifelong member of Cornell's Epsilon of New York Chapter of the Sigma Phi Society.

In addition to serving in these critical advisory roles for Cornell, Roy H. Park, Jr. is president and CEO of Park Outdoor Advertising of New York and serves as the chairman and president of Triad Foundation, Inc. Prior to joining Park Outdoor Advertising of New York, he worked in a variety of organizations including J. Walter Thompson, First Union National Bank (now Wells Fargo), and Park Communications.

Park's work with Triad is especially meaningful to his family and to Johnson, as they jointly strive to honor the Senior and Park's legacy by following Park Senior's entrepreneurial values, hard work and perseverance, humility, integrity and sense of community responsibility. Serving as directors and officers of Triad Foundation, Inc. are Roy H. Park, Jr. and his wife, Tetlow, his children Elizabeth Park Fowler and Roy H. Park III, and their spouses Troy Fowler and Laura Park. In addition to Triad's generous support for the Roy H. Park Leadership Fellowship at Johnson, the foundation also supports graduate fellowships at the University of North Carolina at Chapel Hill. Triad also focuses on early childhood and elementary education programs; marine and tropical ecology; selected scientific research; and human service, youth, and other community-based programs in the local communities of its directors.

Establishing the Roy H. Park Leadership Fellowship

As a Johnson alumnus, Roy H. Park, Jr., MBA '63, was determined to give back to the school in a way that would differentiate it from other distinguished programs. Like his father before him, Park was compelled to positively influence his surrounding communities. To this end, Park established a fellowship through his family's foundation, envisioning a program that would increase Johnson's ability to attract the strongest MBA applicants who, after graduating, would go on to apply the leadership skills learned at Johnson to benefit their future organizations as well as Cornell, Johnson, and their communities.

In 1995, a committee formed to explore ways to achieve these goals and subsequently appointed the fellowship's first program director, Clint Sidle. By comparing scholarships offered at other top MBA programs, Clint and the committee saw an opportunity to make deep, transformative leadership development an integral component of the fellowship, therefore securing its position as a truly unique offering. In fall of 1997, the first class of Park Leadership Fellows matriculated into Johnson.

In 2003, responsibility for the program's support transitioned from Park Foundation, Inc. to Triad Foundation, Inc., and at that time, the fellowship's name was modified to the Roy H. Park Leadership Fellowship to directly honor Roy H. Park, Jr.'s father. Since the program's inception, the Fellowship has provided nearly $46 million to support tuition and enrichment opportunities for more than 500 fellows at Cornell.

ROY H. PARK, JR., MBA '63
Johnson and Cornell
benefactor and
catalyst for the
creation of the Park
Leadership Fellowship

Foundation and family played in the Fellowships including an invitation from Program Director Laura Georgianna. It said "As we mark the 20th anniversary of the Roy H. Park Leadership Fellowship, I invite you to celebrate this milestone with us by reflecting back on the lasting impact that this program has had on your life as well as the lives of those in our surrounding communities. I look forward to seeing many of your at the 20th Anniversary Celebration and continuing to connect with our alumni community for years to come."

The brochure included Spotlight Profiles, examples of Service Leadership and a complete Park Fellow Alumni Directory including pictures of each class and individual listings of the Park Fellows names, locations and business affiliations.

Including Park Fellows spouses and significant others along with Cornell members and Triad family and personnel the dinner meeting accommodated a packed house of some 300 attendees.

The group was welcomed by Martha Pollack, the new President of Cornell University. Other speakers included Johnson

In Celebration of the 20th Anniversary, one-third of the 500 Roy H. Park Leadership Fellows gather after dinner on the 65th floor of the Rockefeller Cente

School Dean Mark Nelson, Soumitra Dutta, former dean of the School and the SC Johnson College of Business, the third largest business school in the world.

Laura Georgianna, a Park Fellow herself, and Park Fellow Jennifer Dulski, an entrepreneur from the first graduating class, and now the head of groups and communities at Facebook, also spoke.

Following the dinner, President Pollack sent a letter saying "exciting to know that there are 500 Park Fellows and inspiring to think of all the good work they are doing now and will continue to throughout their personal and professional lives." She complimented "our compelling vision and extraordinary support for what has been done to advance and differentiate the Johnson School and Cornell."

During my welcoming address to the Fellows I pointed out it was their first class that helped to sell and develop the program by exhibiting leadership combined with a humility that was welcomed by the remainder of the students in the class.

The Waitlisted Park Fellows Celebration in the Rainbow Room in New York City which was only able to accommodate 300 people resulted in a packed house.

Explaining how this all got started I said that few people are given as many as three breaks in their lifetime, with my first break being admitted to Cornell. After blowing this by busting out halfway through my sophomore year, I was given a second chance by the University of North Carolina. I could be admitted to start over as a sophomore if I could earn a B average in eight summer, extension and correspondence courses. Which I did, and graduated with a BA in Journalism. This led me to my third break, when the Johnson School gave me the chance to return to Cornell and earn an MBA.

Thus my desire to repay Johnson for giving me a third break and for Carolina giving me a second chance after my first departure from Cornell. The result: the establishment of Park Fellowships at both schools.

And referring to our Roy H. Park Fellowship program at the University of North Carolina at Chapel Hill for Masters and PhD graduates at the School of the Media and Journalism it brings the combined number of Roy H. Park Fellows to 1000 in the nation and across the world:

"We plan for the 500 Park Fellow Masters and Doctorates from the School to celebrate their own 20th Anniversary in 2019 in Chapel Hill, North Carolina." I said.

With all this said, the most meaningful part of the Park Fellowship programs is captured by one of our newest Park Fellows, Brian Guo, who will graduate in 2019.

He said surviving his first semester in the business school was difficult enough but he always found time to take advantage of an optional but unique opportunity, so he signed up for the 20th Anniversary Celebration in New York.

Arriving with 12 of his other 2019 classmates, he said he was overwhelmed by the sea of 300 people circulating atop Rockefeller Center, the majority being Park Fellows who had traveled near and far to attend the event.

"Seeing 20 different classes of Johnson students interacting, as voices were raised and pictures (selfies) were shamelessly snapped, I was filled with pride and excitement" he wrote. As I

surveyed the room, I paused and noticed how diverse this group was. The business world is often criticized for over-representing Caucasian males in leadership positions, but as I looked at many of the last 20 years of Johnson's Park Leadership Fellows, I see Johnson and the Park program striving to buck the trend. I saw:
- people of all ethnic backgrounds
- an equal distribution of men and women
- tall and short people, young and old people
- people in the public sector and people in the private sector
- employees at *Fortune* 100 companies and small business owners
- introverts and extroverts

"While we sat for dinner," Guo wrote "Jennifer Dulski '93, MBA '99, recounted five powerful stories demonstrating how an individual's leadership can have profound impact on broader audiences. As the head of Groups and Communities at Facebook, and former president and COO of Change.org, Jennifer sees first-hand how leadership can be used to serve our communities. Effective leaders focus on supporting and developing those around them so everyone is able to perform at extremely high levels. Johnson's leadership programming focuses on equipping students with skills to accomplish this as evident through the 'diverse teams' training, abundance of self-reflection based activities, and feedback oriented conversations during teambuilding activities and treks. The Park Fellowship doubles down on these skills through retreats, volunteering, and our community-focused service project.

"When Roy H. Park Jr., MBA '63, took the stage and spoke about what Cornell and Johnson has meant to him, he gave me chills." Guo continues. "A year ago, I was fumbling through the admissions process, unsure of what separated me from other applicants. I always viewed myself as a leader, but could never articulate the type of leader I was. Fast forward a year, and I still haven't exactly labeled my leadership style. What I have done is embrace what the Park Fellowship has taught me, which is to channel my self-awareness and to empathize with and empower those around me. I understand it is OK not having one specific leadership style, and that the best leaders are adaptable in varying situations. I have to continue honing my ability to inspire those

around me to achieve their goals. And although I was wading through the heart of recruiting season with hours of schoolwork awaiting me," Guo concluded, "the few hours I spent at the 20th anniversary dinner clearly reminded me of just how powerful leadership can be."

Addressing the Park Fellows in the Rainbow Room.

APPENDIX O
Marquis Who's Who

In 2017, I was interviewed by Marquis Who's Who as the subject for a biographical record in the hardcover registry of the Who's Who in America which was then issued as a press release. Later in the year I was also contacted for a full-page feature in what was being considered in the future as a *Marquis Millennium* magazine.

Asked how professional and colleagues would describe me, I pointed out that being a workaholic set the pace of teamwork our companies engender resulting in loyalty through shared strong core values by all of our people and outside partners which result in achievable goals.

Asked if my upbringing and family history influenced my career choice, I pointed out that to be a son of a family headed by a workaholic entrepreneur who came off a small farm and worked through four careers to become a billionaire, seeing little of him growing up, made it natural for me to set forth on an independent career before returning to the family business and eventually buying a part of it.

Among the other questions in the interview I was asked about what was my personal definition of success. I replied "Despite some of the obstacles in my path, there is nothing I would change and would personally define success as being able to look back on my life and that of my family's with satisfaction, enabling me, therefore, to live it twice."

The release, which appeared in February 2017, follows on the next two pages and this concludes the Appendices in this book, which I hope you found somewhat illuminating and more importantly, entertaining.

For Immediate Release

Roy H. Park, Jr. Celebrates 55 Years of Invaluable Contributions to His Field

Mr. Park is President and CEO of Park Outdoor Advertising of New York, Inc. and President and Chairman of Triad Foundation, Inc.

ITHACA, NY, January 13, 2017, With nearly five and a half decades of broad-based business experience, Mr. Park is uniquely qualified to oversee a wide range of managerial tasks as president, CEO and director of Park Outdoor Advertising of New York and president, chairman and director of Triad Foundation, Inc.

After graduating from Lawrenceville in 1956, earning a B.A. in journalism from the University of North Carolina, Chapel Hill and an MBA from the Johnson Graduate School of Management at Cornell University, Park joined J. Walter Thompson in New York City in 1963. Spending the next seven years with the world's largest advertising agency in creative, research, personnel and management positions, he was recruited in 1970 by the advertising division of First Union National Bank Corps (now Wells Fargo) in Charlotte, NC as VP Marketing and Account Management.

In 1971 he joined Park Communications, Inc., his father's multi-media empire which eventually reached 25 percent of the American public with its radio, television, newspapers and outdoor divisions. During the next 17 years Park served as VP Advertising and Promotion for its television division, as well as GM, VP and CEO of its outdoor advertising companies, which he purchased from his father in 1988. During this time he received the Chamber of Commerce's Project of the Year Award for bringing the Junior

Olympics to Ithaca, and he founded the Outdoor Advertising Council of New York, Inc., serving as its president from 1986 to 1991, then chairman until 1995. Beginning in 1998 he also served as VP of Park Foundation, Inc., before splitting off in 2002 to form Triad Foundation, Inc. to honor his father's legacy.

Park is Trustee Emeritus of Cornell University and a Presidential Councillor, the highest honor its Board of Trustees can bestow. As a member of the Advisory Council of the Johnson Graduate School of Management since 1996, he was inducted into its Hall of Honor in 2004. He received a Distinguished Alumnus Award from the University of North Carolina in 2005, and having served as a member of the Board of Advisors of UNC's School of Media and Journalism since 1999, he was inducted into its Advertising Hall of Fame in 2011. In 2015, Park was chosen to receive the William Richardson Davie Award, the highest honor given by the University of North Carolina's Board of Trustees.

In 2017, he was inducted into the North Carolina Media and Journalism Hall of Fame and was awarded the *Order of the Long Leaf Pine*, one of the most prestigious awards conferred by the Governor of North Carolina to individuals who have provided exemplary service to their communities and to the state. He was also elected by the Cornell Board of Trustees as a founding member of the Leadership Council of the Cornell SC Johnson College of Business, the third largest business school in the world.

Since 1995, he has also served as a Vice Chairman and member of the Board of Directors of the Boyce Thompson Institute for Plant Research, Inc. located on the Cornell Campus, and is a life member of Cornell's Epsilon of New York Chapter of the Sigma Phi Society.

Mr. Park has parlayed his knowledge into a book called *Sons in the Shadow: Surviving the Family Business as an SOB (Son of the Boss)*, published in 2016. He has been featured in *Town & Country, Seventeen* and *The American Way* magazines as well as in over 30 biographical publications including Who's Who in Advertising, Who's Who in Media and Communication, Who's Who in Finance and Industry, both the Cambridge and Strathmore Who's Who's, Who's Who Among U.S. Executives, Community Leaders in America, and the National Register's Who's Who of Executives and Professionals.

NOTES

[1]"Ashes to Ashes," by Dennis Earle Lambert and Brian August Potter; © 1972 Dutchess Music Corporation; All rights administered by Songs of Universal, Inc./BMI. Used with permission. All rights reserved.

[1a] "Cherry Bomb," by John Cougar Mellencamp. All reasonable efforts have been made to contact the copyright holders.

[2] Dean Koontz, *The Darkest Evening of the Year*, A Bantam Book/published by Bantam Dell, a division of Random House, Inc., © 2007, p. 53. Reprinted by permission of Dean Koontz.

[3] *Business Week*, Communications Section, "Bagging the broadcast limit," July 25, 1977, p. 50.

[4] Virgil Gaither, "What's black, white and owned by a chain?," *The Tulsa Tribune*, August 22, 1979, p. 2B.

[5] Helen Mundell, "Roy Park is ready for $100 million expansion when FCC relaxes rules," *The Ithaca Journal,* circa 1984. Reprinted by permission of *The Ithaca Journal.*

[6] "Keeper of the Castle," by Dennis Earle Lambert and Brian August Potter; © 1973 Music Corporation of America; All rights administered by Songs of Universal, Inc./BMI. Used with permission. All rights reserved.

[7] Ibid.

[8] Jim Dumbell, "Making Money For Fun and Profit," *The Charlotte Observer*, May 2, 1982, p. 1, Section D, p. 1.

[9] Ibid.

[10] Everett Groseclose, "You Have Problems? Consider the Plight of Nation's SOBs," *The Wall Street Journal*, Eastern Edition, March 20, 1975, © 1975 Dow Jones & Company.

[11] Judith Hortsman, "Ithaca's Roy Park: A Man of Many Careers," *The Ithaca Journal*, October 2, 1972, p.3. Reprinted by permission of *The Ithaca Journal.*

[12] Jim Dumbell, *The Charlotte Observer*, May 2, 1982, p. 1.

[13] John Byrd, "Just a Collector. Broadcast-Newspaper Empire Is Roy Park's 4th Career," *Winston-Salem Journal*, Financial Section, February 6, 1983, Section G.

[14] John W. Overacker, "Duesenberg Roadster Brings $5,300 at Sale," *Watertown Daily Times*, October 27, 1961. Copyright *Watertown Daily Times*. Reprinted by permission of the *Watertown Daily Times*.

[15] Rudolph Pate, "A Saga of Success," *NCSU Alumni News*, March/April 1971, Volume 43, No. 5, p. 6.

[16] Joseph V. Junod, "Views differ on Park's style of leadership," *The Ithaca Journal*, Features Section. May 17, 1985, p. 12. Reprinted by permission of *The Ithaca Journal*.

[17] Virgil Gaither, *The Tulsa Tribune*, August 22, 1979, p. 2B.

[18] Ibid.

[19] Jim Dumbell, *The Charlotte Observer*, May 2, 1982.

[20] Virgil Gaither, *The Tulsa Tribune*, August 22, 1979, p. 2B.

[21] Clifton B. Metcalf, Jr., "Park seeks papers to expand his chain," *UNC Journalist*, February/March 1983, Volume 24, Number 1, School of Journalism, Chapel Hill, NC.

[22] *Business Week*, Communications Section, July 1977, p. 50.

[23] Jim Dumbell, *The Charlotte Observer*, May 2, 1982.

[24] Clifton Metcalf, *UNC Journalist*, February/March 1983.

[25] John Byrd, *Winston-Salem Journal*, February 6, 1983.

[26] Jim Dumbell, *The Charlotte Observer*, May 2, 1982.

[27] Ibid.

[28] John Byrd, *Winston-Salem Journal*, February 6, 1983.

[29] Virgil Gaither, *The Tulsa Tribune*, August 22, 1979.

[30] Ken Allen, "Big Operator Owns Small Newspapers," *The Charlotte Observer*, February 11, 1980, p. 1A, 10A.

[31] Dr. Mortimer R. Feinberg, "Feinberg Tells What Makes a Chief Executive Tick," reprinted in *The Sales Executive* from a speech Dr. Feinberg delivered at The Sales Executive Club of New York. Quotes used by permission.

[32] Angelia Herrin, "Life can be hard when business is all in the family," *The News and Observer*, Raleigh, NC, People, Section III, Sunday, June 15, 1989.

[33] Joseph V. Junod, "Ithaca's media baron keeps his eye on the future," *The Ithaca Journal*, Friday, May 17, 1985, p. 12. Reprinted by permission of *The Ithaca Journal*.

[34] C.E. Yandle, "Recession provides opportunity for Park to expand media holdings," *The News & Observer*, Raleigh, NC, Tuesday, January 28, 1992, p. 2D.

[35] Harry Levinson, *The Great Jackass Fallacy* © 1973 by the President and Fellows of Harvard College. Reprinted by agreement with the Division of Research, Harvard Business School, Boston, pp. 128–31.

[36] Richard S. Morrison, "Working for the Old Man," First Person, *MBA* magazine, June 1974, p. 12.

[36a] "Tin Man," Words and Music by Dewey Bunnell; © 1972 (Renewed) WB Music Corp. All Rights Reserved. Used under Print License Agreement Ref. L1408805-9004 between ALFRED PUBLISHING CO. INC. and ROY PARK dated August 5, 2014.

[37] Jeffrey A. Trachtenberg, "Every Decade a New Career," *Forbes*, Profiles, September 30, 1984, pp. 124, 128. Permission granted to republish text excerpt.

[38] Helen Mundell, "Park quits father's firm after magazine appears," *The Ithaca Journal*, local section, Tuesday, September 4, 1984, p. 3. Reprinted by permission of *The Ithaca Journal*.

[39] Helen Mundell, "Park says he regrets son's decision," *The Ithaca Journal*,

Wednesday, September 5, 1984, p. 3. Reprinted with permission by *The Ithaca Journal.*

[40] Helen Mundell, "Younger Park back in family business," *The Ithaca Journal*, Local section, Monday, September 24, 1984, p. 3. Reprinted by permission of *The Ithaca Journal.*

[41] Sherwood Anderson, "Discovery of a Father," *Sherwood Anderson's Memoirs: Critical Edition.* Chapel Hill: University of North Carolina Press, 1969, ed. Ray Lewis White, p. 76. Reprinted from *Reader's Digest*, XXXV (November, 1939), 21–25.

[41a] "Weekend Lover," Words and Music by Rupert Holmes Copyright © 1976 (Renewed) WB MUSIC CORP (ASCAP) and HOLMES LINE OF MUSIC INC. (ASCAP) All Rights Administered by WB MUSIC CORP. All Rights Reserved. Used by Permission from Alfred Music per Print License Agreement Ref: PR140807-2002 dated August 7, 2014 between ALFRED MUSIC and Roy Park.

[42] Ethan Canin, "The Year of Getting to Know Us," *Emperor of the Air*, Boston: Houghton Mifflin Company, 1988, p. 42.

[43] Evan McGlinn, "5 of the Fortunate," *Town & Country*, October, 1992, p. 124.

[44] Helen Mundell, "At 80, the lion of Park still runs this show," *The Ithaca Journal*, Business/Agriculture section, Monday, July 8, 1991, p. 8B. Reprinted by permission of *The Ithaca Journal.*

[45] Ibid.

[46] Ibid.

[47] Sherwood Anderson, *Sherwood Anderson's Memoirs: Critical Edition*, 1969, p. 85.

[48] "Ashes to Ashes," by Dennis Earle Lambert and Brian August Potter; © Dutchess Music Corporation; All rights administered by Sons of Universal, Inc./BMI. Used with permission. All rights reserved.

[49] Ethan Canin, *Emperor of the Air*, 1988, p. 21.

[50] Dean Koontz, *Darkfall*, A Berkley Book/published by arrangement with

the author, ©1984, p. 220. Reprinted by permission of Dean Koontz.

[51] Research by Jenny Magar, proofreader for Elderberry Books found that the verses below reportedly were written on the wall of Mother Teresa's home for children in Calcutta, and are widely attributed to her. Some sources say the words were written on the wall in Mother Teresa's own room, but in any case, their association with Mother Teresa and the Missionaries of Charity has made them popular worldwide, expressing as they do the spirit in which they lived their lives.

They seem to be based on a composition originally by Dr. Kent M. Keith, but much of the second half has been re-written in a more spiritual way. Both versions are shown below, the first "Do It Anyway" version is credited to Mother Teresa:

> *People are often unreasonable, irrational, and self-*
> *centered. Forgive them anyway.*
> *If you are kind, , people may accuse you of selfish ulterior*
> *motives. Be kind anyway.*
> *If you are successful you win, win some unfaithful friends*
> *and some genuine enemies. Succeed anyway.*
> *If you are honest and sincere people may deceive you. Be*
> *honest and sincere anyway.*
> *What you spend years creating, others could destroy*
> *overnight. Create anyway.*
> *If you find serenity and happiness, some may be jealous.*
> *Be happy anyway.*
> *The good you do today, will often be forgotten. Do good*
> *anyway.*
> *Give the best you have, and it will never be enough. Give your best anyway.*
> *In the final analysis, it is between you and God. It was never between you*
> *and them anyway.*

The second, possibly original version, is a work called "The Paradoxical Commandments" written by Dr. Kent M. Keith in 1968 as part of a booklet for student leaders:

> *People are unreasonable, illogical and self-centered. Love*
> *them anyway.*
> *If you do good, people will accuse you of selfish ulterior*
> *motives. Do good anyway.*
> *If you are successful you win false friends and true*
> *enemies. Succeed anyway.*
> *The good you do today will be forgotten tomorrow. Do*
> *good anyway.*

*Honestly and frankness make you vulnerable. Be honest
and frank anyway.
People favor underdogs but follow only top dogs. Fight
for some underdogs anyway.
What you spend years building may be destroyed
overnight. Build anyway.
People really need help but may attack you if you help
them. Help them anyway.
Give the world the best you have and you'll get kicked in
the teeth.
Give the world the best you've got, anyway.*

[52]Annemarie Kropf, "Billboard firm profits by staying local," Business of The Week, *The Central New York Business Journal*, August 24, 2004, p. 19.

[53] Jim Dumbell, *The Charlotte Observer*, May 2, 1982, p. 4D.

[54] John Byrd, *Winston-Salem Journal*, February 6, 1983.

[55] Dan Higgins, "Park Foundation organization to benefit Cornell, N. Carolina," *The Ithaca Journal*, City & Country Section, February 6, 2003, p.1B. Reprinted with permission from *The Ithaca Journal*.

[56] Dan Higgins, "Triad focuses Park mission," *The Ithaca Journal*, February 7, 2003, p.1B. Reprinted by permission of *The Ithaca Journal*.

[57] *Cornell Chronicle*, "Triad is benefactor of Johnson School's Park program," July 10, 2003, Volume 34, p. 4.

[58] Ibid.

[59] "Turn It Up" by Mick Hucknall & Lamont Dozier © 1988 Mick Hucknall & Publisher(s) Unknown. All rights reserved on behalf of Mick Hucknall administered by SONY/ATV Music Publishing, LLC, 424 Church Street, Nashville, TN 37219. All rights reserved. Used by permission via Lyric Reprint License–PRTUS2014138.

[59b] "Turn It Up" Words and Music by Lamont Dozier and Mick Hucknall. Copyright © 1988 Mick Hucknall, Songs of Universal, Inc. and So What Ltd. All rights on behalf of Mick Hucknall Administered by Sony/ATV Music Publishing LLC, 424 Church Street, Nashville, TN 37219. All rights on behalf of So What Ltd. Administered by Songs of Universal, Inc. International Copyright Secured. All Rights Reserved. *Reprinted by*

Permission of Hal Leonard Corporation.

[60] Roy H. Park, Jr., "Why I Busted College," *Seventeen*, October, 1959, pp 118-119, 166-9. Reprinted by permission.

[61] "Your Letters"—College Ins and Outs; *Seventeen,* December, 1959. Reprinted with permission.

[62] Rudolph Pate, *NSCU Alumni News*, March/April, 1971, Volume 43, p. 12.

[63] Helen Mundell, "How Park enraptured a small city," *The Ithaca Journal*, July 8, 1991, p. 8B. Reprinted by permission of *The Ithaca Journal.*

[64] Helen Mundell, "Roy Park stories," and "How Park enraptured a small city," *The Ithaca Journal*, July 8, 1991, p. 8B. Reprinted by permission of *The Ithaca Journal.*

[65] Dean Koontz, *The Darkest Evening of the Year*, A Bantam Book/ published by Bantam Dell, a division of Random House, Inc., © 2007, p. 314. Reprinted by permission of Dean Koontz.

[66] As reported in the July 18, 2014 issue of the *Cornell Chronicle*, the website **Poets and Quants** ranks Dyson No. 2, derived by combining the annual results of the Bloomberg Businessweek and U.S. News and World Report rankings with a university's overall ranking. Also, accredited by The Association to Advance Collegiate Schools of Business, Dyson is one of only two accredited undergraduate business degree programs in the Ivy League.

INDEX

C

cable networks, 184

Cagney, Jimmy, 256

cake mixes

of Duncan Hines, 53, 54, 56, 57, 61, 91, 134, 140, 177,
255, 343, 411

early research on, 45-46

Calcutta, 527

California, 79, 81, 82, 268

"Call for a New Coalition", NCSU address by RHP, 465-467

Cambridge & Strathmore, Who's Who Among U.S. Executives, 537

Cameron, Dan, 204, 213

Cameron-Brown Company, 202

Canada, 51, 153-154, 241, 264, 289, 388

Canadian, 153, 155

Canin, Ethan, 395,403

Canton, NY, 289, 299, 388

Cape Cod, MA, 136, 138, 437

capitalism, 263, 442

Carborro, NC, 111, 112

Cargill, Wilson & Acree, 203, 205

Caribbean Islands, 159

Carlyle Hotel (NYC), 437

Carnauba, 213

Carolina Blue, 111, 435

Carolina Cooperator, 26

Carolina Cotton, 27, 32, 467

Carolina Cotton Growers Association, 39

Carolina Inn, 99, 100, 102, 103, 109, 395, 488

cars, of RHP, 132, 181, 255, 265-271

Carter, Hodding, 346

Carthage, NY, 266-267

The Catcher in the Rye (Salinger), 18, 86, 87

Caulfield, Holden, 18

Cayuga Heights, 67, 83, 175, 197, 214

Cayuga Heights School, 64, 67, 402

Cayuga Lake, 76, 81, 148, 307, 402

Cayuga's waters, 437

CBS Inc., 185, 186, 188, 194, 250, 269, 391, 399, 471

SONS IN THE SUNSHINE. **The beginning of the fourth generation.**
Me with our first grandson on the beach in Boca Grande, FL.

Front row (l-r): Jones, Clines, Nesbitt, Peck, Tiffany. **Center:** Park, Feldman. **Back row (l-r):** Whitson, Stickane, Leipold, Panara, Dugan, Salamida, Magacs, Spencer, Tevyaw, Cottrell.

THANKS A MILLION **from our Park Outdoor Management Team. We wish you all the best and hope you found some things of value in our story.**